The Sovereignty Wars

The Brookings Institution

The Brookings Institution is a private nonprofit organization devoted to research, education, and publication on important issues of domestic and foreign policy. Its principal purpose is to bring the highest quality independent research and analysis to bear on current and emerging policy problems. Interpretations or conclusions in Brookings publications should be understood to be solely those of the authors.

The Council on Foreign Relations

The Council on Foreign Relations (CFR) is an independent, nonpartisan membership organization, think tank, and publisher dedicated to being a resource for its members, government officials, business executives, journalists, educators and students, civic and religious leaders, and other interested citizens in order to help them better understand the world and the foreign policy choices facing the United States and other countries. Founded in 1921, CFR carries out its mission by maintaining a diverse membership, with special programs to promote interest and develop expertise in the next generation of foreign policy leaders; convening meetings at its headquarters in New York and in Washington, D.C., and other cities where senior government officials, members of Congress, global leaders, and prominent thinkers come together with CFR members to discuss and debate major international issues; supporting a Studies Program that fosters independent research, enabling CFR scholars to produce articles, reports, and books and hold roundtables that analyze foreign policy issues and make concrete policy recommendations; publishing *Foreign Affairs*, the preeminent journal on international affairs and U.S. foreign policy; sponsoring Independent Task Forces that produce reports with both findings and policy prescriptions on the most important foreign policy topics; and providing up-to-date information and analysis about world events and American foreign policy on its website, www.cfr.org.

The Council on Foreign Relations takes no institutional positions on policy issues and has no affiliation with the U.S. government. All views expressed in its publications and on its website are the sole responsibility of the author or authors.

The Sovereignty Wars

Reconciling America with the World

To Dirk,

with fond recollections of
earlier collaborations and
hope for future ones!

all the Best,

Stewart Patrick

10-23-17

STEWART PATRICK

A COUNCIL ON FOREIGN RELATIONS BOOK

BROOKINGS INSTITUTION PRESS

Washington, D.C.

The Brookings Institution is a private nonprofit organization devoted to research, education, and publication on important issues of domestic and foreign policy. Its principal purpose is to bring the highest quality independent research and analysis to bear on current and emerging policy problems. Interpretations or conclusions in Brookings publications should be understood to be solely those of the authors.

Library of Congress Cataloging-in-Publication data are available.
ISBN 978-0-8157-3159-7 (cloth : alk. paper)
ISBN 978-0-8157-3160-3 (ebook)

9 8 7 6 5 4 3 2 1

Typeset in Adobe Jenson Pro

Composition by Westchester Publishing Services

Contents

Acknowledgments   ix

Abbreviations   xiii

ONE
Introduction: The Sovereignty Wars   1

TWO
There's No Place Like Home:
Sovereignty, American Style   28

THREE
Power and Interdependence: U.S. Sovereignty
in the American Century   59

FOUR

Do as I Say, Not as I Do:
American Sovereignty and International Law   97

FIVE

Don't Fence Me In: The Use of Force, Arms Control,
and U.S. National Security   142

SIX

Stop the World, I Want to Get Off:
Globalization and American Sovereignty   172

SEVEN

Good Fences Make Good Neighbors:
Immigration and Border Security   196

EIGHT

Don't Tread on Me: The United States and
International Organizations   217

NINE

Conclusion: American Sovereignty and
International Cooperation   252

Notes   265

Index   313

Acknowledgments

I've incurred many intellectual, professional, and personal debts in writing this book, and I offer my sincere thanks to those who inspired me to write it and helped me bring it to fruition.

The topic of sovereignty has fascinated me since my first undergraduate class in world politics at Stanford University—taught by Stephen D. Krasner, who would later write the definitive theoretical work on the concept. That early exposure came in handy two decades later when I became a fellow on the State Department's policy planning staff. Its director, Richard N. Haass, asked me one day to craft a speech on "Sovereignty: Existing Rights, Evolving Responsibilities." A daunting assignment, given Richard's reputation as an exacting boss. Some twelve drafts later he pronounced the text acceptable, allowing me to move on to related topics. I spent the next few years analyzing the connection between weak sovereignty in the developing world and transnational security threats such as terrorism and infectious disease.

What increasingly fascinated me, though, was my *own* country's attitude toward sovereignty—and the often explosive U.S. domestic debates it sparks. I learned just how volatile my fellow Americans' feelings could run when I began directing a program on international institutions and global govern-ance at the Council on Foreign Relations (CFR). I received quite a bit of color-ful email. The most jarring missive had a three-word subject line: "Sovereignty and Treason." My correspondent provided stylized definitions of those con-cepts, and then closed with these cautionary words: "I just want to warn you that if there were ever a change of regime in this country, you might well be brought before a tribunal for the crime of treachery against the United States of America."

I explained to my new pen pal that he'd misunderstood the motivations behind our initiative, which was predicated on cooperation among sovereign states. But I was indebted to him nonetheless. He spurred me to explore how Americans conceive of sovereignty, how those notions have evolved since the republic's founding, and how they inform U.S. attitudes toward international organizations, treaties, alliances, and law. And the deeper I looked, the more I realized that although most Americans regard "sovereignty" as sacred, they often use it to mean very different things—and talk past each other as a re-sult. The way out of this predicament begins with realizing that sovereignty has distinct components, and that these don't always go together.

I could not have written this book without the insights of innumerable scholars, whose contributions I reference in my endnotes. I owe a special debt to Marty Finnemore, Michael Barnett, and Miles Kahler, as well as two anony-mous reviewers, each of whom read the entire manuscript and provided incisive comments. Ted Alden and Matt Waxman, two thoughtful CFR colleagues, critiqued specific chapters. My ideas for the book were also enriched by conver-sations during the annual Princeton workshop on global governance, which I've had the privilege to co-organize with John Ikenberry, Alan Alexandroff, Bruce Jones, Tom Wright, Keith Porter, and Jennifer Smyser.

I can't say enough about my wonderful CFR colleagues, both past and pres-ent, who offered superb research assistance and editorial advice on this project as members of the International Institutions and Global Governance (IIGG) program that I direct. I thank Megan Roberts, my fabulous associate director, and her dynamic predecessor, Isabella Bennett, as well as several talented research associates, including Naomi Egel, Daniel Chardell, Martin Willner, Theresa Lou, Claire Schachter, and Ryan Kaminski, in addition to my wise program coordinator, Terry Mullan. None of my team's work would have been possible, of course, without the generous backing of the Robina Foundation, which has supported IIGG since its creation. In January 2017 the Robina Board provided resources to establish the James H. Binger Chair in Global

Governance at CFR, an endowed position named for the philanthropist whose bequest created the foundation, and which I am honored to hold.

I thank the Council's president, Richard N. Haass—my boss a second time—for supporting this project and pushing me to ask the important questions. I'm grateful to James M. Lindsay, vice president and director of the David Rockefeller Studies Program at CFR, for his invaluable feedback and guidance—including his admonition to write in "plain English." I thank the entire studies team, especially Amy Baker, for their support. Throughout the writing and publishing process, I had the good fortune to work with the terrific Trish Dorff and her crack team in CFR's publications department. Thanks also to Irina Faskianos, the tireless head of CFR's national program, and to CFR's communications and marketing team, particularly Iva Zoric, Anya Schmemman, and Jenny Mallamo, for helping me spread the word to multiple audiences.

I was fortunate to work with the talented Bill Finan and his colleagues at Brookings Institution Press, as well as with John Donohue of Westchester Publishing Services. I'm grateful for their efficiency and professionalism in getting this book to press—and hopefully to a bookstore (or online retailer) near you.

Finally, I owe a huge debt to my three lively and fast-growing children, Oliver, Henry, and Iona. Every day, they remind me what is important in life.

Abbreviations

AB	Appellate Body (World Trade Organization)
ADA	Americans with Disabilities Act
AEI	American Enterprise Institute
AIIB	Asian Infrastructure Investment Bank
ATT	Arms Trade Treaty
BIS	Bank for International Settlements
BRICS countries	Brazil, Russia, India, China, and South Africa
BWC	Biological Weapons Convention
CBP	Customs and Border Protection
CEDAW	Convention on the Elimination of Discrimination against Women
CESCR	Covenant on Economic, Social and Cultural Rights (United Nations)
CFE	Conventional Forces in Europe Treaty
CIS	Center for Immigration Studies
CPAC	Conservative Political Action Conference
CRC	Convention on the Rights of the Child
CRPD	Convention on the Rights of Persons with Disabilities (United Nations)
CSI	Container Security Initiative

CTBT	Comprehensive Test Ban Treaty
CTC	Counterterrorism Committee (United Nations)
CUSFTA	Canada-U.S. Free Trade Agreement
CWA	Chemical Weapons Act
CWC	Chemical Weapons Convention
DEA	Drug Enforcement Agency
DSU	dispute settlement understanding (World Trade Organization)
EC	European Commission
ECOSOC	Economic and Social Council (United Nations)
EEEZs	extended exclusive economic zones
EEZs	exclusive economic zones
EITI	Extractive Industries Transparency Initiative
EU	European Union
FAIR	Federation for American Immigration Reform
G-7	Group of 7
G-8	Group of 8
G-20	Group of 20
G-77	Group of 77
GAO	General Accounting Office
GATT	General Agreement on Tariffs and Trade
GDP	gross domestic product
IAEA	International Atomic Energy Agency
IANA	Internet Assigned Numbers Authority
ICANN	Internet Corporation for Assigned Names and Numbers
ICC	International Criminal Court
ICCPR	International Covenant on Civil and Political Rights
ICE	Immigration and Customs Enforcement
ICJ	International Court of Justice
IDPs	internally displaced persons
IEA	International Energy Agency
IHR	International Health Regulations
IMF	International Monetary Fund
INF	Intermediate-Range Nuclear Forces Treaty
IPCC	Intergovernmental Panel on Climate Change
IRCA	Immigration Reform and Control Act
ISAF	International Security Assistance Force
ISDS	Investor-State Dispute Settlement
ITO	International Trade Organization
JCPOA	Joint Comprehensive Plan of Action

LEP	League to Enforce Peace
NAFTA	North American Free Trade Agreement
NAM	Non-Aligned Movement
NAT	North Atlantic Treaty
NATO	North Atlantic Treaty Organization
NGO	nongovernmental organization
NPT	[Nuclear] Non-Proliferation Treaty / Treaty on the Non-Proliferation of Nuclear Weapons
NSEERS	National Security Entry-Exit Registration System
NWS	nuclear weapons states
OECD	Organization for Economic Cooperation and Development
OIOS	Office of Internal Oversight Services (United Nations)
OPCW	Organization for the Prohibition of Chemical Weapons
PA	Palestinian Authority
PHEICs	public health emergencies of international concern
PSI	Proliferation Security Initiative
PTBT	Partial Test Ban Treaty
R2P	Responsibility to Protect
RTAA	Reciprocal Trade Agreements Act
RUDs	reservations, understandings, and declarations
SARS	severe acute respiratory syndrome
START I and II	Strategic Arms Reduction Treaties I and II
TPP	Trans-Pacific Partnership
TTIP	Transatlantic Trade and Investment Partnership
UNCLOS	United Nations Convention on the Law of the Sea
UNESCO	United Nations Educational, Scientific and Cultural Organization
UNFCCC	UN Framework Convention on Climate Change
UNGA	United Nations General Assembly
UNIDO	United Nations Industrial Development Organization
UNO	United Nations Organization
UNRRA	United Nations Relief and Rehabilitation Agency
UNSC	United Nations Security Council
USAID	U.S. Agency for International Development
USTR	Office of the United States Trade Representative
VCCR	Vienna Convention on Consular Relations
WHO	World Health Organization
WMD	weapons of mass destruction
WTO	World Trade Organization

ONE

Introduction

The Sovereignty Wars

On the eve of March 19, 1919, 3,000 lucky ticket holders gathered in Boston's Symphony Hall for one of the most eagerly anticipated debates in American history. The question posed was whether the United States should approve the Covenant of the League of Nations and become one of its founding members. Arguing in the affirmative was A. Lawrence Lowell, president of Harvard University. In the negative was Henry Cabot Lodge of Massachusetts, the Senate majority leader.

Interest in the debate was intense, both in the United States and abroad. And rightfully so. A month earlier President Woodrow Wilson and fellow negotiators at the Paris Peace Conference had presented humanity with an ambitious scheme to safeguard international peace. In the wake of the Great War, the idea of the League had captured the world's imagination. More than 72,000 Americans had applied to attend what A. J. Philpott of the *Boston Evening Globe* called "the greatest debate staged in this country in 50 years." Below the event stage, telegraph operators prepared to dispatch the speakers' remarks instantaneously around the country and across the Atlantic.[1]

For the United States, League membership would imply reversing its historical aversion to formal international commitments. Less than a month earlier Wilson had returned from France aboard the *George Washington*—christened for America's first president who, as irony would have it, had cautioned the United States to "steer clear of any permanent alliances." Wilson himself had disembarked in Boston, promising throngs of well-wishers to seek speedy ratification of the Covenant. Four days later, Lodge had begun his own campaign to defeat it.

The Lodge-Lowell debate was but one engagement in what became a titanic battle over the League of Nations, still the most divisive, dramatic, and consequential controversy in nearly two and a half centuries of U.S. foreign policy. Many issues were at stake. But the core issue was national sovereignty—namely, the future of the United States as an independent republic, endowed with freedom of action and capable of shaping its own destiny. Three questions were front and center, and they can be summarized under the headings of authority, autonomy, and influence. First, was League membership consistent with the system of government established under the U.S. Constitution, including the liberties of the American people and the separation of powers? Second, would new commitments under the League expand or constrain America's traditional freedom of action, both abroad and at home? Third, as a practical matter, would League membership help or hinder U.S. efforts to remain master of its own fate? Lurking behind these three queries was a fourth: How should the United States balance these objectives of authority, autonomy, and influence?

One hundred years later the concerns and dilemmas that Lodge and Lowell confronted in 1919 have rarely been more topical. Americans are once again debating just what role the United States should play in a complex, shrinking, and unsettling world that brings dangers and risks, as well as opportunities, closer to its shores. For nearly three-quarters of a century, dating from World War II, the United States shouldered the mantle of global leadership, in effect managing world order. But today many Americans have wearied of this role and have endorsed a narrower, more self-interested posture that looks out for America and Americans first—even as transnational threats like climate change, terrorism, and infectious disease cry out for international cooperation. How should the United States navigate between the practical need to go it with others and its instincts for independence? What external commitments should it make, what constraints should it accept, to advance a rule-bound international order?

Revisiting the Lodge-Lowell encounter is compelling for another reason. In our own anxious century, debates over American sovereignty generate more noise than understanding, with the shrillest voices—typically exaggerating the costs of global integration—garnering the most attention. What has been missing is a thoughtful and ultimately more hopeful discussion about the real (as opposed to imaginary) trade-offs the nation needs to consider as it seeks to reconcile its constitutional independence and desire for freedom of action with the practical requirements of influencing its destiny and advancing its interests in a global age. A closer look at the Lodge-Lowell contest not only illuminates what is at stake in these debates. It also shows that reasonable people can disagree about where to strike the balance among sovereign authority, autonomy, and influence.

Today the notion of a debate between a Republican senator and a university president conjures images of a folksy populist pitted against an effete academic. Not so in the case of Lodge and Lowell. Both were Republicans and Boston Brahmins, scions of prominent colonial families who had five Harvard degrees (including a Ph.D. for Lodge) between them. And their positions were not so far apart. Both favored some international league to enforce world peace and promote disarmament. Lowell, who had challenged Lodge to the debate, also found the Covenant "full of holes and full of defects."[2] He hoped to stake out a moderate middle ground between Wilson's unvarnished enthusiasm and the diehard opposition of League skeptics.

Lodge spoke first, on a stage backed by an enormous American flag. "It has been said that I am against any league of nations," the senator observed. "I am not." But the proposed Covenant was fatally flawed in its vaulting ambitions and infringements on U.S. sovereignty. The closer he examined the document, "the more it became very clear to me that in trying to do too much we might lose all."[3]

The Covenant's biggest defect was Article 10, which pledged League members "to respect and preserve against external aggression the territorial integrity and existing political independence" of "every nation." This was "a tremendous promise to make," the senator warned. Were America's "fathers and mothers, the sisters and the wives and sweethearts" actually prepared, he wondered, "to send the hope of their families, the hope of the nation, the best of our youth, forth into the world on that errand?" But the faults of the Covenant went further. It would undercut U.S. freedom of action, embroil the United States in distant disputes, aggravate global tensions, grant foreigners a say over U.S domestic policies, and endanger U.S. constitutional democracy.

Wilson's scheme would have the United States abandon the sound advice of Presidents Washington and Jefferson, who had admonished the nation to steer clear of (respectively) "permanent" and "entangling" alliances. Article 10 would deprive America of its free hand. Had it existed in the eighteenth century, Lodge averred, "France could not have assisted this country to win the Revolution." Neither could the United States have "rescued Cuba from the clutches of Spain" in 1898. And unlike previous treaties the United States had signed, the Covenant contained "no provisions for withdrawal or termination."

Worse, the Covenant would effectively repudiate the Monroe Doctrine, that "invisible line we drew around the American hemisphere . . . to exclude other nations from meddling in American affairs." The Covenant's defenders claimed "that we preserve the Monroe Doctrine by extending it" globally. Such logic was lost on Lodge. "I have never been able to get it through my head how you can preserve a fence by taking it down." Beyond opening the Americas to foreign powers, the League risked embroiling the United States "in every obscure quarrel that may spring up in the Balkans."

The Covenant also threatened America's internal autonomy by granting the League license to interfere with U.S. immigration policy, which "defends this country from a flood of Japanese, Chinese and Hindu labor." This Lodge could not accept. The power "to say who shall come into the United States . . . lies at the foundation of national character and national well being." Nor would he countenance that "other nations meddle with our tariff"—as the Covenant's provisions for economic boycotts would allow. Such a possibility "runs up against a provision of the Constitution," namely Congress's role in raising national revenue. "I think we ought to set our own import duties."

Lowell offered a polite but spirited riposte. He depicted the League as an imperative step toward world peace that posed no threat to American sovereignty, the Constitution, or the Monroe Doctrine. Yes, Lowell acknowledged, it implied new U.S. commitments. But "I think it is safe to say that most Americans believe that a League to prevent war would be worth some inconvenience to ourselves." And in truth the Covenant's obligations were modest. First, it insisted that nations, before resorting to force of arms, "be obliged to submit their differences to arbitration." Second, it required "severe penalties" for aggression, so that any transgressor would "find itself automatically at war with the rest of the League." Contrary to what Lodge had implied, however, it did *not* include any "automatic" provision to go to war against aggressors (something that Lowell himself would actually have favored as a surefire way to enforce the peace). Overall, Lowell considered the Covenant "the minimum . . . the smallest amount of obligations that could be undertaken if you are really to have a League to prevent war at all."

What about claims that the treaty was unconstitutional? After all, did it not require disarmament, violating congressional prerogatives to raise and equip armies? Did it not define and limit conditions under which states could resort to force, usurping Congress's authority to declare war? And did it not oblige the United States to suspend trade with aggressors, heedless of U.S.

legislative authority to regulate commerce and levy and collect duties? Lowell dismissed these complaints by reminding the audience that the Covenant, like all treaties, could be ratified only upon the Senate's explicit and voluntary advice and consent. "When it comes to treaties, the constitutional powers [of Congress] are unaffected," he explained. "If it were not so every treaty that we have made would be always null and void, because practically every treaty you make does to some extent limit or inhibit the power which Congress might otherwise exercise."

What about the Covenant's limits on U.S. freedom of action? Would not the United States be better off by seeking simply to keep order in its own hemisphere, while allowing the Europeans to do the same in theirs? The error in such logic was in believing that the United States could insulate itself from the wider world. "Isolation has passed away," Lowell insisted. Geography was relative rather than absolute, and technological innovation had diminished its importance. How long would it be, he wondered, before "Zeppelins can sail across the ocean and drop tons of bombs on American cities?" In his boldest stroke, Lowell implied that the famous Farewell Address was obsolete. "Things have changed since the days of Washington," and the United States must keep up with the times. "When the world is moving forward . . . it is a great mistake to walk backwards and look backwards."

Then there was "the greatest bugbear of all—the Monroe Doctrine." Far from contradicting that venerable policy, Lowell insisted, "this [League] covenant merely extends it all over the world"—by prohibiting aggressive intervention everywhere. Lodge had claimed that joining the League would require pulling down this fence. "That is perfectly true if your object is to preserve the fence," Lowell responded. "But if your object is to preserve the fruits inside the fence you do not fail to preserve them by making the fence cover two orchards instead of one." More provocatively, Lowell suggested that League membership would temper any "imperialistic" impulses the United States itself might harbor toward its own neighbors. It was time to abandon the presumption that "the Americas are game preserves in which no poachers are allowed, but in which the owner [the United States] may shoot all he pleases."

Lowell did support one amendment, which he hoped would alleviate "a great deal of misunderstanding." Namely, the United States should insist that both the powers of the League and the obligations of its members be limited to those specified by the Covenant. With this specification, the Covenant would "[mean] what it says, and not something else." He also agreed with Lodge that the United States must avoid submitting questions about domestic matters, including immigration and the tariff, to the League. As to the

Covenant's other obligations—to help fund the Universal Postal Union, to exchange information about armaments industries, to register all treaties with the League, to promote "humane treatment of labor" at home and abroad, and to "maintain freedom of transit and equitable treatment of commerce" with all League members—these were "not very important" and "need not . . . delay us."

Finally, Lowell reassured Americans that the League posed no peril. The envisioned nine-member League Council was hardly a "supersovereign body," as some had alleged. It lacked the "power to direct or order anything," even in response to aggression, and League members were "under no obligation, legal or moral, to accept" its advice and recommendations, unless the entire Council—including the U.S. representative—agreed. The proposed League Assembly, composed of all member states, posed even less of a threat to American sovereignty, since "they have practically no powers except to discuss."

Senator Lodge, who was permitted a final rebuttal, insisted that the Covenant would need to be amended significantly to have any chance of approval. And the place to do this under the U.S. Constitution was not in Paris but in Washington. He chastised Wilson for ignoring the Senate's "right to advise and consent," and for breaking with his presidential predecessors—including Washington, Jackson, Lincoln, and Grant—by failing to consult U.S. senators during treaty negotiations. Had the president submitted an early draft to legislators for possible revisions, "he would have had the amendments laid before him to present to the Peace Conference in Paris. The battle would have been more than half won by the mere submission." Instead, Wilson had allowed "the powers, the constitutional functions of one of the great branches of government [to become] atrophied, evaded, denied."

In his closing minutes Lodge waxed patriotic, invoking touchstones of American identity and nationalism. "We are a great moral asset of Christian civilization," he declared. "How did we get there? By our own efforts. Nobody led us, nobody guided us, nobody controlled us." Wilson's Covenant would take the republic down a different, dangerous path, toward "the dim red light of internationalism" (a clear reference to Leninism). He warned his fellow citizens: "You are being asked to exchange the government of Abraham Lincoln, of the people, for the people, by the people, for a government of, for, and by *other* people."

Lodge did not advocate isolationism, but rather a distinctly American internationalism. "I want my country to go forth: I want her to be a help to humanity as she has been"—just as she had helped defeat "autocracy and barbarism" in the Great War. "But I cannot but keep her interests in my mind," he insisted. And these required defending the country's historic freedom of action.

> I want to keep America as she has been—not isolated, not prevent her from joining other nations for these great purposes—but I wish her to be master of her fate. . . . I want her kept in a position to do that work and not submit her to a vote of other nations, with no recourse except to break a treaty which she wishes to maintain. We must not only strive to keep the world at peace, we must try to keep America as she is. I do not mean outside a League, but keep her as she is in her ideals and her principles. . . . Let her go on in her beneficent career, and I want to see her as she has always stood, strong and alive, triumphant, free.

Although partisans on each side claimed that their champion had triumphed, the debate was a draw in intellectual terms. "Both men won," concluded the moderator, Massachusetts governor Calvin Coolidge. As a practical matter, however, the event tilted political opinion slightly in Lodge's direction, by persuading previously undecided Republicans that Wilson's Covenant contained significant flaws—and that the Senate should adopt a prudent, methodical, and cautious approach to U.S. membership. Although media and public skepticism would take longer to emerge, the seeds of doubt had been sown.[4]

Over the next twelve months, the national debate over the League only grew more heated and partisan. In March 1920 the Senate definitively rejected the Versailles Peace Treaty (including the League Covenant), inaugurating an era of relative isolationism in U.S. foreign policy.

MUCH ADO ABOUT SOMETHING: CONFUSION AND CONTROVERSY OVER SOVEREIGNTY

The Lodge-Lowell debate occurred a century ago. But the choices and dilemmas raised that night—and in the broader League fight that unfolded over the ensuing, tumultuous year—endure. Indeed, they are at the heart of contemporary deliberations and disagreements about America's global role. Namely, can the United States best advance its interests and values through international institutions—including formal multilateral bodies and treaty obligations—or through its own national efforts and more flexible cooperative arrangements? How can the United States ensure that the multilateral commitments that it *does* embrace do not infringe on the authority of the U.S.

Constitution, the rights of U.S. citizens, and American national identity? And when the United States does cooperate with others, what constraints should it accept on its external freedom of action and domestic policy choices?

At their core, these questions have one subject: *sovereignty*—namely, the status of the United States as a constitutionally independent, democratic republic, at liberty to shape its own destiny abroad and govern itself at home without external interference.

Sovereignty is among the most frequently invoked, polemical, and vexing concepts in politics—particularly American politics. The concept wields symbolic power, implying something sacred and inalienable—the right of the people to control their fate without subordination to outside authorities. And yet there is little consensus in the United States about what sovereignty actually entails. Individuals can use the term to mean very different things, and they often employ it as a cover for underlying anxieties about an American national identity they see at risk or a country they fear is in terminal decline. Often lost in these heated discussions is that sovereignty has at least three dimensions—authority, autonomy, and influence—and that advancing U.S. interests in a complex world sometimes requires difficult trade-offs among defending the U.S. Constitution, protecting U.S. freedom of action, and maximizing U.S. control over outcomes. Navigating these choices requires sober thinking.

Given its emotive pull, however, the concept of sovereignty is easily hijacked by nationalists, as well as political opportunists, to shut down debate. By playing the sovereignty card, they can curtail more reasoned discussions over the merits of proposed international commitments by portraying supporters of global treaties or organizations as (in effect) enemies of motherhood and apple pie. Secretary of State Dean Rusk bemoaned this dynamic half a century ago in testimony to the Senate Foreign Relations Committee. The problem with discussing the question of American "sovereignty," he noted, was that "immediately people wrap the American flag around themselves and resort to that form of patriotism which Samuel Johnson once referred to as 'the last refuge of the scoundrel.'"[5]

The discourse over American sovereignty has only grown more heated over the past five decades. During the 1990s, Senator Jesse Helms (R-N.C.), chair of the Senate Foreign Relations Committee, angered a generation of liberal internationalists by blocking U.S. membership in multilateral treaties and withholding U.S. dues to the United Nations (UN) in an effort to impose reform on the world body. In more recent years, John Bolton, who served as U.S. ambassador to the UN under President George W. Bush, has warned of "the coming war on sovereignty." John Fonte of the conservative Hudson Institute frames the choice for the United States as a binary one in his book *Sovereignty or Submission: Will Americans Rule Themselves or Be Ruled by Others?*[6] On Capitol Hill, meanwhile, more than two dozen senators have formed the "Sovereignty Caucus." According to Representative Doug Lamborn (R-Colo.), one of its cofounders, the group was established to "protect and defend the rights of American citizens and the interests of American institutions from the increasing influence of international organizations and multilateral agreements. It will promote policies and practices that protect U.S. self-determination, national sovereignty, and constitutional principles and defend American values from encroachment by transnational actors."[7] Not to be left out, state legislatures from Idaho to South Carolina to Texas have passed resolutions reasserting U.S. sovereignty.

On the campaign trail for the 2016 Republican presidential nomination, the New York real estate mogul Donald J. Trump used his first major foreign policy speech to excoriate the "false song of globalism": "The nation-state remains the true foundation of happiness and harmony. I am skeptical of international unions that tie us up and bring America down. And under my administration, we will never enter America into any agreement that reduces our ability to control our own affairs."[8] Accepting the GOP nomination in Cleveland that summer, Mr. Trump pledged to put "America first," resurrecting the pre–World War II phrase associated with American isolationists like Charles Lindbergh.[9] Candidate Trump promised U.S. citizens that if elected he would help them take their country back—and make it great again. This agenda included renouncing international agreements that he claimed hamstrung U.S. freedom of action, including the Paris Accord on Climate Change; restoring U.S. control over the country's southern border with Mexico; disowning "awful" trade deals struck with other countries; and pulling back from entangling overseas alliances and commitments.

Trump's surprising election in November 2016 as the forty-fifth president of the United States placed front and center the question of whether and how the United States can reconcile long-standing sovereignty concerns with the requirements of sustained and effective international cooperation.

In his dark inaugural address, Trump promised to pursue the hypernationalist agenda on which he had campaigned.[10] In his first days in office he drafted several provocative executive orders intended to advance U.S. sovereignty, as he conceived it.[11] He directed his administration to begin construction of a wall along the border with Mexico, to withdraw from the planned Trans-Pacific Partnership (TPP) trade bloc, to renegotiate the North American Free Trade

Agreement (NAFTA), to suspend all refugee admissions to the United States, to ban immigration from seven Muslim-majority countries deemed hotbeds of terrorism, to begin a process to slash U.S. contributions to the United Nations, and to impose a moratorium on all new multilateral treaties. If one conviction animated these disparate actions, it was that the world order the United States had created after World War II no longer served U.S. interests. Americans had to restore their sovereignty—by regaining control of their borders, adopting economic protectionism, withdrawing from global bodies, and reconsidering multilateral conventions.

As his chief strategist, the new president chose Stephen K. Bannon, former executive chairman of the website Breitbart News, a media focal point of the white nationalist "alt-right" movement, which—among many other constituencies— had helped propel Trump to power. Bannon's "worldview, as laid out in interviews and speeches over the past several years," the *Washington Post* helpfully explained, "hinges largely on [his] belief in American 'sovereignty.'" Among other convictions, "Bannon said that countries should protect their citizens and their essence by reducing immigration, legal and illegal, and pulling back from multinational agreements."[12]

Trump and Bannon had tapped into a strain of populist nationalism that commands powerful support in some quarters of American society—but which internationally minded U.S. elites had long ignored. Its adherents depict U.S. sovereignty as under siege, to the detriment of American liberties and U.S. freedom of action. And its rhetoric flows hot. One need not probe deeply on the Internet to find would-be defenders of U.S. sovereignty who warn ominously about nefarious global bodies determined to undermine U.S. constitutional government. They include outfits like Americans for Sovereignty, Council for America, InfoWars, and WorldNetDaily, which invites visitors to its site to sign a "Re-Declaration of Independence: Petition to Protect U.S. Sovereignty."[13]

No doubt these vigilant netizens see themselves as modern-day "minutemen," patrolling cyberspace to expose an insidious international conspiracy— enabled by domestic fifth columnists writing for organizations such as the Council on Foreign Relations or the *New York Times*—to deprive the United States of its God-given sovereignty. But they often traffic in hysteria reminiscent of the fictional general Jack D. Ripper of *Dr. Strangelove*, who famously warned that Communists had designs on Americans' "vital bodily fluids." As such, their most persuasive role is to serve as exemplars of what the historian Richard Hofstadter famously called "the paranoid style in American politics."[14]

Such alarmism does the nation a disservice. It stokes groundless fears that the U.S. constitutional system is at risk, even as it invokes an imaginary past in which the country enjoyed complete freedom of action. It also ignores the extent to which the United States, in pursuit of its own national interests, has already integrated itself into a system of international rules largely of its own making. Finally, such polemics distract Americans from what is really at stake in the sovereignty debate: namely, the ability of the United States to shape its destiny in a global age.

This book is aimed at readers bewildered by the sovereignty debate—including those who wonder what all the fuss is about or find themselves unsure how to weigh competing claims. It is unlikely to win over die-hard, self-styled "defenders" of American sovereignty. But I hope it will reassure those puzzled by current controversies, persuading them that the United States can indeed reap the benefits of international cooperation without significant incursions on its constitutional authorities or undue restrictions on its freedom of action.

To be sure, deepening economic integration, rising security interdependence, and developing international law *do* pose dilemmas for traditional U.S. conceptions of national sovereignty. The United States cannot successfully manage globalization, much less insulate itself from cross-border threats, simply on its own. As transnational challenges grow, the nation's fate becomes more closely tied to that of other countries, whose cooperation will be needed to exploit the shared opportunities and mitigate the common risks inherent in living on the same planet.[15]

To advance their interests and aspirations in today's world, Americans need to develop a more sophisticated understanding of what sovereignty means. And their government must adopt a more pragmatic approach to navigating inevitable trade-offs among its various components. The first steps are to think clearly about the implications of current trends, about what U.S. prerogatives must be protected, and about what circumstances might warrant adjustments in U.S. policy and psychology.

One impediment to a more candid conversation is a widespread failure to recognize that sovereignty has multiple dimensions. Indeed, when Americans invoke the term, they often imply very different things—and thus talk past one another. Disentangling these meanings can help us distinguish between symbolic but often specious claims and real, practical dilemmas—including painful choices between opposing objectives that sometimes arise. Once we recognize that sovereignty can be disaggregated, we see that it is possible—even desirable—to voluntarily trade off one aspect of sovereignty for another.[16]

FIGURE 1-1. The Sovereignty Triangle

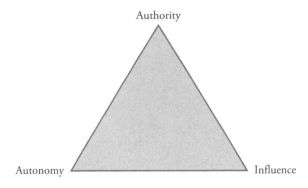

The three core dimensions of sovereignty are authority, autonomy, and influence. *Authority* refers to the state's exclusive and legitimate right to make rules. *Autonomy* refers to its ability to make and implement decisions independently. *Influence* refers to the state's effective capacity to advance its interests. Figure 1-1 depicts these dimensions as distinct poles of a "sovereignty triangle."

As applied to the United States, sovereignty-as-authority implies that the Constitution is the supreme law of the land and no external constraints should limit Americans' right to govern themselves as they see fit. Sovereignty-as-autonomy implies that the U.S. government, acting on behalf of the people, should have the freedom of action to formulate and pursue its foreign and domestic policies independently. Sovereignty-as-influence implies that the United States should be able to shape its own destiny. In sum, American sovereignty means that the United States possesses inherent rights that should not be surrendered, autonomy that should not be infringed upon, and a fate that it should be able to influence.

Each of these three attributes is a valued objective in and of itself. The practical difficulty, as this book will explain, is that sovereignty-as-authority, sovereignty-as-autonomy, and sovereignty-as-influence are often in tension. That is, advancing one dimension may require trade-offs with one or both of the others. When it comes to sovereignty, as in economics, there is no free lunch. The requirements of international cooperation make this clear. In an age of globalization, exercising sovereignty-as-influence requires working with others. But moving in that direction can carry costs for sovereignty-as-autonomy, since a commitment to work with others forecloses notional actions the United States might otherwise take. And it could also infringe on sovereignty-as-authority, if the United States were to accept the political authority of a supranational body or, more commonly, delegate certain authorities to (or pool those authorities within) international organizations.

How grave are these dilemmas? The answer is partly subjective, since it depends on where individuals place themselves on the sovereignty triangle, and which of the three values they seek to privilege. A liberal internationalist, for instance, might place herself at the bottom right corner, prioritizing effective influence in solving a global problem of interest to the United States through cooperative action, even if that implied a loss of autonomy or, conceivably, even authority. A great power nationalist, meanwhile, might consider the lost freedom of action too high a price to pay and insist on retaining autonomy. A constitutional "originalist," finally, might be unwilling to accept the perceived costs to domestic popular sovereignty inherent in subcontracting U.S. foreign policy goals to an international institution that is perceived to lack democratic accountability.

While such trade-offs can be real, their gravity is often exaggerated. Too great a defensiveness against any perceived losses of U.S. sovereignty-as-autonomy or U.S. sovereignty-as-authority can be counterproductive if it deprives the United States of the opportunity to exercise its sovereignty-as-influence—that is, to shape its destiny in a global era.

The United States is hardly the only nation protective of its sovereignty, as chapter 2 discusses. But its dilemma is more acute than for most other countries. The reasons are geopolitical, constitutional, and ideological. To begin with, the unmatched power of the United States, as well as its de facto status as the ultimate guarantor of world order, encourages U.S. insistence on untrammeled freedom of action abroad. Meanwhile, the U.S. Constitution—and the reverence with which it is held—complicates the U.S. assumption of multilateral obligations, particularly those that appear to infringe on the separation of powers, the prerogatives of the fifty states in America's federal system, or the consent of the American people. Finally, the enduring ideology of American exceptionalism, which holds the United States to be unique among nations, makes Americans inherently anxious about submerging themselves in multinational ventures, organizations, or treaties.

These factors help explain why sovereignty has long been a lightning rod issue domestically and why the nation—despite its claims to and legacy of global leadership—is so often the odd man out internationally. No country has done more since World War II to foster a rule-bound international order, spearheading major multilateral treaties and institutions. And yet the United States has repeatedly opted out of international commitments, including conventions supported by overwhelming majorities of nations, perceived to constrain its policy autonomy and freedom of action.

The Comprehensive Test Ban Treaty (CTBT), the Convention on the Rights of the Child (CRC), the Rome Statute of the International Criminal Court (ICC), the Mine Ban Treaty, and the UN Convention on the Law of the Sea (UNCLOS) are but a few examples. More commonly, the United States has carved out special exceptions within treaties to gain unique privileges, while supporting constraints on the behavior of other states.

Debates over U.S. sovereignty have grown louder in the twenty-first century, as the United States tries to reconcile venerable national instincts with new global realities. Self-styled "sovereigntists," predominantly but not exclusively conservative in their orientation, worry that the United States risks sacrificing once-sacrosanct prerogatives on the altar of "global governance," as unaccountable international institutions and haphazard trends in international law infringe on U.S. freedom of action abroad and U.S. regulatory autonomy at home, running roughshod over U.S. democracy and the U.S. Constitution in the process. On the other side of the debate, meanwhile, some apostles of "world government" either dismiss such concerns as unwarranted or, alternatively, welcome these sacrifices on the grounds that sovereignty is an outmoded principle and an obstacle to effective global governance.[17]

In fact, neither sky-is-falling fears nor what-me-worry complacency is warranted. Contrary to sovereigntist mythology, U.S. sovereignty has never been absolute. Since the founding of the republic, the United States has wrestled with how to reconcile its national autonomy and independence with the requirements of international cooperation. At a practical level, moreover, the United States has become well versed in trading off autonomy for influence. Since 1945, in particular, the United States has joined hundreds of international organizations and multilateral treaties, each of which limits its freedom of action, calculating that collective efforts could advance U.S. interests more effectively than could unilateral action. Such bargains have brought tangible benefits. They have nurtured an open world economy that has generated unprecedented wealth, underpinned an international security system with rules governing the use of force and mechanisms to keep weapons of mass destruction (WMD) under lock and key, and undergirded U.S. global leadership by legitimating American power. This last factor is particularly important as U.S. power declines relative to its former dominance.

Contrary to assertions by globalists, however, such choices have not been cost-free: they have required real trade-offs between U.S. prerogatives, including limited delegation of political authorities and constraints on U.S. freedom of action. Traditional concepts and practices of sovereignty *are* being tested by the ever-increasing velocity and volume of cross-border flows of goods, money, services, ideas, and people; by the emergence of new transnational security threats; by the rise of nonstate actors; and by innovations in international law. Deepening globalization also challenges sovereignty's popular dimension, or the expectation that the consent of the governed is the only legitimate basis for political authority, since democratic deficits often plague new multilateral institutions created to manage interdependence.

Fortunately, these challenges are seldom insuperable. The United States is fully capable of cooperating with other nations in multilateral settings that preserve its sovereign authority while accomplishing desired goals, providing that it is willing to sacrifice some notional (but often illusory) freedom of action, by accepting reciprocal obligations alongside its foreign partners. International organizations and treaties will remain imperfect, but the benefits they provide, such as enforcing universal trade rules or arresting potential pandemics, will frequently outweigh the constraints and frustrations. And in many settings, the United States can also avail itself of less formal, à la carte forms of cooperation by forming "minilateral" coalitions of the willing. Such smaller groupings of the capable, interested, and like-minded cannot entirely replace standing institutions. But they are becoming more important features of the global institutional landscape, and their very informality and flexibility can reassure sovereignty-minded Americans worried that the United States is sacrificing too much national authority and autonomy for the sake of global ventures.

SOVEREIGNTY BARGAINS

To shape its own fate, the United States will more often need to consider "sovereignty bargains,"[18] voluntarily delegating some autonomy—but only rarely authority—to gain increased influence over outside forces, advance its national interests, and shape its fate as a nation. The duty of U.S. politicians and diplomats is to ensure that the benefits of sovereignty losses outweigh the costs, and that incursions on traditional U.S. prerogatives or constraints on U.S. behavior are acceptable on prudential, moral, and/or constitutional grounds. American statesmen and -women should design institutions for international cooperation that deliver the same (or better) results while minimizing true sovereignty losses. The purpose of this book is to help U.S. policymakers think more clearly about what is actually at stake in the sovereignty debate, as well as to provide insights about what sorts of bargains may be warranted, based on the relative value they place on authority, autonomy, and influence.

Recognizing that sovereignty can be disaggregated into authority, autonomy, and influence helps to transcend stale debates about whether U.S. sovereignty is (or is not) eroding and, if so, whether this is (or is not) a bad thing. It also becomes clear that the United States can trade off one facet of sovereignty to advance another.

Defined as authority, for instance, U.S. sovereignty is not at risk just because the United States has porous borders or is vulnerable to financial crises. But its sovereignty-as-influence is reduced in both scenarios, and reasserting that influence may require either sacrificing authority (to an outside global entity, for instance) or—far more likely—voluntarily ceding some policy autonomy within a bilateral, regional, or multilateral partnership that constrains its theoretical freedom of action for the benefits of international cooperation.

Similarly, the United States may sacrifice some sovereignty-as-autonomy in joining an international organization like the International Atomic Energy Agency (IAEA) or ratifying a multilateral treaty like the Chemical Weapons Convention (CWC). The former obliges the U.S. government to accept certain international nuclear standards and to abide by the decisions of the organization's board of governors. The latter requires the United States, among other things, to forgo an entire class of weapons. But by joining such frameworks the United States is in fact reaffirming its sovereignty-as-authority, as well as enhancing its sovereignty-as-influence—in this case its capacity to restrain the spread of weapons of mass destruction, a goal that would be unattainable through purely unilateral action.[19]

The most heated debates over U.S. sovereignty today focus on alleged losses of authority. Sovereignty's defenders worry that the U.S. constitutional system of government, which derives its democratic legitimacy from the consent of the governed, is threatened by unaccountable international organizations, proliferating international treaties, and the rampant expansion of international law. Such concerns are overblown. Sovereignty bargains of this sort are rare for the United States, which remains very stingy about transferring real authorities to intergovernmental—much less "supranational"—bodies.

The U.S. decision to join an international body or to be bound by an international convention represents an *expression and exercise* of sovereignty, not its abdication, based on a self-interested calculation that it has more to gain than to lose by throwing its lot in with—and leveraging the contributions of—other like-minded sovereign states. Moreover, the United States always retains the right, if the situation requires, to renounce its membership in any international organization or even to abrogate its treaty commitments.[20] The decision to "exit" may be a costly one, but it remains an ultimate option.

The much more typical trade-off is between autonomy and influence—that is, between independent decisionmaking and action, on the one hand, and enhanced problem solving within collective frameworks, on the other. The question boils down to this: What constraints on its notional range of policy options, both domestic and external, should the United States be prepared to accept in exchange for greater cooperation in exploiting the opportunities, mitigating the risks, and managing the shared dilemmas of globalization?

Although not quite as volatile as debates over sovereignty-as-authority, this question of U.S. freedom of action still generates controversy. Americans naturally resist international constraints on their policy options—an independent streak reinforced by the country's power, geography, and historical identity. However, insisting on national autonomy can undermine America's capacity to advance its objectives and shape its fate in a globalized world. This is obvious when it comes to managing problems that transcend borders, such as the consequences of climate change or the international spread of infectious diseases. In an age of transnational challenges, "effective" sovereignty increasingly implies coordinated responses with other independent states, often within international institutions. And the price of that enhanced problem solving is typically a willingness to cede some sovereignty-as-autonomy for sovereignty-as-influence.[21]

As the world becomes more interconnected, advancing U.S. national security, economic prosperity, and social welfare—and preserving the viability of planet Earth—will require innovative approaches to multilateral cooperation. Whether the United States is prepared to make this shift is unclear. Many of the voters who supported Donald Trump in November 2016 were skeptical of globalization, dubious of international cooperation, and sensitive to lost U.S. freedom of action.

Figuring out when and how to strike sovereignty bargains will be one of the biggest foreign policy challenges facing the United States in the twenty-first century. This is admittedly a different approach to U.S. sovereignty than the one advocated by America's Founders, like Washington and Jefferson. They warned the young United States—at least as long as it remained a weak republic in a world of great powers—to steer clear of international commitments. Times have changed, however. The United States should continue to protect its constitutional system from unwarranted encroachments. But America's ability to shape its fate—that is, to exercise sovereignty-as-influence—will more often require that it relax its insistence on sovereignty-as-autonomy.

Today the best measure of effective sovereignty is not the absence of foreign entanglements, but indeed the extensiveness of a country's links with the outside world. It is not about steering clear of international attachments, but about steering global forces and events in a positive direction. The model to emulate is no longer Greta Garbo, the actor who famously declared, "I vant to be alone." It is Mark Zuckerberg, the CEO of Facebook, who had 93 million "followers" as of July 2017. In an ironic twist, the state's ability to make its influence felt as an independent political unit increasingly depends on the extent of its interdependence with other states.[22]

A ROAD MAP FOR WHAT'S AHEAD

Chapter 2, "There's No Place Like Home: Sovereignty, American Style," introduces the idea of sovereignty and discusses how it has been conceived, expressed, and defended in the United States. It traces sovereignty's emergence as a principle of political order in the late Middle Ages and its consolidation, first in Europe and ultimately globally, as *the* fundamental rule of international relations. It highlights sovereignty's historical attributes, including international legal recognition, supreme political authority, freedom from external intervention, control over cross-border flows, and rule by the consent of the governed. The last of these features—also known as popular sovereignty—is the distinctive American contribution to the concept.

The chapter disputes the frequent contention that globalization has placed sovereignty "at bay" or "on the ropes." The sovereign state remains vital—in both senses of that word. It is fundamental, serving as the bedrock of international order. And it is vigorous, shaping and defining the terms of global integration. There is nothing on the horizon that can take its place as the ultimate source of legitimate political authority and practical capability. And there is no country better placed than the United States to defend its sovereign prerogatives.

Given this state of affairs, why are U.S. sovereignty debates so fraught, vigorous, and volatile? Why do Americans devote such energy to asserting, guarding, and defending their sovereign rights? American vigilance reflects five factors: political ideology, national identity, constitutional structure, geopolitical realities, and accelerating globalization. The first three of these influences date from the republic's founding, and their legacy endures today. The last two (taken up in chapter 3) reflect evolving external forces.

The ideological emphasis that Americans place on sovereignty's popular foundations helps explain U.S. touchiness. The United States was the first modern republic to base legitimate political authority on the consent of the governed, and the heart of the American constitutional order is the principle that the people rule. This legacy makes Americans inherently skeptical of political authority, and they are acutely sensitive to international organizations they perceive to be intruding on the supremacy of the U.S. Constitution and the nation's domestic policymaking processes.[23] They are determined to bring such bodies to heel by making them democratically accountable to American citizens.

Reinforcing this instinct is a pervasive public commitment to American exceptionalism. This is the conviction that the United States is a distinctive and superior political community, founded on unassailable principles and possessing a special global destiny. Americans regularly invoke this noble vocation to justify abstaining from global arrangements or constraints that bind other nations.

The U.S. Constitution, which divides power among three co-equal branches of government and reserves significant powers for the U.S. states, further complicates America's assumption of international obligations. Regardless of executive branch preferences, the separation of powers allows Congress to determine what international treaties get approved and what funds get appropriated for international purposes. The U.S. federal system can also place hurdles before U.S. international engagements by delegating many authorities to the fifty U.S. state governments. Collectively, these three factors help explain the long-standing U.S. discomfort with multilateral cooperation, global organizations, and international law.

Chapter 3, "Power and Interdependence: U.S. Sovereignty in the American Century," turns to the two remaining influences on U.S. conceptions of sovereignty, with a special focus on the past one hundred years. The first is the nation's evolving geopolitical position in relation to other global power centers. The second is globalization, which has buffeted the United States with transnational forces and integrated it into the wider world. Unlike the enduring, essentially static forces of ideology, culture, and institutions, power and interdependence are dynamic factors. Together, they have tempered some traditional American defensiveness with respect to sovereign authority and autonomy.

America's geopolitical position and exposure to globalization have changed profoundly since 1776. The once-tiny, vulnerable republic has become the most powerful nation in history. Meanwhile, ongoing revolutions in technology, communications, transportation, and complex supply chains have deepened and broadened its integration into the world economy.

America's rise to globalism in the twentieth century tempered instinctive U.S. wariness toward international organizations and "entangling alliances." The United States sponsored the creation of the United Nations during World War II and, once the Cold War began, the North Atlantic Treaty Organization (NATO) and the wider U.S. alliance system. The Roosevelt and Truman administrations worked with Congress to reconcile these new commitments with safeguards for American sovereignty, including constitutional authority and U.S. freedom of action. Still, the U.S. conversion to globalism remained ambivalent, selective, and conditional. The United States sponsored new multilateral institutions and shaped global rules, but it resisted encroachments on its Constitution and constraints on its autonomy.[24]

The end of the Cold War left the United States as the world's only superpower and allowed the pace of globalization to accelerate—with ambiguous impacts on U.S. sovereignty. On the one hand, the scale of cross-border flows (both positive and negative) has increased incentives for sovereignty bargains, whereby the United States exchanges some maneuvering room for more effective efforts to reap the benefits and mitigate the downsides of interdependence. On the other hand, the massively powerful United States has often chafed at the restraints of institutionalized multilateral cooperation and preferred advancing its national interests unilaterally—or through flexible, ad hoc frameworks that protect its freedom of action. Presidents George W. Bush and Barack Obama addressed this convergence of U.S. power and global interdependence in different ways—reaping different benefits and incurring different costs in the process.

Chapters 4–8 examine how inherited U.S. concepts of sovereignty shape contemporary American attitudes toward international law, international security, international economics, international borders, and international organizations—and how recent trends are testing and transforming longstanding U.S. policies in each of these five arenas. Each chapter identifies the most serious American sovereignty concerns; addresses the range of potential trade-offs among U.S. authority, autonomy, and influence; and recommends new sovereignty bargains that will allow the United States to secure the gains of interdependence at acceptable cost.

Each chapter begins with a vignette about a recent political controversy, intended to animate what is at stake in quarrels over sovereignty, which otherwise can seem an abstract concept. These incidents illustrate just how pervasive

U.S. sovereignty debates have become—and how much they shape public and private attitudes about America's role in the world.

Chapter 4, "Do as I Say, Not as I Do: American Sovereignty and International Law," explores the ambiguous and fraught U.S. relationship with international law—grist for some of the most contentious U.S. sovereignty disputes.[25] At a rhetorical level, U.S. officials have always supported international law, recognizing America's interest in a rule-bound world order. And yet actual U.S. attitudes and policies have been wary and defensive, thanks to U.S. power, American exceptionalism, and the constitutional separation of powers.

Since World War II, the United States has sought to shape international rules, while sometimes holding itself apart from legal obligations accepted by the vast majority of other states. Two prominent examples are the UN Convention on the Law of the Sea and the UN Convention on the Rights of Persons with Disabilities. At the root of these controversies is whether international law can be made compatible with U.S. sovereignty-as-authority. Can the U.S. Constitution be reconciled with evolving international legal norms?

Conservative politicians, jurists, and scholars worry that that the United States is becoming enmeshed in a thicket of legal obligations that infringe on American popular sovereignty, undermine Congress, and run roughshod over U.S. federalism.[26] They object to what they see as an ever-expanding definition of customary international law, the cross-border activism of left-wing U.S. nongovernmental organizations (NGOs) seeking to define international legal norms, a growing body of "transnational law" that lacks domestic provenance and thus legitimacy, an over-reliance on "self-executing" treaties, and the growing habit of U.S courts to cite foreign law in their judicial decisions.

Chapter 4 finds these concerns excessive. The United States is at no risk of seeing its Constitution subordinated to international law, and U.S. leaders remain vigilant in ensuring that U.S. international legal commitments pass constitutional muster. The United States has multiple mechanisms to protect its sovereign legal authorities. These include placing reservations on its treaty ratification, declaring some treaties to be "non-self-executing," and taking steps to slow the growth of customary international law.

The chapter underscores that the U.S. decision to sign and ratify a treaty is an *exercise* rather than an abdication of sovereign authority. What any treaty does, by design, is limit the autonomy of all parties, so that they can be confident in one another's behavior and realize common aims. While each proposed multilateral treaty needs to be considered on its merits, too great an insistence on U.S. freedom of action would be counter to U.S. national interests.

Finally, the chapter finds overblown the claim that U.S. judges (including Supreme Court justices) undermine the integrity of U.S. constitutional law when they make modest references to foreign jurisprudence. Also, given existing safeguards, international law does not pose any significant threat to the U.S. separation of powers and federal system established under the U.S. Constitution. What international law *does* provide is an opportunity to enhance the dense latticework of international cooperation that has evolved, particularly since 1945, so that the United States can better manage the dilemmas of interdependence.

Chapter 5, "Don't Fence Me In: The Use of Force, Arms Control, and U.S. National Security," asks how the United States can reconcile its traditional desire for sovereign autonomy with the reality of global security interdependence. On the one hand, the United States has an obvious interest in cooperating with others to address terrorism, nuclear proliferation, and other transnational dangers, as well as in securing international legitimacy when it feels compelled to use force. On the other hand, as the world's most powerful nation, with heavy responsibilities, it understandably seeks maximum room for maneuver, and often begrudges the requirements of collective security, particularly within the United Nations. Sovereignty considerations continue to shape U.S. security policy, including the UN Security Council's authorization of military force, U.S. support for (and participation in) UN peace operations, and the U.S. posture toward arms control agreements.

The chapter notes the paradoxical U.S. position with respect to national sovereignty and rules governing the use of force. Since the end of the Cold War, the United States has intervened militarily both with an explicit UN Security Council mandate (as in the Gulf War in 1991 and in Libya in 2011) and without one (as in Kosovo in 1999 and in Iraq in 2003). Meanwhile, it has been a leading exponent of the doctrine of "contingent sovereignty"—the notion that countries forfeit any presumption against external intervention when they support terrorism, pursue WMD, or commit (or fail to prevent) mass atrocities. The United States has also been a major proponent of UN peacekeeping, even as it resists placing U.S. soldiers under the direct command of foreign officers.

The U.S. stance toward arms control and nonproliferation efforts reveals similar ambivalence. As a practical matter, the United States has joined numerous international organizations and multilateral initiatives to combat the spread and use of WMD. Each framework obliges it to forgo certain options, reducing its notional range of maneuver, and some bodies include intrusive multilateral verification schemes to address cross-border threats. In rare instances the United States has even traded a bit of sovereign authority in return for more effective cooperation. Despite these benefits, American "sovereigntists" routinely complain that such arrangements unacceptably constrain U.S. freedom, infringe on U.S. legislative prerogatives, and even endanger U.S. constitutional liberties. Few of these broad critiques hold water. They also ignore a reality of the modern world: the spread of lethal technologies gives the United States a huge incentive to enter into reciprocal, consensual arrangements with other nations to jointly contain these emerging threats.

A similar logic applies when it comes to preserving stability in the global commons—including the oceans, outer space, and cyberspace—as these domains become more crowded, cutthroat, and conflictual.[27] In all three spheres the United States has a fundamental interest in negotiating new rules to preserve a stable, predictable, and regulated arena, even if these reduce its freedom of maneuver. Although the United States must always reserve the right to act alone to defend its national security, the pursuit of maximal autonomy would undercut cooperative efforts to achieve objectives that the nation cannot achieve on its own.

The United States will need to strike similar sovereignty bargains to reap the benefits and mitigate the downsides of global interdependence. In recent years, both conservatives and progressives alike have complained that the United States has sacrificed its sovereignty to the dictates of the international economy. This is the topic of chapter 6, "Stop the World, I Want to Get Off: Globalization and American Sovereignty." It addresses the contemporary U.S. backlash against global integration and the vocal insistence, so prominent in the 2016 presidential campaign, that the United States must reassert sovereign control over its economy.

Since 1945 the United States has been the world's leading champion of an open, nondiscriminatory system of international trade and payments, governed by multilateral rules and institutions. The economic gains have been impressive, if unevenly shared. At the same time, the quickening pace and swelling quantity of international transactions—including flows of ideas, information, goods, services, money, and people—is straining the capacity of all states to manage their own domestic economies, cushion themselves from volatility, and deliver on social goals. These trends help explain the populist backlash against globalization in the United States and many other countries.

The contemporary crisis reflects in part the collapse of a previous sovereignty bargain that was at the heart of the post–World War II global economic system. The major institutions created to govern the postwar economy—including the International Monetary Fund, the World Bank, and the General Agreement

on Tariffs and Trade (GATT)—were intended to reconcile a broad commitment to openness with sovereign flexibility for governments to mediate the
pace and terms of their countries' integration into the new system so that they
could pursue social welfare goals such as full employment. Over time, however, this compromise broke down. The forces of capital were liberated, and
governments—including in the United States—either abandoned or found it
harder to uphold their end of the domestic bargain.

In the mid-1990s the United States doubled down on globalization, promoting the creation of the North American Free Trade Agreement, as well as
the World Trade Organization (WTO) to succeed the GATT. Significantly,
both arrangements included legal provisions that both limited U.S. sovereign
autonomy and impinged (albeit modestly) on U.S. sovereign authorities, most
notably in binding dispute settlement mechanisms.

Chapter 6 recommends that the United States restore balance between
global economic integration and its own national economic and social welfare
needs by making greater use of the sovereign autonomy it retains to pursue
those domestic objectives. This is not a counsel of autarky. Rather, the United
States should negotiate new multilateral bargains with major trading partners
that offer nations greater protections against an unregulated global market
and help American workers and firms adjust to international competition.
The United States should also collaborate with like-minded governments to
strengthen mechanisms of global economic governance so that these are capable of withstanding sudden shocks, building on the initial steps that the international community took in the wake of the global financial crisis of 2007–08.

Recent American anxieties about globalization have merged with fear that
the United States has lost control of its borders, permitting the entry of illegal
immigrants that not only displace U.S. workers but also endanger the safety
of American citizens. This is the subject of chapter 7, "Good Fences Make
Good Neighbors: Immigration and Border Security." In 2016 Donald Trump
successfully exploited these concerns in his quest for the presidency. He
promised to build a "great wall" along the southern U.S. border, to round up
and deport 11 million undocumented individuals, and to bar, at least temporarily, Muslims from entering the United States. Such "solutions" were simplistic, unrealistic, and coldhearted, but they resonated with a visceral public
understanding of a core dimension of sovereignty—namely, the state's ability
to control its borders, including to regulate who enters and is allowed to stay
in the country.

Chapter 7 argues that the vision of complete U.S. border control has always been a mirage—and that making headway on illegal immigration and

other cross-border threats will require more rather than fewer sovereignty bargains with other countries, not least with Mexico. Improving border security will also depend on crafting tailored approaches to the very distinct challenges posed by illegal immigration, narcotics trafficking, and transnational terrorism, which have too often been conflated in American political discourse and the public imagination. Finally, a sustainable U.S. policy toward immigration—legal as well as illegal—will require a more honest public conversation about the societal dimensions of U.S. sovereignty, including how best to assimilate new arrivals and encourage social cohesion within a single, increasingly diverse nation.

The trade-offs between traditional conceptions of U.S. sovereignty and the growing need for multilateral cooperation are nowhere more obvious than in international organizations. A century after Lodge and Lowell squared off in the Boston Symphony Hall, the terms of U.S. membership in global bodies continue to roil U.S. domestic politics. These debates are the subject of chapter 8, "Don't Tread on Me: The United States and International Organizations."

American resistance to the constraints of multilateral bodies is ironic, of course, since the United States more than any other country is responsible for their proliferation. And yet from the earliest postwar years, many Americans—particularly conservatives—have vociferously opposed any perceived infringements that international organizations might place on the nation's sovereign authorities and autonomy.

Ground zero for these debates has been the sprawling UN system, which critics depict as a threat to U.S. democratic sovereignty and freedom of action. In their dystopian scenario, the world could well become a giant version of the European Union. Such a fevered critique overlooks the profound differences between U.S. participation in intergovernmental bodies like the United Nations and membership in a supranational organization like the EU. It also ignores how tarnished the EU has become as a model for economic and political integration.

More generally, sovereigntist warnings about the UN disregard just how little independent power that body actually wields and how modest are the resources at its disposal. By the same token, such alarums fail to explain how the United States could possibly achieve many international objectives purely through its own efforts. Rather than constraining U.S. policy options, international organizations often *expand* them, by allowing the United States to share burdens with others as well as to gain legitimacy for its purposes.

That said, the UN and other international organizations do raise inherent dilemmas for U.S. sovereignty, particularly with regard to democratic accountability. Multilateral organizations require members to delegate some authority to their secretariats and to accept collective decisionmaking within intergovernmental boards created to supervise them. The first of these challenges, "delegation," makes it hard to ensure that the UN (or any other organization) fulfills its mandate rather than pursuing an independent agenda. The second, known as "pooling," means that U.S. influence over any organization may well be diluted by other member states.

These are real and persistent challenges. International organizations can and sometimes do take on a life of their own, doing things at odds with their initial purposes (not to mention U.S. interests) and with little opportunity for American citizens to seek redress through processes of representative democracy. Such risks are manageable, however. The chapter identifies several strategies and tactics that the United States can adopt to limit or rein in dysfunctional behavior by international organizations and reduce some of the democratic deficit that afflicts them. These include insisting on transparency and information sharing, promoting vigilance by independent watchdogs, and requiring "sunset" provisions to phase out initiatives or agencies that cease to be relevant. There is, lastly, the ultimate option of renouncing U.S. membership. As long as this remains a credible threat, the United States can be said to have preserved its sovereign authority.

Reconciling international organizations with the principle of national sovereignty is a very different goal than world government, an objective that one still sometimes hears on the left-wing, utopian fringe. For centuries, dreamers have envisioned that humanity might one day put aside its divisions and embrace a planetary political system in the form of a world government, or even a global state. This is an awful idea, on many grounds. Rather than striving for some misguided cosmopolitan paradise, the United States must work to rejuvenate international cooperation within the sovereign state system.

Building on the previous chapters, chapter 9, "Conclusion: American Sovereignty and International Cooperation," argues that there is both less and more at stake in the sovereignty debate than is conventionally asserted. Contrary to the arguments of many sovereigntists, the United States faces few threats to its sovereignty-as-authority—or the supremacy of the U.S. Constitution and the popular sovereignty that it embodies. What the United States does and will be more likely to confront is a trade-off between sovereignty-as-autonomy and sovereignty-as-influence. As global power diffuses, economic integration deepens, and cross-border challenges proliferate, the imperative for multilateral cooperation will expand and the scope for U.S. freedom of action will shrink. To promote acceptable international outcomes and to shape its destiny in a global age, the United States will at times need—paradoxically—to accept voluntary constraints on its room for maneuver. Clinging to sovereign autonomy will be both difficult to sustain and detrimental to U.S. interests.

The good news is that multilateral cooperation comes in various forms, and the United States will often be able to rely on more flexible, informal frameworks, as opposed to standing and often rigid international organizations. Such à la carte multilateralism has a lot going for it, allowing the United States to create ad hoc coalitions of the interested, capable, and like-minded in ways that allow it to protect its sovereignty-as-authority and maximize its sovereignty-as-autonomy, while still delivering on its sovereignty-as-influence. Still, it would be a mistake to believe that such flexible minilateralism can entirely replace standing international organizations, or that nonbinding arrangements carry the same weight as commitments grounded in international law. The key for the United States is to harmonize its reliance on flexible frameworks with the international organizations and treaties upon whose resources, expertise, and legitimacy it will rely over the long haul.

TWO

There's No Place Like Home

Sovereignty, American Style

The United States has been at war overseas for most of this young century. Meanwhile another conflict, not bloody but shrill, has been brewing at home. It is the political struggle over American sovereignty in an age of interdependence. As global integration accelerates, swells, and deepens, the security, prosperity, and ecological health of each nation is ever more tightly intertwined with the well-being of others. Managing transnational threats and risks, as well as seizing opportunities created by globalization, requires unprecedented international cooperation. But that practical reality collides headlong with traditional U.S. concepts and practices of national sovereignty—whether framed as constitutional independence, external freedom of action, domestic autonomy, border control, or the will of the people.[1]

Americans are famously defensive of their sovereignty. All nations, of course, value independent decisionmaking and freedom of action. But in no other country do domestic sovereignty debates carry such symbolic weight or elicit such emotional intensity. The tenacity with which Americans cling to sovereignty and resist symbolic incursions on their constitutional prerogatives has had—and continues to have—a profound influence on national political life, U.S. foreign policy, and prospects for international cooperation.

At first glance, U.S. anxieties over sovereignty seem mystifying. After all, on most measures the United States remains by far the world's most powerful nation. None is better placed to protect its independence, to act as it desires, or to make its influence felt globally. And yet a persistent domestic drumbeat portrays U.S. sovereignty as fragile and beleaguered by mighty global forces, including unaccountable multilateral organizations and overreaching international law.

Among the most ardent defenders of U.S. sovereignty is the conservative nationalist firebrand John Bolton, a senior fellow at the American Enterprise Institute (AEI), a prominent Washington-based think tank. After serving as undersecretary of state and then UN envoy under President George W. Bush, Bolton returned to his perch at AEI, where he regularly warns that American sovereignty is in peril.[2] In 2008, with Bolton's encouragement, AEI and the Federalist Society launched "Global Governance Watch," an initiative and website designed to monitor and expose emerging international trends ostensibly menacing U.S. sovereignty, in areas ranging from human rights to environmental protection to corporate regulation.[3]

Bolton is hardly alone in claiming that global trends present the United States with an existential crisis. Since 2000, a legion of "new sovereigntists" (as law professor Peter Spiro christened them) has sounded the tocsin. The expanding tentacles of international organizations, they caution, are strangling America's constitutional liberties, freedom of action, self-government, and national security. One of their number is John Kyl, formerly a Republican senator from Arizona. He depicts America as besieged by a legion of "leading academics and some high-level government officials," who "view sovereignty as an outmoded notion . . . not as a principle to be upheld, but a problem to be remedied." In league with activist allies, he claims, these individuals are executing an "end run around the democratic process," by declaring "new" international law, so as to entrap the nation in global obligations to which U.S. citizens have never agreed.[4]

Sovereigntism has a strong constituency on Capitol Hill. Over the past decade, Republican majorities have engineered "sense of Congress" resolutions in the House and Senate opposing any international agreements, including those on climate change and the International Criminal Court. Legislators have warned that such conventions would "compromise" or "undermine" the sovereignty of the United States, whether by conflicting with U.S. constitutional principles, constraining America's ability to defend itself, or "requiring the United States to submit to decisions of international inspection, compliance, and enforcement mechanisms." More radically, since 2001, Republican legislators have repeatedly introduced a bill titled "The American Sovereignty Restoration Act." The most recent version, which Representative Mike Rogers (R-Ala.) offered in January 2017, would if passed and signed into law terminate U.S. membership in the United Nations and close America's UN mission; eject the UN's headquarters from the United States; repudiate all UN conventions to which the United States is party; cease U.S. funding for all UN agencies, departments, and programs; terminate U.S. financial support and participation in UN peacekeeping operations; void the diplomatic immunity of UN officials; and eject those same officials from all U.S. government facilities.[5]

With the election of Donald Trump, sovereigntists appeared to gain a powerful ally in the White House—a man convinced that his predecessors had sold out the nation by allowing it to become entrapped in international institutions and foreign adventures. A month after his inauguration, the president inveighed against such globalist policies. "There is no such thing as a global anthem, a global currency, or a global flag," the president declared at the Conservative Political Action Conference (CPAC) in February 2017. "I'm not representing the globe," he promised. "I'm representing the United States of America."[6]

American neuralgia on the topic of sovereignty is ironic, since the United States has done more than any other nation to weave the institutional fabric of world order. Thanks to U.S. exertions, common international norms, standards, rules, and laws now regulate—or at least shape cooperation in—virtually every global arena, from civil aviation to nuclear safety to international finance. But having toiled to construct this multilateral world, some Americans now perceive themselves to be enmeshed in a dense and thickening web of international commitments and expectations, and they chafe at these real and imagined constraints.[7] America today seems to run from its own record of achievement, resisting binding obligations and carving out exemptions to preserve its authority and autonomy. What gives?

To get a handle on contemporary U.S. sovereignty anxieties, it helps to start with a bit of history. Since 1776, five factors have shaped how Americans conceive of, defend, and occasionally compromise their national sovereignty. One might label these influences ideological, cultural, institutional, geopolitical, and global.

The ideological factor is a political conviction that the consent of the governed is the ultimate foundation of U.S. sovereignty. When Americans speak about sovereignty, they mean first and foremost *popular* sovereignty. The cultural factor is a widespread societal attachment to American exceptionalism. This attitude takes for granted that the United States is unique among nations and, in fulfilling its destiny, may be justified in holding itself apart from rules and constraints binding on others. The institutional influence is the U.S. Constitution, which complicates American assumption of multilateral obligations.

By distributing the people's power among three co-equal branches of the federal government, as well as between national and state governments, America's founding document places multiple hurdles in the way of international cooperation.

These three factors—ideology, political culture, and constitutional structure—have endured since the late 1700s. Two other influences—America's geopolitical circumstances and its interdependence with the world—have been more variable and ambiguous in their impact. In 1776 the United States was a weak republic on the periphery of a world dominated by rival imperial powers. Today it is the most powerful nation in history and the fulcrum of international politics. The impact of this rise to global dominance on U.S. concepts of and policies toward sovereignty has been equivocal, however. At times, sheer power has tempted Americans to recast the world in their own image as an open community under law. At other times it has reinforced U.S. claims to remain apart from global rules and obligations so as to preserve America's unique domestic values and self-assigned role as the ultimate guarantor of world order.

Finally, American attitudes toward sovereignty have evolved in response to globalization. Over the past century, innovations in technology, transportation, and communication have shrunk the planet in ways previously unimaginable, increasing humanity's economic, strategic, epidemiological, ecological, and even moral interdependence. Inevitably, these trends have reshaped U.S. calculations about the global institutions and sovereignty trade-offs required to advance U.S. national security, prosperity, and values. A recurrent U.S. choice is whether to hunker down in order to preserve U.S. freedom of action, or instead to explore new forms of cooperation that may reduce its notional autonomy but promise greater influence over the terms of interdependence.[8] The United States has offered no single answer about how it intends to navigate this new world, or about the sovereignty bargains it is willing to strike to mitigate the risks, tame the excesses, and reap the gains of globalization.

A BRIEF HISTORY OF SOVEREIGNTY

Before delving more deeply into what has made the American approach to sovereignty so distinctive, it makes sense to review the historical origins and political significance of the concept. For several centuries sovereignty has been *the* bedrock principle of international order. It refers in the first instance to supreme, exclusive political authority over a particular territory and its inhabitants.

Today the term applies exclusively to states. In the Middle Ages, by contrast, the word encompassed a wider range of hierarchical social relations, from the legal rights of royalty to the obedience that a wife (in those unenlightened times) owed to her husband. To the degree that one "true" sovereign existed in medieval Europe, it was of course God.[9]

Although we now take it for granted as the fundamental unit of world politics, the sovereign territorial state is a modern invention, dating from seventeenth-century Europe. For millennia beforehand humans had coalesced in diverse groupings, among these hunter-gatherer bands, warring tribes, feudal kingdoms, and sprawling empires. The emergence of state sovereignty as the basic principle of political authority is what separates the modern political order from the Middle Ages.

Medieval Europe was a collage of crosscutting and overlapping authorities and jurisdictions, reflecting the complexities of the feudal system and the blurring of temporal and religious spheres. Personal bonds defined political relations, political borders could be discontiguous, and hierarchies were not absolute. Across the continent, kingdoms (or *regna*) competed with the Holy Roman Empire, city-states, and leagues of the same. Complicating matters, these *regna* comprised a broader Christian commonwealth (*respublica Christiana*). Under the "two swords" doctrine, the bishop in Rome exercised not only spiritual authority (*sacerdotium*) but also political authority (*regnum*) within Latin Christendom. All earthly princes owed their thrones and legitimacy to the pope.[10]

This arrangement guaranteed repeated clashes between the Papacy and the Holy Roman Empire, a decentralized, multiethnic complex of territories at the heart of Europe whose elected ruler threatened the Church's religious authority as well as its political pretensions. The most famous confrontation, between Pope Gregory VII and Emperor Henry IV, culminated in the latter's excommunication and penitential prostration in the snow at Canossa, Italy.[11]

The political shift from medieval to modern Europe involved the disintegration of a unified *respublica Christiana* and the eclipse of the Holy Roman Empire—and their replacement by sovereign kingdoms that recognized no superior authority. The Reformation and Counter-Reformation propelled this transformation, fragmenting the unitary and hierarchical *ecclesium* centered on Rome into a system of separate national churches, Protestant as well as Catholic, subject to the temporal authority of kings and princes. The Peace of Augsburg (1555) institutionalized this shift by acknowledging the prerogative of rulers to enforce their own faith in their own territories.[12]

The historical moment most widely associated with sovereignty is the Peace of Westphalia of 1648, which ended the Thirty Years War. As Robert

Jackson observes, the Westphalian settlement is best understood symbolically rather than literally. It was less an abrupt discontinuity between two eras than one important milestone in the gradual emergence of a new European order based on independent, sovereign states, which trumped transnational claims of universal authority, both papal and imperial.[13]

As might be expected, the Westphalian settlement was unpopular with the Vatican. Pope Innocent X sputtered that it was "null, void, invalid, iniquitous, unjust, damnable, reprobate, inane, empty of meaning and effect for all time."[14] And yet sovereignty brought welcome order to Europe. Beyond ending the wars of religion, it allowed the emergence of a stable "society of states" whose members recognized each other's legitimate rights and (increasingly) resolved differences through diplomacy and international law.[15] Sovereignty did not eliminate war. But it reduced its frequency and ferocity by narrowing its causes and moderating its conduct.

During the nineteenth and early twentieth centuries, the emergence of nationalism in Europe would give the concept of sovereignty even greater vigor by elevating the nation-state as the only legitimate form of political organization— and self-determination as the baseline aspiration of self-identified national communities.[16] From Europe the principle of state sovereignty spread worldwide. Still, it was not until the mid-twentieth century, with the advent of decolonization, that it became *the* universal principle of political authority, delegitimating other forms of political organization.[17] Today the entire terrestrial surface of the planet save Antarctica is neatly delineated into mutually exclusive territorial jurisdictions that strictly distinguish the "foreign" from the "domestic."

Sovereignty's Components

Today we tend to associate sovereignty with five main characteristics. The first is *supreme political authority within a given territory*, including a monopoly on the legitimate use of armed force. This is the aspect of sovereignty that preoccupied the political philosopher Thomas Hobbes. Writing in the context of Europe's (un)civil wars, Hobbes envisioned an all-powerful state—a Leviathan—that could bring order and justice to a given territory. By controlling the instruments of violence and making rules binding on all actors, the state would make life less "nasty, poore, brutish and short" for its inhabitants.[18]

Sovereignty has an outward as well as an inward-looking face. Its second inherent property is *international legal recognition*. The state is a juridically independent, geographically defined actor eligible to participate in international relations. Indeed, it is the mutual recognition by states of their political independence—or "sovereign equality"—that enables conventions of diplomacy and international law.[19] One corollary of sovereign equality is that state consent is the primary basis of international law. In America's case, independence from Great Britain provided international legal recognition—including the ability to enter into treaties and (later) to join international organizations.

Sovereignty's third attribute is *autonomy in the formulation and pursuit of policy choices*, including freedom from external intervention. Often associated with Westphalia, autonomy is akin to a "no trespassing" sign. It is codified within the United Nations Charter, Articles 2.4 and 2.7 of which prohibit both the world body and its member states from interfering in matters within the "domestic jurisdiction" of UN members, as well as infringing on their political and territorial integrity.[20]

Sovereignty's fourth generally accepted characteristic is *influence over the terms of interdependence*, particularly when it comes to controlling cross-border flows. As long as sovereign states have existed, national governments have claimed the right—and sometimes enjoyed the ability—to regulate traffic across their national frontiers. This includes determining what people and goods can enter and exit their country, levying duties on such transactions, and restricting flows of items or actors deemed injurious.[21]

Sovereignty's fifth attribute is a distinctive American contribution: *rule by the consent of the governed*. It holds that the people alone are sovereign, and that just government arises only when citizens delegate a portion of their power to agents of their will chosen through constitutional, democratic processes. Popular sovereignty, as this concept is also known, gained its first major expression in the American Revolution. It has since spread globally, although its application remains uneven. The United Nations includes many autocracies, after all. Still, global expectations have grown that sovereign state governments should reflect democratically expressed popular aspirations. At home, U.S. attachment to popular sovereignty reinforces mistrust of formal international bodies and treaties that appear removed from the will of the American people.

Significantly, these five generally accepted attributes of sovereignty—supreme authority, legal recognition, policy autonomy, influence over interdependence, and consent of the governed—are not always present in equal measure. States may enjoy legal (de jure) sovereignty, for instance, but struggle to exercise empirical (de facto) sovereignty. This distinction is obvious in the world's forty-odd fragile or failing states, of which Somalia provides the starkest post–Cold War example.[22] In addition, states frequently trade off among different aspects of their sovereignty.

Recognizing these separate dimensions of sovereignty can shed light on debates over American sovereignty, helping clarify what is at stake, or even (allegedly) under assault. Of the five components of sovereignty, we can take international legal recognition for granted in the U.S. case. More relevant for our purposes are three properties that are often in tension—namely authority, autonomy, and influence, as well as sovereignty's final, popular attribute: the consent of the governed.

Viewed as *authority*, sovereignty implies that a state has the legitimate and supreme right to rule and administer its territory, including to make laws binding on citizens, implement policies, use coercion against usurpers, police its frontiers, provide for national defense, enter into commercial and diplomatic relations, sign treaties, and, if need be, declare and make war. The scope of these authority claims is not fixed, however, but evolves as state functions expand or contract. For example, a century ago there was little expectation that sovereign states should provide basic social welfare, much less have the authority to generate funds for that purpose by taxing personal income or domestic commercial transactions.[23]

Sovereignty-as-authority implies that the state has the "last word": there is no superior or higher entity to which it must appeal in crafting and implementing rules within its jurisdiction. Whether or not that state enjoys actual *autonomy* (that is, can independently determine its national policy) much less *influence* (that is, can impose its will and shape outcomes in critical domains) are different questions.[24]

Sovereign authority is commonly depicted as both absolute and unitary: it is either present or not, and it cannot be divided. The reality is more complex. Such authority can be "pooled," as it is within the European Union. It can even be "shared," as in the international administration of war-torn countries, which occurred in UN-led missions in Kosovo and East Timor that both began in 1999.

Sovereign autonomy and influence, meanwhile, are inherently relative. They depend on numerous factors, among these the capacity of state institutions to extract domestic resources, to provide internal security, and to rebuff meddling outsiders. Even a powerful nation like the United States, which has unquestioned authority to control its borders, may struggle to do so in practice.

More relevant for the United States, governments can make trade-offs among sovereignty's components, particularly authority, autonomy, and influence. Although purported sacrifices of U.S. sovereign authorities generate the most attention and controversy, the far more common trade-offs are between autonomy and influence. The quandary for the United States—as for other nations—is how much freedom of action to sacrifice in return for the anticipated benefits of cooperation.

This recognition—that sovereignty can be disaggregated and that states can make trade-offs among its components—helps us avoid a zero-sum mindset, according to which sovereignty, being unitary, can only be safeguarded or surrendered. Under many circumstances, institutions or treaties help states adjust to new realities and become more effective in using their sovereignty.

On the Ropes or Alive and Kicking?

There is a widespread perception that sovereignty—whether conceived as supreme authority, legal recognition, policy autonomy, border control, or democratic consent—is under unprecedented siege. Indeed, some wonder whether it remains a viable form of political organization. States, after all, face intrusive demands both from above, in the form of international organizations, and from below, in the form of vibrant nonstate actors, even as they struggle to regulate swelling cross-border flows of goods, services, money, microbes, information, ideas, and people. Sovereign statehood presumes a clear distinction between what is "foreign" and what is "domestic." But can it survive the rise of "problems without passports," ranging from financial volatility to climate change, transboundary pollution, networked terrorism, uncontrolled migration, WMD proliferation, and pandemic disease?

Skeptics of sovereignty, particularly on the left, concede that it provided a modicum of predictability and order in the past. But they regard it as "morally dangerous, conceptually vacuous, and empirically irrelevant," particularly "in light of new global imperatives." Ken Booth, a prominent British professor of international relations, dismisses it as "a tyrant's charter" that thwarts the spread of universal liberties, giving repressive regimes license to crush dissent.[25] Others view it as obsolete, not least for the dozens of weak and failing states that face existential threats from insurgent groups challenging their territorial integrity, and which are easily exploited by malevolent terrorist and criminal networks that hopscotch among national jurisdictions. Still others dismiss sovereignty as an impediment to effective global action, whether in curbing greenhouse gas emissions or coping with global financial instability. More practically, skeptics note, sovereignty is being hollowed out, as long-standing norms of nonintervention are made "contingent" on fulfillment of specific obligations—among these not committing atrocities or sponsoring terrorism. Finally, formerly independent states have at times chosen to pool sovereignty, with the European Union being the premier example.[26]

Given these trends, should we dismiss sovereignty as an institution that has run its historical course—and whose moral claims have evaporated? Is this the twilight of sovereignty?

Not at all. Sovereignty remains relevant and resilient. Several points merit stressing. To begin with, sovereignty has never been sacrosanct or inviolable. Conventional mythology notwithstanding, states have rarely enjoyed absolute territorial control; borders have long been porous; intervention has been a recurrent fact of life; global interdependence is not new; and the state has long shared the global stage with influential nonstate actors. Claims that sovereignty is suddenly "at bay" are thus ahistorical, alarmist, and exaggerated.[27]

Equally important, state sovereignty remains the fundamental ordering principle of world politics and a bedrock of international stability. It defines who is—and by extension who is not—a legitimate actor in global affairs. Only independent, territorial states are entitled to receive ambassadors, to negotiate diplomatically, to use military force, or to recognize similar actors as sovereign. Others need not apply. Sovereignty is also flexible enough to permit occasional violations and derogations without undermining the entire edifice. Consider the norm of nonintervention. States violate this norm only rarely, at least when it comes to military action, and when they do so, others expect them to offer justifications. Rather than disappearing, sovereignty will continue to evolve in response to new forces, as states bargain and trade off across its different components.[28]

And there is nothing on the horizon to replace the sovereign state. The prospect of a "world state" remains implausible, even in the distant future—and that is a good thing because, although deeply imperfect, the sovereign state has the best record of any institution yet devised when it comes to expressing the will of the people.[29] To be sure, state sovereignty offers no guarantee of political liberty. But it offers the greatest prospect of balancing the reality of international pluralism with democratic self-determination. As chapter 8 explains in greater detail, there are few grounds for assuming that a global Leviathan would be nearly as successful.

In addition, neither private corporations nor nongovernmental organizations (NGOs) can compete with sovereign states as independent sources of political power. Given the hype that these nonstate actors sometimes generate, a little historical perspective is warranted. Influential private corporations and transnational movements have existed for centuries, from the British (and

Dutch) East India Company to the Catholic Church. Certainly the absolute number of transnational NGOs has exploded—from an estimated 176 globally in 1909 to 32,446 in 2014.[30] Under certain conditions, civil society networks, as well as multinational corporations, can advance new norms and influence the course of multilateral deliberations, thereby shaping global agendas, informing negotiations, and even assisting with the implementation, monitoring, and enforcement of multilateral commitments.[31]

For all that, states remain "the most densely linked institutions in the contemporary world."[32] Over the past four centuries, the state system has also proven flexible enough to accommodate multiple types of states, among these "monarchies, republics, military regimes, theocracies, imperial states, unitary states, federal states, democracies, dictatorships, and others besides."[33] No doubt it will remain capable of doing so in the future.

Prophets of sovereignty's demise often argue that globalization confronts nation-states with unprecedented challenges. But globalization is not an entirely new phenomenon or necessarily a threat to the state. Consider U.S. immigration rates, which were higher as a proportion of the U.S. population at certain points in the nineteenth century; or the volume of private capital flows as a percentage of the global economy, which were arguably greater during the years 1890–1913 than at any time since; or the scope of pandemics, such as the Spanish influenza outbreak of 1919–20, which killed more people in absolute numbers than any scourge since.[34] More generally, it is misleading to conceive of state sovereignty and globalization as inherently opposed. After all, the world economy did not arise magically from invisible market forces: it was shaped by the conscious choices of major governments, which believed that creating space for transnational commercial activity was in their national interest. Far from being the passive objects of global integration, states have been its driving forces, even as they seek to tame it.[35]

Rather than being locked in a zero-sum game, in which globalization's gain is sovereignty's loss, the two have co-evolved, mutually transforming each other. States respond to rising global interdependence by expanding (and more rarely contracting) the scope of their authority claims and functional activities, in an effort to exploit the upsides and manage the risks and downsides of globalization. The emergence of the modern welfare state and its safety nets, for example, was partly a response to the vulnerabilities associated with increased trade. To the degree that states struggle to manage aspects of interdependence, this may reflect their efforts to extend their authority into novel domains where domestic and international rules (and the means to enforce them) have previously been lacking.[36] It may also reflect the state's decision to abandon authority claims in certain areas or its neglect to make full use of them. (Chapter 6, for example, attributes contemporary U.S. public discontent with globalization in part to the failures of successive U.S. administrations to use their sovereign powers to help American society adjust to the dislocations of global economic competition.)[37]

Finally, it is an error to depict the sovereign state as inherently threatened by international organizations. Yes, the United States has chosen to join scores of multilateral organizations, each of which in some way limits its absolute freedom of action. But these decisions were expressions of American sovereignty—which membership has typically *reinforced* rather than undercut. As rising interdependence complicates the ability of states to make good on authority claims, governments naturally turn toward collective efforts to manage globalization, voluntarily trading off notional (but often illusory) policy autonomy for a semblance of influence over shared problems that exceed their national response capabilities. Indeed, the only alternative is for states to cede sovereign claims in areas they cannot manage. Viewed in this light, multilateral cooperation is not an abdication or derogation of sovereign authority but its manifestation. Sovereignty is definitely an obstacle to world *government*, but it is certainly compatible with global *governance*, if we define the latter as purposeful, institutionalized international cooperation to advance common interests in peace, security, and justice.

How Distinctive Is the U.S. Attachment to Sovereignty?

Nearly all countries, large and small, seek to preserve their national sovereignty. There are partial exceptions, of course. The most notable is Germany, which since the catastrophe of Nazism and World War II has sought to embed its national power and destiny within a European bloc. But most other nations—even within the EU—continue to value sovereignty-as-authority and sovereignty-as-autonomy (as well as sovereignty-as-influence). A recent case in point was the United Kingdom's "Brexit" decision of 2016, in which a bare majority of British voters determined that the benefits of European integration did not compensate for the perceived costs to constitutional independence and freedom of action.

Sovereignty retains a powerful allure not only for large but also for smaller countries, particularly postcolonial nations that have been (or fear being) the target of external intervention. It remains a fundamental justification for the persistence of the Non-Aligned Movement (NAM), for instance, nearly three decades after the end of the Cold War. At its August 2012 summit in

Teheran, the NAM reaffirmed that "the Movement will continue to uphold the principles of sovereignty and the sovereign equality of States, territorial integrity and non-intervention in the internal affairs of any State."[38]

Among contemporary big powers, Russia, China, and India are especially insistent on defending their sovereignty prerogatives. Russian president Vladimir Putin underscored this in his 2014 State of the Nation address: "If for many European countries, sovereignty and national pride are forgotten concepts and a luxury, then for the Russian Federation a true sovereignty is an absolutely necessary condition of its existence." He continued, "I want to stress: either we will be sovereign, or we will dissolve in the world. And, of course, other nations must understand this as well."[39] Domestically, Russian officials have invoked sovereignty to justify laws limiting foreign media ownership as well as activities by foreign NGOs. Externally, they have sought to restore Russia's territorial sovereignty and political influence over portions of the country's "near abroad" (including in Georgia and Ukraine), where a significant number of Russian speakers remained after the dissolution of the Soviet Union.

China's own attitudes toward sovereignty have deep historical roots, having been shaped by ancient concepts of China's civilizational superiority and, more recently, by its nineteenth- and twentieth-century humiliations at the hands of Western imperial powers.[40] Thanks to relative geographic isolation and weaker neighbors, China under successive dynasties developed a hierarchical and centralized approach to international relations, known as *tianxia*. This depicted China as the "Middle Kingdom" of the known world and its emperor as possessing the mandate of heaven, accepting tribute from suzerain states on the country's periphery. Unfortunately, as Fei-Ling Wang notes, this "*tianxia* system came to a fatal clash with the expanding Westphalia system in the mid-nineteenth century." China was compelled to make degrading concessions to European powers and the United States. Since Mao tse-Tung's victory in 1949 brought the Chinese Communist Party to power, this shameful memory has reinforced a determination to defend Chinese "sovereignty" (*zhuquan*), as well as to assert China's territorial claims over Tibet, Taiwan, and the East and South China Seas.[41]

India, Asia's other emerging giant, has since 1947 pursued a foreign policy based on maximizing self-determination at home and freedom of action abroad. Indeed, "sovereign" is the first word describing the republic in the Indian constitution. Independence leader Mahatma Gandhi conceived of sovereignty in terms of *swaraj*—"the capacity for self-rule on the part of individuals and civil society," and his famous Salt March was intended to demonstrate "the sovereignty of the people."[42] After freeing themselves from British imperialism, Indians sought to protect their hard-won liberty by refusing to join either camp in the Cold War. India's first postcolonial leader, Jawaharlal Nehru, cofounded the NAM in 1961 as part of this "quest for autonomy," and India remains an active member. "Unlike neutrality," Gopal Krishna explains, non-alignment is "an activist policy" designed to promote a more peaceful world "through the spread of principles of territorial integrity, and mutual non-aggression and non-interference."[43] Sovereignty concerns inform contemporary Indian foreign policy, as reflected in the country's moralist isolationism (for example, staying clear of promoting human rights abroad or validating human-itarian intervention), as well as the nation's ferocious defense of its territorial integrity. Sovereignty considerations are also front and center in India's refusal to join the Nuclear Non-Proliferation Treaty (NPT), as well as the International Criminal Court (ICC).[44]

THERE'S NO PLACE LIKE HOME: THE SOURCES OF AMERICAN CONDUCT

The United States, then, is hardly alone in its attachment to national sover-eignty. What is distinctive and curious about America is how Janus-faced it has been on the issue. Since 1945 the United States has been simultaneously the main driving force behind international cooperation *and* among those nations most defensive of its sovereignty. What explains this striking ambivalence?

Five factors have been at play. Three of these—the country's ideology, political culture, and constitutional structure—have been enduring. Two others—the country's geopolitical position and exposure to globalization—have been more changeable.

The first influence on the American concept and practice of sovereignty is the conviction that legitimate political authority flows from the people. The United States was the first modern republic founded on the consent of the governed, and when Americans speak of "sovereignty," they mean *popular* sov-ereignty. They imply—as Lincoln declared at Gettysburg—a government of, by, and for the people. Any infringement on this principle of self-rule, whether real or perceived, is liable to raise Americans' hackles. This ideological com-mitment helps explain recurrent U.S. ambivalence and often resistance toward multilateral cooperation, particularly binding international obligations that appear to impinge on U.S. domestic authority structures, policy choices, or freedom of action.

A second long-standing source of sovereign defensiveness is American exceptionalism—the conviction that the United States is an irreplaceable political community with a unique mission among nations. America is at once a beacon for humanity—a "city on a hill," in the words of colonial Massachusetts governor John Winthrop—and a redeemer nation possessing a "special providence."[45] To fulfill this dual destiny, the United States cannot accept external constraints on its internal liberties or international behavior.

Beyond these ideological and cultural influences, a third, institutional factor has long complicated the U.S. assumption of international obligations. This is the distinctive political order established by the U.S. Constitution. The separation of powers, which divides responsibility for foreign affairs among three co-equal branches of government, combined with the principle of federalism, which preserves important prerogatives for the fifty constituent U.S. states, can make it difficult for the United States to commit to credible multilateralism. It also provides self-styled defenders of U.S. sovereignty with outsized opportunities to make their opinions felt, particularly when it comes to treaty ratification.

To these enduring features one must add fourth and fifth factors that have had more variable impacts on how the United States defends and expresses its sovereignty—and which are the subject of chapter 3. These are America's evolving geopolitical situation and its growing interdependence with the rest of the world. Since the founding of the republic the United States has shifted from a position of acute vulnerability to one of global primacy, with ambiguous implications for its sovereign sensitivities. More recently, traditional U.S. attitudes toward sovereignty—including sovereignty-as-authority, sovereignty-as-autonomy, and sovereignty-as-influence—have been challenged by globalization. The United States faces growing pressures to create new frameworks of multilateral cooperation to manage the shared challenges of interdependence, as well as to determine its fate as a nation.

Before addressing factors four and five, we first turn to the influence of America's ideology, political culture, and institutional inheritance on U.S. thinking about sovereignty.

Born Free: Popular Sovereignty in the United States

The United States did not invent sovereignty, which had become a bulwark of world order by the seventeenth century. But America's Founders made a revolutionary contribution by insisting that sovereign authority was legitimate only if it reflected the consent of the governed and—even more boldly—by building the first modern democracy on that basis. "In Free governments," Benjamin Franklin observed in a speech to the Constitutional Convention in

Philadelphia on July 26, 1787, "the rulers are the servants and the people their superiors and sovereigns."[46] The principle that sovereignty resides ultimately in the people was embedded in the Declaration of Independence and the Constitution—the preamble of which begins, "We, the people of the United States, in order to form a more perfect union . . ."

John Jay, the first chief justice of the United States, explained the U.S. concept of popular sovereignty in one of the court's first major rulings, *Chisholm v. Georgia* (1793). Whereas the European political order was founded on "feudal principles" that designated "the Prince as the sovereign, and the people as his subjects," he wrote, "No such ideas obtain here; at the Revolution, the sovereignty devolved to the people, and they are truly the sovereigns of the country."[47]

To be sure, the American doctrine of popular sovereignty did not emerge out of thin air. It was informed by evolving British constitutionalism, as well as by the writings of contractarian philosophers like Hobbes and (more importantly) John Locke, with which the U.S. Founders were intimately familiar.

By the late sixteenth century, as noted earlier, the sovereign state had emerged as the fundamental political unit in Europe. But *in whom or what*, precisely, did sovereign authority reside? The first answer was that it was vested in the physical person of the king or queen. Europe's monarchs claimed legitimacy and commanded obedience by invoking their divine right to rule as God's agents on Earth. The Frenchman Jean Bodin defended royal absolutism in *Les Six Livres de la République* (1576), written in the midst of a civil war between France's Catholic monarchy and Calvinist Huguenots. Across the Channel, British monarchs asserted the same right. Thus the "Epistle Dedicatory" to the King James Bible referred to James I as "England's most dread souveraine." William Shakespeare also depicted royal authority in personal terms, as when Horatio warns Prince Hamlet that pursuing his father's ghost "might deprive your sovereignty of reason and draw you into madness."[48]

During the early seventeenth century, a less personalistic formulation of sovereignty arose, thanks to power struggles between the king and parliament. Monarchs and their mortal bodies might come and go, but the "body politic" would endure in the dynastic line. By the 1640s, the English parliament had begun to set limits on the king's authority. Royal rule was made contingent on his fulfillment of core obligations. If he failed, parliament could even depose him. Such was the fate of King Charles I, who was brought to trial and executed in 1649. As the prosecution stated in that case: "Sir, if this bond be once broken, farewell sovereignty."[49]

Two years later, Hobbes published his influential *Leviathan*, which reframed sovereign authority as an implicit social contract: in exchange for protection,

the people transferred their rights to the state and accepted the ruler's authority to create law. That arrangement could become null and void if the king
abused his prerogatives, however. Although the Stuart monarchy was restored
in 1660, the king's rights were no longer divine, or even supreme. William of
Orange, after ascending to the British throne with his wife, Mary, in the Glorious Revolution, signed a historic Bill of Rights on December 16, 1689.
Henceforth, the monarch would share sovereignty with parliament.[50]

Contemporaneously, Locke published his *Second Treatise on Government*
(1689), the classic defense of popular sovereignty. "In a constituted Commonwealth . . . there can be but one supreme power," which was not the monarch
but "the people." Whereas Hobbes had depicted the social contract as a
grudging response to insecurity, Locke portrayed it as a voluntary arrangement, whereby the people accepted the legitimacy of the state in return for the
latter advancing the "Publick Good." Locke's writings—along with William
Blackstone's later *Commentaries on the Laws of England*, which became the
most influential legal text in the thirteen colonies—helped cement intellectual and political support for popular sovereignty in America. In Blackstone's
view, "There must be in all [governments] a supreme, irresistible, absolute,
uncontrolled authority, in which . . . the rights of sovereignty reside." And
that authority was grounded, ultimately, in the will of the people.[51]

The doctrine of popular sovereignty found fertile soil in the colonies. Already the colonists enjoyed a measure of self-government within representative assemblies, and their deference to the British monarchy and parliament
would erode with perceptions of corruption in Westminster. Distance reinforced their growing disaffection. Americans considered it absurd to be represented in parliament by men they had never seen, much less elected, and who
knew little of their circumstances. Colonial assemblies became more assertive
as quarrels with the crown grew, especially as parliament imposed new tax
schemes through the Sugar Act of 1764 and the Stamp Act of 1765.[52] In 1775
open hostilities broke out. The following year the colonies declared their
independence.

Viewed through a twenty-first-century lens, the American Revolution can
seem conservative. It vindicated the concept of popular sovereignty but defined the "people" narrowly, as property-owning white males. Those without
land, as well as women, slaves of African descent, and Native Americans, were
denied basic liberties, which they gained only slowly during the nineteenth
and twentieth centuries. And unlike later upheavals in France, Russia, and
China, the American Revolution neither sought nor brought about societal
transformation. The colonists rebelled to assert their rights as Englishmen on

the grounds that George III and parliament had denied them the freedoms to which they were entitled, thus violating the liberal social contract.[53]

The essential moderation of the American Revolution is clear in the Founders' preference for Lockean liberalism over the radical leanings of the French contractarian Jean-Jacques Rousseau, who envisioned the state as an organic embodiment of people's "general will." As Rousseau explained in *The Social Contract* (1762), "Sovereignty, or the general will, is inalienable . . . it is indivisible . . . it is infallible and always right."[54] This illiberal approach to popular sovereignty, which excluded the very possibility of pluralism, would be integrated into the French Constitution of 1791: "Sovereignty is one, indivisible, inalienable, and imprescriptible; it belongs to the Nation." In the wrong hands, such an absolutist conception lent itself to totalitarianism. That is precisely what happened in France, where Jacobin leaders of the revolution, having swept aside the monarchy and aristocracy, seized the reins of power and created an apparatus of ruthless repression. Many other popular revolutions have repeated the pattern.[55]

Fortunately for the United States, the Founders rejected the notion of direct democracy, choosing instead to embed the people's sovereignty within a "compound republic." The people might have ultimate authority, but, as John Jay, Alexander Hamilton, and James Madison counseled in *The Federalist Papers*, they should delegate it to their elected leaders. This preference for Locke over Rousseau had significant consequences, making both the American Revolution and the U.S. constitutional order less radical than their French counterparts. Sovereignty would rest with the people rather than the state. But it would be "recessed" rather than expressed through direct democracy.[56]

And yet the American Revolution was momentous in its time. It was the first revolution to place sovereignty in the hands of the people, as opposed to the person of the king—or even a sitting parliament. Throughout history, the people had been the object of government. They would now be its motive force, who by their consent and will brought it into being. As the Massachusetts legislature declared in 1776: "Supreme, Sovereign, absolute and uncontrollable Power . . . resides, always, in the Body of the People." In the American conception, the historian Gordon Wood observes, the people held "final, supreme, and indivisible lawmaking authority." They might delegate this authority temporarily to elected representatives, but "on an always recallable loan."[57]

The power of popular sovereignty in the United States impressed early foreign visitors. "The American Revolution broke out, and the doctrine of the sovereignty of the people came out of the townships and took possession of the state," Alexis de Tocqueville wrote in *Democracy in America* (1835). "It became the law of laws." He marveled at the resulting political order: "The people reign in the American political world as the Deity does in the universe. They are the cause and the aim of all things; everything comes from them, and everything is absorbed in them."[58]

As an expression, the phrase "popular sovereignty" began to gain wide currency only in the late 1840s, in connection with U.S. sectional disputes over whether to allow slavery to spread into the huge new territories recently acquired through war with Mexico. Seeking to bridge Northern and Southern differences on this question, Senator Stephen A. Douglas of Illinois proposed that the residents of these territories decide this question on the basis of "popular sovereignty." (Douglas would subsequently invoke the principle to help secure passage of the Kansas-Nebraska Act of 1854.)[59]

The principle that sovereignty remains forever in their own hands has long made Americans distrustful of government—and more insistent on accountability from those who would claim to speak on their behalf. This skepticism is even more pronounced at the international level, particularly when global bodies claim—or are perceived to be seeking—governing authority above the U.S. Constitution itself. Two centuries ago, in the case *Schooner Exchange v. McFaddon* (1812), Chief Justice John Marshall established the principle that any external limitation on the nation's sovereignty was unacceptable unless it was based on the principle of consent: "The jurisdiction of the nation within its own territory is necessarily exclusive and absolute. It is susceptible of no limitation not imposed by itself. Any restriction on it, deriving validity from an external source, would imply diminution of its sovereignty to the extent of the restriction, and an investment of that sovereignty to the same extent in that power which could impose such a restriction."[60]

The zero-sum nature of sovereign authority is something most Americans instinctively understand—and it is one that contemporary defenders of U.S. sovereignty play on when raising fears of international organizations. "I think that since most Americans think we don't have enough control over our own government, the last thing we want to do is give what we have up in whole or in part" to global bodies, John Bolton explains.[61]

Twenty-four decades after the United States won its independence, it remains political suicide for any U.S. aspirant to national office to speak of moving "beyond sovereignty" or indeed to speak the language of "global governance," given the widespread impression—reinforced by conservative nationalists—that unaccountable international institutions and law are running roughshod over the U.S. Constitution and the principle that legitimate government is based on popular consent.[62]

These concerns deserve to be taken seriously, for globalization does create significant dilemmas for popular sovereignty. On the one hand, the surging volume and quickening speed of cross-border transactions and interactions has obliterated distance between previously unconnected locales, increasing humanity's political, security, economic, ecological, epidemiological, informational, and moral interdependence and generating transnational problems (from terrorism to financial instability) that no single state can address on its own. On the other hand, Americans rightly insist that the consent of the people—as mediated through democratic politics—is the sole legitimate foundation for making authoritative choices about the rules, institutions, and policies that should govern the lives of individuals within the United States (as well as in other democracies).

There is no obvious way to translate the people's democratic will into multilateral organizations—or to hold those entities directly accountable.[63] What is to ensure that international bodies do not circumvent or ignore domestic structures established to ensure the people's voice and right to rule? But if the dilemma is real, its dangers should not be exaggerated. There are strategies (discussed more comprehensively in chapter 8) that the U.S. government can take to help increase the democratic accountability of multilateral organizations—as well as to shift the focal point of international cooperation to more informal arrangements that infringe less on U.S. sovereign authority and autonomy.

It's Not You, It's Me: American Exceptionalism

Reinforcing this sovereign defensiveness is the *liberal exceptionalism* that has permeated American political culture and discourse since 1776. Throughout U.S. history, American leaders and citizens have agreed overwhelmingly that the nation's domestic values and institutions offer the most desirable model for political and economic life and that the United States, by virtue of its founding principles, has a unique destiny in world affairs. Moreover, many believe that fulfilling this mission justifies exempting the United States from some rules that are binding on other nations.

The United States is distinctive on many counts, including its geographic location and its demographic makeup. But what truly sets the nation apart, as Louis Hartz observed more than six decades ago, is its "absolute and irrational attachment" to the liberal principles enunciated by Locke. All nations are in some sense "imagined communities": that is, their cohesion relies on the mutual perception of countless individuals who have never met that somehow they constitute a distinct cohesive group. In much of the world, citizenship is viewed as a birthright, based on bonds of blood, ethnicity, language, religion, or soil. Not so in the United States. To be an "American" is a political commitment, available (at least in principle) to anyone who embraces the Enlightenment values on which the country is established. "America is the only nation in the world that is founded on a creed," as G. K. Chesterton wrote. Citizenship is not about being someone but believing in something.[64] In practice, of course, the United States has not always lived up to these liberal principles— as demonstrated by periodic eruptions of racial and ethnic chauvinism, including white nationalism, throughout American history. And yet the idealism endures.

Americans resist the notion that they are an ideological people. But they are deeply so, being committed to "self-evident" truths that Jefferson referenced in the Declaration of Independence. Writing in 1835, Tocqueville described Americans as "unanimous on the general principles that ought to rule human society." The American creed, as outlined in the Constitution, comprises individual liberty, representative government, the rule of law, freedom of speech and religion, private property, commercial freedom, and equality of opportunity. This liberal dogma is so taken for granted that it has become synonymous with "the American way of life." Indeed, most U.S. political dissidents in the United States have framed their arguments not as a rejection of the country's founding principles but as disappointment that the nation has failed to live up to its ideals.[65]

The conviction that the United States has a unique destiny among nations is as old as the republic. "What is most extraordinary about the Revolution," the historian Wood notes, "is the world-shattering significance the Revolutionaries gave it." When they declared independence from the powerful British Empire, the thirteen colonies had only 2.5 million inhabitants. And yet already they saw themselves as being present at the creation (as Dean Acheson would later write of his State Department years). Their aspirations were audacious. "We have it in our power," Thomas Paine declared in 1776, "to begin the world over again."[66]

Exceptionalism permeated U.S. popular culture in the nineteenth century, helping underpin and justify America's "manifest destiny" to expand across the continent. Herman Melville, author of the quintessential American novel *Moby Dick*, warmed to this theme in another maritime yarn, *White Jacket* (1850):

We Americans are the peculiar chosen people—the Israel for our time; we bear the ark of the liberties of the world. God has predestined, mankind expects, great things of our race; and great things we feel in our souls. The rest of the nations must soon be in our rear. We are pioneers of the world; the advance guard, sent on through the wilderness of untried things, to break a path into the New World that is ours.[67]

American exceptionalism is evergreen. As the Cold War ended in 1990, President George H. W. Bush donned destiny's raiment, promising a "new world order" under U.S. leadership. Several years later, Madeleine Albright, Bill Clinton's secretary of state, christened the United States the world's "indispensable power," proclaiming that it "stands taller and sees farther" than any other.[68] Undergirding America's sense of national predestination has been the powerful influence of religion—particularly Protestantism—in U.S. society. Even today, the United States has by far the most religious population in the Western world, with nearly 90 percent of citizens believing in God, 77 percent identifying with a religious faith, and six in ten believing that the Bible is God's word.[69]

Faith in American exceptionalism is a touchstone of national identity that spans the U.S. political spectrum. It has been invoked by presidents both Democrat and Republican, from Woodrow Wilson, John F. Kennedy, and Bill Clinton to Teddy Roosevelt, Ronald Reagan, and George W. Bush. And when presidents deviate from this orthodoxy, expect fireworks. In 2009, Barack Obama offered only tepid endorsement of U.S. uniqueness. "I believe in American exceptionalism, just as I suspect that the Brits believe in British exceptionalism and the Greeks believe in Greek exceptionalism." Republican critics pounced. Obama's remarks, thundered AEI's Bolton, had exposed him as the first "post-American" president.[70]

In 2012, Republican leaders chose "American Exceptionalism"—"the conviction that our country holds a unique place and role in human history"—as the title of the foreign policy plank of the party's electoral platform. Four years later, they invoked the concept in the opening lines of the preamble to the 2016 GOP platform:

We believe in American exceptionalism.

We believe the United States of America is unlike any other nation on earth.

We believe America is exceptional because of our historic role—first as refuge, then as defender, and now as exemplar of liberty for the world to see.[71]

As for the Democrats, they learned from Obama's mistake. During their own 2016 convention in Philadelphia, which nominated former secretary of state Hillary Clinton, party leaders offered repeated paeans to American exceptionalism, complete with Reaganesque invocations of the United States as a "shining city on a hill."[72]

American exceptionalism has long shaped how U.S. decisionmakers perceive American sovereignty and power, define U.S. national interests, design and pursue policies to advance them, and justify those choices. To be sure, this mindset has drawbacks. It can blind U.S. leaders to global complexities, encourage crusades that devolve into quagmires, and expose the United States to charges of hypocrisy as it navigates a complicated world. And while the notion of U.S. benevolence is seductive to Americans, foreigners regard the United States with a more skeptical eye, given its checkered history of meddling in others' affairs for baser motives.[73]

But if exceptionalism is embedded in the U.S. national psyche, little unanimity exists about how it should inform U.S. foreign policy. For much of American history, U.S. leaders invoked it to justify an insular, defensive foreign policy stance. Washington, Jefferson, John Quincy Adams, and others admonished the young nation to avoid international entanglements that might corrupt or endanger its values and institutions. Rather than remaking the world, the republic should be a beacon to inspire and guide other nations.

For the revolutionary generation, the United States was a novel political community, the first in modern history in which authority flowed not through dynastic bloodlines but from the consent of the people. The Founders considered it axiomatic that a nation based on liberal Enlightenment principles should adopt more pacific and cooperative foreign policies than those of decadent Old World monarchies, which competed ceaselessly for power and territory. "As war is the system of Government on the old construction, the animosity which Nations reciprocally entertain, is nothing more than what the policy of their Government excites, to keep up the spirit of the system," Paine wrote in *Common Sense*. "Man is not the enemy of man, but through the medium of a false system of Government."[74] It stood to reason that as liberal democracy spread globally, humanity's warlike proclivities would dissipate.

Contemporary American advocates of international cooperation, particularly when bemoaning U.S. unilateralism or failure to ratify this or that international treaty, frequently invoke the Declaration of Independence, which speaks of a "decent respect for the opinions of mankind." The implication is that the Founders recognized the need not to alienate other countries. But there is an alternative reading of this phrase, according to the sovereigntist legal scholar Jeremy Rabkin. What the Declaration's authors meant was that re-spect for foreign opinion obliged them to explain precisely *why* they had to break with Great Britain and pursue their own, independent destiny, embrac-ing that "separate and equal station to which the Laws of Nature and Nature's God entitle them."[75]

To many observers, the election of Donald J. Trump in November 2016 suggested that the era of American exceptionalism was over.[76] The president reinforced this sense early in his term when he seemed to draw a moral equiv-alence between the United States and authoritarian Russia, creating a media firestorm.[77] But in his desire to "make America great again" by protecting and insulating the nation, Trump was arguably echoing another, venerable strand of American exceptionalism, one frequently undergirded by anxiety, which regards U.S. sovereignty as a fragile, precious heirloom in a savage, alien world. Without vigilance this birthright could be irrevocably lost. Those who share this view seek to insulate the United States from binding international com-mitments that might constrain U.S. freedom of action or sacrifice the U.S. Constitution to a misguided global consensus, haphazard trends in interna-tional law, and the actions of unaccountable multilateral organizations and the meddling bureaucrats who staff them.[78]

And yet American exceptionalism does not always imply hunkering down. It can also cut in the opposite direction, particularly when U.S. power waxes. At such moments, American leaders have invoked exceptionalism to justify international activism, including reformist efforts to recast world politics along liberal lines. Periodically, the United States dons the mantle of a re-deemer nation, seeking to secure the global triumph of values that are deeply American but also in principle universal. Woodrow Wilson, who took the United States into World War I not merely to defeat the Central Powers but to establish a new international organization to preserve postwar peace, remains the preeminent exemplar of this approach.

Although Wilson failed, Franklin D. Roosevelt and Harry Truman resurrected much of this agenda and oversaw a flurry of international institution building. Given unprecedented opportunities to recast world order, the United States sponsored multilateral organizations as pillars of an open, rule-bound inter-national system in which independent nations could pursue peace and pros-perity. Their effort was intended, in the words of historian Anton DePorte, to "Lockeanize a hitherto Hobbesian world"—that is, to transform an anarchic, conflictual arena into an open, universal community under law, mirroring America's own free domestic political economy. Just as "many" had become "one" in America's plural society, so new multilateral institutions grounded in international law might reconcile international diversity through shared principles. In short, U.S. officials projected outward their domestic values, hoping to transfer to the international realm the same legal, political, and economic principles that sustained security, order, prosperity, and justice at home.[79]

America's own early history inspired these mid-twentieth-century U.S. architects of world order. As Secretary of State Cordell Hull explained in his memoirs, "We Americans should return again and again to the fountainhead of our national greatness, the founding fathers. Their thinking, their struggles to obtain cooperation, among the thirteen states, are magnificent prototypes for the thinking and struggles we must undertake to bring cooperation among the nations."[80]

Such messianism did not escape foreign notice. In 1912 the minister of state at the British Foreign Office alerted his colleagues in the U.K. cabinet office of U.S. ambitions. The Americans were convinced "that the United States stands for something in the world—something of which the world has need, something which the world is going to like, something in the final analysis the world is going to take whether it likes it or not."[81]

And yet even at the height of American global dominance, U.S. exceptionalism often translated into "exemptionalism"—and continues to do so today. That is, U.S. officials and pundits frequently invoke America's unique status to keep the United States apart from international rules, treaties, or institutions that they believe might infringe on U.S. sovereignty. "Sovereignty is vital for America because we are an exceptional nation, one uniquely blessed with a vibrant Judeo-Christian heritage, as demonstrated both through its founding documents and by the witness of history," Representative Doug Lamborn (R.-Colo.) wrote in a 2009 op-ed shortly before launching the Congressional Sovereignty Caucus. "For any nation, and I believe especially for America, to give up any degree of control of its destiny to transnational bodies is irresponsible and wrong."[82]

The ironic result is that the United States itself frequently opts out of the world that America made. Conservatives in particular seek to return the United States to a (largely mythical) past of lost innocence, when the nation was more insulated from and less buffeted by the world. Much of Trump's appeal as a presidential candidate in 2016 was precisely his promise to restore things to how they once had been for U.S. workers—and for the broader American society. Such a romantic image ignores how interconnected with the rest of the world the United States has become. As interdependence deepens, American exemptionalism will be increasingly difficult to sustain.[83]

An Invitation to Struggle: Sovereignty and the U.S. Constitution

America's distinctive governing system, which emerged from the Constitutional Convention in Philadelphia in 1787, reinforces U.S. resistance to incursions on national sovereignty. The U.S. Constitution not only vests sovereignty in the people but also disperses power among three co-equal branches of government *and* between the federal government and the constituent U.S. states. The resulting U.S. political system has repeatedly hamstrung the U.S. assumption of international obligations, not least multilateral treaties.

For America's Founders, the question of how to translate popular sovereignty into a new political order raised two main dilemmas. The first was how to ensure that governmental authority flowed from the people without degenerating into crude majoritarianism or mob rule. It was one thing to declare that "the people rule," and quite another to place power directly in their hands. On one level, the Founders conceived of American society as without formal rank—at least among property-owning white males. And yet they also presumed the existence of a "natural aristocracy"—a subset of men whose virtue and intellect marked them for distinction—and they sought a new political system that might identify and elevate such men of merit above the masses.[84]

"The Consent of the People" was "the only moral Foundation for Government," John Adams of Massachusetts conceded in 1776. And yet he mistrusted the "common Herd of Mankind." His fellow Federalists, Alexander Hamilton and James Madison, harbored similar prejudices. Anti-Federalists, for their part, held a more egalitarian and optimistic outlook. "The decisions of the people, in a body, will be more honest and more disinterested than those of wealthy men," Jefferson believed. But not even he endorsed direct democracy, which he feared would generate anarchy and ultimately tyranny, as an authoritarian government arose to reimpose order upon chaos.[85]

The Founders' second quandary was deciding how to apportion the people's sovereignty between the American republic as a national unit and its constituent states. The answer was not obvious in 1776. The colonies had declared their independence as "the thirteen united States of America"—accounting for the use of plural verbs throughout the Declaration. The document further insisted, "That these United Colonies are, and of Right ought to be, Free and Independent States," with "full Power to levy War, Conclude Peace, contract Alliances, establish Commerce, and to do all other Acts and Things which Independent States may of right do." But how should these thirteen units— each of which emerged from the war with its own constitution, governor, senate, and/or assembly—now relate to one another?

In its first incarnation, the United States bore little resemblance to today's federal union. The Articles of Confederation (issued in 1778 and formalized in 1781) established a league, or confederacy, of thirteen republics. Article 2 expressly declared: "Each State retains its sovereignty, freedom, and independence, and every power, jurisdiction, and right, which is not, by this confederation, expressly delegated to the United States, in Congress assembled."[86] The confederation's central government was weak. It took the form of a Congress whose representatives were chosen by state legislatures. It had only limited powers, among these the right to wage war, conclude peace, make alliances, regulate coinage, establish a post office, handle Indian affairs, mediate disputes among states, borrow money, and build a navy. In discharging these duties, Congress depended on the cooperation of state governments, whose assemblies and legislatures could refuse to carry out its directives. Congress could borrow funds but not levy taxes or regulate interstate commerce, leaving it perpetually cash-strapped.[87]

During the 1780s many U.S. leaders concluded that the confederation government was too flimsy. Madison bemoaned that it was "nothing more than a treaty of amity of commerce and of alliance, between so many independent and Sovereign states." With an eye toward amending the Articles, Congress convened a constitutional convention in Philadelphia in May 1787. As it happened, the delegates wound up scrapping the Articles and drafting an entirely new constitution. The final document would strengthen the powers of the federal government, notably in the areas of diplomacy, national defense, and commerce.[88]

A major point of contention in Philadelphia was how much of the people's sovereignty should remain with the states. Anti-Federalists regarded the Articles as a treaty among independent republics that could be changed only if the states gave their explicit consent. Federalists retorted that the colonies had declared and secured their independence as a union, not individually, meaning that there was only one true sovereign: the American people, as a collective body. "The Idea which has been so long and falsely entertained of each being a sovereign State must be given up," Charles Pinckney of South Carolina declared, "for it is absurd to suppose that there can be more than one sovereignty within a Government." Writing in *The Federalist*, Madison reassured anti-Federalists that individual U.S. states would retain significant powers, while warning that confederacies had failed throughout history.[89]

Still, federalism might present dangers of its own, including an oppressive state. The trick was to avoid the twin dangers of anarchy (too little order) and despotism (too much). The Constitution must bring the states to heel but also constrain its guardian. To vest sovereignty in the people while discouraging democratic excesses, the Founders embedded a system of internal checks and balances within a federal structure. The Constitution apportioned political authority at the national level among co-equal executive, legislative, and judicial branches, while reserving significant rights for the states. It divided war-making authority between the executive branch, which commanded the armed forces, and the legislature, which could declare war, raise taxes, and approve treaties. The overall impact was "to bind—to set limits to—any single sovereign power within the American constitutional order." The ultimate locus of popular sovereignty was not to reside in any single individual or institution, but in the U.S. Constitution itself. As Chief Justice Marshall wrote in 1821 in *Cohens* v. *Virginia*, the Constitution is "the creature of their [the people's] will and lives only by their will."[90]

Although the Constitution shifted the people's sovereignty from the states toward the federal government, the transfer was incomplete. The states retained multiple rights, including over militia, policing, and criminal prosecution. During the republic's early decades, as Daniel Deudney observes, "It was customary to speak of the states retaining sovereignty in certain spheres."[91] Respect for states' rights explains why each, regardless of population, received two senators, and why (until ratification of the Seventeenth Amendment in 1913) senators were elected indirectly by state legislatures. As Madison explained in Federalist 62, "The equal vote allowed to each State is at once a constitutional recognition of the portion of sovereignty remaining to individual States, and an instrument for preserving that residual sovereignty." Or as the Supreme Court ruled in the 1995 case *U.S. Term Limits, Inc.* v. *Thornton*, "The Framers split the atom of sovereignty. It was the genius of their idea that our citizens would have two political capacities, one state and one federal, each protected from incursions by the other."[92]

Despite the Constitution's ratification, Americans continued to disagree over the balance between these twin sovereignties well into the nineteenth century. On one side were those who insisted that the republic constituted a unitary, indissoluble sovereignty, embodied in the people. Their paragon was Daniel Webster, the Whig senator from Massachusetts and secretary of state under three presidents. On the other were those, exemplified by Senator John C. Calhoun of South Carolina, who insisted with equal vehemence that the United States remained an assemblage of sovereign states that had voluntarily joined together and delegated some powers to the federal government but that might—under "the law of compact"—voluntarily dissolve these binding ties. The tensions between these opposing views produced periodic confrontations, including the Virginia and Kentucky resolutions, as well as the Nullification

Crisis of 1832–33. In a last-ditch effort to balance national sovereignty with states' rights on the question of slavery, Senator Henry Clay of Kentucky brokered the Compromise of 1850.[93]

Clay's stopgap dampened the controversy over slavery, but only temporarily. The political truce collapsed a decade later, when eleven Southern states invoked the principle of state sovereignty as legal justification for seceding from the Union to form the Confederate States of America. South Carolina was the first to do so. Its declaration of secession, issued on December 24, 1860, argued that the failure of Northern states to honor the constitutionally protected property rights of Southern slaveholding states released the latter from their obligations to the Union, which was accordingly "dissolved." By seceding, the document declared, "the State of South Carolina has resumed her position among the nations of the world, as a separate and independent State."[94]

The federal government repudiated this logic, of course, on the grounds that the Union was indissoluble, possessing a unitary sovereignty. "What is a 'sovereignty' in the political sense of the term?," inquired President Lincoln. "Would it be far wrong to define it as 'a political community, without a political superior?' Tested by this, no one of our states . . . ever was a sovereignty. . . . The Union, and not themselves separately, procured their independence and their liberty."[95]

It would take four bloody years, including more than 620,000 deaths, to establish the Union's indivisibility and supremacy over its constituent states as the main repository of the people's sovereign authority under the Constitution. The Civil War witnessed a dramatic expansion of the federal government, particularly the executive branch. Still, the issue of "states' rights" remained a flashpoint in U.S. constitutional debates, not least during the civil rights struggle of the 1950s and 1960s. And, as chapter 4 describes, the issue of state prerogatives within the U.S. federal system can complicate U.S. conformity with international legal obligations.

It bears noting, as well, that the U.S. federal system recognizes not only the residual sovereignty of the fifty American states but also certain sovereign rights of the more than 560 officially recognized Native American tribes. Beginning with the tenure of Chief Justice John Marshall (1801–35), the Supreme Court has repeatedly established that American Indians are entitled to self-government in the conduct of their affairs, and that these rights are protected by the U.S. Constitution, legal precedent, and treaties. The roots of tribal rights "lie in the fact that Indian nations pre-exist the United States and their sovereignty has been diminished, but not terminated."[96]

Under U.S. law, tribal authorities have the power to form their own government, make and enforce laws, levy taxes, establish and determine tribal
citizenship, license and regulate activities within their jurisdictions, exclude
people from tribal lands, administer justice and set rules of conduct through
tribal ordinances, regulate the domestic relations of their members, pass zon-
ing ordinances, prescribe rules of inheritance for reservation property, and set
voter criteria in their reservations. Tribal authorities do *not* have the right to
make war, engage in foreign relations, issue their own currency, or do anything they have relinquished in past treaties with the United States.[97]

The separation of powers established under the Constitution cannot but
shape U.S. foreign policy and the nature of America's international commitments. The president enjoys great leeway in foreign affairs, serving as the nation's chief diplomat and commander in chief of its armed forces. At the same
time, the Constitution accords an independent legislative role to Congress,
one absent in parliamentary democracies. This includes the power of the purse
in appropriations for an army, a navy, and foreign missions, as well as the overall federal budget; the right to approve all treaties and appointments, to which
the Senate must give its advice and consent; and responsibilities for oversight,
including through hearings and investigations. Congress also retains the power
to declare war and to regulate commerce. Legislators have used these tools
to shape and limit U.S. membership in and obligations to multilateral
institutions—not least international treaties, whose approval requires a two-
thirds supermajority in the Senate.

Competition between the executive and the legislature can provide creative tension, as well as check dangerous impulses. But it can also complicate
credible U.S. diplomacy, as foreign interlocutors quickly learn that the president's word is rarely final. The famous economist John Maynard Keynes implied as much in 1941, during wartime financial negotiations. "One can take
nothing whatever for settled in the U.S.A.," he told his colleagues. Whereas
representatives of the U.K. prime minister could make credible commitments,
any promise made by American officials "can and does bind no one," since
Congress would make the final decisions.[98]

As the negotiations over the League of Nations revealed, executive-legislative
disagreements over U.S. international commitments can be especially volatile
when partisanship runs high and different parties control opposite ends of
Pennsylvania Avenue. They tend to be smoother when a single party controls
both branches or in those rare moments when executive and legislative officials nurture bipartisan comity. As chapter 3 describes, the 1940s stands out
as a rare and remarkable period of bipartisan leadership, thanks to the exertions

of statesmen like Democratic presidents Franklin D. Roosevelt and Harry Truman and Senator Arthur Vandenberg (R.-Mich.). While politics never truly ended "at the water's edge," Democrats and Republicans worked together to forge agreement on sovereignty bargains that fundamentally reoriented U.S. foreign and national security policy. Some seventy years later such enlightened bipartisan leadership seems a world—and sometimes a galaxy—away.

THREE

Power and Interdependence

U.S. Sovereignty in the American Century

The previous chapter stressed the enduring influence of America's political principles, national identity, and domestic institutions on how the United States defines, expresses, and defends its sovereignty. That is, American conceptions about sovereignty are rooted in a conviction that the will of the people is the foundation for political legitimacy, in a broadly shared belief that the United States is an exceptional nation, and in the distribution of domestic power and authority established by the U.S. Constitution. Given these ideological, identity, and institutional realities, U.S. attitudes toward sovereignty can seem immutable.[1]

And yet fixity is not the entire story. Two other factors, external to the United States itself, have shaped how American leaders and citizens interpret and express U.S. sovereignty. The first is the geopolitical position that the United States occupies within an always shifting landscape of global power. Having secured its independence as a weak republic in a world of expansionist empires, the United States has since become the most powerful nation the world has ever known—and this changing position has naturally affected Americans' conception of their national sovereignty. The second external influence on U.S. understandings of sovereignty is globalization, which has linked Americans' security, prosperity, health, and social welfare ever more tightly with developments in other parts of the world.

Over the past century these two forces—the rise of U.S. power and deepening global integration—created new opportunities and dilemmas for the United States. Growing might gave the United States unprecedented scope to spread its influence and ideas abroad. Simultaneously, the emergence of global markets brought benefits of commercial and financial integration—as well as more nefarious cross-border flows. The impact of power and interdependence on U.S. attitudes toward sovereignty has been uneven. Although the dominant U.S. mode has been internationalist, latent isolationist sentiments have lingered. And throughout, Americans have been torn over how much sovereign autonomy they should be prepared to trade for the promise of more effective multilateral cooperation.

THE GEOPOLITICS OF SOVEREIGNTY

The United States was born free but vulnerable. In 1776 fewer than 3 million Americans were scattered along the narrow, 2,000-mile strip of Atlantic seaboard from Georgia to Maine. The new republic's population was overwhelmingly rural, with 95 percent employed in agriculture. Only twenty-one towns exceeded 2,500 people, and just five cities had more than 10,000 inhabitants.[2] At sea, the United States was exposed to potential naval assaults; on land, to attacks from acquisitive European powers and their Native American allies. Preserving American sovereignty meant gaining a capacity for self-defense—while avoiding conflicts that did not involve the United States.

National security considerations helped justify replacing the Articles of Confederation with a more federal Constitution in 1789. Only a strong central government, Federalists insisted, could defend the United States from centrifugal tendencies at home and aggression from abroad. Without a strong core, sectional jealousies and rivalries might rip the republic apart. And as the nation disintegrated into competing blocs, a miniature version of the European balance of power might even arise, as U.S. states armed to the teeth, entered into shifting alliances, and engaged in recurrent warfare. History's lesson was clear, Hamilton warned: "To look for a continuation of harmony between a number of independent, unconnected sovereignties in the same neighborhood, would be to disregard the uniform course of human events, and to set at defiance the accumulated experience of ages." Innumerable clashes, he predicted, would arise from "acts of independent sovereignties consulting a distinct interest."[3]

Outside powers would surely exploit such disarray, playing different U.S. states against one another—when not seizing U.S. territory for themselves.

These dangers would increase as westward expansion lured U.S. settlers into the arms of Britain, Spain, and other colonial powers. As early as 1775, John Adams warned his fellow revolutionaries of America's sovereign vulnerability. Foreign governments "would find means to corrupt our people, to influence our councils, and, in time, we should be little better than puppets, danced on the wires of the cabinets of Europe. We should be the sport of European intrigues and politics."[4] Indeed, the republic's early years were rife with rumors and paranoia about foreign plots and subversion. A strong national government seemed the only defense against internal dissolution or vassalage to powerful empires.

National security considerations were thus front and center in at the Constitutional Convention that assembled in Philadelphia in 1787, and in the arguments for ratification. The first four *Federalist* papers endorsed a robust U.S. central government capable of standing up to big powers, enforcing international treaties, punishing violations of the law of nations, and establishing a common tariff to generate revenue for national defense. They also informed the "Virginia Plan," which would form the basis for the Constitution. The plan's authors endorsed a new federal system capable of defending U.S. sovereignty under international law, including a stronger central government with the authority to finance a standing army and navy to defend these rights.[5]

The young United States adopted a distinctive grand strategy of political and military self-reliance. This was not isolationism—that is, a withdrawal from world affairs—so much as unilateralism plus neutrality: an orientation the Founders believed would simultaneously safeguard America's independence (or sovereign authority), its freedom of action (or sovereign autonomy), and its ability to shape its destiny (or sovereign influence). During the republic's first century, Americans' main preoccupations were to defend their independence and rights against external threats, extend their territorial control across the continent, and preserve their internal unity in the face of sectional rivalry and, ultimately, civil war. Abroad, the United States supported foreign trade but minimized political commitments, avoiding overt participation in the global balance of power.

George Washington laid the intellectual foundations for this stance in his oft-cited Farewell Address of 1796, which admonished the United States to "steer clear of permanent alliances with any part of the foreign world." The trade-dependent nation should of course engage in international commerce— as well as harmonious cultural interchange—on a nondiscriminatory basis. But it must assiduously avoid foreign intrigues and warfare of the sort that had repeatedly engulfed Europe. "Our detached and distant position invites and enables us to pursue a different course," Washington observed. "Why forgo the advantages of so peculiar a situation? Why quit our own to stand on foreign ground?" Accordingly, "The great rule of conduct for us in regard to foreign relations is, in extending our commercial relations to have with them as little political connection as possible."[6]

Unilateralism appealed both to Federalists, who wanted to expand the federal government, and to members of the Democratic-Republican Party, who sought to limit it. By standing apart from the Old World, Hamilton argued in Federalist 7, the United States could "aim at an ascendant in the system of American affairs" (that is, within the Western Hemisphere). Eventually it might even "become the arbiter of Europe in America . . . able to incline the balance of European competitors in this part of the world as our interests may indicate." Jefferson, for his part, reaffirmed the doctrine of nonentanglement in his first inaugural address. The republic's policy, he declared on March 14, 1801, must be: "Peace, commerce, and honest friendship with all nations, entangling alliances with none."[7]

Nonentanglement did not mean rejecting international law. As chapter 4 discusses in greater detail, the revolutionary generation was steeped in the "law of nations," and the Declaration of Independence began and ended by invoking America's natural rights under international law. In 1789 the U.S. Constitution would recognize international treaties as the "supreme law of the land." Beyond respect for legal principle, Americans understood that the international rule of law had a particular value to their fragile and exposed republic in helping to make world politics less savage and unpredictable.

Diplomatically, the early United States clung to neutrality, in an effort to preserve its freedom of action, safeguard its political system, and influence its destiny. The Napoleonic Wars tested this stance. After repeated seizures and humiliations that mocked its sovereignty, the United States in 1812 declared war on Great Britain, which some refer to as America's "second war of independence."[8]

A decade later, the revolutions sweeping Spanish America presented another quandary. Worried that by meddling abroad the United States might endanger its own liberties, Secretary of State John Quincy Adams pledged only moral support to those trying to throw off the Spanish yoke. "America goes not abroad in search of monsters to destroy," he famously declared on July 4, 1821. Were she to do otherwise, she might become "dictatress of the world" and "no longer be the ruler of her own spirit." Accordingly, the United States would remain a "well-wisher to the freedom and independence of all," but "the champion and vindicator only of her own."[9]

That was not the final word, however. Aware that Europe's imperial powers might have fewer scruples, John Quincy Adams penned for President James Monroe a more forceful statement, which the latter delivered to Congress on December 2, 1823. The president unilaterally announced the birth of a new "American System" off limits to any new colonization, as well as any transfer of existing colonies to other powers or any reimposition of the colonial yoke where it had been thrown off. He warned the Europeans, "We should consider any attempt on their part to extend their system to any portion of this hemisphere as dangerous to our peace and safety."[10] Given U.S. weakness, Monroe's doctrine was a bluff—albeit one that he was confident the British Royal Navy would enforce for him.

Closer to home, the United States gradually shored up its vulnerable borders and extended its sovereignty across the continent, acquiring territory through a combination of settlement, negotiation, seizure, and purchase. Monroe justified U.S. acquisitiveness in geopolitical terms, telling Congress: "It must be obvious to all [Americans] that the further the expansion is carried . . . the greater will be . . . [their] freedom of action . . . and the more perfect their security." Moreover, "Extent of territory . . . marks . . . the difference between a great and a small power."[11] Pivotal steps in American expansion included the Northwest Ordinance in 1787; the admission of new states, including Vermont, Kentucky, and Tennessee in the 1790s; the purchase of Louisiana from France in 1803 and Florida from Spain in 1819; the annexation of Texas in 1845; negotiations with British Canada over Oregon Territory in 1846; the acquisition of California and the future American Southwest through war with Mexico (1846–48) and the Gadsden Purchase (1853); and the purchase of Alaska from Russia (1867).

As the United States expanded westward, so did the Monroe Doctrine. The shield of the republic became its sword, helping to consolidate U.S. territorial sovereignty on the continent and—in an irony not lost on America's neighbors—to justify intervention within the hemisphere. In 1845 President James K. Polk endorsed the annexation of the Republic of Texas, lest it become "an ally or dependency of some foreign nation more powerful than herself."[12] The next year he invoked the doctrine to justify war with Mexico, a conflict that increased America's land area by 50 percent—and made the United States a Pacific power. Two decades later President Andrew Johnson summoned Monroe's doctrine to rationalize the Alaska purchase.

In the late nineteenth century the Monroe Doctrine was revived to transform the Caribbean basin into a fenced preserve, with the United States (as Lowell would note in his 1919 debate with Lodge) serving as game warden.

U.S. secretary of state Richard Olney laid any doubts to rest in 1895, when intervening in a dispute between Britain and Venezuela over the boundary of British Guiana. "Today the United States is practically sovereign on this continent," he declared, "and its fiat is law upon the subjects to which it confines its interposition." Sharpening his corollary to the Monroe Doctrine, he added that America's "infinite resources combined with its isolated position render it master of the situation and practically invulnerable as against any or all other powers."[13]

Three years later the United States edged closer to great power status, defeating Spain in a short war that ranged from the Caribbean to the Pacific and acquiring its first colonial possessions in the Philippines, Guam, and Puerto Rico, as well as a protectorate over Cuba. Underscoring America's growing interests in the Asia-Pacific, Secretary of State John Hay in 1899–1900 issued his Open Door Notes on the future of China, demanding that the imperial powers respect that nation's territorial integrity and that China open itself to U.S. commerce on terms equal to what the Europeans enjoyed.

As these nineteenth-century experiences reveal, the United States showed far more reverence for its own sovereignty than for that of others. This dichotomy would become even clearer in the twentieth century. Overall, in the more than two centuries since 1798, the United States has intervened in other countries militarily on more than 200 separate occasions, for reasons as varied as eliminating piracy, acquiring territory, liberating colonies, restoring governance, bolstering friendly governments, toppling radical populists, apprehending criminal leaders, protecting U.S. lives and companies, attacking terrorist safe havens, ending genocide and ethnic cleansing, and eliminating dangerous regimes.[14]

THE DEFEAT OF THE LEAGUE OF NATIONS

The U.S. emergence as a global power around 1900 touched off a momentous domestic debate about America's international role, including how it should define and pursue its interests in a shrinking world. At the heart of this dispute was whether America's burgeoning might, combined with rising global interdependence, required the United States to adapt its traditional conceptions of sovereignty—and, if so, what trade-offs it should be prepared to make in balancing its objectives of authority, autonomy, and influence.

Despite its broadly internationalist orientation, the United States would repeatedly exhibit discomfort with the constraints that multilateralism placed on its freedom of action—that is, its sovereignty-as-autonomy. To some degree this was inevitable. Surging power provided U.S. officials with new opportunities to act unilaterally (as well as bilaterally or through narrow coalitions), just as expanding U.S. international responsibilities offered new justifications for the United States to act as it saw fit.

A pivotal moment in this century-long debate was of course the epic confrontation over the League of Nations, introduced in this book's opening pages. The core point of contention was whether the United States should participate in a global collective security system and, if so, what corresponding constraints it should be willing to accept on its sovereignty. Participants in this debate fell into three camps. Isolationists, truest to the vision of the Founders, were skeptical of crusades to remake foreign societies, believing that the United States could best promote and protect its ideals and interests by serving as a beacon for others. Convinced that events outside the Western Hemisphere were none of America's business and wary of Old World entanglements, they advocated a focus on regional rather than global affairs and embraced unilateralism to preserve U.S. freedom of action and American constitutional liberties.

Internationalists, meanwhile, rejected U.S. detachment as both impractical and imprudent in a shrinking world. But they disagreed among themselves on the appropriate scope and terms of U.S. global engagement. Great power internationalists, like Lodge and Theodore Roosevelt, emphasized U.S. responsibilities to uphold world order but insisted that America remain master of its fate. They thus rejected universalist schemes that might undermine America's sovereign authority and autonomy. Globally, they recommended that the United States cooperate flexibly with powers that truly mattered. Regionally, they advocated a hegemonic role whereby the United States would provide order unilaterally in the Western Hemisphere.[15]

In contrast, liberal internationalists like Woodrow Wilson embraced the ideal of collective security, arguing that the United States should be willing to compromise its sovereign autonomy—and even a degree of sovereign authority—to make such a scheme work. Three premises informed their thinking. First, international peace had become indivisible, implying that the outbreak of war anywhere could endanger U.S. security. Second, traditional diplomacy—including the balance of power, standing alliances, and exclusive treaties—were bankrupt, since they had failed to prevent World War I. Third, only a universal international organization grounded in international law and committed to deterring and defeating aggression could ensure lasting peace.

The defeat of the League was both ironic and unnecessary. By the time Lodge and Lowell squared off in Boston, most U.S. politicians, Republicans and Democrats alike, wanted America to pursue a more internationalist future. Where they disagreed was on the desirable structure of postwar peace, what powers any new international organization should possess, and what limitations the United States should accept on its sovereign prerogatives.

Paradoxically, Republicans themselves had issued the first call for a post-war multilateral framework for peace. In September 1914, a month after war had erupted in Europe, former president Teddy Roosevelt declared the time ripe for "a great world agreement among all civilized military powers to back righteousness by force." He blasted Wilson and his secretary of state, William Jennings Bryan, for pusillanimous inaction. "I regard the Wilson-Bryan attitude of trusting to fantastic peace treaties, to impossible promises, to all kinds of scraps of paper without any backing in efficient force, as abhorrent."[16]

Eight months later William Howard Taft, who had succeeded TR and preceded Wilson as president, launched the League to Enforce Peace (LEP), a private group composed of prominent Americans committed to a postwar international organization. "We have got to depart from the traditional policy of this country," he declared in May 1915, and "step forward and assume some obligations in the interest of the world." One year later Senator Lodge spoke to the LEP's annual meeting and endorsed the same goal. As he explained: "I do not believe that when Washington warned us against entangling alliances he meant for one moment that we should not join the other civilized nations of the world if a method could be found to diminish war and encourage peace."[17]

Lodge's interpretation of the Farewell Address was both novel and news-worthy. But it was overshadowed by the more sweeping vision that Wilson himself presented to the same audience that very day. What the world needed, the president announced, was a "universal association of . . . nations" capable of providing "a virtual guarantee of territorial and political independence to every nation." Sovereignty was at the core of Wilson's dream. But in a sharp break with U.S. history, its defense would no longer be limited to the United States:

> We believe these fundamental things: First, that every people has a right to choose the sovereignty under which they shall live. . . . Second, that the small states of the world have a right to enjoy the same respect for their sovereignty and their territorial integrity that great and powerful nations insist upon. And third, that the world has a right to be free from every disturbance of the peace that has its origin in aggression and disregard of the rights of peoples and nations.[18]

This was an audacious departure from U.S. diplomatic traditions. But in a feat of rhetorical gymnastics, Wilson depicted it as consistent with the Founders' intent. "I will never myself consent to an entangling alliance," he explained. "But I would gladly consent to a disentangling alliance—an alliance which would disentangle the peoples of the world from those combinations in which they seek their own separate and private interests and unite the people of the world upon a basis of common right and justice." Such a universal arrangement would bring America "liberty . . . , not limitation, . . . freedom, not entanglement."[19]

As the war proceeded Wilson's vision assumed an increasingly utopian aspect. In January 1917 the president delivered his famous "peace without victory" speech, calling for a world order in which there would exist "not a balance of power, but a community of power; not organized rivalries, but an organized, common peace." Henceforth, he declared "the doctrine of President Monroe" must become "the doctrine of the world: that no nation should seek to extend its policy over any other nation or people."[20]

For Republicans, this was a bridge too far. Wilson's proposal was "a departure from the hitherto unbroken policy of this country," Lodge complained. "If we have the Monroe Doctrine everywhere, we may be perfectly certain that it will not exist anywhere." To Senator William Borah (R.-Idaho), a staunch isolationist, Wilson's universalism spelled nothing but trouble. "What this passion-torn world needs and will need, are not more leagues and alliances, but a great, untrammeled, courageous, neutral power."[21]

America's entry into the war in April 1917 sharpened U.S. debates over the appropriate postwar structure of peace—and the U.S. role in upholding it. Wilson's own ambitions, meanwhile, expanded. The nation had entered the war not simply to defeat the Central Powers, he declared, but to "make the world safe for democracy." It would work with other victor nations to establish "a universal dominion of right . . . by such a concert of free peoples as shall bring peace and safety to all the nations and make the world itself at last free." The centerpiece would be the League of Nations, which Wilson foreshadowed in his Fourteen Points speech of January 1918 as "a general association of nations . . . under specific covenants . . . affording mutual guarantees of political independence and territorial integrity of great and small states alike." In September he promised that the United States was "prepared to assume its full share of responsibility of the common covenants."[22]

To secure such a dramatic reorientation of America's global role, the president would need to nurture bipartisan consensus, as well as comity between the White House and Capitol Hill. Unfortunately, Wilson lacked the temperament for this delicate task. Despite being a scholar of American government, he treated Congress with disdain and the question of League membership as a purely executive branch decision. He made a starkly partisan appeal for the League before the November 1918 midterm elections, only to see the GOP win control of the Senate and increase its margin in the House. He then compounded these mistakes by omitting prominent Republicans from the U.S. delegation to the Paris Peace Conference. Thanks to these errors of commission and omission, the League fight deteriorated into a rancorous partisan battle pitting executive and legislative branches against each other, with disastrous results.

Within Congress, all protagonists in the League fight considered the United States to be a uniquely principled nation with a special global destiny. Where they disagreed was over what global role this exceptional country should play. At one pole were wholehearted proponents of collective security; at the other the so-called irreconcilables, opposed to the League on any terms. Most legislators fell in the middle, being open to membership provided that it protected U.S. sovereignty—variously conceived as constitutional supremacy, autonomous decisionmaking, and external freedom of action.

Wilson presented his draft Covenant in Paris on February 14, 1919. Critics at home quickly rejected the proposed League as imprudent, futile, unconstitutional, and un-American. It would, they claimed, embroil the United States in unnecessary wars, seek vainly to freeze the imperial status quo, trample congressional prerogatives, and repudiate U.S. foreign policy traditions. The Covenant's most controversial clause, as noted in chapter 1, was Article 10: "The members of the League undertake to respect and preserve against external aggression the territorial integrity and existing political independence of all members of the League."[23]

For Republicans, Article 10 contained "nothing but peril." Roosevelt objected that it would make the United States an "international meddlesome Matty," intervening wherever troubles arose. Elihu Root, former secretary of state and GOP wise man, groused that it "completely abrogated the Monroe Doctrine," sanctioning foreign intervention in the Western Hemisphere and compelling U.S. intervention outside of it. But lost autonomy was not the only concern. Senator Philander Knox (R-Pa.) viewed Wilson's League as "a world state" and "a great catalogue of unnatural self-restraints" that would run roughshod over American independence. He preferred "a new American doctrine" that "entangles us in no way," whereby the United States would simply "consult with other powers" in the face of threats. Borah too hoped America would remain "a free, untrammeled Nation," able "to determine for itself and in its own way where duty lies and where wisdom calls." This was "not isolation but freedom to do as our people think wise and just."[24]

The League's defenders accused its critics of scaremongering. Taft, unlike many Republicans, regarded the Covenant as a reasonable trade-off, offering the promise of peace in return for modest U.S. responsibilities. The League "does not create a super-sovereignty," he insisted. "It is only a loose obligation among the nations of the world."

> It does not impair our just sovereignty in the slightest—it is only an arrangement for the maintenance of our sovereignty within its proper limits: to wit, a sovereignty regulated by international law and international morality and international justice, with a somewhat rude machinery created by the agreement of nations to prevent one sovereignty from being used to impose its unjust will on other sovereignties. Certainly we, with our national ideals, can have no desire to secure any greater sovereignty than this.[25]

Wilson did the League no favors, however, by speaking of "sovereignty" in global rather than national terms. In conversation with Taft, the president even anticipated a time "when men would be just as eager partisans of the sovereignty of mankind as they were now of their own national sovereignty."[26] Such tone-deafness played into nationalist anxieties that the president was trading America's birthright for a global Leviathan.

Hoping to make the League more palatable to Congress, Wilson ultimately renegotiated the Covenant with European allies to exempt the Monroe Doctrine. But he left Article 10 untouched, on the grounds that removing it would emasculate the League. Lodge remained defiant—he was determined that no U.S. soldiers, "not even a corporal's guard . . . can ever be ordered anywhere except by the constitutional authorities of the United States." Knox agreed that America's priority should be to "reserve complete liberty of action either independently or in conjunction with other powers in taking such steps as we determine for preserving the peace."[27]

The president tried to reassure League skeptics that Article 10 was "a moral not a legal obligation," but he also criticized them for seeking "special privileges" and "exceptional advantages . . . to exempt [the United States] from the obligations other [League] members assume." Hoping to sway public opinion, Wilson in September 1919 embarked on a grueling, nationwide whistle-stop tour, delivering forty speeches in twenty-one days. Growing interdependence, he declared, made it "impossible for the United States to be isolated . . . to play the lone hand." At the same time, the president conceded, "Some of our sovereignty would be surrendered for the good of the world."[28]

Meanwhile, on October 24, 1919, Lodge offered his own Fourteen Reservations to the Covenant. These were intended, in his words, "to release us from obligations which might not be kept, and to preserve rights which ought not to be infringed."[29] Among other provisions, these insisted that the United States would: brook no interference with the Monroe Doctrine; be the sole judge of whether it had fulfilled its League obligations; retain the right to withdraw at any time; assume no duty to go to war under Article 10 or to deploy military or naval forces without congressional approval; accept no League commitment precluding national military preparedness; oppose any League sanctions that overrode U.S. economic sovereignty; reject any terms of the Versailles Treaty that restricted the individual rights of U.S. citizens; tolerate no interference on domestic or political questions; and determine for itself which matters—including commerce, immigration, labor, tariffs, and illicit trafficking—fell within its own "domestic jurisdiction."[30]

The Senate approved Lodge's reservations on November 17, but Wilson was intransigent, instructing League supporters to oppose the treaty with the Lodge reservations. They did so, defeating the treaty 55–39 and returning it to the White House. The treaty suffered the same fate in a second and final Senate vote exactly four months later, on March 19, 1920.

Still hoping to salvage victory, Wilson implored voters to treat the 1920 presidential election as a "solemn referendum" on the League. His appeal fell flat. The Democratic Party gave the League only tepid endorsement, subject to reservations "making clear and more specific the obligations of the United States." Meanwhile the Republican nominee, Warren G. Harding, stated in unambiguous (if turgid) prose that "America's present need is not . . . submergence in internationality, but sustainment in triumphant nationality." Harding reaffirmed these sentiments after his lopsided victory, announcing in an address to a joint session of Congress on April 12, 1921: "In the existing League of Nations, world-governing with its super-powers, this republic will have no part."[31]

The League fight thus had an ironic result. Thanks to Wilson's obduracy, the two opposing schools of internationalism wound up canceling each other out, and the United States assumed a more modest global role than its power might otherwise have permitted. During the 1920s the U.S. government pursued policies of economic nationalism, while limiting binding formal entanglements. President Calvin Coolidge reflected this new attitude in his first state of the union address, on December 16, 1923. Referring to the League as a "foreign agency," he insisted that "the United States sees no reason to limit its own freedom and independence of action by joining it."[32]

Interwar America did not entirely ignore international diplomacy, of course. The Harding administration hosted the Washington Naval Conference of 1921–22, for example, which culminated in a five-power agreement to prevent a naval arms race, particularly in the Asia-Pacific. Still, the United States resisted any enforcement measures that would give that accord real teeth. The pattern repeated itself in 1928, when the United States cosponsored and signed the idealistic Kellogg-Briand Pact renouncing war as an instrument of national policy. Once again, Washington rejected any international machinery to implement the agreement.

Senator Borah spoke for many of his colleagues in 1931 when he explained the U.S. global posture to an audience at the Council on Foreign Relations in New York: "In all matters political, in all commitments of any nature or kind, which encroach in the slightest on the free and unembarrassed action of our people, or which circumscribe their discretion and judgment, we have been free, we have been independent, we have been isolationist."[33]

Isolationism would reach its apogee in the mid- to late 1930s, with passage of the first Neutrality Acts, the Nye Committee hearings on the "merchants of death" who had allegedly conspired to drag the nation into the Great War, and the rise of the America First movement, for which the aviator Charles Lindbergh became the most prominent spokesman.

Gradually, however, Axis aggression in Europe and Asia undermined the twin premises of isolationism: that what happened abroad had little bearing on U.S. security and that detachment was the best strategy to keep the country safe. In Congress, isolationists like Senator Arthur Vandenberg, the powerful chair of the Senate Foreign Relations Committee, continued to take comfort in America's geographic situation. "True, we do live in a foreshortened world, in which, compared with Washington's day, time and space are relatively annihilated," Vandenberg conceded in February 1939. "But I still thank God for the two insulating oceans." President Franklin D. Roosevelt disagreed: "Beyond question, within a few scant years air fleets will cross the oceans as easily as today they cross the closed European seas." On July 4, 1941, he warned the public: "The United States will never survive as a happy and fertile oasis of liberty surrounded by a cruel desert of dictatorship."[34]

The president proved prescient. The Japanese attack on Pearl Harbor, on December 7, 1941, brought the United States into the war and—as Vandenberg himself conceded—"ended isolationism for any realist."[35] Once again the nation confronted the questions that had bedeviled the previous generation:

What postwar structure of peace should the United States promote? And what compromises (if any) to its sovereign autonomy or sovereign authority should it accept to bring about such an order?

The answers to these questions would be shaped not only by geopolitics, including the threats posed first by fascism and then by Soviet communism, but by the lessons that Americans learned about the need for international cooperation to exercise U.S. sovereignty-as-influence in a world of growing security and economic interdependence.

THE LESSONS OF INTERDEPENDENCE

It is tempting to attribute the U.S. turn to internationalism after World War II simply to the meteoric rise in American power. The problem with this explanation is that the economic might of the United States, relative to that of its potential competitors, had arguably changed as much between 1900 and 1919 as it did between 1919 and 1940—and yet America had retrenched in the 1920s and become isolationist in the 1930s.[36] What led the United States to embrace internationalism after World War II—and to readjust its attitude toward national sovereignty in the process—was a revolution as much intellectual as geopolitical. To be precise, the Roosevelt and Truman administrations, as well as a majority of members of Congress in both parties, drew an object lesson from their recent cataclysmic experiences of depression and war: namely, that what happened in Europe and Asia affected vital U.S. interests— meaning that the country could no longer afford to go it alone. To influence and shape its destiny, the United States would need to go it with others.

The Great Depression and World War II convinced U.S. political leaders, foreign policy elites, and eventually a majority of American citizens that advancing U.S. security, prosperity, and freedom required robust international institutions to promote those goals abroad. Americans also came to believe that multilateral cooperation could be made consistent with U.S. constitutional interdependence, and that the benefits of international organizations would outweigh any modest constraints on U.S. policy autonomy and freedom of action.

From the origins of the republic, successive U.S. administrations had operated on the assumption that a detached global posture, including scrupulous avoidance of international entanglements, offered the United States the best odds of advancing its national security, economic prosperity, and political liberties. Wilson had challenged this premise in 1917–19, but the nation had quickly reverted to an insular and unilateral posture after Congress rejected the Treaty of Versailles—and the League Covenant along with it. But the subsequent litany of disasters—the world's descent into depression, the quickening march of fascism, and the outbreak of an even more devastating world war—discredited former orthodoxies. Liberal internationalism triumphed over American isolationism and unilateralism.[37]

These hard lessons informed the Roosevelt administration's planning for the postwar world. FDR's core objective was to embed the postwar United States within a new international system that allowed nations to cooperate harmoniously to advance their common security and prosperity. This new world order would be girded by steady American leadership and supervised by an interlocking system of legitimate international institutions. These multilateral bodies promised to transform a world racked by rivalry and violence into a stable international community governed by the rule of law, in which nations coordinated and reconciled their national policies rather than engaging in power politics and zero-sum economic competition. Roosevelt also believed that international institutions would pay domestic dividends. They would discourage the United States from retreating to isolationism or oscillating unpredictably in its global engagement, as well as provide Americans with the material benefits of an open, stable, and rule-bound trading system.

The new order was supported by security and economic pillars. A new international organization to preserve global peace would supplant previous expedients like the balance of power, spheres of influence, and bilateral alliances. Likewise, an open, reciprocal system of trade and payments—governed by multilateral institutions—would replace discriminatory imperial preferences, bilateral arrangements, and mercantilist state barriers. The Roosevelt administration saw the new order's political and economic components as mutually reinforcing: Collective security, predicated on great power comity, would provide a foundation for peaceful dispute resolution, the pursuit of common interests, and shared prosperity. Commercial multilateralism would increase interdependence among nations, reduce the likelihood of conflict, and advance political liberty and democracy.

This economic piece was critical because the breakdown in interwar order had been commercial as well as political. In response to the prolonged slump, the world's major trading nations had adopted self-defeating protectionist and discriminatory policies. These included prohibitive tariffs, preferential trade agreements, and competitive devaluations designed to insulate them from foreign competition while exporting their economic woes. The United States had exacerbated the resulting global downturn in 1930 by passing the Smoot-Hawley tariff, which imposed steep import duties for access to the U.S. market. Three years later the United States undercut the London Economic Conference, a vain effort to stabilize the world's major currencies, by rejecting any U.S. commitment to the effort. American "sovereignty was protected," the scholar Jeffrey Legro notes, "but at terrible cost."[38] Such mercantilist trade and beggar-thy-neighbor monetary policies fragmented the global economy, prolonged the depression, accentuated social disruption, and poisoned bilateral relations and the global political climate, contributing to the outbreak of World War II. In the aftermath of these disastrous economic policy decisions, FDR and senior officials in his administration committed the United States to building and leading an open postwar world economy, in which global trade and monetary relations would be governed by accepted rules and anchored by multilateral institutions.[39]

As the State Department postwar planner Harley Notter later recalled, the U.S. decision to create and underwrite an entirely new international order "implied fundamental departures from the traditional American position." For the first time the United States would be "embracing cooperative action with other powers on an agreed basis" rather than "seeking security by our own efforts alone."[40] In other words, sovereignty-as-autonomy would cede ground to sovereignty-as-influence. This new posture required Americans to place unaccustomed faith in international institutions.

Recent domestic experiences helped ease their anxieties. Between 1930 and 1945 the size and scope of the U.S. federal government had expanded dramatically, and Americans' faith in the government had reached historic highs. Some of this optimism transferred into the global arena. Borrowing from recent domestic regulatory innovations, U.S. planners sponsored wartime multilateral conferences to lay the groundwork for new international agencies in spheres ranging from financial and monetary affairs to humanitarian relief, civil aviation, education, and food and agriculture. Roosevelt administration officials also drew inspiration from U.S. history, likening their efforts to draw the world closer together in a multilateral system to America's own constitutional experience in constructing a federal state that balanced order and liberty.[41]

THE CREATION OF THE UNITED NATIONS AND AMERICAN SOVEREIGNTY

The most important wartime negotiations concerned the postwar structure of peace. FDR's goal was to find a middle ground between traditional power politics—based on the balance of power, spheres of influence, and standing military alliances—and pure collective security, epitomized by the League of Nations. The League had failed for numerous reasons. Beyond the absence of the United States, the lack of any real teeth was its major debility. Accordingly, the Roosevelt administration determined to create a standing, universal forum that included all countries but to place responsibility for peace in the hands of a concert of great powers. As Undersecretary of State Sumner Welles explained to FDR in March 1943, the postwar international organization must balance "the sovereign equality of all states with the inevitable demand by the major military powers for such freedom of action as might be required." The premise of the new organization was that "Nations should retain, and will insist on retaining, a large degree of freedom of action." Accordingly, "no international super-government is feasible at this time, even if it were desirable."[42]

Avoiding Wilson's errors, Roosevelt worked to forge bipartisan U.S. consensus behind UN membership. This included cultivating Wendell Willkie, his Republican opponent in the 1940 election. But it was Vandenberg who became the most influential GOP convert to internationalism. The senator sought a middle ground between his own previous isolationism and "those extremists at one end of the line who would give America away." With his support, the Republican Party advisory council on September 8, 1943, endorsed the watershed Mackinac Declaration. This document advocated "responsible participation by the United States in a postwar cooperative organization among sovereign nations and to attain permanent peace with organized justice in a free world"—while also stressing the need "to protect the nation's sovereignty and freedom of action."[43]

Nine days later the House easily passed the Fulbright Resolution (the vote was 360–29), supporting "the creation of appropriate international machinery, with power adequate to establish and maintain a joint and lasting peace, among nations of the world." Astonishingly, most prewar isolationists voted for it. One was Karl Mundt (R-S.D.). "I shall never be for any commitment that gives away one iota of our national sovereignty," he averred. But "within . . . [the] boundaries [of Fulbright's resolution] is haven for the most ultra-isolationist in the country as well as the most 'super-duper' internationalist in the world." In the Senate, meanwhile, legislators overwhelmingly supported (85–5) a resolution sponsored by Tom Connally (D-Tex.), chair of the Foreign Relations Committee, authorizing U.S. participation in a postwar "international authority." Even Senator Robert Taft (R-Ohio), the quintessential Midwestern isolationist, voted in favor, notwithstanding grumbling from his colleague Robert Reynolds (R-N.C.), who complained: "It contemplates the submergence of our American sovereignty into some yet undiscovered form of super-government."[44]

Remarkably, given the acrimonious League debate just a generation earlier, the issue of UN membership never became a flashpoint in the 1944 presidential campaign. Hull persuaded FDR's Republican opponent, New York governor Thomas E. Dewey, that the administration had no desire to create an international "superstate with its own police force and other paraphernalia of coercive power." Hull subsequently worked with Dewey's foreign policy adviser, John Foster Dulles, to craft a bipartisan public statement declaring that the United States should "not only be a part of the [new international organization] but also take her share of the responsibilities such leadership implied."[45]

Roosevelt reassured the public that the United States would retain complete independence under this new scheme. The goal of the UN was to establish "some machinery of talking things over with other Nations, without taking away the independence of the United States . . . or destroying . . . the integrity of the United States in any shape, manner, or form." As *Time* magazine noted approvingly, "Franklin Roosevelt was not going to yield any U.S. sovereignty to any international organization." On August 23 the Roosevelt and Dewey campaigns released an unprecedented joint statement declaring that U.S. membership in the world body should not become an issue of partisan debate in the 1944 election.[46]

During the 1944 Dumbarton Oaks negotiations with Great Britain and the Soviet Union over the United Nations, Hull consulted with senators from both parties, assuring worried legislators that the planned postwar organization posed no dangers to U.S. sovereign authority and autonomy. Vandenberg's early reactions to the blueprint were auspicious. "The striking thing about it is that it is so conservative from a nationalist standpoint. . . . This is anything but a wild-eyed internationalist dream of a world State." At one point, Senator Guy Gillette (D-Iowa) complained to Hull that the envisioned veto for permanent Security Council members constituted "discrimination against small nations." The secretary of state was unapologetic. That provision was "in the document primarily on account of the United States," which "would not remain there for a day without retaining its veto power."[47]

Hull also promised the senators that the UN Charter would not alter congressional war powers under the U.S. Constitution. One tricky question was whether the president would need Congress's explicit consent before America's UN envoy cast a Security Council vote authorizing UN enforcement action. FDR appealed for legislative flexibility, offering a homespun analogy. Just as a police officer ought to be able to address a robbery in progress without having to call a town hall meeting, so "our American representative [on the new body] must be endowed in advance by the people themselves, by constitutional means through their representatives in Congress, with authority to act." Congress ultimately agreed that the U.S. representative could authorize UN enforcement action, while insisting that any provision of U.S. troops to such an operation would require separate legislation.[48]

The U.S. negotiating team at Dumbarton Oaks aimed to create a multilateral security organization capable—unlike the League—of responding forcefully to aggression, but without unduly restricting U.S. freedom of action (that is, its sovereign autonomy) or challenging the Constitution (its sovereign authority). American diplomats insisted that the Security Council be able to impose sanctions and order military force—and that these decisions be legally binding on all UN member states. But the Charter omitted any open-ended commitment (along the lines of Article 10 of the League Covenant) to guarantee the independence and territorial integrity of UN member states. All enforcement decisions would be left to the discretion of the Security Council, particularly its five veto-wielding permanent members. At the behest of the United States, the document also included other sovereignty protections, including Article 2(7), which read in part: "Nothing contained in the present Charter shall authorize the United Nations to intervene in matters which are essentially within the domestic jurisdiction of any state."[49]

American, Soviet, and British negotiators also debated the military tools to be placed at the Security Council's disposal. One obvious alternative, mobilizing coalitions on an ad hoc basis, had failed under the League. But another—creating a standing UN military force—risked running afoul of U.S. sovereign authority and autonomy, not least by raising complex issues of command and control. U.S. negotiators thus endorsed the third approved option: UN members would earmark national contingents for potential use by the United Nations.[50]

Would Congress and the American people accept the responsibilities and constraints of UN membership? The cloud of 1919 hung over the nation as the November 1944 presidential elections approached. In October 1944, Willkie, the 1940 GOP candidate, chastised both Republicans and Democrats for prioritizing U.S. freedom of action over collective security: "We are presented with an extraordinary proposition. We jealously guard our sovereignty; other nations likewise guard their sovereignty; but somehow all nations are to be welded together into an international organization with the power to prevent aggression and preserve peace."[51]

Following FDR's defeat of Dewey and reelection to a historic fourth term, the administration launched a massive public relations campaign to build domestic political support for the United Nations. It distributed millions of pamphlets within the United States, as well as a fifteen-minute documentary, *The Watchtower over Tomorrow*.[52] These efforts depicted isolationism and unilateralism as impractical in a shrinking world. At the same time, executive branch officials underscored their rock-solid commitment to American sovereignty. "The thought of any kind of superstate is to us wholly repugnant," the new secretary of state, Edward Stettinius, declared on New Year's Day 1945. But the UN was essential to avoid a third world war. As Vice President Harry S. Truman explained in February 1945, "The only rational alternative to existing international anarchy lies in some reasonable form of international organization among so-called sovereign states." Assistant Secretary of State Joseph Grew framed the challenge of postwar international organization as akin to "the problem which confronted our forefathers in 1789: The necessity of creating an effective organization for the maintenance of the peace."[53]

Returning from Yalta in February 1945, FDR himself offered the boldest prediction for the United Nations. "It ought to spell an end of the system of unilateral action, the exclusive alliance, the spheres of influence, the balances of power, and all the other expedients that have been tried for centuries—and have always failed."[54] Alas, the president would not live to see his baby born, dying in mid-April. It would be up to his successor, Harry S. Truman, to watch it emerge.

In June 1945 delegates from fifty nations approved the UN Charter at the San Francisco conference. That document established a United Nations Organization with six distinct organs: a Security Council, a General Assembly, an Economic and Social Council, a Trusteeship Council, an International Court of Justice, and a Secretariat. President Truman celebrated the accomplishment at a closing ceremony at the city's Opera House, reminding the assembled nations that success would depend on how "united" they in fact remained. "We all have to recognize—no matter how great our strength—that we must deny ourselves the license to do as we please. . . . This is the price each nation will have to pay for world peace." American journalists depicted the Charter as a judicious balance among national independence, great power privilege, and the requirements of collective security—in short, among the goals of sovereign authority, autonomy, and influence. While it "does not and could not produce anything resembling a world government," the editors of the *New York Times* noted, "it does, on paper, involve some voluntary relinquishment of sovereignty by the leading powers."[55]

It was now up to the Senate to offer a verdict different from the one it had delivered in 1919. On July 9 Connally opened hearings in the Foreign Relations Committee. The UN, he implied, was a careful balance between the desire for U.S. freedom of action and the need for collective means to halt aggression. "Those Senators who believe we should tread our path alone will vote against the Charter," he acknowledged. "But those who realize that . . . the United States cannot live in a cellophane wrapper will favor the Charter." Prospects for approval were strong, thanks to Vandenberg's own intellectual journey from isolationism to internationalism. "I have always been frankly one of those who has believed in our own self-reliance," the Michigan senator conceded. "But I do not believe that any nation hereafter can immunize itself by its own exclusive action."[56]

To underline his own commitment to American independence, Connally strengthened a proposed U.S. reservation to the Charter, which exempted the nation on "matters which are essentially within the jurisdiction of the United States," by adding the phrase: "as determined by the United States." As the senator explained, "I do not want to surrender the sovereignty or the prestige of the United States on any question which may be merely domestic in character and contained within the boundaries of this Republic."[57] The committee approved the Charter overwhelmingly (21–1), highlighting its "safeguards for American sovereignty," including the veto provision and the Monroe Doctrine. The entire Senate approved the Charter in late July, by a vote of 89 to 2, and President Truman ratified the result on August 8, 1945, making the United States the first member of the new United Nations organization.

THE COLD WAR: CONTAINMENT, THE "FREE WORLD," AND AMERICAN SOVEREIGNTY

Unfortunately, the United Nations would never enjoy the golden age the Roosevelt and Truman administrations had envisioned. Superpower confrontation abruptly quashed U.S. dreams of an open world and sidelined the UN on most major issues for decades. Still, Americans did not turn their back on multilateral institutions, even as the Cold War transformed their national security and foreign policy. As the world fractured into two, the United States traded in its vision of universal collective security for a more circumscribed strategy of collective defense, focused on bolstering a "Free World" community that enjoyed a preponderance of global power.[58]

In planning for post–World War II structures of peace, the United States had sought to balance the principle of sovereign equality among all UN member states with a recognition of the special role of the great powers. As permanent Security Council members, the latter were not only empowered to make legally binding decisions but also endowed with vetoes allowing them to block any enforcement action they considered counter to their national interests. The rationale for the veto was plain: no structure of peace could be viable if war could be authorized against the wishes of one of the world's policemen.

The veto provision enhanced America's own sovereignty, protecting its constitutional independence and freedom of action. But it also meant that the UN Security Council, by design, could be paralyzed by great power disagreement. The Soviet Union cast the first Security Council veto in February 1946 (in an effort to hasten the removal of French forces from Syria and Lebanon). Vandenberg's response was instructive. "The system worked," he told his Senate colleagues, by making great power consensus a requirement for Security Council action.

The American architects of the UN had hoped that the Soviet Union, given a stake in the postwar system, would abide by Atlantic Charter principles, thus minimizing the scope of future great power disagreement. But Stalin's government was deeply threatened, ideologically and geopolitically, by the American vision of an open, rule-bound international order. By 1947 it was clear to all, as U.S. diplomat Charles Bohlen concluded, that there were "two worlds instead of one"—and that the United States must devote itself to trying to unite the "non-Soviet world . . . politically, economically, and in the last analysis militarily."[59]

Collective security would give way to alliance and coalition building, complemented by international institutions (including the International Monetary Fund, the World Bank, and the General Agreement on Tariffs and Trade) to govern the capitalist world economy. The United States was the undisputed leader of this order. But unlike the Soviet Union, which imposed its own vision on others, the United States would adopt a more consensual leadership style, helping to legitimate its power.

The centerpiece of the Western alliance became the North Atlantic Treaty Organization (NATO), established in April 1949. Significantly, the United States insisted, despite its overwhelming might, that NATO take a multilateral form. This was an intriguing choice. After all, Washington might have maximized its sovereign autonomy (that is, its freedom of action) by negotiating a set of unequal bilateral arrangements with individual Western European states. Alternatively, as the U.S. diplomat George Kennan advocated during 1947–48, it could have forged an alliance between two freestanding European and North American pillars. Finally, it might have unilaterally extended the Monroe Doctrine eastward, declaring external meddling in Western Europe off-limits—and subject to a U.S. response. These alternatives would have expanded U.S. freedom of choice, negotiating room, and leverage to extract concessions and resources from allies.[60]

Instead, the United States insisted that Atlantic nations treat their security as indivisible. When European leaders all but clamored for institutionalized subordination to Washington, the Truman administration rebuffed them, insisting that NATO be a multilateral regional defense pact. The costs to U.S. sovereignty-as-autonomy were significant: A multilateral alliance made it harder for the United States to throw its weight around or punish individual countries, while allowing others to "free ride" on U.S. contributions to collective defense. Collective defense made it impossible for the United States to discriminate against allies based on their material or geopolitical importance, while creating collective action problems, resulting in unending disputes over burden sharing that continue to this day (and indeed have been front and center under President Donald Trump).[61] In sum, NATO placed constraints on U.S. autonomy and permitted other, lesser players to influence U.S. national security decisions. Simultaneously, the United States pushed mightily for integration among its West European allies—arguably the first time a great power had tried to promote unity over division in a region where it had major interests. This was in historical perspective a remarkable turn of events.[62]

Why would the United States, which had long avoided entangling alliances, choose to restrict its sovereign autonomy within NATO? The Cold War provides part of the answer. American officials recognized that America would reap long-term benefits by behaving as if it had less power than it actually did. By exercising restraint, treating partners as equals, and guaranteeing the security as well as economic stability of the free world, the United States helped legitimate its own power and leadership, particularly when contrasted to heavy-handed Soviet behavior. Restraint would also have "downstream" benefits, underpinning U.S. leadership even after relative U.S. power had begun to decline.[63] Finally, the common political heritage of NATO members—most of which were democracies united by political and cultural values—bred a distinctive, egalitarian ethos. Disputes occasionally arose, but a shared commitment to democratic norms encouraged members to determine alliance policies jointly, while delegitimating hard-nosed coercion by the United States and other large members during difficult negotiations.[64]

Of course, the Truman administration still had to sell the entangling alliance at home. It had to convince legislators—and the American people—that NATO membership was consistent with popular sovereignty, American exceptionalism, and the separation of powers, and that it would not unduly infringe on either the authority of the U.S. Constitution or U.S. freedom of action. Once again, the former isolationist Arthur Vandenberg played an essential role, this time by marshalling support for an eponymous resolution authorizing negotiations on a North Atlantic Treaty (NAT). American diplomats had to tread a fine line. They had to persuade anxious Europeans that any U.S. security guarantee was ironclad while reassuring U.S. legislators precisely the opposite: there would be no "automatic" U.S. response to aggression reminiscent of Article 10. After Vandenberg and Connally objected to an early draft, Secretary of State Dean Acheson softened the phrasing of Article 5 of the draft treaty. In case of an armed attack, each NATO member was obliged only to take "such action, including the use of armed force, as it deems necessary to restore and maintain the security of the North Atlantic area." The treaty also included an important caveat to preserve U.S. sovereign authority. Any response by members would be "carried out in accordance with their respective constitutional processes."[65]

The United States, Canada, and ten European nations signed the NAT in Washington on April 4, 1949. By the time the Senate began public hearings three weeks later, a clear plurality of senators supported it. Senator Robert Taft, along with a dozen other conservatives, remained skeptical. "Mr. Republican" preferred a unilateral American security guarantee for Western Europe, instead of a "pact which binds us for twenty years to come to the defense of any country, no matter by whom it is attacked and even though the aggressor may be another member of the pact." Vandenberg sought to reassure him. He conceded that the treaty was "a literal departure from orthodox American diplomacy." Still, it was consistent with a U.S. "philosophy of preventive action against aggression" dating from the Monroe Doctrine. Taft remained unpersuaded, calling the treaty's Article 3 provisions for rearming Europe "an incitation to war." Nevertheless, the Senate approved the treaty handily, 82–13, on July 21.[66]

The ratification of the NAT symbolized America's transition from "one world" wartime dreams to a more pragmatic "free world" approach tailored to Cold War realities. The vision of a universal collective security community had yielded, at least temporarily, to a more circumscribed multilateral alliance among market democracies (as authorized by Article 51 of the UN Charter). Although U.S. dominance within NATO would become more obvious as the allies moved to create an integrated force under a U.S. supreme commander, the treaty itself accorded the United States no special status within the alliance's political or military structure. Indeed, U.S. officials hoped that Europe would quickly emerge as a strong bloc capable of defending itself. As events transpired, the United States wound up enmeshing itself in a highly structured alliance, providing billions of dollars in military aid, and adopting a forward strategy to defend its European allies. Far from "recruiting" client states as a security buffer—like a traditional great power—the United States actually assumed new burdens at great risk to itself, including by providing a nuclear umbrella.[67]

NATO placed unprecedented obligations on the United States, reducing its diplomatic flexibility. The core commitment was Article 5, which obliged each NATO member to regard an attack on one as an attack on all, and to come to one another's aid. In signing the Washington Treaty establishing NATO, the United States ceased going it alone and began going it with others. In short, U.S membership in NATO implied sacrificing some sovereignty-as-autonomy for the prospect of sovereignty-as-influence—in the shape of collective defense.

Nor was this the end of U.S. commitments. Far from steering clear of "entangling alliances," the United States by the mid-1950s stood at the center of a vast global alliance system, involving more than forty countries and some 450 U.S. military bases and installations in foreign lands, whose members were committed to "collective effort and mutual obligations."[68] This alliance structure would remain largely intact for the next four decades, through nine successive U.S. administrations, Democrat and Republican alike.

SECURITY AND SOVEREIGNTY AFTER THE COLD WAR

The rapid end of the Cold War—a transition bookended by the fall of the Berlin Wall in November 1989 and the dissolution of the Soviet Union less than two years later—vindicated the U.S. policy of containment. It also inaugurated a brief, "unipolar moment" in which the United States faced no challengers.[69] And yet the more complex, diffuse threat environment posed its own quandaries. One was whether the United States should redouble its support for multilateral security cooperation or instead revert to a unilateral posture to protect its sovereign prerogatives, including freedom of action to use military force as it deemed fit.

Initially, the answer seemed clear. The victory of the UN-mandated, U.S.-led coalition in the 1991 Gulf War generated euphoria about multilateral cooperation. President George H. W. Bush lauded a "new world order" based on collective security, the rule of law, democratic governance, and expanding trade. His Democratic successor, Bill Clinton, doubled down on this vision. He committed the United States to the path of "assertive multilateralism," in which alliances and international organizations would advance a new grand strategy: the "enlargement of the world's free community of market democracies."[70]

The dawn of multilateralism proved false—or at least cloudy. In Somalia and Bosnia the Clinton administration found collective security tougher in practice than in theory. After winning control of Congress in late 1994, Republicans placed restrictions on support for UN peace operations. The administration retreated to a more pragmatic stance, embodied in the phrase "multilateral when we can, unilateral when we must." The most symbolic blow to U.S. multilateral security cooperation would come in 1999, when the Senate rejected the Comprehensive Test Ban Treaty (CTBT), in a rebuke to Clinton that commentators likened to the rejection of the Versailles Treaty eighty years earlier.[71]

More generally, the reality of unipolarity was often hard to square with multilateral cooperation, making the United States more sensitive to external constraints on its foreign policy choices—that is, its sovereignty-as-autonomy. This was particularly true in the military arena. By 2000, the United States was spending more on national defense than the rest of the world combined. Such a vast disparity in national capabilities for destructive power coexisted uneasily with rules enshrined in the UN Charter governing the collective legitimation of armed force.[72] Moreover, the widely shared notion that the United States was the world's "indispensable power," in the words of Secretary of State Madeleine Albright, implied that it had unique responsibilities, shared not even by other members of the UN Security Council, to serve as the ultimate guarantor of world order. In discharging these custodial obligations, some U.S. leaders and analysts argued, the United States could not be subject to constraints binding on others.[73]

To be sure, the Clinton administration continued to value cooperative defense institutions, particularly NATO, which it relied on to end the Bosnian war in 1995 and to force Serbia out of Kosovo in 1999. But when it came to the United Nations, the president faced a wary public and skeptical Congress. In an effort to build bridges between Capitol Hill and the United Nations, Clinton's UN envoy, Richard Holbrooke, invited Jesse Helms, the powerful Republican chair of the Senate Foreign Relations Committee, to make an unprecedented appearance before the UN Security Council. The senator used the occasion to remind the world body who was boss. "Candor compels that I reiterate this warning: the American people will never accept the claims of the United Nations to be the 'sole arbiter of legitimacy on the use of force' in the world," he declared. "No institution—not the Security Council, not the Yugoslav tribunal, not a future ICC—is competent to judge the foreign policy and national security decisions of the United States."[74]

The Bush Revolution in U.S. Foreign Policy

The ascendance of George W. Bush to the presidency in January 2001 underscored Helms's message: the United States would protect its sovereign authority and sovereign autonomy. Whereas the president's father had pursued pragmatic internationalism, the younger Bush and his closest advisers favored the forthright and unapologetic use of American might in the service of U.S. interests and values, regardless of whether those actions unsettled long-standing institutions and partnerships. To drive home this point the new administration in short order renounced the Anti-Ballistic Missile Treaty with Russia, "unsigned" the Rome Statute of the ICC, repudiated the Kyoto Protocol, blocked a verification protocol to the Biological Weapons Convention (BWC), opposed a draft UN convention to reduce illicit trafficking in small arms and light weapons, and reaffirmed the Senate's 1999 rejection of the CTBT. These actions sent a clear message: America's unique power gave it unique interests, which the United States would pursue without compromise, regardless of international perceptions.[75]

Bush's approach departed both in substance and in tone from long-standing U.S. foreign and national security policy. From FDR to Clinton, the United States had promoted international security institutions as a foundation for U.S. leadership. It had accepted modest but real constraints on its sovereign freedom of action, calculating that self-restraint in the exercise of U.S. power offered the promise of greater international legitimacy for its purposes and the prospect of burden sharing in advancing them. To return to the "sovereignty triangle" outlined in chapter 1, the United States had ceded some sovereignty-as-autonomy for the promise of greater sovereignty-as-influence.

From the moment it assumed office, the George W. Bush administration signaled a desire to escape these institutional constraints and embrace the robust pursuit of American primacy, a grand strategy that the president's father had explicitly rejected. Its objective, captured in the title of Ivo Daalder and James Lindsay's incisive account of these years, was an "America unbound."[76] This sometimes expressed itself in unilateralism, including acting alone or opting out of international treaties or regimes endorsed by the vast majority of other nations.[77] The more common position was to embrace an alternative form of collective action through selective coalitions of the willing.

Several convictions underpinned this skepticism of standing international institutions, from the United Nations to NATO: First, multilateralism must be a means to concrete foreign policy ends, rather than an end in itself. Whereas the Clinton administration had (allegedly) regarded a multilateral imprimatur as "essential to the legitimate exercise of power," Bush adviser Condoleezza Rice promised in 2000 that Clinton's successor would be far more discriminating, assessing proposed treaties and organizations on a case-by-case basis. Second, the United Nations in particular was hopelessly dysfunctional—given to lowest-common-denominator policymaking and reflecting a consensus at odds with American interest and ideals.

Third, the expanding reach of international law, most notably the ICC, not only challenged the supremacy of the Constitution but increased the vulnerability of globally deployed U.S. military forces to a tribunal lacking democratic accountability—not least to the American people. Fourth, growing asymmetries in military and technological capabilities reduced the value of traditional multilateral alliances like NATO, which constrained U.S. freedom of action without any appreciable benefit. Beyond criticizing NATO's "war by committee" over Kosovo in 1999, the Bush administration believed that Europe's modest contributions to burden sharing undermined its claims to decision sharing in alliance policy. Fifth, the Bush administration argued that unilateralism—or at least its threat—could at times be an essential catalyst to jump-start collective action.[78]

Most significantly, the Bush administration argued that formal international organizations were only one (and often a second-best) approach to multilateral cooperation. The United States could often achieve its aims more efficiently (that is, optimize its sovereignty-as-influence) by working through flexible coalitions of the willing that presented fewer constraints on its options (sovereignty-as-autonomy) and posed little threat to its constitutional prerogatives (sovereignty-as-authority). Instead of relying on a "prix fixe" menu of standing alliances and formal organizations that would circumscribe its freedom of action and achieve only bland consensus, the United States should adopt an opportunistic, "à la carte" approach, selectively assembling coalitions of capable, like-minded states to address discrete tasks and specific challenges.[79] Besides excluding those with little to offer, as well as potential spoilers hoping to subvert collective objectives, such frameworks would permit the United States to deploy coalition assets in the service of U.S. priorities.

The Impact of September 11

The attacks of September 11, 2001, accentuated the instinct to enlarge U.S. freedom of action. In an age of unpredictable, potentially catastrophic threats, U.S. officials concluded, the nation could not accept limits on its military choices or tolerate time-consuming multilateral diplomacy. Anticipation, flexibility, and speed were imperative. At home, the attacks aroused a Jacksonian outburst of nationalism, as a wounded society lashed out with a "don't tread on me" ferocity. Sensitive to the mood, Congress provided President Bush with a blank check to pursue a new, revolutionary foreign policy based on the unchecked assertion of American might—a maximalist approach to sovereign autonomy.

To be sure, the administration welcomed statements of international solidarity. The day after the attacks, NATO invoked for the first time the alliance's Article 5 collective defense provisions, while the UN Security Council authorized "all necessary steps" against the 9/11 perpetrators. Later that month Security Council Resolution 1373 required all member states to crack down on terrorist financing and report on their efforts to a new UN Counterterrorism Committee (CTC). But from the outset, the Bush administration signaled that it alone would define the war against terrorism and brook no interference in its prosecution.

Secretary of Defense Donald Rumsfeld explained this logic to CNN host Larry King: "There is no coalition," Rumsfeld insisted. "There are multiple coalitions. . . . It's the mission that determines the coalition." Indeed, the emerging U.S. antiterror alliance was less a multilateral undertaking with mutually agreed obligations than a "hub and spoke" arrangement founded on specific bilateral deals between a U.S. "sheriff" and members of its diverse "posse." This approach gave Washington a free hand in setting and pursuing goals. But abroad, as EU commissioner for external relations Christopher Patten observed in February 2002, U.S. allies perceived America as shifting into "unilateralist overdrive."[80]

Insistence on sovereign autonomy was at the heart of the Bush administration's 2002 National Security Strategy, released one year after 9/11. It emphatically endorsed a unilateral approach to U.S. national security, including a policy of "preemption" to forestall catastrophic threats. The twin themes were conjoined in a single sentence: "While the United States will constantly strive to enlist the support of the international community, we will not hesitate to act alone, if necessary, to exercise our right to self-defense, by acting preemptively against such terrorists, to prevent them from doing harm against our people and our country." The administration argued that the convergence of "shadowy" terrorist networks, unpredictable rogue states, and spreading WMD technology had rendered traditional containment and deterrence obsolete, since devastation could come without warning. Rather than waiting until emerging threats became acute, the United States would respond preventively—and alone if necessary.[81]

To be sure, the world *did* need new norms defining the criteria for principled preemption. What made Bush's strategy controversial was that it elevated the right of preemption to a doctrine and expanded the definition of "imminence" to encompass emerging threats that were not yet fully realized. To many observers around the world, Bush's failure to build an international consensus *before* enunciating this doctrine signaled a determination to marginalize the UN Security Council and lower the threshold for preventive war.

The administration's pursuit of freedom of action was on full display in Afghanistan, where Washington rebuffed any formal role for NATO in toppling the Taliban or pursuing the al Qaeda terrorist network. Not until September 2003 did it agree to place the International Security Assistance Force (ISAF) under NATO command and permit its gradual expansion beyond Kabul. Even then, U.S. officials regarded NATO's involvement as a mixed blessing, since resource-strapped, casualty-averse allies strained to generate even modest forces, funds, and materiel, and they often placed restrictive "national caveats" on the use of their troops.[82] Skepticism about NATO would only increase during the subsequent transatlantic crisis over Iraq, in which major U.S. allies France and Germany voted against a U.S.-sponsored UN Security Council resolution to authorize armed force against the regime of Saddam Hussein. In 2006 one senior State Department official predicted that NATO would play a declining role in U.S. defense policy. Henceforth the United States would "'ad hoc' our way through coalitions of the willing."[83]

Exhibit A in this coalition approach was the Proliferation Security Initiative (PSI). Created in 2003, this innovative partnership of like-minded countries was designed to intercept illicit maritime, air, and land shipments of nuclear, chemical, and biological weapons; ballistic missiles; and related technologies. The genius of PSI, its champions said, was its nimble response to a growing menace. "Rather than rely on cumbersome treaty-based bureaucracies," Undersecretary of State John Bolton explained in 2004, "the robust use of the sovereign authorities we and our allies possess can produce real results."[84]

Bush administration officials touted PSI as a potential model for addressing other threats. Unlike universal organizations, which permitted Lilliputians to gang up on the American Gulliver, thwart his purposes, and exploit his resources, the coalition approach left control in the hands of the U.S. giant. Washington could convene a small core group of like-minded countries, get them to endorse specific principles that narrowly defined the network's mandate and activities, and only then mobilize others to join on U.S. terms. Over time, the Bush administration employed this general approach in other spheres, from nuclear materials to climate change to pandemic disease. In each case the intent was to shift cooperation from dysfunctional formal organizations to flexible, responsive coalitions.[85]

There was a lot to be said for mixing and matching among multilateral vehicles, administration officials reckoned. Informal, flexible, and transitory coalitions would allow the United States to preserve its sovereign authority and maximize its sovereign autonomy, while advancing its sovereign influence. But the tumultuous Bush years also suggested that there was no free lunch— that focusing on authority and autonomy could at times limit U.S. influence. By marginalizing the United Nations, in particular, the United States risked squandering the legitimacy of its leadership, forfeiting opportunities for burden sharing, and eroding the foundations of world order.

It was also unsustainable. Whatever his instincts, President Bush was forced to return repeatedly to the UN Security Council to win authorization and endorsement for concrete U.S. objectives. These goals included international recognition of the Iraqi Governing Council; UN aid for Iraqi elections; renewal of the UN Assistance Mission in Afghanistan; a binding legal commitment (under Resolution 1540) to keep WMD out of the hands of terrorists; and the establishment of new UN missions in Haiti, Lebanon, Darfur, and elsewhere. More broadly, the United States relied daily on standing UN agencies to confront emerging threats to U.S. national security. These ranged from the International Atomic Energy Agency (IAEA), which monitored the nuclear weapons activities of North Korea and Iran, to the World Health Organization (WHO), which helped to contain the severe acute respiratory syndrome (SARS) pandemic in 2003.

THE POLITICS OF "ENGAGEMENT": OBAMA'S "RETURN" TO MULTILATERALISM

Barack Obama, who succeeded George W. Bush as president in January 2009, promised to return the United States to a multilateral course. As a candidate, the junior senator from Illinois had criticized Bush for allegedly alienating U.S. friends and allies, violating fundamental American values, and tarnishing the nation's once-sterling reputation by going it alone in global affairs. He

pledged if elected not only to reverse Bush's disastrous unilateralism but also
to spearhead a new era of international cooperation.

Obama delivered his first major foreign policy address as a candidate at the
Chicago Council on Global Affairs in April 2007. He harkened back to the
mid-1940s, when farsighted U.S. leaders had "built the system of international institutions that carried us through the Cold War." What the giants of
the mid-twentieth century had understood was that "instead of constraining
our power, these institutions magnified it." America's task was to update these
creaky organizations to today's new realities: the dramatic shift of economic
power to the developing world, the rise of shared security threats like climate
change, and the emergence of malevolent nonstate actors like terrorists.
Obama promised "a new chapter in American leadership," in which the United
States would "rebuild the alliances, partnerships and institutions necessary to
confront common threats and enhance common security."[86]

Obama's foreign policy vision was predicated on a conviction that U.S.
national security and prosperity were increasingly intertwined with those of
other nations. In such a world, too great a reliance on sovereignty-as-autonomy
risked undercutting U.S. sovereignty-as-influence. The president proposed a
"new era of engagement" in which the United States would work with both
established and rising powers to retrofit international institutions to match
the new global agenda and shifting power dynamics.

Obama's commitment to a multilateral renaissance was commendable, but
it was also based on two shaky premises. The first was that the main object of
statecraft was no longer navigating great power rivalries but managing the
shared vulnerabilities of an interconnected planet. The president intimated as
much in his first National Security Strategy, which declared, "power, in an
interdependent world, is no longer a zero-sum game." The second assumption
was that the United States had the will, to say nothing of the capacity, to engineer a grand bargain between established and rising powers on the contours of
global institutional reform. Established players would grant emerging players
a seat at the high table. In return, rising powers would help to sustain and
manage an agreed global order.[87]

Both assumptions would be sorely tested during Obama's eight years in
office. This was not a moment of creation—or even of re-creation—akin to
the mid-1940s. It was true that global problems increasingly dominated the
international agenda. But the world remained much more conflictual than
Obama's technocratic vision of international politics suggested. And even where
broad interests and values aligned, formal international organizations defied
fundamental reform.

In retrospect, it should have been clear to the Obama administration how fierce were the headwinds against global institutional reform. Four major differences between the current world and the era of the "wise men" made reconfiguring the bedrock institutions of world order a Herculean challenge.

First, the world was no longer a clean slate. In the 1940s, U.S. architects of the postwar order could design institutions out of whole cloth, without dismantling existing institutions or reallocating power and privilege within them. They were, as Dean Acheson titled his memoirs, "present at the creation." The Obama administration had no such luxury. It confronted a landscape teeming with international organizations and treaties. Member states and agency bureaucrats fiercely resisted efforts to alter the mandate, membership, management, and funding of existing multilateral treaty bodies. Consider the UN Security Council, to which Russia and China adamantly opposed adding any permanent members—or the International Energy Agency (IEA), whose own membership remains limited to Organization for Economic Cooperation and Development (OECD) countries and in which voting shares still reflect oil consumption in the mid-1970s. Within the UN system especially, retrofitting existing institutions has proved more daunting than creating them in the first place—encouraging the search for workarounds.

Second, the urgency of the 1940s was lacking. In the absence of major policy failure, institutions evolve incrementally at best. In a perverse way, Acheson's generation had it easy, operating on the heels of the most devastating economic crisis and most destructive war in modern history. While the contemporary world has been spared such catastrophes, the very absence of crisis reinforced institutional inertia. The recent exception that proved the rule was the Great Recession of 2007–08, when fears of economic implosion created a transitory incentive for world leaders to adopt significant reforms to global economic cooperation, including elevating the Group of 20 (G-20) to the leaders' level, creating a new Financial Stability Board, and adopting the Basel III capital account requirements for major banks.

Third, by the time of Obama's election the global agenda had become more ambitious and intrusive than immediately after World War II, making major breakthroughs elusive. Much of the "low-hanging fruit" of multilateral cooperation had long been picked. Consider trade: Early GATT rounds focused on lowering tariffs and eliminating subsidies. The more recent trade agenda had shifted to harmonizing behind-the-border standards and regulations on matters like fiscal policy, health and safety, or intellectual property. Such agreements impinged more deeply on state sovereignty. The world had also become more crowded—with states. At its founding the UN had only fifty members. By 2009 it had 193, many wedded to bloc identities and entrenched regional positions, complicating global consensus within forums like the UN General Assembly.

Fourth, the global distribution of power had changed since the 1940s. The Roosevelt-Truman administration operated at the zenith of American hegemony. During the Cold War decades the United States and its Western allies dominated the capitalist world economy. In 1990, when that conflict ended, the members of the OECD represented more than three-fifths of global gross domestic product (GDP). By 2015, despite its addition of a dozen new members, the OECD share had slipped to 47 percent, while the BRICS countries (Brazil, Russia, India, China, and South Africa) accounted for almost 25 percent of global output.

To the degree that emerging and established countries shared values and preferences, this power shift might have been managed. But as the Obama administration would learn, integrating emerging powers was not just about offering them a place at the global high table and expecting them to foot the bill. It also implied allowing them to shape the agenda. Unfortunately, major Western and non-Western countries often diverged over important international norms, such as the appropriate boundaries of national sovereignty, criteria for humanitarian intervention, role of the state in the market, and balance between national security and civil liberties.

All rising powers sought greater voice and prerogatives within international institutions. But they were also tempted to free ride rather than assume greater burdens within international institutions, in part because of their status as "poor" countries facing extraordinary development challenges and rising demands from citizens.[88] Such considerations help explain why the Obama administration chose not to pursue Security Council reform, despite its initial sympathy for that agenda. Senior U.S. officials ultimately concluded that the most likely developing world aspirants to permanent membership—even fellow democracies like India, Brazil, and South Africa—would often oppose U.S. preferences.

Even more alarming, the Obama years witnessed a resurgence of traditional great power competition that took the administration by surprise—and complicated cooperation on international peace and security, in particular. The "return of geopolitics" was most obvious in relations with Russia and China.[89] Washington's much hyped "reset" with Moscow, intended to improve U.S.-Russian relations, proved illusory, and Vladimir Putin's 2014 decision to seize the Crimea peninsula and support separatists in eastern Ukraine brought

Russo-American relations to their lowest point since the Cold War. The United States and its Western partners responded to Moscow's aggression by imposing sanctions on Russia and suspending Russian membership in the Group of 8 (a collection of the world's most important market democracies, within which Russia had always been an odd bedfellow).

Meanwhile, under the leadership of Xi Jinping, who became general secretary of the central committee of the Chinese Communist Party in 2012 and China's president in 2013, China became more assertive both in its region and globally. In the East and South China Seas, Beijing advanced expansive and controversial jurisdictional claims over territorial waters and the island features therein, while challenging customary norms of maritime law.[90]

It was in the conflict in Syria, above all, where geopolitical frictions posed the most obvious impediment to international cooperation. Russia, supported by China, repeatedly blocked effective Security Council action to end the carnage in that country. Both countries cited the bitter legacy of Libya, where (they claimed) the West had exploited a 2011 UN resolution to protect the lives of civilians to engineer regime change—specifically, to depose Libyan strongman Moammar Gaddafi. In Syria, Russia would eventually intervene militarily to prop up the dictator Bashar al-Assad.[91]

This combination of resurgent great power rivalry and anemic international organizations created a quandary for the United States. On the one hand, the seemingly inexorable momentum of global integration placed new pressures on all nations, increasing their vulnerability to negative spillovers. The United States found it harder to advance the security, prosperity, and well-being of American citizens through purely national means. This was true whether the challenge was regulating volatile financial flows, harmonizing trade rules, mitigating greenhouse gases, controlling pandemic disease, governing cyberspace, controlling migration, combating transnational terrorism, preventing proliferation of weapons of mass destruction, policing criminal networks, or preserving the openness of an increasingly congested global commons. The imperative of international cooperation, in other words, had created incentives for "sovereignty bargains," in which the United States delegated some notional autonomy for the promise of greater influence.

On the other hand, many global institutions were flailing in responding to contemporary challenges. What was the United States to do? If one were to focus purely on formal international organizations, one might have been tempted to despair. But that pessimistic view obscured a more complicated, promising picture of global cooperation that had gained momentum in the still young twenty-first century.

What sets the contemporary global era apart is not the absence of international institutions but their astonishing diversity. Faced with resistance to sweeping transformational change within more encompassing global bodies, U.S. and foreign policymakers have generated and then exploited a messier form of multilateralism.[92] The Obama years—like the George W. Bush years before them—suggested that a hallmark of twenty-first century multilateralism might be the rising prominence of alternative forms of collective action as complements to—and sometimes substitutes for—traditional intergovernmental cooperation. Formal organizations would persist, but governments will continue to participate in a sprawling array of flexible networks whose membership varies based on situational interests, shared values, or relevant capabilities.

Faced with blockages in formal international organizations, the United States and its partners abroad have experimented with informal, ad hoc, and selective approaches to global cooperation. These institutions are often "minilateral" rather than universal, voluntary rather than legally binding, disaggregated rather than comprehensive, transgovernmental rather than just intergovernmental, regional rather than global, multilevel and multistakeholder rather than state-centric, and "bottom-up" rather than "top-down."[93] States continue to negotiate and collaborate within conventional bodies like the United Nations and the Bretton Woods institutions. But extensive policy coordination also occurs within parallel frameworks that are ad hoc and temporary rather than formal and permanent.

As this book's conclusion spells out in greater detail, these more flexible forms of multilateralism have the potential to cushion—although not entirely eliminate—some of the otherwise painful trade-offs among U.S. sovereignty-as-authority, sovereignty-as autonomy, and sovereignty-as-influence. Although no panacea, such informal, ad hoc arrangements offer the promise of enhancing U.S. influence over its destiny, in the form of effective international cooperation, at no cost to its constitutional authorities and with fewer constraints on U.S. freedom of action.[94]

CONCLUSION

In the century since the United States entered World War I—and emerged as the world's most powerful nation—Americans have debated their nation's proper role in the world. With the exception of the interwar period, U.S. foreign, national security, and commercial posture has been overwhelmingly internationalist. The primary disagreements have been among variants of American internationalism—between unilateralists and multilateralists, and between realists and idealists. This bipartisan globalist consensus was shaken by the end of the Cold War, and challenged after 9/11, but it did not collapse. Advocates of American detachment and withdrawal remained a distinctive minority, at least within the U.S. foreign policy establishment.

The question today is whether that era is ending. The populist wave that helped elect Donald Trump as the forty-fifth president of the United States in November 2016 challenged a number of long-standing orthodoxies about America's role in the world. Trump's triumph has opened a new, more free-wheeling debate over the appropriate contours and purposes of U.S. foreign policy. Trump's campaign slogan—"Make America Great Again"—was open to diverse interpretations and attracted voters for disparate reasons. But a core message was that the time had finally come to put America first.

Trump's rhetoric tapped into public anxieties about globalization and fatigue with unending wars and nation building abroad. But it also drew on a venerable school of thought that had dominated U.S. foreign policy from the founding of the American republic until the early twentieth century. This tradition portrays the United States as exceptional but also vulnerable, best able to retain what is unique and to advance peace and prosperity by keeping to itself. It holds that the nation must be prepared to defend itself, but that it should abandon any pretense of ordering the world, much less remaking other societies in the American image.

The 2016 U.S. presidential campaign exposed a collision between the logic of globalization and American domestic politics. As global interdependence increases, the rationale for more extensive and intrusive forms of multilateral cooperation grows, implying greater sacrifices of sovereignty-as-autonomy (and perhaps at times even sovereignty-as-authority). And yet growing global integration elicits defensiveness in many parts of American society, in the form of cultural anxiety, ideological opposition, and institutional resistance to perceived incursions on U.S. prerogatives and traditions. Today the main threat to the post-1945 Western liberal order comes less from potential adversaries, though they exist (notably China and Russia), than from Americans themselves, no longer confident that the world that they built, and the institutions they created to manage it, are still in the U.S. interest or worth the burdens of American leadership. And at the heart of contemporary debates between American "nationalism" versus "globalism" is the question of U.S. sovereignty.[95]

The following chapters examine how this collision between growing global interdependence and U.S. sovereignty concerns are playing out in critical spheres, influencing American attitudes and policies toward international law, international security, global economic integration, border control, and international organizations. The overall thesis is that while U.S. sovereignty-as-authority remains largely untroubled by current trends, the United States is more often finding it difficult to reconcile its aspirations for freedom of action with its desire to shape its own destiny.

FOUR

Do as I Say, Not as I Do

American Sovereignty and International Law

Antonin Scalia was beside himself. The U.S. Supreme Court had just ruled 5–4 in *Roper* v. *Simmons* (2005) that it was unconstitutional to impose the death penalty on individuals who had committed capital crimes as minors. But what most offended the associate justice was the majority's invocation of international opinion to justify its decision. What possible relevance could the findings of foreign courts and jurists have for Supreme Court deliberations?, Scalia inquired. "I thought it was the Constitution of the United States that we were discussing."[1]

The target of Scalia's ire was Associate Justice Anthony Kennedy, the court's frequent swing voter. Writing for the majority, Kennedy had argued that imposing capital punishment on juvenile offenders constituted "cruel and unusual punishment," based on "evolving standards of decency"—a principle the court had endorsed in the 1965 case *Trop* v. *Dulles*. Noting "the overwhelming weight of international opinion against" putting minors to death, Kennedy observed: "The United States now stands alone in a world that has turned its face against the juvenile death penalty."[2]

Scalia's dissent, joined by Chief Justice William Rehnquist and Associate Justice Clarence Thomas, was withering. "What a mockery today's opinion makes. . . . The court thus proclaims itself sole arbiter of our Nation's moral standards—and in the course of discharging this awesome responsibility purports to take guidance from the views of foreign courts and legislatures." In the minority's view, "the basic premise of the Court's argument—that American law should conform to the laws of the rest of the world—ought to be rejected out of hand."[3]

This conservative determination to protect American legal sovereignty from international law is not limited to the judiciary. In early December 2012 the Senate debated U.S. accession to the UN Convention on the Rights of Persons with Disabilities (CRPD). Among those looking on was eighty-nine-year-old, wheelchair-bound Robert Dole. The former Senate majority leader and 1992 GOP standard-bearer, himself a disabled World War II veteran, had returned to support the treaty's passage.

On the surface the CRPD was innocuous, already ratified by 126 other governments. It had been negotiated and signed under a Republican president, George W. Bush, and U.S. diplomats had drafted most of the text. The treaty was modeled closely on the Americans with Disabilities Act (ADA), which the president's own father, George H. W. Bush, had championed and signed into law in 1990. It imposed no new legal burdens on the United States, while promising to universalize the basic rights that handicapped U.S. citizens already enjoyed at home. Beyond easing the lives of millions globally, it would facilitate travel for disabled Americans, including veterans like Dole. Nevertheless, the treaty encountered extraordinary hostility in the Senate, where it failed to secure the required two-thirds support for passage.[4]

Why? The CRPD's detractors depicted it as a mortal threat to the freedom and sovereignty Americans enjoyed under the U.S. Constitution. "Experience shows," critics alleged, that "once a UN treaty is ratified, a UN committee takes charge of interpretation . . . to impose the political agenda of the global hard left," making common cause with Democratic administrations and activist U.S. judges to foist socialist policies on the American people.[5]

Senators Mike Lee (R-Utah), Rick Santorum (R-Pa.), and James Inhofe (R-Okla.) led the charge. "Our concerns with this convention . . . have everything to do with protecting U.S. sovereignty, protecting the interests of parents in the United States and the interests of families," Lee declared. Santorum and Inhofe warned that the CRPD would allow UN officials to dictate U.S. social policy, prevent parents from home schooling their children, and force the United States to expand legal access to abortion. These were absurd allegations, but ones that resonated well beyond Congress. Not content with "surrender[ing] our nation's sovereignty to unelected bureaucrats," the Home School Legal Defense Association charged, "The CRPD would override existing state laws, seriously damaging states' rights."[6]

These concerns were groundless. The treaty explicitly protected the independent decisions of parents and required no changes in U.S. law. While the treaty would establish a UN committee to monitor country compliance with the CRPD, its reports would have no legal status in the United States. To underline this point, the Obama administration had included safeguards in the proposed instrument of ratification, declaring that the CRPD could not override inconsistent laws within the fifty U.S. states.

A handful of moderate Republicans sought to inject reason into the debate. Former attorney general Richard Thornburgh, point man for the ADA under George H. W. Bush, assured legislators that any recommendations emerging from treaty bodies would be purely advisory and create no new legal rights in federal or state courts. Dole himself denounced opponents' "scare tactics."[7]

In the end, hysteria carried the day. The final tally was 61–38 in favor, six votes short of passage, with Republican senators accounting for all the "no" votes. Even in triumph, Senator Orrin Hatch (R-Utah) warned his conservative colleagues to remain vigilant against any effort to revive the treaty. It was, he reminded them, a "threat to American sovereignty and self-government," one that "would endorse an official ongoing role for the United Nations in evaluating virtually every aspect of American life."[8]

These twin episodes—*Roper v. Simmons* and the CRPD—are part of a larger ongoing debate about the relationship between U.S. domestic law and international law. What makes this debate so volatile is that it impinges not simply on sovereignty-as-autonomy (that is, the potential loss of freedom of action though international cooperation) but also on sovereignty-as-authority (the potential subordination of the U.S. Constitution to outside authorities). The central question at stake is whether international legal trends—including evolving international rules, expanding multilateral treaties, and exposure to foreign jurisprudence—are compatible with U.S. sovereignty under the Constitution.

The answer is yes. A closer look shows that international law poses little threat to U.S. sovereign authorities, while expanding U.S. sovereignty-as-influence. The United States remains quite adept at resisting incursions on the supremacy of the Constitution—and in defending democratic self-government under it. More positively, the United States benefits both when it respects international law and when it takes active steps to shape the evolution of that law. There is no guarantee, of course, that America will always get its way in negotiations over international legal standards. (As transatlantic disputes with the EU over privacy law in the digital age illustrate, sometimes parties may simply agree to disagree.) But the overriding conclusion is clear:

By influencing and upholding the rules by which all nations must play, the United States supports a stable and legitimate international system broadly consistent with U.S. interests and values.

This is not what one hears from conservative nationalists, whose "conception of sovereignty . . . focuses on minimizing ties to the community of nations, rather than seeking to lead that community."[9] Their stance is both misguided and shortsighted. First, it wrongly depicts the U.S. decision to ratify an international treaty or to join an international organization as a *surrender* of sovereignty; it is in fact its *exercise*. Second, it ignores the limits of legal isolationism in an age of globalization. The United States cannot hope to constrain other countries through international law while claiming special exemptions from those very same obligations. True sovereignty today implies the power to shape and support a rule-bound international order.

INTERNATIONAL LAW AND THE U.S. CONSTITUTION

To understand contemporary U.S. debates, it helps to define terms: *International law* refers to the body of rules and principles of action that are binding on states in their relations to one another, as well as toward other international actors, including individual human beings.[10] It has two primary sources: formal agreements negotiated among states, and customary international law—or rules of behavior derived from established state practice. In the United States, international agreements can be further divided into actual treaties, which require the advice and consent of the U.S. Senate, and executive agreements, whereby the executive branch (in most instances with prior congressional authorization) reaches an accord with another government or other governments.

In comparison with domestic law, international law is inherently fragile. No supranational global authority, analogous to the government of an individual state, exists to impose its rules. The emergence, development, and enforcement of international law thus relies on consensus among independent states. That dependence is often its Achilles' heel. As the famous political theorist Hans Morgenthau observed, "national sovereignty is the very source of [international law's] decentralization, weakness, and ineffectiveness."[11]

That international law should raise hackles with respect to U.S. sovereignty is unsurprising, given America's power and constitutional structure. On the one hand, the United States requires international cooperation—including in its legal form—to manage global integration. On the other, it has an obvious interest in retaining freedom of action (including action to defend itself), as well as preserving its system of government—not least the supreme political authority of the Constitution.

These countervailing impulses are mirrored in the two main U.S. schools of thought about the appropriate relationship between domestic and international law. The first, the "sovereigntist" view, is self-contained and inward-looking. It emphasizes that the Constitution—and the statutes enacted under it by elected representatives of the people—is the fundamental source of U.S. law. It is wary of both treaty commitments and international legal norms. The second, the cosmopolitan perspective, is outward-looking. It respects the Constitution but believes that "American law needs to be considered alongside international law and (legitimate) national legal traditions" in other countries.[12]

America's Founders were well read in and supportive of international law.[13] A stable world under law appealed to the U.S. revolutionary generation for expedient as well as principled reasons. It promised to temper "might" with "right," helping their vulnerable nation resist great power bullying, assert its neutral rights, and insist on fair treatment for its commerce. In 1793 John Jay, first chief justice of the United States, opined that the "peace, prosperity and reputation of the United States, will always greatly depend on their fidelity to their engagements"—that is, on their respect for international legal obligations. A decade later Jay's successor, John Marshall, established what became known as the *Charming Betsy* Doctrine (1804), arguing, "An act of Congress ought never to be construed to violate the law of nations if any other possible construction remains."[14]

In fact, the relationship between U.S. domestic and international law—the subject of the legal field known as "foreign relations law"—has been anything but straightforward.[15] The Constitution provides only modest guidance about how the two should interact. Article VI, Section 2 designates treaties to which the United States is party as the "supreme Law of the Land," alongside the Constitution and U.S. statutes enacted under it. The Constitution also delegates treaty-making power solely to the federal government, rather than to the fifty states (Art. I, Sec. 10), and establishes that this power is shared between the president, who leads negotiations, and the Senate, whose "advice and consent" (by a two-thirds majority) is required for ratification (Art. II, Sec. 2). In addition, the Constitution gives the judicial branch power to interpret treaties (Art. II, Sec. 2). Finally, the United States has insisted since its founding that it alone possesses the sovereign authority to interpret U.S. treaty commitments, as well as to renounce them in extreme cases.

Consistent with Washington and Jefferson's admonitions against overseas entanglements, the United States accepted few international political or military obligations for most of its history. By 1900 it was party to some 456 treaties.[16] But most were bilateral and focused on commerce and navigation.

This pattern changed in the twentieth century. The United States' rise to world power status coincided with growth in the scope and reach of international law, which increasingly took a multilateral form and touched on new issues, from global health (covered by the International Sanitary Convention of 1903) to world peace (the topic of the Hague peace conferences of 1899 and 1907). Suddenly U.S. ambivalence toward international law took on global implications, since the republic could now shape—as well as seek to insulate itself from—the emerging international legal order. That ambivalence generated shocking results in 1918–19, when the United States first promoted and then failed to join an entirely new global body grounded in international law, the League of Nations.

A generation later, under Presidents Roosevelt and Truman, the United States once more promoted—and this time delivered on—a rule-bound international order. The most important of these foundational institutions, as noted in chapter 3, was the United Nations Organization (UNO), whose Charter became the bedrock of international law and the authoritative framework for global treaties. And yet even in those halcyon, world-order-building days, U.S. ambivalence toward international law was apparent. This was particularly true in Congress, where many legislators resisted legal obligations that might constrain the nation, challenge the Constitution, or infringe on states' rights in the U.S. federal system.

Why So Two-Faced?

The Janus-like U.S. attitude reflects countervailing instincts. On the one hand, Americans appreciate that international law can make others' actions more predictable, stabilize expectations, and legitimate rule enforcement, and they aspire to legislate international law that binds others. But many resist subjecting themselves to those same constraints, seeking to safeguard U.S. freedom of action and policy autonomy and to uphold the Constitution as the ultimate source of law.[17] They confront a perceived trade-off, in other words, between their desire to preserve U.S. sovereignty-as-autonomy and sovereignty-as-authority, on the one hand, and their aspiration to advance U.S. sovereignty-as-influence on the other.

Three main factors underpin U.S. exceptionalism—or what some call "exemptionalism"—in international law: power, culture, and institutions. As the world's dominant actor, the United States has more options than other countries, including wide latitude to choose among unilateral, bilateral, coalitional, and multilateral approaches to advance its policy objectives. And when the United States does make international commitments, it prefers that these be voluntary rather than legally binding.

Moreover, given its unique obligations and exposure as the ultimate guarantor of world order, a case can be made that America should not be hamstrung by rules that constrain lesser actors. In the late 1990s the United States invoked this custodial role in rejecting both the Mine Ban Treaty and the Rome Statute of the ICC, citing (respectively) its defense commitment to South Korea and its vulnerability to ICC prosecutions, given worldwide deployment of U.S. military forces. Indeed, U.S. policymakers and politicians often interpret foreign support for international law as a way to clip America's wings and reduce its scope for unilateralism. (This is not an unreasonable assumption, since foreign governments often desire to rein in U.S. power and restrict U.S. freedom of action.)

Political culture, notably U.S. attachment to popular sovereignty, reinforces American exemptionalism. The United States won its independence and became the first modern democracy after revolting from its colonial master. This legacy makes Americans naturally suspicious of any outside authority that might undermine their Constitution as the ultimate source of U.S. law. At the same time, Americans insist that their country's founding political and legal principles are inherently universal—and ought to be shared globally. The result is an odd (and to foreigners exasperating) amalgam of defensiveness and messianism. What distinguishes this from pure hypocrisy is the perception, widespread among Americans, that the United States is an inherently benevolent and disinterested global force.[18]

Finally, the constitutional separation of powers complicates U.S. attitudes toward international law by inviting competition between executive and legislative branches to determine the scope of U.S. global commitments. The cumbersome division of labor is most obvious in the case of treaties. The executive first negotiates and signs a treaty with a foreign government (or governments). The president then submits it to the Senate Foreign Relations Committee, which then reports the treaty to the full Senate by majority vote, often attaching reservations and amendments. Following floor debate, the Senate gives its consent by a two-thirds vote. Finally, the president formally "ratifies" the treaty by signing that legislation. (Complicating matters, some treaties, deemed "non-self-executing," require subsequent congressional legislation to give U.S. bodies the domestic legal authority to comply and allow them to be judicially enforced.)[19]

The separation of powers makes treaty ratification far more onerous for the United States than for parliamentary democracies, since delay or failure can occur at any step. The highest hurdle is the two-thirds Senate supermajority, which allows motivated legislative minorities to block ratification of proposed conventions. Given these odds, many treaties are never brought to vote. In rare cases the Senate may reject a treaty outright, as it has done on twenty-four occasions since 1789, the most famous being the Versailles Treaty in 1919. (The two most recent cases are the Comprehensive Test Ban Treaty in 1999 and, as discussed earlier, the Convention on the Rights of Persons with Disabilities in 2012.) Treaties may also languish for years, as the Genocide Convention did for four decades before its ratification. Historically, treaty gridlock has been most common during periods of high partisanship, especially when Democrats control the White House, Republicans dominate the Senate, and a conservative chairs the Senate Foreign Relations Committee.

The Legacy of the Bricker Amendment

All three factors were at play in the early 1950s during debates over the Bricker Amendment. In 1951, Republican senator John Bricker of Ohio proposed amending the Constitution to limit the president's treaty-making power and rein in the Truman administration's support for international organizations. Under Bricker's proposed scheme, U.S. accession to treaties would require not only a Senate supermajority but also separate congressional implementing legislation giving domestic effect to those commitments. Henceforth, all U.S. treaties would be "non-self-executing." Even more onerous, any UN treaty would need to be approved by *all* of the (then) forty-eight U.S. state legislatures. Finally, the amendment would invalidate any treaty provision that conflicted with the Constitution.

Racial politics motivated the Bricker Amendment. Its most ardent champions worried that UN human rights treaties would empower civil rights activists to challenge segregationist policies. That said, supporters couched their objections in broader constitutional concerns that still resonate among conservatives. They argued that UN conventions would infringe on U.S. sovereign legal authorities, usurp Congress's legislative functions, downgrade already-protected American rights, and empower the federal government to legislate in areas within the jurisdiction of individual U.S. states. UN treaties, they warned, were but the vanguard of "world government."[20]

These fears were unwarranted, since any ratification of UN treaties would occur through constitutional processes, including the assent of Congress.

Legislators would need to approve implementing legislation (if any), and there would be no external enforcement mechanism. Still, a diluted version of the Bricker Amendment came perilously close to passage in 1954. It fell just one vote shy of the two-thirds majority needed to override President Dwight D. Eisenhower's veto—and only after the administration had reassured wavering senators that it would not seek approval for any other UN human rights treaty. The grueling episode helps explain why the Senate took until 1988 to approve the Genocide Convention (signed in 1948), nearly three decades (from 1966 until 1994) to approve the Convention on the Elimination of All Forms of Racial Discrimination, and a quarter century (from 1967 until 1992) to approve the International Covenant on Civil and Political Rights (ICCPR).

Although the amendment's original racial motivation has faded, the "ghost of Senator Bricker" survives in resistance to treaties among conservatives skeptical of intergovernmental bureaucracies and determined to defend traditional values on issues like abortion, capital punishment, gun control, and the role of religion in society.[21]

Conservative Critiques and Liberal Defenses of International Law

Today the boldest U.S. criticisms of international law come from conservative legal scholars. Many deny that international law is really "law," depicting it as a mere set of "political obligations." In this view, states may conform to international law when it meets their situational needs. But they quickly cast it aside when it collides with expedient reasons of state, as the United States did in leading NATO's 1999 air campaign over Kosovo and the 2003 invasion of Iraq.[22] Placing faith in international law is thus naive, "encouraging states to sacrifice elements of their sovereignty, adopt multilateralism, and compromise their ability to act independently."[23] In addition, many conservatives insist that international law becomes "real" law only if Congress, as the repository of the people's democratic sovereignty, passes relevant implementing legislation to "domesticate" it. They also regard customary international law as inherently undemocratic, and they believe that all treaties should be "non-self-executing."[24]

Liberal scholars and jurists retort that international law is real law—and that it affects state behavior in tangible ways. Their point of departure is the observation of Louis Henkin, arguably the most prominent U.S. scholar of international law in the second half of the twentieth century, that "almost all nations observe almost all principles of international law and almost all of their obligations almost all of the time." International law exerts a "pull to compliance," in this view, because it embodies a shared conception of what is legitimate and permissible, creates a web of obligations, and carries material and reputational costs for those who violate it.[25] Liberals also believe that the United States should be open to integrating evolving international rules into domestic law, and to delegating regulatory powers to multilateral bodies, even if the relevant agencies and officials are not directly accountable to U.S. citizens. This equanimity reflects a conception of "sovereignty" that (in terms of the sovereignty triangle presented in chapter 1) emphasizes U.S. influence on international law (and international outcomes) above U.S. autonomy and even (for some) U.S. constitutional authority.[26]

From a liberal perspective, "sovereigntist" efforts to keep the United States unfettered actually harm U.S. interests by depriving America of the credit it would otherwise get for advancing the global rule of law, and also by undermining the legitimacy of international rules. Sovereigntists, meanwhile, offer little guidance about how the United States can mitigate the downside of globalization, much less reduce its vulnerability to transnational threats, without global rules. They also do not explain how international cooperation would be possible were all 193 UN member states to mimic the maximalist sovereignty posture they endorse for the United States.[27]

A Threat to U.S. Sovereignty?

The United States, then, has long been ambivalent about international law. It values the order and predictability law lends to global affairs, even as it chafes at perceived incursions on U.S. sovereignty-as-authority and sovereignty-as-autonomy. And for self-appointed defenders of U.S. sovereignty the stakes have never been higher: The United States, they argue, faces growing pressure to embrace dubious international standards emerging from global legal processes that lack democratic provenance. In the past, conservatives argue, sovereign states made law by consciously negotiating treaties and recognizing the slow accretion of state custom. But that traditional legal order is being upended, as new forms of "transnational" law penetrate sovereign borders and "supranational" law is imposed from above.[28]

Sovereignty's defenders cite several worrisome global legal trends threatening the U.S. political and legal system. These include a proliferation of intrusive and unwarranted multilateral treaties; an ever-expanding definition of "customary international law"; efforts by left-wing NGOs to hijack the agendas of UN treaty-making bodies; new "transnational law" emerging from freelancing global networks of judges and regulators; unwarranted activism by unaccountable international organizations; and growing references to foreign law and decisions in U.S. court rulings. This "new" international law, warn David Rivkin and Lee Casey, is "profoundly undemocratic at its core," constituting nothing less than "a frontal assault on sovereignty as the organizing principle of the international system."[29] Slowly but surely, the U.S. Constitution will be subordinated to a global legal system, and the Supreme Court will be relegated to ensuring that domestic statutes conform to international law.

The main obstacle to this global governance project, U.S. sovereigntists claim, is the United States, which heroically clings to exceptionalism in its national identity, politics, and jurisprudence. This explains why, they say, legal progressives in the United States and abroad have taken aim at America, using "lawfare" in the hopes of bringing the United States "to heel" and entrapping it in a web of international obligations that limit its maneuvering room, trample its constitutional democracy, and impose alien values on its people.[30] In short, warns former senator John Kyl (R-Ariz.), they have launched "a campaign against American sovereignty."

> Multilateral treaties delegate power to new international bodies with little or no accountability, as transnationalists seek to subordinate the U.S. government and U.S. law to international norms. We have seen this movement in many levels, from laws of war to arms control to climate change, women's rights, the death penalty. Advocates are bypassing the domestic political processes and going to the international level to accomplish their aims.[31]

In sum, the United States is in for a world of hurt.

Time to Take a Deep Breath

Such hyperventilating makes good copy. But the alleged risks that international legal trends pose to U.S. sovereignty—and particularly to sovereignty-as-authority—are overblown. The United States is fully capable of defending its constitutional system of government from international encroachments and managing the inevitable tensions between emerging international law and domestic principles about the legitimate uses of national power.

Globalization *is* placing unprecedented demands on sovereign governments. The swelling volume and quickening pace of cross-border flows makes it harder for states acting independently to defend their national security, manage their economies, and deliver social welfare. To exploit the upside and minimize the downside of global integration—that is, to exercise their sovereignty-as-influence—national governments need agreed rules of the road. Settling on these will require more extensive multilateral collaboration in negotiating new legal obligations, setting common standards, regulating international behavior, monitoring and verifying compliance with commitments, and resolving disputes among parties. It also implies deeper involvement by international organizations, institutions, and treaty bodies in policy arenas historically reserved for sovereign state authorities, to manage crossborder flows in fields as diverse as finance, trade, terrorism, pollution, disease, weapons of mass destruction, and crime.

Such new international legal rules could create tensions with domestic rules about the legitimate uses of governmental power. The pivotal questions are: Can the United States embrace international law without undermining its constitutional sovereignty? Can it protect democratic decisionmaking without stymieing multilateral cooperation?

The answer to both questions is yes. To begin with, the "sovereigntist" position grossly exaggerates the transfer of authority that occurs in the creation of international law and institutions. Nearly all the multilateral legal instruments to which the United States is party take an *inter*national rather than a *supra*national form. That is to say, they emerge through horizontal negotiation and agreement among sovereign governments, rather than vertical imposition by some higher, global political authority. Moreover, under most international agreements, it is states parties themselves (the sovereign states that are party to an agreement), rather than international bodies, that implement the relevant accord.

Second, the transnational legal trends to which "sovereigntists" most object—including the expanding scope of customary international law, the machinations of radical transnational NGOs, and the cross-border activities of networks of jurists, regulators, judges, and technocrats—are less extensive and worrisome than alarmists allege, as the following sections will demonstrate. The United States retains ample scope to determine which evolving norms it recognizes as customary international law. It is also fully capable of exploiting transgovernmental networks to grapple with shared challenges while improving their transparency and accountability to elected U.S. officials. Accordingly, the "suicide of liberal democracy," of which John Fonte warns, is not in the cards.[32]

Third, to clarify a common misconception, a decision by the United States to sign, ratify, and accede to an international treaty or to join an international organization is not an abdication of democratic sovereignty but indeed its *expression*. The U.S. president only ratifies treaties after elected U.S. representatives, operating through domestic political processes and acting on the people's behalf, calculate that the benefits of such collective arrangements outweigh the costs. The sovereigntist position thus fails on its own terms, since there is nothing in the Constitution that prevents the United States from voluntarily entering into international legal arrangements and organizations that affect U.S. citizens.

This is not to say that all proposed treaties or other multilateral institutional commitments warrant support, or that international organizations should not be reformed. When the president or Congress considers the costs of joining to be exorbitant, they can easily opt out of conventions—and have done so on numerous occasions. They have also conditioned treaty accession on explicit provisions that limit U.S. legal obligations, as well as requiring separate implementing legislation to allow certain treaties to take domestic legal effect. What is worthy of debate is how extensively the United States should use such caveats and preconditions.

Finally, the U.S. judiciary's invocation of foreign and international law continues to remain limited and, if handled prudently, need not endanger the integrity of the U.S. constitutional system and the historical precedents on which U.S. jurisprudence rests. At the same time, exposure to the findings of foreign courts can teach U.S. judges how counterparts abroad have addressed similar legal questions, helping them discharge their responsibilities with greater wisdom. This is far from requiring that they copy the decisions of foreign courts.

The remainder of this chapter takes on these sovereigntist claims and disposes of them one by one.

THE SPECTER OF SUPRANATIONALISM

The first fear to dispense with is the specter of supranationalism—that is, that the United States risks subordinating its hallowed Constitution to a higher global legal authority.

The EU Bogeyman

For the past two decades, there has been no greater bogeyman for sovereigntists than the European Union. They regard it as an unnatural agglomeration of once-proud nation-states that have sacrificed their independence in a misguided desire to "pool sovereignty"—only to find themselves in thrall to a Brussels-based Leviathan staffed by officious and unaccountable Eurocrats intent on expanding their power and preserving an overly regulated welfare state, even as membership in the EU brings transnational challenges, from refugees to terrorists, to individual countries' doorsteps. American sovereigntists have long described the EU as a harbinger of world government.[33]

Sovereigntists correctly point out that the EU's twenty-eight members have ceded not only significant policy autonomy but also a measure of constitutional authority. The EU's supranational features include a powerful European Commission that sets regulatory standards in multiple fields; a European Parliament composed of legislators elected from member states; and a European Court of Justice empowered to override incompatible domestic legislation and high court decisions in member states. The Treaty of Lisbon (2009) deepened EU integration by establishing a president of the European Council, a high representative for foreign affairs and security policy, and an External Action Service (analogous to a foreign ministry). It also expanded the EU's authority in traditional national spheres of crime, justice, and homeland security. Finally, the nineteen EU members in the Eurozone have accepted sweeping infringements on national authority and autonomy, in adopting a common currency, a European Central Bank, and (in the aftermath of the Eurozone crisis) a banking union.

In sum, the EU is not simply an intergovernmental association of sovereign states bound by horizontal treaties. The "constitutionalization" of the EU has enmeshed national governments, as well as citizens and private corporations, in a set of "vertically integrated legal regimes conferring juridically enforceable rights and obligations."[34] Bemoaning the EU's fate, Kyl notes, "What they have now is a situation where their sovereignty has largely been supplanted by others who are not accountable to voters in included European countries." Even worse, declares George Mason University law professor Jeremy Rabkin, "Euro-governance poses a direct challenge to American ideas of constitutional government and national sovereignty."[35]

The root of this anxiety is suspicion that the EU is not simply an isolated regional experiment but an alternative model for global order. Within such a future "Global Union," Walter Russell Mead explains, national autonomy would be limited by "an increasingly dense framework of commonly agreed upon laws and norms, and an increasingly complex and effective web of global institutions would supplement and in many cases replace the authority of national governments." American sovereigntists point forebodingly to the words of William W. Burke-White and Anne-Marie Slaughter, two leading transnational legal progressives: "Once those laws are passed [by European governments], EU institutions . . . look over national shoulders to ensure that they do what they actually commit to do," they write. "This European way of law is precisely the role that we postulate for international law generally around the world." The nightmare scenario for sovereigntists, write Julian Ku and John Yoo, is the emergence of "a full-blown European-style system of global governance."[36]

Such anxieties are overwrought. The United States is in no danger of following the EU's path. To begin, the European Union is a sui generis historical phenomenon, the product of political dynamics and cultural affinities among member states and (during its formative years) of superpower conflict. Moreover, whatever luster the EU once enjoyed is by now badly tarnished, thanks to years of economic malaise, the grinding Eurozone crisis, the EU's flailing response to massive flows of migrants and refugees, and public disillusionment with democratic deficits at the heart of the "European project." The most dramatic indication of this disenchantment was the shocking triumph on June 23, 2016, of the "Leave" campaign in the historic referendum on whether Great Britain should exit the European Union. The victory for "Brexit" (discussed more in chapter 8) was a massive repudiation of the elite-driven European project—at least within the United Kingdom. Centrifugal forces could well gain momentum in other member states, redirecting the EU away from the dream of a federal (and ultimately supranational) union, associated with its godfather, Jean Monnet, and toward Charles de Gaulle's alternative vision of a looser, confederal, *Europe des patries*.[37]

Drawing a Line: The ICC

But perhaps the clearest signal that the United States remains determined to preserve its own sovereignty-as-authority is the continuing U.S. decision not to accept the jurisdiction of the International Criminal Court. Although President Bill Clinton signed the Rome Statute in December 2000, toward the end of his administration, he chose not to submit it to the Senate for its advice and consent. Indeed, he recommended that his successor, George W. Bush, not do so until U.S. concerns were addressed. Even President Barack Obama chose not to seek U.S. accession, despite an increasingly close U.S. working relationship with the court.

The United States has indicated several concerns about the ICC. One is that the court could deprive accused U.S. citizens of rights of due process protected under the Constitution. Another is that it could reduce U.S. freedom of action in conducting military operations. But the fundamental source of U.S. skepticism is the ICC's supranational character. Unlike other, ad hoc tribunals established to address war crimes issues, such as for Rwanda and the former Yugoslavia, the ICC possesses an institutional identity separate from the authority of the UN Security Council. It also has universal jurisdiction, including over the nationals of nonparty states, as well as an independent special prosecutor empowered to sit in judgment on the adequacy of domestic legal proceedings undertaken by member states.[38]

To be sure, the court has competence over only a narrow range of crimes (for the present, genocide, war crimes, and crimes against humanity) and is meant to operate only when a state party is incapable of or unwilling to conduct its own credible investigations and trials. However, those restrictions have not reassured critics, who retort—not unreasonably—that granting sweeping discretionary powers to an independent and unaccountable prosecutor and tribunal sacrifices the sovereign authority of ICC member states and creates a situation ripe for abuse, including the potential for politically motivated prosecutions.

Following the 2000 presidential election, the administration of George W. Bush quickly affirmed its opposition to the ICC. John Bolton, who "unsigned" the Rome Statute in May 2001 as undersecretary of state, declared that the ICC "runs contrary to fundamental American precepts and basic constitutional principles of popular sovereignty, checks and balances, and national independence."[39]

To protect U.S. civilian and military personnel from the court's reach, the Bush administration subsequently negotiated more than 100 bilateral agreements under Article 98 of the Rome Statute to ensure that states parties would not transfer any U.S. citizens to the court "without U.S. consent." To underscore the U.S. position, Congress passed and Bush signed into law the American Servicemembers' Protection Act (2002). Its provisions prohibited any U.S. tax dollars from going to the ICC, as well as the sharing of any classified information with the court, restricted U.S. participation in UN peacekeeping operations unless U.S. troops were exempted from ICC jurisdiction, and prohibited any military aid to ICC parties that had not signed Article 98 agreements with the United States (though waivers could be granted on national security grounds). Finally, the law authorized the president to "take any action necessary" to free U.S. officials or soldiers held by the court (leading wags to dub it the "Hague Invasion Act"). In 2010 the House of Representatives reaffirmed U.S. opposition to ICC membership, declaring, "The Rome Statute undermines national sovereignty . . . conflicts with the principles of the United States Constitution . . . and hinders its ability to defend itself and its allies with military force."[40]

Based on the court's record to date, the scenarios that most concern sovereigntists seem implausible (though certainly not impossible). For one thing, an ICC that pursued unfounded prosecutions against U.S. officials would be committing suicide. For another, the United States has developed a quiet, pragmatic working relationship with the court, which began in the Bush administration and expanded under Obama. This has included providing evidentiary and other support related to cases on the ICC's docket, as well as supporting Security Council referrals to the ICC of certain atrocity situations (including those in Darfur in 2005 and Libya in 2011).[41] By 2016 many international observers regarded the United States as a de facto member of the ICC—albeit one that remained outside its jurisdiction.

The broader lesson is that the United States has proven itself wholly capable of rejecting supranational challenges to its sovereign authority. In the case of the ICC, this involved negotiating side agreements to guarantee that other states that embraced such schemes did not employ those supranational arrangements to infringe on the supremacy of the U.S. Constitution.

THE "TRANSNATIONAL LEGAL PROCESS"

So much for the supranational threat to U.S. sovereignty-as-authority. What about the transnational threat? According to conservative legal scholars, U.S. sovereignty is increasingly besieged by an unholy alliance of progressive advocacy groups, left-wing jurists, liberal politicians, and unelected technocrats, all seeking to "smuggle" new international norms into domestic law while riding roughshod over representative democracy. As evidence for this proposition, American sovereigntists point to the role of NGOs in "hijacking" UN treaty negotiations, to the growing legal influence of cross-border networks of judges and regulators, and to the alacrity with which some U.S. lawyers declare the existence of "new" customary international law. Conservatives look on these trends with dismay, believing that they embody the new "transnational legal process" championed by the progressive legal scholar Harold Hongju Koh, who served as State Department legal adviser during President Obama's first term. Back in 2006, writing in the *Penn State International Review*, Koh had heralded the emergence of a new era, in which evolving international norms could be "downloaded" into U.S. law.[42]

NGOs Gone Wild

To self-styled defenders of U.S. sovereignty like John Fonte of the Hudson Institute, progressive civil society groups are the "shock troops" of global governance. Having failed to secure political and legal victories home—including in areas like gun control, capital punishment, abortion, gender policy, and racial discrimination—these American "globalists" have adopted an "indirect" approach, shifting their attention and resources to UN conferences, where they can get a second bite at the apple. Arriving en masse at multilateral negotiations, they distort international agreements in ways that constrain the United States, without having to deal with the difficult, messy requirements of American democracy. The resulting influence enjoyed by unaccountable nonstate advocacy groups, two Heritage Foundation scholars complain, "undermines responsible diplomacy and the sovereignty of the United States and other nation-states."[43]

This "NGOs gone wild" thesis is overblown. To begin with, global civil society is more diverse ideologically than such alarums suggest. When conservatives critique the international agendas of NGOs, they mean progressive outfits like Greenpeace or Human Rights Watch, ignoring the long-standing global role of the Catholic Church and the growing international activism of the National Rifle Association. This is to say nothing of the massive influence and resources that private corporations bring to bear in influencing national negotiating positions and global deliberations, which dwarf NGO clout.

More important, multilateral negotiations remain firmly in the hands of sovereign state actors. Yes, civil society groups can mobilize, write "amicus briefs," and advise national governments. But they are essentially lobbyists, whose advice may well be rejected. Fonte's own book, *Sovereignty or Submission*, is telling in this regard. It presents no evidence that NGO advocacy groups have *ever* significantly altered the U.S. negotiating position at a major multilateral conference.[44] In practice, the U.S. government routinely ignores NGOs' demands, just as it brushes aside the findings of UN special rapporteurs and monitoring committees who judge U.S. performance. On some occasions, as with the Mine Ban Treaty (1997), the Rome Statute (2000), and the Cluster Munitions Convention, grassroots movements have helped mobilize global political will for new conventions—at times making common cause with governments whose positions are at odds with those of the U.S. government. But the actual negotiations of these treaties, to say nothing of their ultimate signature and ratification, reflects the sovereign decisions of state authorities, who are—particularly in the case of the United States—capable of pushing back against provisions they find misguided and, in the final analysis, rejecting a treaty they deem ill-advised.

Unaccountable Transgovernmental Networks

Sovereigntists also worry that transnational networks of government officials, acting beyond legislative oversight, may unduly influence the content of international norms and rules. Here, there are modest grounds for concern. One way that national governments have adapted to global interdependence, as Slaughter notes, is by becoming "disaggregated." That is, even as foreign, finance, and defense ministries continue to conduct traditional diplomacy, governments are also more frequently linked through informal cross-border networks of regulators, judges, and even parliamentarians, who may interact on a daily basis. Such transnational linkages can improve international cooperation by helping governments harmonize standards, share best practices, and improve compliance. And because networked cooperation tends to be faster than conventional negotiations within traditional intergovernmental organizations, it can help governments respond to and manage the shared challenges of interdependence quickly and flexibly. To the degree that sovereignty is about "influence" on a nation's destiny, this type of cooperation has a lot going for it.[45]

But it does carry risks. Informal networks can undermine sovereignty-as-authority, particularly when their relevant activities lack accountability, transparency, and legislative oversight. Indeed, some conservatives suspect that transnational networks are "a deliberate device to make an end run around the formal constraints imposed on global governance . . . by traditional international organizations." Slaughter herself feeds such worries when she writes: "The disaggregation of the state creates opportunities for domestic institutions, particularly courts, to make common cause with their supranational counterparts against their fellow branches of government."[46]

These risks should be acknowledged but not overstated, since they can be managed without jettisoning nimble networks. One logical approach would be for the U.S. Congress to mandate that the heads of relevant U.S. agencies provide and publish online annual reports on the scope of their transnational activities—and to require those agencies to appear more regularly before their relevant oversight committees. Congress could also authorize and require the U.S. State Department to report on the transnational activities of U.S. government agencies, including any ramifications for U.S. international legal obligations.

Customary International Law Run Amok

The greatest threat that legal transnationalism poses to sovereignty, according to conservative critics, is the unwarranted expansion of customary international law. For centuries, sovereign states have agreed to be bound not only by negotiated agreements but by norms and rules embodied in accumulated state practice. Traditionally, to qualify as "customary" an observed practice must be "general, consistent, and (typically) longstanding." Moreover, parties must embrace the practice out of "a sense of legal obligation," regardless of any explicit agreement. Some customary international law has become so universal and embedded in state practice that it is recognized as *jus cogens*, or "peremptory rules which permit no derogation." The prohibition against slavery is one example. The U.S. Supreme Court recognized the validity of customary international law more than a century ago, in the *Paquete Habana* (1900) case, and—with caveats—considers it to be part of U.S. law. Despite this venerable history, the definition, status, and application of customary international law depend on subjective determinations.[47]

What incenses contemporary sovereigntists is their perception that today customary international law is being declared and recognized instantaneously. Rather than waiting for custom to accumulate gradually, through enduring state behavior, transnational "legal entrepreneurs" now declare new "norms" on the basis of what states and other actors *say* rather than *do*, and without any criteria or authoritative process to justify this elevation. As a case in point, conservatives cite the Additional Protocol I to the Geneva Conventions of 1949, which they complain "would grant prisoner-of-war privileges to terrorists" (under Article 75). Although the United States has not ratified the protocol, Secretary of State Hillary Clinton declared in March 2011 that America would henceforth accept the protocols' "fundamental guarantees" for illegal combatants, "out of a sense of legal obligation."[48]

Conservatives also worry that activist U.S. judges may incorporate alleged new global "norms" into their domestic court rulings, rather than simply interpreting established U.S. law. To prevent this possibility, Curtis A. Bradley and Jack L. Goldsmith propose that the United States recognize customary international law only if Congress first "domesticates" it—namely, by passing legislation explicitly incorporating it into U.S. statute law.[49]

Such a radical reform is unwarranted, since the alleged risks that custom poses to the U.S. Constitution are overblown. As John Ruggie observes, critics have failed to demonstrate "that any *actual* case has ever adversely skewed constitutional arrangements or practices as a result of a bad call by a court involving domestic incorporation of international norms." Accordingly, the concern is "entirely hypothetical."[50]

Overall, conservative warnings about the "transnational legal process" are inflated. America is not about to lose its sovereign authorities to a nefarious alliance of progressive legal scholars, radical NGOs, and freelancing globalist bureaucrats. Customary international law poses little risk to the United

States. Indeed, it frequently serves to promote U.S. values, interests, and norms on the global stage.

COMMITMENT PROBLEMS: SOVEREIGNTY OBJECTIONS TO MULTILATERAL TREATIES

If customary international law poses little danger to U.S. sovereignty, what about multilateral treaties, which critics liken to ropes restraining an American Gulliver? At its 2016 national convention in Cleveland, the Republican Party underscored its own wariness. "We . . . affirm the wisdom of President George Washington's warning to avoid foreign entanglements and unnecessary alliances," the party platform explained. "We therefore oppose the adoption or ratification of treaties that would weaken or encroach upon American sovereignty or that could be construed by courts to do so."[51]

This suspicion of international ties that bind was apparent during Donald Trump's first week as president, when his senior staff drafted an executive order declaring a moratorium on any new multilateral treaties. The draft order, leaked to the press, directed the creation of a "high level executive branch committee" to review not only any pending treaty negotiations but also "whether the United States should continue be a party to" existing treaties. "Recent decades," the author(s) explained, had witnessed a "proliferation of multilateral treaties." Such conventions had been "used to force countries to adhere to often radical domestic agendas that could not, themselves, otherwise be enacted in accordance with a country's domestic laws."[52] The basic premise of the draft order was false: that the United States had become party to multiple treaties that were "not in our national interests" and involved "ceding sovereignty."[53]

To begin with an obvious point: the United States retains complete sovereign authority over whether to become party to any international treaty, and it does not suddenly lose that aspect of its sovereignty when it ratifies a multilateral convention. To be sure, the U.S. government has an obligation to citizens to weigh the costs and benefits of accession, and it may withhold U.S. consent to be bound by a treaty regardless of the opinions of other nations. But the decision to join a treaty is an exercise rather than a surrender of sovereign authority.

The frequent trade-off the United States *does* face in considering treaties is between sovereignty's two other dimensions: sovereignty-as-autonomy and sovereignty-as-influence. How much policy freedom should America yield in return for enhanced cooperation on shared challenges? Such dilemmas have grown sharper and more common as nations confront more cross-border problems requiring collective responses. Sovereigntists tend to bemoan this trend as a license for outsiders to meddle in U.S. affairs.[54] But they typically overstate the constraints such treaties place on U.S. autonomy, while failing to explain how the United States could possibly accomplish its aims unilaterally. They focus on sovereignty-as-autonomy, in other words, but ignore sovereignty-as-influence.

The United States has ratified hundreds of multilateral treaties since 1900, with the number rising dramatically since World War II (see figure 4-1). More than 600 such conventions are in force today, addressing matters ranging from defense cooperation to environmental protection, communications standards, peaceful uses of outer space, child abduction, response to pandemics, and trade preferences.[55] Each reduces U.S. sovereignty-as-autonomy, by obligating (or proscribing) certain conduct. At the same time, such treaties expand U.S. sovereignty-as-influence, helping the United States to achieve outcomes otherwise beyond its reach.

As former State Department legal adviser John Bellinger told the *Washington Post* in January 2017, the United States is party to "many hundreds of multilateral treaties that help Americans every day in concrete ways." In their absence, "Americans could not have our letters delivered in foreign countries; could not fly over foreign countries or drive on foreign roads using our state driver's licenses; could not have access to a foreign consular official if we are arrested abroad; could not have our children returned if abducted by a parent; and could not prevent foreign ships from polluting our waters."[56]

More than fifty years ago, in 1965, Secretary of State Dean Rusk explained this sovereignty trade-off in Senate testimony.

> We are, every day, in one sense, accepting limitations upon our complete freedom of action.... We have more than 4,300 treaties and international agreements, two-thirds of which have been entered into in the past 25 years ... each one of which limits our freedom of action. We exercise our sovereignty in going into these agreements.... Law is a process by which we increase our range of freedom.... We are constantly enlarging our own freedom by being able to predict what others are going to do.[57]

The WTO Charter, for instance, obliges the United States to grant all parties "most favored nation" trade status and to seek resolution of trade disputes

FIGURE 4-1. Multilateral Treaties in Force in the United States

Number of treaties

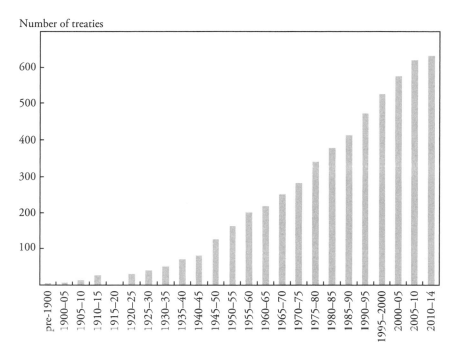

Source: Compiled from U.S. State Department data.

within the WTO's Appellate Body. Similarly, the Chemical Weapons Convention requires the United States to destroy its entire stockpile of chemical weapons, to forswear their production, and (in principle) to open its domestic chemical facilities to short-notice challenge inspections. Likewise, the WHO's strengthened International Health Regulations commit the United States to improving its infectious disease surveillance and response capacities, as well as to reporting to the WHO any major public health emergency.[58] In each case the United States has voluntarily agreed to limit its notional policy options in order to reap promised benefits of collective action: respectively, preserving an open, nondiscriminatory global trading system; eliminating a heinous category of weapons of mass destruction; and preventing the rise and spread of pandemics.

On several high-profile occasions, U.S. political leaders have calculated that the anticipated trade-offs are not worth it and have accordingly chosen not to sign or ratify major multilateral conventions endorsed by most UN member states, even ones that the United States led in championing, drafting, and negotiating. These include the United Nations Convention on the Law of the Sea (UNCLOS), the Convention on Biological Diversity, the Kyoto Protocol, the Comprehensive Test Ban Treaty (CTBT), and the Rome Statute. Table 4-1 identifies seventeen such treaties and the justifications policymakers and critics offered for remaining apart. The reasoning for opting out varied. In some instances U.S. officials were skeptical that the envisioned conventions would achieve their aims or worried they would complicate competing U.S. policy goals. In such circumstances U.S. political leaders concluded that it did not make sense to sacrifice U.S. autonomy for (questionable) influence. In other cases the principal objection was to (perceived) infringements on U.S. sovereignty-as-authority—including the exercise of popular sovereignty under the U.S. Constitution. As Republican senators Inhofe and James DeMint (S.C.) observe, "The debates about these treaties are not about the legalistic minutiae they contain but the sovereign citizenry they threaten."[59]

How distinctive is the U.S. attitude toward international treaties? In terms of the number of multilateral treaties to which it is a party, the United States falls in the middle of the pack in comparison with its most important European allies, including the United Kingdom, Germany, and France. Among other major powers, it is on a par with China, though lags behind both India and Russia. More striking than simple numbers is the fact that many of the conventions that the United States has chosen not to join (such as UNCLOS and CTBT) were actually the handiwork of U.S. administrations. Moreover, these treaties have generated extraordinary controversy in the United States.

Equally distinctive, in comparative perspective, is the long legislative delay that typically occurs between the initial U.S. signing of a treaty and its ultimate ratification. Of the thirty-two treaties deposited with the UN secretary general between 1945 and 1989, the United States ratified just eight in the decade in which they were concluded, and the average wait time for ratification was ten years. But treaties may languish far longer—four decades in the case of the Genocide Convention.

Treaty type also matters. Historically, the U.S. Senate has been more favorably disposed toward contract-like treaties that facilitate mutual exchange, such as those related to trade and investment or international legal assistance, than with treaties that establish laws constraining U.S. autonomy or empowering international authorities, particularly in the spheres of arms control and disarmament, environmental protection, and human rights.

Common U.S. objections to arms control treaties include the arguments that they limit U.S. defense options, undercut the U.S. military edge, fail to prevent cheating by adversaries, and expose the United States to unacceptably intrusive verification regimes. Such worries help explain the Senate's long delay

Table 4-1. *Major Treaties to Which the United States Is Not a Party*

A. Arms control treaties	Objections raised by opponents
Arms Trade Treaty	Would supersede the U.S. Constitution, allowing amendments to be approved by a three-quarters majority vote of parties, "circumvent[ing] the power and duty of the Senate" and "placing political and legal pressure on United States to comply in practice with amendments it was unwilling to accept." Also, "the treaty could be used to justify the imposition of controls within the U.S. that would pose a threat to the Second Amendment."[a]
Biological Weapons Convention Verification Protocol	The protocol's invasive on-site inspection measures would jeopardize the security of U.S. biodefense programs, as well as proprietary commercial information, while still allowing determined proliferators to evade verification by "conceal[ing] efforts in legitimately undeclared facilities."[b]
Cluster Munitions Convention	Would limit U.S. forces' freedom of action and ability to protect U.S. interests by eliminating a category of weapons that "have demonstrated military utility" and that "often result in much less collateral damage" than other bombs or shells.[c]
Comprehensive Test Ban Treaty	Would bring no substantial benefits and instead limit the U.S. ability to maintain a safe and reliable nuclear weapons stockpile—and thus a credible nuclear deterrent—while not foreclosing cheating by other parties, including Russia and China.[d]
Mine Ban Treaty	Would limit U.S. freedom of action in national security and ability to protect U.S. interests, notably on the Korean Peninsula, by expanding the enemy's freedom of maneuver, jeopardizing the safety of U.S. military personnel, and complicating the U.S. defense of South Korea.[e]

B. Environmental treaties	
Basel Convention on the Transboundary Movement of Hazardous Wastes and Their Disposal	Would limit free trade and impose unnecessary burdens not only on the United States and other wealthy countries (by increasing disposal costs and health risks) but also on poorer countries (by depriving them of increased national income from accepting hazardous wastes).[f]
Convention on Biological Diversity	Would not adequately protect intellectual property of U.S. corporations, including biotechnology and pharmaceutical firms, and could subject the United States to the authority of a mandatory, international dispute resolution body.[g]
Kyoto Protocol	Would disadvantage the U.S. economy because it has no limits for developing countries. Would give international bureaucrats control over U.S. energy policy.[h]

(continued)

Table 4-1. *(continued)*

B. Environmental treaties

Rotterdam Convention on the Prior Informed Consent Procedure for Certain Hazardous Chemicals and Pesticides in International Trade	Would cede U.S. authority to set standards banning or limiting certain chemicals to the UN, an unelected, unaccountable body. Such a transfer of power from U.S. federal government to international agencies outside U.S. control would create "troubling and dangerous precedents . . . in American law."[i]
Stockholm Convention on Persistent Organic Pollutants	Would cede to an unelected, unaccountable UN the authority to determine standards for the United States.

C. Human rights treaties

Additional Protocol I to the Geneva Conventions	Would alter and undermine the laws of war by granting combatant status and POW privileges to terrorists and irregular forces who hide among civilian populations. Giving concealed adversaries advantages over U.S. forces would hamper U.S. combat operations and limit the U.S ability to defend itself.[j]
Convention on the Elimination of All Forms of Discrimination against Women	Would erode core U.S. principles of democratic self-government and individual liberty by legitimating an intrusive role for unaccountable UN monitors in foisting alien values on American society, families, and individuals.[k]
Convention on the Rights of Persons with Disabilities	Would surrender parental rights, U.S. state laws, and national sovereignty to unelected and unaccountable UN bureaucrats, while authorizing a UN committee to implement the treaty, supervise compliance with it, and impose new recommendations on parties.[l]
Convention on the Rights of the Child	Would cede national sovereignty, state laws, and parental rights to unelected and unaccountable UN bureaucrats, including an international committee of experts authorized to issue interpretations of treaty commitments binding on U.S. courts and legislatures, as well as to "override" the U.S. Constitution.[m]
Optional Protocol to the Convention against Torture	Would impose "overly intrusive" inspections on the United States, conflict with constitutional law regarding searches and seizures, and infringe on the rights of individual U.S. states.[n]
Rome Statute of the International Criminal Court	Would leave the United States vulnerable to politically motivated prosecutions of its citizens and soldiers, limit its ability to defend itself and its allies, and subordinate the U.S. Constitution and domestic courts to an unaccountable tribunal and independent prosecutor.[o]

Table 4-1. (*continued*)

D. Global commons	
UN Convention on the Law of the Sea	Would undermine "American sovereignty" by transferring "ownership" of the high seas to the UN, allowing global bureaucrats to veto U.S. naval operations, and require U.S. deep-sea mining companies to pay exorbitant royalties to an unaccountable International Seabed Authority.

a. Letter sent to President Obama by a bipartisan group of fifty senators opposed to the Arms Trade Treaty, October 15, 2013, http://kelly.house.gov/sites/kelly.house.gov/files/Kelly%20Member%20 Letter%20to%20Obama%20on%20UN%20Arms%20Trade%20Treaty%20FINAL%2010-15-2013.pdf.

b. Rebecca Whitehair and Seth Brugger, "BWC Protocol Talks Collapse in Geneva Following U.S. Withdrawal," September 1, 2001, Arms Control Association, www.armscontrol.org/act/2001_09/bwcs.

c. "Cluster Munitions," U.S. Department of State, www.state.gov/t/pm/wra/c25930.htm.

d. *America's Strategic Posture: Final Report of the Congressional Commission on the Strategic Posture of the United States* (2009), www.usip.org/strategic-posture-commission/view-the-report.

e. "U.S. Landmine Policy," September 23, 2014, www.state.gov/r/pa/prs/ps/2014/09/231995.htm.

f. Jay Johnson, Gary Pecquet, and Leon Taylor, "Potential Gains from Trade in Dirty Industries," *Cato Journal* 27, no. 3, https://object.cato.org/sites/cato.org/files/serials/files/cato-journal/2007/11/cj27n3-6.pdf; Robert F. Blomquist, "Ratification Resisted: Understanding America's Response to the Convention on Biological Diversity, 1989–2002," *Golden Gate University Law Review* 32, no. 4 (January 2002), http://digitalcommons.law.ggu.edu/cgi/viewcontent.cgi?article=1844&context=ggulrev.

g. Sense of the Senate Resolution, July 11, 1994, www.gpo.gov/fdsys/pkg/BILLS-103sres239pcs/html /BILLS-103sres239pcs.htm.

h. "S.RES.98—A Resolution Expressing the Sense of the Senate Regarding the Conditions for the United States Becoming a Signatory to Any International Agreement on Greenhouse Gas Emissions under the United Nations Framework Convention for Climate Change," 105th Congress, July 25, 1997, www.congress .gov/bill/105th-congress/senate-resolution/98.

i. In 2006, Representative Ralph Hall (R-Tex.) expressed concern that the implementing legislation proposed for these conventions (H.R. 4800) would create "troubling and dangerous precedents to set in American law." Hearing before the Subcommittee on Environment and Hazardous Materials, 109th Congress, March 2, 2006, p. 2, www.gpo.gov/fdsys/pkg/CHRG-109hhrg27145/pdf/CHRG-109hhrg27145.pdf.

j. Ronald Reagan, "Message to the Senate Transmitting a Protocol to the 1949 Geneva Conventions," January 29, 1987, https://reaganlibrary.archives.gov/archives/speeches/1987/012987b.htm; R. Jeffrey Smith, "Bush White House Sought to Soften Treaty on 'Enforced Disappearances,'" *Washington Post*, September 8, 2009.

k. John Fonte, congressional testimony on CEDAW before the U.S. Senate, November 18, 2010, www .hudson.org/content/researchattachments/attachment/845/cedaw-senate-testimony-fonte-john-11182010 .pdf.

l. Testimony by Jeremy Rabkin on the CRPD, November 21, 2013, www.foreign.senate.gov/imo/media /doc/Rabkin_Testimony.pdf; "Inhofe Praises Senate Rejection of CRPD," www.inhofe.senate.gov/newsroom /press-releases/inhofe-praises-senate-rejection-of-crpd.

m. Michael P. Farris, "Nannies in Blue Berets: Understanding the UN Convention on the Rights of the Child," Home School Legal Defense Association, January 2009, www.hslda.org/docs/news/20091120 .asp.

n. Human Rights Watch, "United States Ratification of International Human Rights Treaties," July 24, 2009, www.hrw.org/news/2009/07/24/united-states-ratification-international-human-rights-treaties.

o. H. Concurrent Resolution 265 (2010), www.gpo.gov/fdsys/pkg/BILLS-111hconres265ih/html/BILLS -111hconres265ih.htm.

in ratifying the Limited Test Ban Treaty; the numerous conditions it attached when approving and ratifying the Intermediate-Range Nuclear Forces Treaty (INF), Strategic Arms Reduction Treaties (START) I and II, the Conventional Forces in Europe Treaty (CFE), and the Chemical Weapons Convention (CWC); and its outright rejection of both the CTBT and the Mine Ban Treaty. Sovereigntists also worry that vaguely worded treaty language could entrap the United States in open-ended obligations. Theodore Bromund of the Heritage Foundation objects that the UN Arms Trade Treaty includes fuzzy concepts like "international humanitarian law" and "international human rights law." He predicts: "By signing the treaty, the United States has tied itself to a conveyor belt: It is no longer in control of where it is going."[60]

Environmental treaties also face tough sledding. Although the United States is party to narrow-scope treaties such as the Montreal Protocol on Ozone-Depleting Substances and the Straddling Fish Stocks Convention, it has remained outside more far-reaching arrangements, including the Kyoto Protocol, the Convention on Biological Diversity, the Stockholm Convention on Persistent Organic Pollutants, and the Basel Convention on Hazardous Wastes. In part, this reflects cost-benefit calculations: Kyoto, for instance, would have imposed heavy economic costs. More generally, the U.S. private sector often seeks to convince legislators that U.S. accession to environmental treaties will undercut U.S. business and economic competitiveness. In other cases, the relative strength of U.S. domestic environmental protections gave it fewer obvious incentives to join. But opponents have also argued that environmental treaties, by creating new international authorities to monitor compliance, could empower global bureaucrats to dictate rules for the United States.

The Human Rights Paradox

There is no bigger bugaboo for defenders of American sovereignty than international human rights treaties. This is ironic. Few countries match the U.S. record in protecting human rights at home, promoting them abroad, and shaping international rights conventions. The United States is home to the world's most dynamic human rights advocacy organizations, and most U.S. sovereigntists are themselves committed to individual liberty and, where possible, the global expansion of human freedom. Historically, the United States helped launch the global human rights revolution in the 1940s—a period punctuated by FDR's "Four Freedoms" speech (1940), the Atlantic Charter (1941), the UN Charter (1945), the Universal Declaration on Human Rights (1948), and the Genocide Convention (1948).

Thanks in large part to U.S. exertions, international law has come to encompass not simply the rights of states but the rights of individual human beings as possessors of inherent rights and dignity.[61] And yet even during the early post–World War II era, Americans debated whether they should ratify formal human rights treaties, insist on voluntary agreements, or "simply oppose [human rights agreements] in their entirety as unacceptable intrusions into sovereign domestic space." Even today, the United States stands apart from other mature democracies in resisting major human rights treaties. Expressions of American exemptionalism include failing to sign or ratify conventions despite spearheading relevant negotiations, acceding to such treaties only after protracted delays, and conditioning their ratification so heavily as to limit U.S. obligations ("Swiss cheese ratification").[62]

The United States is one of only two countries not to have ratified the UN Convention on the Rights of the Child (the other is Somalia) and one of only six not party to the Convention on the Elimination of Discrimination against Women (CEDAW). The United States refuses to accept the jurisdiction of international tribunals (including the ICC) or to allow its citizens to bring suit in either domestic courts or international tribunals for violations of rights codified in international conventions.

When the United States does ratify human rights conventions, it includes extensive, substantive reservations, understandings, and declarations (known as RUDs),[63] while also insisting such treaties are non-self-executing. Even so, the United States has often failed to cooperate with UN human rights rapporteurs and committees seeking to assess U.S. domestic conformity with UN standards.[64]

Several factors underpin America's ambiguous posture on human rights. One is the natural desire of a globally dominant power to avoid external constraints or supervision. The emergence of international human rights law is the most profound legal challenge to state sovereignty since 1945, implying that how governments treat citizens within their own borders is no longer a purely domestic matter. It is understandable that the world's most powerful nation would resist such scrutiny. Moreover, the costs of human rights treaties are modest but real, requiring parties to adopt uniform domestic standards and open themselves to external scrutiny by treaty bodies. Given robust human rights protections at home, Americans see few obvious incentives to accept such domestic constraints.

Still, as the Princeton scholar Andrew Moravcsik notes, the intensity of U.S. debates over human rights treaties suggests other factors are also at play. They include a distinctive U.S. "rights culture," America's perceived national identity and global role, the durability of U.S. political and legal institutions, the many "veto" players in the U.S. political system, and the conservatism of America's polity and elected leaders.[65]

First, America's Founders were heirs to the Enlightenment, and the U.S. conception of human rights bears the imprint of that era. The U.S. Constitution, including the Bill of Rights, focuses on "negative rights," or eliminating state and other restraints on individual liberties, including freedom of speech, assembly, and faith. This classically liberal approach persists, even as the global rights dialogue shifts toward asserting "positive rights" such as guaranteed access to food, employment, shelter, health, and education. This explains why the United States, although a signatory to the nonbinding Universal Declaration of Human Rights, has never ratified the UN Covenant on Economic, Social and Cultural Rights (CESCR).[66]

Second, American exceptionalism is not easily squared with the diplomatic give-and-take inherent in multilateral negotiations over human rights. If the United States is indeed the world's leading embodiment of human freedom, it clearly has a lot to teach the world about the appropriate content of international norms. But it has precious little to learn (or borrow) from others. As the CRPD debate reached its zenith, Senator James E. Risch (R-Idaho) explained the stakes: "I will not vote to hand our sovereignty and constitutional protections over to people who are not accountable to U.S. citizens and, in many instances, advance a liberal international agenda."[67]

American sovereigntists get incensed when international officials presume to sit in judgment of the U.S. legal and judicial system. In April 2012 Navi Pillay, who was then UN high commissioner for human rights, commented on the killing of Trayvon Martin, an unarmed African American teen, by neighborhood watch coordinator George Zimmerman. "Justice must be done for the victim," Pillay declared. "I will be awaiting an investigation and prosecution and trial and of course reparations for the victims concerned." To American conservatives like John Kyl, this statement transcended simple hubris from a UN busybody. "Such comments express the desire, and growing power, of a global progressive elite to pierce the shield of U.S. sovereignty and influence the outcomes of the country's domestic debates."[68] Human rights advocacy groups stoke such sovereigntist fears when they incorrectly suggest that the findings of Geneva-based groups of experts, who issue comments on compliance with UN human rights groups, are legally binding. The fact that dictatorial regimes that routinely abuse their citizens can obtain seats on the UN Human Rights Council and other global bodies merely reinforces this resistance to outside scrutiny.

Third, Americans view their political institutions, including domestic human rights standards, as having been vindicated historically. In contrast, democracies with troubled, authoritarian, or totalitarian pasts often try to bind themselves to global human rights regimes as a check against domestic backsliding. Such historical differences also help to explain why the United States protects freedom of speech absolutely, whereas other democracies restrict "hate speech" (or Holocaust denial) to ensure civility.[69]

Fourth, America's decentralized system of federal lawmaking complicates U.S. accession to human rights treaties by empowering multiple players to veto new international obligations. Partisan dynamics influence ratification. Most successful human rights treaties have been signed and submitted by Democratic presidents, and no treaty has ever been approved (even with reservations) with fewer than fifty-five Democrats in the Senate.[70]

This history hints at a fifth, ideological factor—namely, a powerful current of U.S. conservatism that regards international human rights treaties as embodying an alien, socialist agenda. Senator Bricker expressed this view in 1951 when he declared that the proposed UN International Covenant on Human Rights "would be more appropriately entitled as a Covenant on Human Slavery or subservience to government," since it "repudiated the underlying theory of the Bill of Rights—freedom to be let alone."[71]

Similar mistrust persists today among social conservatives who believe human rights treaties portend social engineering and threaten traditional "family values." As the Republican Party explained in its 2016 platform, "Precisely because we take our country's treaty obligations seriously, we oppose ratification of international agreements whose long-range implications are ominous or unclear."[72]

Taken at face value, this position seems eminently reasonable. Why would anybody support a convention with "ominous and unclear" implications? What is unreasonable is the alarmist, unfounded rhetoric sovereigntists often use to discredit treaties. The Convention on the Rights of the Child (CRC) is a case in point. The document has few domestic implications. American children already enjoy significant legal protections; the treaty lacks enforcement provisions; and the Senate can include extensive RUDs in any instrument of ratification. Despite these facts and safeguards, a vocal coalition of opponents, including the Family Research Council and the National Center for Home Education, has mobilized to oppose it, describing it as a grave threat to "parental rights" that would permit minors to sue their parents in court, refuse to attend church, and obtain abortions without parental consultation. The CRC, critics allege, "overrides our own Constitution" by "effectively transfer[ring] ultimate authority" over American children to "a committee of 18 experts from other nations, sitting in Geneva," whose "official interpretations of the treaty . . . are entitled to binding weight in American courts and legislatures." None of these claims is true. And yet such statements carry political weight.[73]

Treaty Gridlock and Its Costs for the United States

The Senate has long been known as the "graveyard of treaties," but that metaphor was especially apt during the Obama presidency, when the United States ratified only six multilateral treaties. The Senate either rejected or failed to approve six treaties the president personally signed. It also declined to move on the vast majority of the multilateral treaties signed by previous presidents that the White House had included on its "treaty priority list" in 2009, among them CTBT, UNCLOS, CEDAW, the Stockholm Convention on Persistent Organic Pollutants (POPs), the Rotterdam Convention, and conventions addressing labor rights and UN peacekeeping.[74] At the advent of the Trump administration, forty-four treaties were pending before the Senate.

Both ends of Pennsylvania Avenue have contributed to treaty logjams.[75] President Obama's use of Article II treaty powers and his success rate lagged behind those of his post–World War II predecessors. Over eight years, Obama averaged only eight treaty transmittals to the Senate per congressional session, whereas the average for 1949–2008 was 31.6 treaties per session; and his batting average in securing ratification was far lower than that of other modern presidents. The Senate, meanwhile, consented to a smaller fraction of submitted treaties than average, thanks to partisan ideological divides. As Bellinger explained in the New York Times, "an increasing number of Republicans have come to view treaties in general (and especially multilateral ones) as liberal conspiracies to hand over American sovereignty to international authorities."[76]

American exemptionalism on treaties harms the United States by undercutting U.S. national interests and weakening America's global stature. Consider UNCLOS. The United States signed the treaty in 1994 but at this writing in 2017 has never ratified it, despite its being endorsed by every living former president, secretary of state and defense, and chairman of the joint chiefs of staff, as well as major industry and environmental organizations. Senate conservatives blocked the treaty, claiming spuriously that it would subject the United States to a supranational legal authority and a massive international tax scheme. In a typically ill-informed statement, Senators James Inhofe and Jim

DeMint declared, "This treaty would convey ownership of the oceans to a United Nations agency and give international bureaucrats veto over U.S. naval operations."[77] Both claims have no basis in fact.

What is clear is that remaining outside of the treaty deprives the United States of an effective instrument for *extending* its sovereignty. As an outsider, the nation cannot participate in the world's last major territorial partition: namely, the allocation to states parties of hundreds of thousands of square miles in extended exclusive economic zones (EEEZs). It thus forfeits an opportunity to extend its own jurisdiction over vast areas along its Arctic, Atlantic, Gulf, and Pacific Coasts.[78] As chapter 5 explains in more detail, the UNCLOS experience provides a textbook example of how unfounded fears of sacrificing sovereignty-as-authority and sovereignty-as-autonomy through international law can undermine U.S. interests by diminishing American sovereignty-as-influence.

Second, failure to become party to a multilateral treaty endorsed by the vast majority of other UN member states carries reputational costs, undermining faith in the country's dedication to the international rule of law and the credibility of its commitments. America's inability to ratify UNCLOS, after spearheading its negotiation and shaping its provisions to reflect U.S. interests, weakens U.S. defense of an open maritime commons. It also reduces U.S. diplomatic leverage in countering China's provocative territorial claims in the South China Sea,[79] as well as Russia's own controversial claims in the Arctic Ocean. The American domestic debate over UNCLOS underscores the importance of clear thinking about sovereignty trade-offs. In this case, the United States would be wise to yield some absolute freedom of action to support and enforce a stable, open maritime order.

Finally, multilateral treaty gridlock prevents the United States from influencing the terms of major international conventions. In the not-so-distant past, U.S. negotiators often persuaded other countries that conceding to U.S.-desired treaty provisions was the price for Senate passage. As the Senate moves toward blanket rejection of multilateral treaties, such negotiating tactics may no longer work. Failure to ratify also prevents the United States from influencing committees typically established to interpret and monitor compliance with treaties, from the Convention on Biological Diversity to CEDAW. "Treaty-making . . . is an expression of sovereignty, not a threat to it," the legal scholar David Kaye explains. But "by excluding itself from the process," the United States becomes a mere bystander, forfeiting the chance "to influence global problem solving."[80]

The Rise of Treaty Workarounds

Faced with treaty gridlock, U.S. administrations have tried to achieve similar results through executive agreements. In the nation's first half century, treaties outnumbered executive agreements 60 to 27. From 1939 to 2012, the nation concluded a total of 17,300 executive agreements but only 1,100 treaties (both bilateral and multilateral). While multilateral agreements are still more likely than bilateral ones to take the form of formal treaties, multilateral executive agreements now outnumber multilateral treaties. Although some legal academics applaud this trend as superior to the treaty clause route to international agreements, it has created consternation among sovereigntists.[81]

Sovereigntists contend that such arrangements run counter to the intentions of the Founders, allowing activist presidents to usurp the Senate's treaty-making powers and make imprudent international commitments that would be beyond their reach under the two-thirds supermajority provision. The Founders understood, Bolton and Yoo write, that "America needs to maintain its sovereignty and autonomy, not to subordinate its policies, foreign or domestic, to international control." Consistent with this position, Republicans declared in their 2016 party platform that any executive agreements reached during the Obama years "must be deemed null and void as mere expressions of the current president's preferences."[82]

Beyond making greater use of executive agreements, recent U.S. administrations have resorted to "stealth multilateralism," as Kaye terms it, relying on flexible and informal tools to achieve results consistent with unratified treaties. Thus although the Senate rejected the CTBT in 1999, Presidents George W. Bush and Barack Obama both quietly funded a global system of monitoring stations, envisioned in that treaty, to analyze evidence of nuclear tests.

More generally, treaty gridlock has accelerated America's turn toward à la carte forms of cooperation. As the conclusion of this book discusses at greater length, this approach substitutes informal arrangements and "minilateral" coalitions for binding conventions and formal international organizations. While such ad hoc-ism introduces speed and flexibility, it also lacks the binding force of law, making it harder for the United States and others to make credible commitments, verify compliance, and punish violators.[83] Nevertheless, in some circumstances it can make sense, allowing the United States to strike the best balance among the three goals of protecting U.S. sovereign authorities, preserving sovereign autonomy, and exercising sovereign influence.

Strategies to Limit the Scope of Treaty Obligations

Although opting out of treaties is one way to protect sovereign rights, the pre-ferred U.S. approach is to insist on special privileges and limit U.S. obliga-tions. Examples of American prerogatives include the UN Charter, which grants the United States permanent membership and veto power within the Security Council; the NPT, which accords elevated status to the United States and other recognized nuclear weapons states; and the executive boards of the IMF and the World Bank, which employ a system of weighted voting that favors large countries, not least the United States.

A second strategy is for the United States to make treaty signature, ratifi-cation, and accession contingent on RUDs that limit U.S. obligations. In sign-ing the Convention against Torture, for instance, the United States insisted that it would interpret the convention's prohibition on "cruel and degrading treatment" according to the Fifth, Eighth, and Fourteenth Amendments to the Constitution. Other countries also insist on RUDs, of course. But the un-matched frequency and scope of U.S. caveats elicits frequent criticism from close U.S. allies and partners, including Portugal and Sweden, which complain that U.S. practice "undermines basic principles of international law."[84] To date, U.S. administrations have calculated that taking this reputational hit is an acceptable price for protecting U.S. sovereignty.

A third approach to protecting U.S. sovereignty is to expand the doctrine of *non-self-execution*. This means that international agreements produce no do-mestic legal effects without separate congressional implementing legislation giving U.S. agencies authority to meet international legal obligations, or allow-ing private parties to make them enforceable in court. Legal conservatives favor a "general presumption of non-self-execution," arguing that it would reinforce U.S. popular sovereignty. Progressive legal scholars disagree, noting that the Supremacy Clause designates treaties (alongside the Constitution and Acts of Congress) as "the supreme law of the land." They cite in their defense Alexan-der Hamilton, who wrote that a blanket doctrine of non-self-execution would render hollow the treaty power authorized in the Constitution.[85]

In sum, the United States has a well-stocked arsenal of weapons to reduce the constraints that multilateral treaties place on U.S. sovereignty, whether conceived as constitutional authority or policy autonomy.

REFERENCES TO FOREIGN LAW BY U.S. COURTS

Among the most contentious issues in U.S. jurisprudence, as measured by the political attention it generates, is whether U.S. courts, including the Supreme Court, should consider international legal sources and foreign judicial opinions in interpreting the U.S. Constitution and U.S. domestic statutes. References to foreign law by U.S. courts are nothing new. As long ago as 1815 the Supreme Court noted that the "decisions of the Courts, of every country, so far as they are founded upon a law common to every country, will be received, not as authority, but with respect." Historically, U.S. courts have periodically looked to foreign jurisprudence for "persuasive value," including a better understanding of how foreign governments interpret international law and treaties. But foreign law has never been treated as binding precedent.[86]

More contentious is whether domestic U.S. courts should be free to refer more extensively to foreign jurisprudence in interpreting U.S. statutes and the U.S. Constitution. Conservatives usually oppose this practice, arguing that allowing judges to decide what international laws should be "domesticated to bind Americans at home" violates the separation of powers by allowing judges to appropriate an inherent lawmaking function. The Republican Party adopted this stance at its 2016 convention. "The legitimate powers of government are rooted in the consent of the American people," the GOP platform declared. "Judicial activism that includes reliance on foreign law or unratified treaties undermines American sovereignty."[87]

Whether the Supreme Court should make use of foreign jurisprudence has divided justices themselves. The late Antonin Scalia, consistent with his "originalist" position, regarded foreign law as irrelevant in interpreting U.S. constitutional law, inasmuch as "we don't have the same moral and legal framework as the rest of the world, and never have." He also believed that progressive judges invoke foreign jurisprudence only "selectively"—namely, when they cannot cite existing American practice or statutes that conform to their own biases. The invocation of foreign materials thus "invites manipulation."[88]

Democratic sovereignty lies at the heart of this conservative critique. Even if one accepts the notion of an "evolving Constitution" (which Scalia did not), elite justices have no standing as arbiters of "what the moral values of America should be on all sorts of issues, such as penology, the death penalty, abortion, whatever." If the American people change their positions on such matters, it is up to their representatives in Congress, not an unelected judiciary, to legislate those shifts.[89]

In contrast to Scalia's originalism, Associate Justice Stephen Breyer advocates a more flexible stance: "Law emerges from a complex interactive democratic process," he observes, and it is impossible to insulate this "conversation" from global influences. Although "the decisions of foreign courts do not bind American courts," U.S. judges can and should learn how their counterparts abroad apply their own legal texts to grapple with legal problems similar to those the United States confronts.[90]

Debates over citing foreign law revolve around two concerns.[91] The first is about the relevance of international materials in U.S. judicial reasoning. Liberals argue that awareness of foreign jurisprudence makes for more informed U.S. judicial decisions. Conservatives retort that divergent legal traditions and sociopolitical contexts make it easy to misinterpret and misuse foreign opinions. Even worse, judges may cherry-pick among foreign sources to reinforce preferred positions.

The second, more profound debate is about how constitutional lawmaking should occur in a sovereign democracy. Conservatives worry that U.S. judges who cite opinions from other nations' courts or from international tribunals create new U.S. law that lacks democratic provenance and accountability. In this view, the legitimacy of U.S. constitutional (and other domestic) law depends on whether it emerges from and remains embedded in the will of the American people, as expressed through their elected representatives. By using foreign law to interpret domestic law, the judicial branch gains unwarranted legislative power, allowing it to impose its own social and moral views on American society.[92]

These debates expose divergent ideological preferences: Conservatives fear (while liberals hope) that comparative analysis will favor progressive interpretations of the U.S. Constitution on topics such as the death penalty, affirmative action, abortion, and gay rights. But the ferocity of conservative resistance suggests something even more fundamental is at stake. After all, no sitting liberal justice—or even prominent judge or legal scholar—has proposed subordinating U.S. constitutional traditions and their normative authority to a global legal consensus.[93] So why such antipathy to the suggestion that U.S. judges might learn from foreign peers about how to think about certain common legal situations—and the potential consequences of alternative decisions?

The source of conservative disquiet is worry that invoking foreign law will adulterate a coherent body of U.S. constitutional reasoning that has evolved since 1789. The assumption here is that there exists an unbroken, largely self-contained U.S. discourse on constitutional law. Introducing foreign legal materials into U.S. court cases would, in this view, threaten the integrity of America's constitutional tradition and expose it to alien principles, norms, and values. It could undermine the Constitution's critical role, within America's heterogeneous society, of providing a neutral procedural framework in which to reach decisions on controversial matters.[94]

Such fears are understandable but alarmist. The U.S. constitutional tradition can retain its coherence and identity while opening itself to foreign influences. As a practical matter, U.S. judges are increasingly connected with counterparts abroad, as members of a common judicial enterprise. Some of the most pressing and complex legal challenges on today's Supreme Court's docket involve transnational issues, reflecting the globalization of commercial exchanges. Judges regularly confront cases (such as bankruptcies of multinational corporations) that cannot be decided without an understanding of foreign legal systems. Meanwhile, at a personal level, judges are now regularly exposed to international jurisprudence. These experiences and insights cannot but affect their thinking.

The wisest course is for judges to honestly acknowledge these influences, open themselves to comparative analysis, and give "weight" to any "visible international consensus." Associate Justice Sandra Day O'Connor took this position in a celebrated 2002 address to the American Society of International Law. "Although international law and the law of other nations are rarely binding upon our decisions in US courts," she reasoned, the "conclusions reached by other countries and by the international community should at times constitute persuasive authority in American courts."[95]

Determining the relationship between foreign law and U.S. constitutional jurisprudence is becoming more pressing as the dynamic center of international law shifts from the United States to other countries. During the twentieth century, the international flow of legal discourse tended to be one-way: from the United States to the rest of the world. Today the traffic flows in multiple directions, increasing opportunities for cross-fertilization or (in the view of purists) cross-contamination. Foreign judges and legal scholars look for guidance and insights not just from U.S. counterparts but from colleagues in Canada, South Africa, and elsewhere. Indeed, some countries' constitutions, including those of Germany and South Africa, explicitly take international or foreign law into account. By contrast, the U.S. Constitution recognizes no legal authorities outside those of the United States itself.[96]

The Supreme Court, once a historic guide to other nations, is gradually losing its pole position as the primary international influence on the high courts of foreign nations, and its reluctance to engage its foreign counterparts simply accelerates this trend. For as Associate Justice Ruth Bader Ginsburg asked in 2008, "If we don't cite them, why should they look to us?"[97] The lesson here is straightforward and can be expressed in terms of the "sovereignty triangle" presented in chapter 1: Paying too much attention to sovereignty-as-authority can jeopardize U.S. sovereignty-as-influence—in this case, a capacity to shape the global framework of norms and rules in which all countries operate.

The challenge is thus for U.S. courts to open themselves to comparative legal analysis without jeopardizing the integrity of the U.S. constitutional system. This is not as implausible as it sounds. Rather than convergence, exposure to foreign law could even encourage "informed divergence"—a reassertion of U.S. legal traditions, based on distinctive historical, cultural, political, economic, social, religious, or other grounds.[98]

Whether the Supreme Court should consider foreign materials is not a new debate. Six decades ago the court invoked international legal opinion in *Trop v. Dulles* (1958), ruling that it was cruel and unusual punishment to deprive an army deserter of American citizenship. Writing for the plurality, Chief Justice Earl Warren observed that "civilized nations of the world are in virtual unanimity that statelessness is not to be imposed as a punishment for crime."[99] Today most U.S. legal scholars agree that U.S. judges should be able to refer to foreign cases in their constitutional jurisprudence—for instance, to illustrate contrasts or make factual propositions. At the same time, scholars overwhelmingly reject allowing foreign cases to be "outcome determinative." And they remain divided on whether judges may, as O'Connor suggested, cite foreign law as a "persuasive" basis for their decisions.[100]

Conservatives have long argued that invoking foreign sources for more than banal purposes is an attack on U.S. constitutional sovereignty. In *Stanford v. Kentucky* (1989), for instance, Scalia dismissed as irrelevant Associate Justice William Brennan's observation that the world "overwhelmingly disapproved" of the juvenile death penalty. "We emphasize," Scalia rejoined, "that it is *American* conceptions of decency that are dispositive." A decade later Associate Justice Clarence Thomas took to the parapet in *Knight v. Florida* (1999), launching volleys at Associate Justice Stephen Breyer for invoking foreign jurisprudence in arguing that a twenty-five-year delay in carrying out capital punishment constituted "cruel and unusual" punishment. Surely, Thomas wrote, Breyer would have no need to invoke support from "the European Court of Human Rights, the Supreme Court of Zimbabwe, the Supreme Court of India, or the Privy Council," had he been able to find support from either "the American Constitutional tradition" or "this Court's precedent."[101]

Four years later the court's conservative and liberal wings clashed again in *Lawrence v. Texas* (2003), which struck down a Texas antisodomy law for violating the Fourteenth Amendment's due process clause. That ruling overturned an earlier decision, *Bowers v. Hardwick* (1986), that had depicted sodomy as contrary to "Western" and "Judeo-Christian" civilization. Writing for the majority in *Lawrence*, Kennedy marshalled rulings from the European Court of Human Rights, as well as other foreign courts, to bolster his argument that consensual adult sexual relations were constitutionally protected. He added for good measure that "the evolution of other countries' understanding of human freedom" could inform America's own. Scalia disparaged these foreign materials as "meaningless dicta." The relevant question was whether any such right was "deeply rooted in *this* Nation's history and traditions."[102]

The most full-throated battle over the place of foreign law in Supreme Court deliberations remains *Roper v. Simmons* (2005), the case introduced at the start of this chapter. Among the intriguing aspects of that case was O'Connor's separate, dissenting opinion. Although she determined that a genuine *national* consensus against the death penalty did not yet exist, "Nevertheless, I disagree with Justice Scalia's contention, that foreign and international law have no place in our Eighth Amendment jurisprudence." O'Connor continued: "Obviously, American law is distinctive in many respects. . . . But this Nation's evolving understanding of human dignity certainly is neither wholly isolated from, nor inherently at odds with, the values prevailing in other countries."[103]

The question of whether U.S. judges should consider foreign jurisprudence in interpreting the Constitution has not been limited to dueling Supreme Court justices and legal scholars. On May 3, 2007, Representative Tom Feeney (R-Fla.) introduced a "Sense of the House" resolution cosponsored by forty-eight other representatives. "Whereas inappropriate reliance on foreign judgments, laws, or pronouncements threatens the sovereignty of the United States, the separation of powers and the President's and the Senate's treaty-making authority," the legislators declared, no such materials should be employed by U.S. courts unless consistent with the "original meaning" of the Constitution.[104]

The aftermath of *Roper v. Simmons* highlights one of the chief concerns of sovereignty-minded conservatives: the worry that once foreign law is cited in court decisions, it may continue exerting an influence in less obvious ways. In *Roper*, the court relied on the fact that most U.S. states did not put minors to death for capital crimes, using the practice of foreign nations only in a complementary manner, to help define "cruel and unusual." But only five years later, in *Graham v. Sullivan* (2010), the court used foreign law in a more integral manner, to supplement the ruling where no national consensus existed regarding life sentences for minors. And by the time the court ruled in *Miller v. Alabama* (2012), foreign law was no longer cited, because precedents from the two previous rulings in *Roper* and *Graham* (both based in part on foreign law) provided sufficient justification. Such a progression demonstrates, for better or worse, how foreign law may continue to influence U.S. law, even when the connection no longer seems apparent.[105]

This is likely to be true only at the margins, however. As Associate Justice Breyer concludes his book *The Court and the World*, "Those who hold a negative view of cross-referencing at best overstate their concerns." There is little danger that reference to "foreign legal concepts and values" will "corrupt" American legal traditions. At the same time, consideration of foreign law and practices is an indispensable dimension of the world that U.S. judges inhabit and the sort of legal questions that come before them—whether in interpreting treaty obligations, settling investment disputes, or considering the foreign reach of U.S. regulatory and other statutes. "At most, cross-referencing will speed the development of 'clusters' or 'pockets' of legally like-minded nations whose judges learn things from one another, either as a general matter or in particular areas of law, such as security, commerce, or the environment," Breyer concludes. "But these groupings need not be formal, and their members can insist on the conformity of any legal rule with their own nation's basic legal values."[106] In short, the integrity of the U.S. constitutional tradition remains secure.

FEDERALISM UNDER ATTACK?

Finally, a special category of U.S. sovereignty concerns pertains to the impact of international law on the prerogatives reserved to the fifty U.S. states under the Constitution—as opposed to the authority of the United States as a union. The issue here is federalism. As Associate Justice O'Connor argued in *New York v. the United States* (1992), the Constitution "leaves to the several States a residual and inviolable sovereignty" (quoting Federalist 39). Defenders of states' rights routinely depict international treaty obligations, in particular, as infringing on the Tenth Amendment, which declares that the powers not explicitly delegated to the federal government are reserved to the individual U.S. states and the American people.[107]

As chapter 2 explained, the debate over the scope of states' rights is as old as the Constitution. For the first several decades after its ratification, the former colonies constituting the new American "states-union" vied with the federal government for supremacy in many arenas. To the Frenchman Alexis de Tocqueville, writing in 1835, it appeared that "there are twenty-four small sovereign nations" that constituted the United States.[108] Although the Civil War tilted the balance strongly toward the federal government, state governments retain significant legal authorities in and jurisdiction over certain public spheres, from law enforcement to education, family law, and private commercial law. These prerogatives are under increasing strain, however, as globalization creates pressures to expand intergovernmental cooperation on behind-the-border issues, including in regulatory arenas traditionally under the purview of U.S. states.

The potential collision between states' rights and U.S. treaty obligations was on display in Idaho in April 2015, when the Judiciary, Rules, and Administration Committee of the State Assembly rejected a state bill pertaining to child support. The bill's offending provision, according to the committee's Republican majority, was its link to an obscure multilateral treaty that requires all national parties to enforce child support decisions made in foreign courts. Under the terms of U.S. ratification, however, all fifty U.S. states had to approve the mechanism of the treaty for it to take effect, and Idaho was now opposing the measure.[109]

On the surface, the treaty was entirely unobjectionable. The product of five years of international negotiations, it was intended to track down delinquent parents around the world. The United States, under President George W. Bush, had been the first country to sign it in 2007, and the U.S. Senate had approved it unanimously. Moreover, Idaho's failure to approve the bill jeopardized tens of millions of dollars in federal funds to support the state's child welfare system. Still, GOP legislators balked, arguing without merit that the legislation could impose on Idaho decisions made by foreign tribunals, including those based on *shariah*, the Islamic legal code. As Republican state representative Kathleen Sims explained, "It's a sovereignty issue." She simply opposed "involving foreign nations in our laws." The bill eventually passed, but only after Republican governor Butch Otter called grumpy legislators back for a special session.[110]

As global integration proceeds, international legal obligations are more likely to bump up against the Tenth Amendment. Among the trickiest questions that federalism raises is whether the executive branch and Congress may enact legislation implementing treaty obligations that infringe on areas of traditional state competence. For nearly a century the guiding precedent has been *Missouri v. Holland* (1920). That Supreme Court ruling upheld the constitutionality of the Migratory Bird Treaty (1918) between the United States and the United Kingdom, the enforcement of which Missouri had sought to block on Tenth Amendment grounds. Over time, *Missouri* has become increasingly controversial, with legal advocates for states' rights under the U.S. Constitution arguing that it should be overturned.[111]

The more recent case of *Medellin* v. *Texas* (2008) illuminates the complex relationship between federalism and international law. *Medellin* originated in an earlier complaint that Mexico had lodged against the United States before the International Court of Justice (ICJ). In that case, *Avena* (2005), Mexico accused the United States of violating the Optional Protocol to the Vienna Convention on Consular Relations (VCCR) by failing to inform fifty-one detained Mexican nationals of their right to communicate with their consulates. After the ICJ ruled in Mexico's favor, President George W. Bush announced that the United States would "discharge its international obligations ... by having State courts give effect to the decision." However, when detainee José Medellin appealed to overturn his conviction in a capital murder case, the Court of Criminals Appeals in Texas, where he had been arrested, refused to hear the case because he had not raised his claim in a timely manner.[112]

The Supreme Court then heard *Medellin* to answer two questions: First, was the ICJ's *Avena* decision directly enforceable as domestic law in state courts? Second, did the president's memorandum require states to comply with *Avena* regardless of state procedural default rules? In a 6–3 decision, the Court answered "no" on both counts. It declared the Optional Protocol to the VCCR to be non-self-executing, meaning that it required separate congressional legislation to make ICJ judgments directly enforceable. And it ruled that the president had exceeded his exclusive constitutional powers. In sum, the Court conceded that Texas had violated international law, but also that the executive branch could not compel the state's compliance with an international obligation. Having lost his appeal, Medellin was executed in Texas.

At the heart of the court's decision was the issue of sovereignty-as-authority. As Noah Feldman explains: "By its own lights, the Supreme Court in the *Medellin* case was reading the Constitution to guarantee us control over our destiny. This meant turning away from international law in a systematic and profound sense. The cost to the United States might be real, but the court considered it justified by the preservation of our democratic sovereignty."[113] The State Department has tried to comply with *Avena*, but no relevant legislation has been passed.

More recently, the Tenth Amendment's constraints on treaty-making emerged in *Bond* v. *United States* (2014). The case arose when Carol Anne Bond, who had tried to poison an acquaintance, was charged with violating the Chemical Weapons Act (CWA), a domestic statute implementing U.S. obligations under the CWC. As in *Medellin*, a core question in *Bond* was whether the president and Congress, in acceding to a treaty, had the authority to implement domestic legislation required to comply with it, when the sphere in question was one otherwise reserved for the fifty U.S. states. Bond's counsel, meanwhile, argued that the defendant should have been charged with a criminal offense under state rather than federal law. All nine Supreme Court justices sided with the plaintiff, reasoning that Bond's local poisoning did not fall within the CWA's scope. Separately, Justices Samuel Alito, Scalia, and Thomas all agreed that the *Holland* precedent should be overturned.[114]

Together, *Medellin* and *Bond* caused a commotion in legal circles, since they indicated a presumption against self-executing treaties—potentially calling into question the enforceability of up to seventy existing conventions.[115] Many conservatives depicted *Medellin* as a victory for the sovereignty of the fifty U.S. states over the federal government and international law. One was Senator Ted Cruz (R-Tex.), who as solicitor general of Texas had argued the *Medellin* case before the Supreme Court. Writing in the *Harvard Law Review* in 2014, Cruz concluded: "The President, even with Senate acquiescence, has no authority to make a treaty with a foreign nation that gives away any portion of the sovereignty reserved to the states."[116] *Medellin* demonstrates just how complicated it can be to implement international obligations in a federal system that reserves power to the states. And were *Holland* to be overturned, the United States would be even more limited in its ability to enforce treaties it has ratified, reducing its credibility as a treaty partner.

In their provocative book *Taming Globalization*, Julian Ku and John Yoo propose that individual U.S. state governments should be granted a greater role in "interpreting, incorporating, and implementing international legal norms." The authors concede that this "radical proposal" could create inconsistency in the U.S. approach to international law. But it would be worse, they say, to override established principles of federalism. Their recommendation, however, is an invitation to legal anarchy, since it would allow separate U.S. states to determine whether they will implement U.S. treaty obligations. In their quest to defend principles of federalism, they offer a remedy that runs athwart of the popular sovereignty of the American people, conceived as a union, and the nation's ability to make credible international commitments.[117]

CONCLUSION

As the preceding pages testify, the "sovereigntist" approach to international law seeks to protect the United States from threats that are largely imaginary and from dangers against which it is well insulated. Contrary to the warnings of conservative legal scholars, the United States is in little danger of subordinating its constitutional authorities to ambitious supranational bodies, to expanding customary law, to unaccountable networks and freelancing NGOs, to vaguely worded multilateral treaties, or to foreign jurisprudence.

Sovereigntist warnings also run counter to U.S. long-term interests. This is true in at least two senses. First, the sovereigntist approach reinforces a split personality—and to foreign eyes and ears, a hypocritical U.S. approach—toward international law, whereby the United States aspires to be both a rule maker and exempt from those same rules. Whatever its past value, America's "exemptionalism" toward international law and treaties is no longer prudent or sustainable. Even if other states tolerate such exemptionalism, they are likely to begin emulating U.S. "cherry-picking" strategies themselves.

The second point is more fundamental. In an age of globalization, the test of sovereignty is no longer the power to be left alone, with pristine authority and unencumbered autonomy. Rather, as the international lawyers Abram and Antonia Chayes note, it is measured by the degree of "connection to the rest of the world and the political ability to be an actor within it," capable of exercising influence over others and one's destiny. In a world of interdependence and shared transnational challenges, true sovereignty resides not in the pursuit of absolute independence and freedom of action, but in the ability of states to operate within a "tightly woven fabric of international agreements, organizations, and institutions that shape their relations with one another and penetrate deeply into their international economics and politics."[118]

The "sovereigntist" case suggests that the United States benefits from a hierarchical, often unilateral approach to international law. In truth, the United States is more likely to achieve its aims, control its fate, and legitimize its power and purposes by adopting a more egalitarian approach to the global legal order. As a sovereign people, of course, Americans have the inherent democratic right, should they so choose, of trying to seclude themselves from international legal trends. But both they and their elected representatives should do so with their eyes open, aware of the relative balance of costs and benefits in making this trade-off.

FIVE

Don't Fence Me In

The Use of Force, Arms Control, and U.S. National Security

Senator John Kerry (D.-Mass.) stood stiffly, but his condemnation of President George W. Bush was forthright. It was not simply that the Iraq invasion had been based on a false premise—that Saddam Hussein possessed weapons of mass destruction. It was that Bush had rushed to war without securing international support. Yes, there were times when a "preemptive strike" might be warranted, Kerry told Jim Lehrer, who was moderating the first presidential debate in Coral Gables, Florida, on September 30, 2004. "But if and when you do it, Jim, you have to do it in a way that passes the test, that passes the global test . . . and you can prove to the world that you did it for legitimate reasons."[1]

Kerry's choice of words would haunt him for the remainder of the campaign. Bush spotted the gaffe immediately. "I'm not exactly sure what you mean, 'passes the global test,' you take preemptive action if you pass a global test," he wondered aloud. "My attitude is you take preemptive action in order to protect the American people, that you act in order to make this country secure." Under his watch, the president implied, the United States would never ask for a permission slip from the United Nations to defend its vital national interests.[2]

Kerry walked back his answer in the ensuing days. "I will never cede America's security to any institution or any other country," Kerry reassured a New Hampshire audience. "No one gets a veto over our security. No one." But the damage was done. Kerry had played into the Republican narrative that

Democrats were squishy on national security—handing the Bush campaign a cudgel with which to beat him. Conservative media outlets pilloried Kerry as an out-of-touch internationalist willing to subordinate sovereign decisions to international bodies unaccountable to U.S. citizens and at odds with American interests and values.[3]

Bush pressed the attack at their second, town hall–style debate at Washington University in St. Louis, on October 8. "My opponent said that America must pass a global test before we use force to protect ourselves," he observed incredulously. "That's the kind of mindset that said, 'Let's keep it at the United Nations and hope things go well.'"[4] Bush's assault distracted attention from other issues on which Kerry had hoped the public would focus— namely, the manipulation of intelligence about Iraqi WMD, the chaotic aftermath of the intervention, and the weakened U.S. diplomatic position. Within a month Bush had won reelection.

Nearly eleven years later, in the summer of 2015, another U.S. president, Barack Obama, perceived that a deal was within reach to dismantle Iran's nuclear weapons program. After years of negotiations, the permanent members of the UN Security Council (UNSC), along with the European Union and Germany, had secured the Islamic Republic's agreement to a Joint Comprehensive Plan of Action (JCPOA). The president's biggest headache was no longer in Tehran but in Washington, where skeptical legislators hoped to block the deal. To thwart them, Obama went international, engineering the UNSC's passage of Resolution 2231, which endorsed the JCPOA just a week after the agreement was struck.

The president's move outraged conservatives. "The President has maneuvered to box [U.S. legislators] in by having the United Nations approve it first," the editors of the *Wall Street Journal* seethed. "Mr. Obama deliberately structured his Iran negotiations to make Congress a secondary party to the UN."[5] The president had already sidestepped the Senate's advice and consent by fashioning the JCPOA as an executive agreement. Now he could depict any congressional obstruction as pitting the United States against the world.

But what really offended the *Journal* was Obama's riding roughshod over U.S. sovereignty. "The bigger issue here is self-government. The U.S. Constitution gives presidents enormous clout on foreign policy. . . . But Mr. Obama doesn't have authority to let the United Nations dictate to America's elected representatives." Over at *Investor's Business Daily*, the editorial verdict was the same. "Sovereignty: Few constitutional scholars thought it possible for a president to give away unilaterally American representative government to an international body. The United Nations' Iran vote just did."[6]

At the root of both controversies—Kerry's "global test" and Obama's UN resolution—was the idea that a U.S. president would turn to an international body to legitimate, shape, or even determine vital U.S. national security decisions. The very notion that the United States might place its faith in collective security, elevate international over domestic authorities, or allow itself to be constrained by outside forces contradicted traditional U.S. conceptions of self-reliance, constitutional independence, and freedom of action.

Such concerns are hardly new, of course. During the fight over the League of Nations, William Jennings Bryan, Wilson's former secretary of state, worried that the Covenant might portend "the surrender of the right of each League nation to control its own military and naval policy." Bryan declared that "no nation, however small, could for a moment consider such an abandonment of sovereignty."[7] For the past century Americans have debated how much sovereign autonomy—or even authority—to exchange for the potential gains of multilateral security cooperation. This dilemma becomes ever more acute as American security and that of other nations grow increasingly interdependent.

Early in its history, the republic could try to quarantine itself from global "bads," confident that what happened in the world outside would stay there— as they now say of Las Vegas.[8] No longer. Revolutions in telecommunications, trade, and transport connect distant lands more closely every day. New networks of malevolent nonstate actors, with potential access to technologies of mass destruction, accentuate global risks. Today, terrorists bent on violent jihad can board commercial airliners. Tomorrow, smugglers might conceal a radiological or even nuclear device in a shipping container bound for a U.S. port. The contemporary world looks less like Vegas, in other words, and the United States now seems more like Rome, to which all roads lead.

Navigating and securing this interconnected world raises quandaries for the United States, accentuating long-standing dilemmas about how to prioritize among U.S. sovereignty-as-authority, sovereignty-as-autonomy, and sovereignty-as-influence. For as much as Americans might yearn for all three simultaneously, the current global threat environment does not always permit it.

On the one hand, the rising number and growing severity of transnational threats creates incentives for the United States to cooperate with others in negotiating new rules of the road and standards of behavior, as well as mechanisms to coordinate action. In a world of security interdependence, purely unilateral and even bilateral efforts are often inadequate, as well as unsustainable. To exert its sovereignty-as-influence—in this case, to advance its national security—the United States must be more open to multilateralism.

On the other hand, the United States retains an obvious interest, when it comes to such pivotal security choices, in preserving both its sovereignty-as-authority and its sovereignty-as-autonomy: It wants to be the final judge and jury in these grave decisions, and it wants to keep as much freedom of action as it can, particularly given its many global responsibilities.

This quandary is front and center in several ongoing U.S. policy debates, which are the subject of this chapter. To begin with, what authority should the United States grant the UNSC when it comes to legitimating America's use of force? Second, should the United States be prepared to act alone to put an end to rogue regimes that sponsor terrorism, pursue WMD, or commit atrocities? Third, under what circumstances, if any, should the United States allow its soldiers to serve under UN command in peace operations? Fourth, should the United States support intrusive international arms control regimes, even if those include stringent provisions for monitoring and verification of U.S. policies, capabilities, and facilities? Fifth, what multilateral commitments and constraints should the United States accept to secure the "global commons"—including the oceans, outer space, and cyberspace? Finally, when it does pursue multilateral security cooperation, what balance should the United States strike between formal collective security (via the UN), collective defense (especially through NATO), and ad hoc coalitions of the willing?

A long-standing justification for defending U.S. sovereign prerogatives in national security affairs is that world politics is ultimately a self-help system. When the chips are down, no country can count on international law or international organizations, much less an illusory "international community," to come to its defense.[9] The only reliable protection lies in amassing lots of power and pursuing national interests ruthlessly, while retaining complete sovereign authority over U.S. capabilities and maximum freedom of action (or sovereign autonomy) in using them.

As a presidential candidate, Donald J. Trump embraced his own hyper-sovereigntist logic, enunciating a U.S. national security vision that not only dismissed the United Nations but also belittled the transatlantic alliance and other U.S. defense pacts. Trump derided NATO as "obsolete" and depicted European and Asian allies as freeloaders on U.S. security guarantees and military might. He suggested that unless allies ponied up money and troops, the United States should be prepared to walk away, reneging on its treaty commitments. Trump's transactional approach—which continued after his election—reduced alliances to a protection racket, implying that the U.S. goal was to secure the best possible bilateral deal with each ally.[10]

For a professional dealmaker like Trump, such a hardboiled approach has an obvious appeal. But in its most dogmatic guise, the self-help doctrine is hardly realistic, for it fails to see the world as it is or U.S. options as they are. Today's transnational threats—whether terrorism, nuclear proliferation, or pandemic disease—seldom lend themselves to purely unilateral solutions. Self-reliance may sound noble, but it is often futile, posing an unenviable choice of doing everything oneself, at exorbitant cost and with uncertain results, or doing nothing at all. The image of Uncle Sam as Lone Ranger also ignores just how much the United States already relies on others to promote its own security.

Consider the "global war on terrorism" since 9/11. Yes, the initial, dramatic U.S. successes in Afghanistan, including toppling the Taliban and ejecting al Qaeda, were accomplished primarily through U.S. force of arms, as the United States insisted on complete liberty of action. But that phase was short-lived. The subsequent U.S. counterterror campaign was overwhelmingly multilateral, involving scores of governments and international institutions working to clamp down on illicit financing, expose terror cells, interdict foreign fighters, lock down WMD, and combat violent extremism. Drone strikes and commando raids may generate headlines, but as Bruce Jentleson notes, it is on "lower-profile fronts such as intelligence sharing, border security, economic sanctions, and law enforcement" that the struggle will be won or lost. In these endeavors, "The freedom of action given up by acting multilaterally tends to be outweighed by the capacity to achieve shared objectives."[11]

As interdependence deepens, incentives for multilateral security cooperation will only grow. In terms of the "sovereignty triangle," the United States will need to move from autonomy toward influence, exchanging some (notional) freedom of action for increased sway over outcomes that enhance its security. Before choosing to trade freedom of action for influence, of course, U.S. officials must be confident that the anticipated benefits—for example, increased burden sharing, reciprocal obligations, and greater legitimacy for U.S. purposes—will outweigh any sacrifices, including constraints on U.S. behavior.

At the same time, the United States cannot afford to place all of its trust in collective security through the UN. While the UN can ameliorate many threats—and retains unparalleled international legitimacy—it has never lived up to the 1945 dreams of its architects and remains a fragile and incomplete foundation for world order. Meanwhile the United States, for all its own challenges, remains the single most important determinant of international peace and regional stability. The task for U.S. elected leaders and policymakers is to reconcile these two parallel security orders: the world of formal multilateral organizations, grounded in the UN Charter, and the U.S.-centered framework of alliances and less formal partnerships, based on American power and shared interests and ideals.[12]

Today, the most relevant national security debate is not over going it alone or with others but over the merits of alternative forms of multilateralism. Here there is room for creative thinking. The United States needs to balance its reliance on standing, formal international organizations like the United Nations, narrower alliances like NATO, and flexible, purpose-built "minilateral" coalitions of the capable, interested, and like-minded.[13]

PASSING THE "GLOBAL TEST"? THE UN CHARTER AND THE USE OF FORCE

As Senator Kerry learned to his dismay in 2004, few sovereignty debates are as sensitive as those pertaining to military force, where the potential collision between international authority and national authority is real. The central question is: Should the United States be required to obtain Security Council approval before resorting to armed force? As a legal matter, the answer is yes. With the sole exception of self-defense (Article 51), UN member states may employ such coercion only if the Council authorizes it under Chapter 7 of the UN Charter. Otherwise, military action is illegal, regardless of whether its defenders argue that it is "legitimate" (as many did in the Kosovo intervention).

Those, at any rate, are the formal rules. Other than chastity vows, it is hard to think of another injunction so commonly flouted. The United States, certainly, has never accepted these Charter constraints as the final word. Since World War II, the United States has used significant military force on at least twenty occasions, not including covert action (for example, in Guatemala and Nicaragua) or material support to friendly governments (such as El Salvador) or rebel forces (such as Angola's). In fewer than half of those cases did the United States obtain prior, explicit UNSC authorization. The most prominent case of nonauthorization is the decade-long U.S. involvement in the Vietnam War.[14]

Since the end of the Cold War, Republican and Democratic presidents alike have ordered major military action both with and without UNSC approval. George H. W. Bush and Barack Obama obtained such authorization before the 1991 Gulf War and the 2011 intervention in Libya, respectively, while Bill Clinton and George W. Bush proceeded without it in, respectively, the 1999 NATO bombing campaign in Kosovo and the 2003 invasion of Iraq. In April 2017 Donald Trump unilaterally ordered a barrage of fifty-nine cruise missiles against Syrian air installations in response to the government of Bashar al-Assad's use of chemical weapons against civilians in rebel-held areas.[15] All U.S. presidents, moreover, insist that their constitutional authority to defend the American people trumps the UN Charter in legitimating the U.S. use of force.

Given this track record, cynics might well dismiss the Charter as a fig leaf to conceal Thucydides' dirty secret that the powerful do what they want (and the weak what they must). And yet one cannot but be impressed by America's "willingness to incur significant costs in terms of time, policy compromise, and side-payments, simply to obtain the stamp of approval from the UN Security Council," as Eric Voeten writes.[16] This suggests at a minimum that U.S. officials believe that securing a multilateral endorsement carries value. Also noteworthy is the energy the United States puts into justifying military actions not authorized by the UNSC as being consistent with Charter principles such as the preservation of democracy, protection of human rights, and right to self-determination.

American leaders have practical international and domestic reasons to seek UNSC endorsement, as well as to justify American unilateralism when they fail to secure it. Most UN member states consider the Security Council the only entity competent to authorize military intervention, and their ultimate diplomatic support may be contingent on whether the United States at least tries the UN route. Likewise, a majority of American citizens believe that the UNSC has unique legitimacy to authorize military intervention. (By contrast, Americans overwhelmingly oppose using U.S. military force without a UNSC mandate, except in self-defense or to protect vital U.S. interests.)[17]

Still, hard-core sovereigntists argue that seeking UN authorization is unwise, unrealistic, and unnecessary. It is imprudent because collective security is a mirage, based on a fantasy that independent states will perceive threats identically and assume similar risks and burdens to combat them. It is impractical because it ignores the unparalleled freedom of action the United States requires as the ultimate custodian of world order. And it is extraneous because the only authorities needed to legitimate the U.S. use of military force are the elected representatives of the American people, who require no global by-your-leave. As John Bolton puts it, "The Constitution trumps international law."[18]

Despite these sovereigntist admonitions, U.S. presidents typically seek and welcome the UN's imprimatur for major military action, seeing it as political asset in securing diplomatic and material support for U.S.-led interventions— as well as a way to bring on board some skeptical members of Congress. In their joint memoir, George H. W. Bush and his national security adviser Brent

Scowcroft recount the lengths they went to in 1990–91 to obtain Security Council authorization to reverse Iraq's invasion of Kuwait. "We . . . believed that the United States should not go it alone, that a multilateral approach was better," they explain. "Building an international response led us immediately to the United Nations, which could provide a cloak of acceptability to our efforts and mobilize world opinion behind the principles we wished to project."[19]

Like Father, Like Son?

What an apparent contrast, at least at first glance, with George W. Bush's own decision twelve years later to invade Iraq without an explicit UNSC mandate. White House spokesman Ari Fleischer explained the forty-third president's thinking in response to a skeptical question from the press at a news conference on March 10, 2003, nine days before the United States launched Operation Iraqi Freedom. "You seem to be equating an ad hoc coalition that the United States has been able to form around one issue and one task with permanent bodies like the UN and NATO, which have charters formed by treaties," a reporter noted. "Does the President believe that international affairs can be conducted entirely through ad hoc bodies like the one he's putting [together]?" To which Fleischer responded, "The point I'm making here is that there are many ways to form international coalitions. The United Nations Security Council is but one of them."[20]

And yet one should not overstate the divergence between the two Bushes, since the father was also prepared to bypass the United Nations. "We would ask the Council to act only if we knew in advance we had the backing of most of the Arab bloc and we were fairly certain we had the necessary votes," the elder Bush and Scowcroft recall. "If at any point it became clear we could not succeed, we would back away from a UN effort and cobble together an independent multinational effort built on friendly Arab and allied participation."[21] In other words, as Clinton would later do in Kosovo and Bush's son in Iraq, George H. W. Bush would assemble a purpose-built grouping that might lack the UNSC's legal authority but still lend a surrogate multilateral legitimacy to the undertaking.

Going forward, the United States should work assiduously to secure explicit UN Security Council authorization, especially for major military action. Beyond being preferred by the American people, the UN route promises greater international legitimacy as well as diplomatic and material support. At the same time, as former deputy national security adviser James B. Steinberg explains, the United States should resist making the UNSC the "final arbiter" of the U.S. use of force.[22] The hard reality is that America will sometimes perceive threats, assume obligations, and define interests very differently from the other permanent members of the Security Council, not least China and Russia. There may be occasions when its use of force is legitimate and warranted, even if international lawyers deem it illegal.

But if the United States must retain the sovereign right to act in its own interests, it should employ this prerogative sparingly, to avoid setting precedents that others can easily exploit—with the result that the exception eventually becomes the rule. In addition, while privileging U.S. sovereign authority can maximize U.S. autonomy, it may also leave the United States in a weaker position to garner burden sharing, as well as legitimacy, for its purposes, resulting in less U.S. influence over long-term outcomes.

Beyond the matter of UNSC authorization, American policymakers should consider how broad they want the corresponding intervening coalition to be, as well as what influence they want to give partners in shaping and implementing its war strategy. Since the Cold War's end, the U.S. interventions pursuant to UNSC authorization have sometimes involved many other states (see the Gulf War in 1991), but at other times elicited only token contributions (for example, Somalia, 1992–93). The United States has also led interventions without UNSC authorization, both on its own (as in Panama, 1990) and alongside others, whether through NATO (Kosovo, 1999) or a "minilateral" coalition (Iraq, 2003).[23]

The case for America intervening through a narrow coalition is stronger when the threat is urgent, leaving little time for protracted multilateral diplomacy; when the situation requires military firepower that only the United States and a handful of others possess; or when the intervention requires likemindedness. By contrast, the scholar Sarah Kreps writes, intervening with a greater number of participants can make more sense if the time horizon is long, resource requirements are high, and diplomatic (or local) sensitivities require it.[24] Finally, the United States may wish to preserve maximum autonomy during early, heavy war-fighting phases, as in the first weeks of the post–9/11 Afghanistan campaign, before transitioning to less-intensive but protracted stabilization operations.

Contingent Sovereignty—for Others

Whereas the United States vigorously defends its own sovereign right to use force when its national interests warrant, it is far from circumspect about violating the sovereignty of *other* nations that it perceives as threats to U.S. national interests or regional order. While this has long been true—not least in hemispheric relations—recent U.S. interventionism rests on new justifications. Since the 1990s the United States has contributed by word and deed to a nascent doctrine of "contingent sovereignty." This holds that a state jeopardizes its expectation of nonintervention in two situations: first, when it fails to meet fundamental obligations to its own citizens, notably by committing mass atrocities against them; and second, when it fails to discharge baseline obligations to other countries, for instance by sponsoring (or harboring) terrorists or pursuing WMD in contravention of treaty commitments.[25]

The first impulse behind contingent sovereignty is an ethical one, namely revulsion over mass atrocity crimes. Although the nonintervention and human rights thrusts of the UN Charter have long been in tension, these frictions ignited during the 1990s, as murderous regimes or their proxies slaughtered civilians in Rwanda, Bosnia, Kosovo, and East Timor. In 1999, UN secretary general Kofi Annan spoke for many when he declared that state sovereignty could not constitute a license to commit mass murder. Subsequently, a Canadian-sponsored International Commission on Intervention and State Sovereignty helped crystallize a new international norm, the "Responsibility to Protect" (R2P). It holds that each UN member state has an unconditional obligation to protect its citizens from genocide, war crimes, crimes against humanity, and ethnic cleansing. And when any state fails to protect (or makes war on) its citizens, this responsibility devolves to the international community, which may take corrective actions—including military intervention.[26] The R2P concept helped shift global conversations away from fruitless debates over a "right to intervention" and toward an affirmative doctrine of "sovereignty as responsibility." UN member states unanimously endorsed R2P at the World Summit in September 2005.

The second, prudential impulse behind contingent sovereignty is the threat to global security posed by catastrophic terrorism. The nightmare scenario of a "nuclear 9/11" convinced George W. Bush, and Barack Obama after him, that sovereignty cannot be a shield behind which terrorists operate with impunity. Where possible, the United States would cooperate with vulnerable governments to eliminate terrorist threats. But where states had ceased to exist (as in Somalia), lacked control over "ungoverned spaces" (as in Yemen), or played a double game (as in Pakistan), the United States would take direct action to eliminate terrorists—including, most famously, al Qaeda leader Osama bin Laden in 2011.

Exploiting advances in drone technology, the Bush administration began launching "targeted killings" of suspected terrorists, beginning (according to news reports) in Yemen in November 2002. President Obama dramatically accelerated drone strikes, launching an estimated 500 through January 2016—ten times the number his predecessor authorized.[27] For U.S. national security officials, drones were irresistible. They permitted the United States to pierce the shell of sovereignty in target countries, but without incurring the high political costs of inserting visible U.S. troops. The strikes were surgical enough to deny plausibly (at least for a time), and they carried no immediate risk of U.S. casualties. At the same time, their champions overlooked the ethical and legal quandaries of remote-control assassination, mounting evidence that such strikes often killed innocent victims, and the likelihood that they would prove a powerful recruiting tool for violent jihadists.

Together, the resurgence of atrocity crimes and the rise of mass-casualty terrorism strained long-standing UN rules on nonintervention. And yet the notion of contingent sovereignty also raised difficult practical and normative questions about threshold criteria, right authority, and the responsibilities of interveners. What severity must be reached before atrocity crimes or terrorist activities warrant intervention? What entity should determine when that line is crossed? What limits must intervening nations observe?

These questions have no easy answers. Under the Charter, the Security Council alone has the legal standing to authorize external intervention against a recalcitrant state. But the United Nations has no independent intelligence capacity to help inform UNSC decisions, no explicit oversight mechanism to ensure that intervening powers stick to UN mandates, and only limited capability to restore order in postconflict countries.

All of these dilemmas—concerning trigger mechanisms, right authority, follow-through, and accountability—came to the fore in the NATO-led intervention in Libya in 2011. Within the Security Council, members debated the scale and trajectory of violence, ultimately agreeing with Hillary Clinton that, "left unchecked, [Libyan leader Moammar] Qaddafi will commit unspeakable atrocities." The resulting UNSC Resolution 1973 authorized a "no-fly zone" and "all necessary means" to protect civilians. But as the intervention proceeded, Russia, China, the African Union, and others accused the West of hijacking the R2P norm to pursue regime change. Moscow and Beijing later cited this bitter experience when they blocked a vigorous Security Council's response to the slaughter that unfolded in Syria over the next several years.[28]

MULTILATERAL PEACE OPERATIONS AND AMERICAN SOVEREIGNTY

Tensions between U.S. sovereignty and collective security have also arisen in the context of UN multilateral peace operations. These often messy contingencies raise tricky choices that touch on both U.S. sovereignty-as-authority and U.S. sovereignty-as-autonomy. Practical questions include: What military capabilities should the United States—and other UN members—place at the UN's disposal when the UNSC authorizes peace enforcement or peacekeeping missions? What command and control arrangements should govern the deployment of such assets? What limits should the United States place on its own involvement?

Late in World War II, U.S., British, and Soviet negotiators at Dumbarton Oaks had wrestled with how to provide the United Nations—an assemblage of sovereign states—with sufficient military force to maintain international security. In lieu of creating a standing UN army, the conferees agreed that member states should designate standby forces and make them available on request to the United Nations. The Charter (Article 47) also anticipated that the UNSC's permanent members would establish a joint Military Staff Committee to command and control these forces. As events transpired, they never created this body.[29]

Although it is tempting to blame this failure on Cold War divisions, the American decision not to revisit this option after the Berlin Wall fell suggests deeper U.S. misgivings about placing control in the hands of the United Nations. During the Gulf War, Washington insisted that U.S. military officers command the UN-authorized coalition, just as they had in the Korean War (1950–1953). "We opposed allowing the UN to organize and run a war," Bush and Scowcroft explain. "It was important to reach out to the rest of the world, but even more to keep the strings of control tightly in our hands."[30]

The question of whether U.S. troops should *ever* be placed under foreign command remains politically explosive at home, despite a clear historical record of U.S. flexibility in practice. In the Revolutionary War, General George Washington placed 2,000 American militiamen under a French general, the Marquis de Lafayette. During the twentieth century, U.S. soldiers reported to foreign commanders no fewer than seventeen times, including during both world wars, Operation Desert Storm, and NATO's Kosovo Force. At the same time, as the Congressional Research Service notes, "U.S. soldiers serving in multinational commands always retain their ultimate allegiance to the United States of America: they wear their national uniforms and insignia; and no oaths are given to other powers or organizations." Even while under the *operational* command of foreign officers, U.S. soldiers remain bound to defend the U.S. Constitution and still subject to the National Command Authority that flows from the president.[31]

Despite these safeguards, American nationalists rebel at the notion that U.S. soldiers might temporarily report to commanders operating under a flag other than the Stars and Stripes. Some of these objections reflect prudential concerns. Skeptics doubt that the United States ought to entrust the lives of its soldiers to foreign officers who might lack adequate judgment or training. Others fear that a U.S. presence could make UN contingents tempting targets for terrorists or other adversaries. But the high passion the topic arouses hints at deeper worries, notably "concerns about whether the United States cedes any degree of sovereignty when it participates in collective security mechanisms."[32]

The issue erupted during the 1990s, when the United States increased its involvement in post–Cold War multidimensional UN peace operations. In October 1993 a team of U.S. Army Rangers supporting the second phase of the UN-led peace operation in Somalia (UNOSOM II) was ambushed in Mogadishu, with eighteen killed and several soldiers' corpses dragged through the streets in what became known as the "Black Hawk Down" episode. Although the soldiers were operating under U.S. command, Republicans blamed the UN for the disaster and the Clinton administration also scapegoated the world body, fostering the impression that UN commanders were at fault.

In the debacle's aftermath, the White House formulated a more restrictive doctrine for peace operations. It insisted, "The President retains and will never relinquish command authority over U.S. forces." Henceforth, "Any large scale participation of U.S. forces in a major peace enforcement mission that is likely to involve combat should ordinarily be conducted under U.S. command and operational control or through competent regional organizations such as NATO or ad hoc coalitions."[33]

Such reassurances fell on deaf ears on Capitol Hill. Six weeks before the 1994 midterm elections, Minority Leader Newt Gingrich (R.-Ga.), hoping to deliver the House of Representatives to the GOP for the first time in forty years, persuaded Republican colleagues to sign a "Contract with America." It included a pledge to pass legislation mandating "no U.S. troops under UN command."[34] In 1995 President Clinton vetoed a defense authorization bill containing similar language.

That same year Michael G. New, a U.S. Army Specialist serving in the UN Preventive Deployment (UNPREDEP) mission in Macedonia, made headlines when he refused an order from his operational commander, a Finnish general, to wear the designated blue beret and UN patch on his uniform. Spec. New "argued that he owes allegiance to the United States, not to the

U.N., that the insignia are not authorized, that the chain of command was not constitutional, and that the operation was not legal." New's case quickly became a cause célèbre in conservative circles. House Majority Leader Tom Delay (R-Tex.) quickly drafted a bill, cosponsored by one hundred colleagues, to "prevent the president from forcing American soldiers to wear the uniform of the United Nations."[35] Despite these efforts, New was court-martialed and convicted.

Still, resistance to placing U.S. soldiers under foreign command has endured. In 2015, Representative Mike Rogers (R-Ala.) introduced the latest version of the American Sovereignty Restoration Act (H.R. 1205)—the first having been introduced by Representative Ron Paul (R-Tex.) in 2001. Beyond terminating U.S. membership in the UN, it would prohibit participation by any U.S. service member in—as well as U.S. funding for—any UN peacekeeping operation.[36] Such sovereignty anxieties help explain the paltry U.S. participation in UN peace operations. In April 2016, Americans accounted for only 74 out of 104,000 soldiers, military experts, and police deployed in UN missions worldwide, a figure that left the United States tied with Namibia as the seventy-fifth largest contributor.

Such a low profile can be defended, given the broader U.S. role in providing global security, as well as the risk that U.S. involvement would be controversial or create tempting targets. Still, U.S. troop contributions are trifling alongside those of China, which by 2016 was the eighth largest contributor to UN missions, with 3,042 personnel deployed.[37]

ARMS CONTROL AND AMERICAN SOVEREIGNTY

As chapter 4 argued, the voluntary U.S. decision to enter into a treaty is an exercise rather than abdication of sovereign authority. This is true even though treaties by design constrain national freedom of action. Arms control and disarmament agreements, for instance, limit U.S. sovereignty-as-autonomy as part of a sovereignty bargain. The United States agrees to forgo certain military options (related to weaponry, force structure, and defense posture, for example) in exchange for limiting other nations' ability to threaten America, thus gaining more sovereignty-as-influence. This is what Jeffrey Lewis of the Center for Nonproliferation Studies implies when he writes, "States that submit themselves to international norms and law have more sovereignty, not less."[38]

This is particularly true in the nuclear realm, where cooperation is the alternative to Armageddon. Six weeks before his assassination, President John F.

Kennedy delivered a sober message to the UN General Assembly. "The science of weapons and war has made us all . . . one world and one human race, with one common destiny," the president explained. "In such a world, absolute sovereignty no longer assures us of absolute security. The conventions of peace must pull abreast of the inventions of war."[39]

Fortunately, modern arms control and disarmament treaties typically include three features designed to *safeguard* state sovereignty. The first is the principle of state consent, which preserves sovereignty-as-authority. Each party must agree voluntarily to accept not only the treaty's initial terms but also any new obligations that the secretariat subsequently elaborates. "This requirement of concrete consent for any new rule," Mika Nishimura explains, "hinders the dynamic development of a multilateral framework, which would in return place a greater constraint on sovereignty," by usurping a state's authority to determine its own commitments.[40]

Second, arms control treaties preserve a measure of sovereignty-as-autonomy because they are founded on reciprocity. That is, treaty obligations are interdependent, or contingent on acceptable performance by other parties. When one party fails to comply, whether through cheating or incapacity, others have the right to restore balance. They can do so by imposing sanctions or otherwise punishing the offending state until it changes its behavior or, alternatively, by suspending or withdrawing from the treaty.

Finally, traditional arms control and disarmament conventions recognize each party's sovereign right to interpret its treaty obligations and to assess whether others are complying, rather than accept the judgments of an independent mechanism. Both the Partial Test Ban Treaty (PTBT) and the Nuclear Non-Proliferation Treaty (NPT) contain an explicit "auto-interpretation" clause, which reads: "Each State Party shall, in exercising its national sovereignty, have the right to withdraw from the Treaty if it decides that extraordinary events, related to the subject matter of this Treaty, have jeopardized the supreme interests of its country." Testifying to the Senate in 1963, Secretary of State Dean Rusk explained the significance of this clause: "Under this treaty we alone will decide whether extraordinary events have occurred and whether they jeopardize our supreme national interests. We need answer to no tribunal and to no authority other than our own consciences and requirements."[41]

Since 1945 the United States has become party to several major multilateral (as well as bilateral) arms control agreements, from the NPT to the BWC to the CWC (see table 5-1). Each required difficult sovereignty bargains, including accepting constraints on U.S. behavior in return for greater strategic stability, predictability, and reassurance.

To complement these formal conventions, the United States has also sponsored multiple informal, "minilateral" arrangements, ranging from the Proliferation Security Initiative (PSI) to the Nuclear Suppliers Group (see table 5-1). These frameworks entail specific commitments, but unlike treaties are not legally binding and permit significant flexibility. As such, they not only protect U.S. sovereignty-as-authority but also preserve greater U.S. sovereignty-as-autonomy—while still promising some sovereignty-as-influence over international outcomes. While they cannot replace formal treaties, of course, they represent a useful complement to them. And being more attentive to sovereign prerogatives, they tend to raise fewer domestic hackles.

A dyed-in-the-wool "sovereigntist" might well dismiss this tangle of commitments as a surrender of American independence, reflecting naive faith in parchment promises. But enlightened self-interest offers a more persuasive explanation for U.S. conduct. Successive U.S. administrations (and the Senate in the case of treaties) have calculated that a measured, voluntary, and reciprocal delegation of sovereign autonomy is the best—and perhaps only—way to address the relevant threat.

Consider the NPT, which came into effect in 1970 and remains the cornerstone of efforts to control the spread of nuclear weapons. It rests on three pillars: nonacquisition of nuclear weapons by states that did not have them in 1970; access for all countries to nuclear energy for peaceful uses; and eventual disarmament by nuclear weapons states (NWS). In the early Cold War years U.S. officials feared the number of NWS would rise to dozens. The NPT helped prevent this. Today there are just nine nuclear weapons states, and only one party to the treaty—North Korea—has acquired a weapon since 1970. The United States, meanwhile, has reduced its own nuclear stockpile from more than 26,000 weapons to approximately 4,600 in 2015.[42]

Informal frameworks, too, can include reciprocal commitments in U.S. interests. The Container Security Initiative (CSI) is one such arrangement. Created under President George W. Bush, CSI is a partnership among some thirty trading nations designed to prevent terrorists and other illicit actors from exploiting shipping containers loaded and unloaded at the world's busiest seaports. According to U.S. Customs and Border Protection (CBP), "CBP's 58 operational CSI ports now prescreen over 80 percent of all maritime containerized cargo destined to the United States."[43] In public documents CBP lauds CSI for extending the U.S. border outward, allowing U.S. officials to protect U.S. citizens by walking docks from Singapore to Rotterdam. More fascinating, from a U.S. sovereignty perspective, is the (less publicized) fact that partner countries enjoy the same privilege in the United States. As the State Department

Table 5-1. *Major Multilateral Arms Control and Nonproliferation Treaties and Initiatives the United States Has Joined*

Treaty or initiative	Description	Implementing body
Treaty on the Non-Proliferation of Nuclear Weapons	The five recognized nuclear weapon states agree to disarm, states without nuclear weapons agree to not acquire them, and all states parties may use nuclear energy for peaceful purposes.	International Atomic Energy Agency
Biological Weapons Convention	States agree to not develop, acquire, or use biological weapons and to destroy any stockpiles.	Implementation Support Unit
Chemical Weapons Convention	States agree to not develop, acquire, or use chemical weapons and to destroy any stockpiles.	Organization for the Prohibition of Chemical Weapons
Nuclear Suppliers Group	Members set export control guidelines for transfers of nuclear technologies and materials to prevent the proliferation of nuclear weapons.	None
Wassenaar Arrangement	Members set export control guidelines for transfers of conventional arms and dual-use technologies and goods to promote international security and stability.	None
Hague Code of Conduct against Ballistic Missile Proliferation	States commit to principles to curb the proliferation of WMD-capable ballistic missiles and promote transparency in their missile development and testing.	None
Australia Group	Members set export controls guidelines to ensure exports do not contribute to the development of chemical or biological weapons.	None
Proliferation Security Initiative	States voluntarily interdict shipments of illicit WMD-related materials.	None
Container Security Initiative	High-risk containers are screened at participating ports before they are shipped to U.S. ports.	None
Nuclear Security Summits	Participating states take measures individually or collectively to improve nuclear security and prevent nuclear terrorism.	None
UN Security Council Resolution 1540	All UN member states must take measures to prevent nonstate actors from developing, acquiring, or using nuclear, chemical, or biological weapons.	1540 Committee
Global Partnership against the Spread of WMD	G-8 members take a variety of measures to prevent WMD proliferation and terrorism.	None

Table 5-1. *(continued)*

Treaty or initiative	Description	Implementing body
Convention on the Physical Protection of Nuclear Material (and amendment)	States must protect nuclear facilities and materials against physical theft and damage, and take measures to detect and punish offenses relating to nuclear materials.	International Atomic Energy Agency
Global Initiative to Combat Nuclear Terrorism	States strengthen their capacity to prevent, detect, and respond to nuclear terrorism through multilateral activities.	None

explained in 2004, "A reciprocal program, CSI also authorizes participating countries to station their customs officers at U.S. seaports to screen cargo that is exported to their countries via ocean-going containers." Accordingly, "Japanese customs officers are working at the port of Los Angeles/Long Beach," even as "Canada has customs personnel stationed at the ports of Newark and Seattle."[44]

The most dramatic instance of the United States trading sovereign autonomy (and even a measure of sovereign authority) for effective arms control may be the 1997 Chemical Weapons Convention (CWC). The first international treaty to outlaw the possession, stockpiling, and use of an entire category of weapons, the CWC requires all states parties (189 as of 2016) to declare their chemical weapons holdings and production facilities and to submit and carry out plans to destroy both. The Organization for the Prohibition of Chemical Weapons (OPCW), a permanent implementing body based in The Hague, ensures that states actually fulfill these obligations. Indeed, the OPCW's Technical Secretariat is authorized to conduct highly intrusive, short-notice challenge inspections of any country's facilities, "anytime, anywhere," with no right of refusal by a state party.[45]

The effort to control chemical weapons is daunting, given the so-called dual-use dilemma. That is, many subcomponents of chemical weapons, as well as the machines that fabricate and deliver them, have legitimate industrial applications. Globally, there are tens, perhaps hundreds, of thousands of facilities where precursor and toxic chemicals could be diverted into illicit weapons programs.

To get a handle on this complex challenge, CWC parties have accepted treaty provisions that remove or at least qualify the three (aforementioned) sovereignty protections typical of arms control agreements: interdependent obligations, auto-interpretation, and concrete consent.[46] First, any state that challenges another for breaching the CWC is not permitted to suspend its own participation. Instead, it must allow the OPCW to respond. Second, states must accept the OPCW's interpretations and evaluations. Indeed, the Technical Secretariat's decisions "are not reviewable by any domestic governmental body."[47] Third, the OPCW includes provisions for majority voting within the Conference of the States Parties, which can in principle make binding rules without explicit consent of all members. To be sure, the CWC includes as an ultimate safeguard the right to withdraw. Still, it clearly intrudes on parties' sovereign authority (not just autonomy), as well as their territorial control, since OPCW inspectors can (in theory) walk into any suspect facility.

Despite these provisions, the United States Senate—with a Republican majority, no less—approved the treaty in 1997, by a 74–26 vote.[48] Supporters understood that voluntarily ceding some U.S. sovereignty was required to get others to do the same and thus restrict the spread of dangerous, inhumane weapons. Such is the price of global security in a world of potentially catastrophic cross-border threats.

In a 2003 speech, State Department policy planning chief Richard N. Haass explained the rationale for U.S. accession: "Having already foresworn chemical weapons, we have little to lose from inspections. And we have a great deal to gain from a CWC that helps us to verify compliance by 140 other signatories and ostracize governments—like Saddam Hussein's—that continue to resist the abolition of these horrific weapons."[49]

The CWC proved its worth in 2012, after Syrian President Bashar al-Assad used chemical weapons on civilians in areas held by rebels seeking to overthrow him. For its subsequent work to remove chemical arms from Syria, the OPCW earned the Nobel Peace Prize.[50]

Reasons for Opposition to Arms Control

American sovereigntists offer several generic objections to arms control treaties. One is that they limit America's freedom to defend its national security. "Long-term limits on arms, by requiring far-reaching constraints on building and deploying weapons systems, strike at the very core of national sovereignty: the ability to defend ourselves," write Yoo and Bolton. As a case in point, they allege that the CTBT would prevent modernization of the U.S. nuclear arsenal, casting doubt on its reliability and undermining deterrence. Second, sovereigntists worry that America, which respects laws, will fulfill its obligations whereas cheaters like Russia, which has "violated many of its arms-control treaty commitments," will play the United States for a sucker.[51]

Third, sovereigntists worry that arms control treaties will expand White House authorities at the expense of Congress, allowing progressive-minded U.S. administrations to interpret treaty ambiguities expansively, in a manner that conservatives consider reckless. Along these lines, the Heritage Foundation's Theodore Bromund warned in 2012 that the proposed Arms Trade Treaty (ATT) would jeopardize "the sovereignty of the United States" by handing Obama administration officials "a blank check" in interpreting the treaty.[52]

Fourth, critics allege that some arms control treaties endanger U.S. constitutional liberties. In October 2013, 181 members of the House sent a letter to President Obama objecting that one provision of the ATT, which allowed it to be amended by just three-quarters of its member states, would "steadily subject the U.S. to the influence of internationally-defined norms, a process that would impinge on our national sovereignty." Such a prospect would "violate the right of the American people, under the Constitution, to freely govern themselves," including by exercising their Second Amendment rights to bear arms. As National Rifle Association president Wayne LaPierre told Fox News, Americans "just don't want the UN to be acting as a global nanny with a global permission slip stating whether they can own a gun or not. It cheapens our rights as American citizens, and weakens our sovereignty."[53]

These generic sovereigntist objections are unpersuasive. The first—that such treaties inordinately impinge on U.S. freedom of action—ignores the reciprocal nature of the obligations and the sovereignty safeguards the United States retains if it discovers parties to be cheating—something that the United States possesses the technical means to do. Likewise, specific complaints that the CTBT would hinder the reliability of the U.S. nuclear stockpile are unconvincing. What the CTBT *would* do is strengthen the international taboo against nuclear testing—an important step in preventing the further spread of nuclear weapons—as well as bolstering the world's capacity to monitor nuclear tests by rogue states like North Korea. The fear of an executive branch power grab is also not credible. Given legislative powers of oversight of U.S. treaty commitments, as well as powers of the purse over their implementation, Congress has instruments at its disposal to prevent mission creep.

What really worries conservatives is that a progressive president might pursue his or her foreign policy preferences rather than theirs. But the shoe is often on the other foot when it comes to partisan control of branches of the U.S. government, and the electorate has regular opportunities to weigh in on the country's direction. None of this is to argue that all potential multilateral arms control agreements deserve to be ratified—or that they offer a panacea to the problem they purport to address. It is merely to conclude that most common sovereignty-based objections do not withstand scrutiny.

Reconciling Sovereignty and Arms Control

Most important, arms control skeptics ignore that the spread of technologies of mass destruction requires changes in how Americans conceive of—and defend—their national sovereignty. Among the most common justification for rejecting multilateral agreements is that they tie America's hands. But such arguments are persuasive only if the proposed agreement is unlikely to achieve its objectives—or if the United States can better ensure its own security by retaining complete freedom of action. If not, sacrificing some sovereignty-as-autonomy may be a price worth paying if it engenders restraint as well as encourages cooperation from others in containing the world's most dangerous threats.[54]

Preserving U.S. and global security in an age of WMD will require unprecedented levels of international cooperation—and an acknowledgment by sovereign states that their mutual vulnerability implies mutual obligations. All national governments retain the inherent authority—even duty—to preserve their internal ("homeland") security. But "responsible sovereignty [also] requires all states to be accountable for their actions that have impacts beyond their borders," as Bruce Jones, Carlos Pascual, and Stephen Stedman write.[55] These state obligations include opening themselves up to external scrutiny in the form of monitoring schemes to verify their compliance with commitments, as well as containing injurious "spillovers" that might otherwise emanate from their territories.[56]

To be compatible with sovereignty-as-authority, international regimes to control WMD must be based on the principle of consent. That is, states must agree voluntarily to be bound by any new rules and standards of behavior. At the same time, as former secretary of homeland security Michael Chertoff insists, states must be held accountable for actions that injure other nations, in a global extension of "the legal principle of nuisance."[57]

AMERICAN SOVEREIGNTY AND THE GLOBAL COMMONS

Much like they can enhance the U.S. ability to combat transnational threats, sovereignty bargains can also help the United States secure the "global commons." This fancy term denotes those physical (as well as virtual) spaces upon which all countries depend for their security and prosperity, but which are not under the exclusive jurisdiction of any single state. Three of the most important are the oceans, outer space, and cyberspace. These collectively constitute the sinews of globalization, facilitating the integration of the world economy. In each domain America has long called the shots. But as its relative dominance fades, the United States must contemplate new trade-offs between autonomy and influence, sacrificing some freedom of action for more robust international agreement on the boundaries of legitimate state conduct. Failure by the United States to lead on these issues could encourage rising powers to offer alternative ordering principles and assert their own exclusive sovereign rights over parts of the global commons.[58]

At Sea

The United States has been an ardent defender of the freedom of the seas, which cover 71 percent of Earth's surface, from the very origins of the republic. And since 1945 the U.S. Navy has guaranteed an open ocean commons, in the process serving as the handmaiden of globalization. Today, 90 percent of global exports are carried on the world's container ships, and 40 percent of humanity lives within 100 kilometers of a coast. However, this historically open domain is now at risk as new maritime powers seek blue-water capabilities, try to deny others access to regional waters, and make controversial territorial claims.

In East Asia, China is embroiled in maritime disputes with multiple neighbors, including in the South China Sea, through which more than $5 trillion of commerce passes each year. China claims sovereignty over more than 80 percent of those waters. To back up these assertions, it has harassed the vessels of rival claimants, occupied and reclaimed multiple islets and reefs, and insisted that foreign warships obtain permission to transit those waters. Such actions risk precipitating a Sino-American confrontation, either in the form of a direct naval clash or as a result of reckless actions by a formal U.S. treaty ally (for example, the Philippines) or an emerging partner (for example, Vietnam).[59]

Meanwhile, geopolitical and economic competition has heated up in the warming Arctic, as littoral nations argue over extended continental shelves, the control of new sea routes, the definition of territorial waters, and rights to exploit undersea mineral and fossil fuel deposits. Russia has staked assertive claims to the Arctic Ocean seabed that extend under the North Pole. Such geopolitical maneuvering has raised fears of a regional arms race pitting Russia against the United States and its NATO allies.[60]

The single most important step the United States could take to strengthen a stable and open maritime commons is to strike a sovereignty bargain and finally accede to the UN Convention on the Law of the Sea (UNCLOS), the legal bedrock of contemporary ocean governance since it came into force in 1994. Among other provisions, UNCLOS recognizes national jurisdiction over "territorial seas" within twelve nautical miles from shore; establishes "exclusive economic zones" (EEZs) extending 200 miles from shore; and clarifies rules for transit through "international straits." It also provides a forum for resolving ocean-related disputes. To date, 162 countries (and the EU) have ratified UNCLOS. Unfortunately, the United States is not among them, despite staunch support for the treaty from the last five U.S. presidents, all living secretaries of state and defense, senior U.S. military leaders, the American business community, and environmental groups. The diehard opposition of sovereigntist senators and their allies outside Congress continues to block ratification. (As of August 2017, the Trump administration had not announced its position on UNCLOS.)

The U.S. failure to join not only reduces the effectiveness of UNCLOS but also undermines American national interests and global leadership.[61] Because it is absent—ironically due to sovereignty objections—the United States cannot take part in the last great partitioning of sovereign space on the planet. Neither can the United States serve on the International Seabed Authority, where (thanks to assertive U.S. diplomacy during treaty negotiations) it would enjoy an effective veto. The U.S. stance also undermines the credibility of U.S. commitments to a rules-based international order, while emboldening revisionist powers seeking to throw their regional weight around. In this case, a misguided defense of U.S. sovereignty-as-authority and sovereignty-as-autonomy is weakening U.S. sovereignty-as-influence, empowering potential adversaries to make sovereignty claims of their own in the world's oceans, while weakening the U.S. diplomatic hand in opposing them.

Lost in Space

Outer space is another domain that the United States has long dominated but where a "sovereignty bargain" is warranted. Like freedom of the seas, guaranteed access to outer space is a cornerstone of U.S. security and global prosperity. Space-based systems and satellites facilitate communications, commerce, and finance; enable navigation, transportation, and meteorological and scientific observations; and support intelligence gathering and military operations. American corporations and citizens use satellites and the global positioning system (GPS) to transfer money, ship goods, enjoy smartphone service, and map current locations and travel destinations.

Like the oceans, the outer space commons are becoming more "congested, contested, and competitive," in the words of former deputy secretary of defense William Lynn. The United States confronts renewed geopolitical competition from Russia and China, as well as new "space-faring nations" like India and Brazil. Assured access to space is endangered by the rapid accumulation of space junk and, more worrisome, by looming space weaponization. Unfortunately, the 1967 Outer Space Treaty has failed to keep pace with either technological developments or geopolitical trends. It lacks a dispute resolution mechanism, says nothing about space debris or congestion, and does not address interference with other countries' space assets. To avoid a "Wild West" scenario, the world needs agreement on new rules of the road that ensure secure access, promote responsible conduct, and prevent arms races in space. To achieve this result, all nations—including the United States—must accept some constraints on their freedom of action.[62]

To this end, the Obama administration promoted the goal of a nonbinding international code of conduct for outer space activities, designed to mitigate space debris, minimize collisions, and prohibit intentional interference with another country's orbiting space objects. But the prospect of even an informal agreement raised sovereigntist hackles. In February 2011, thirty-seven Republican senators declared themselves "deeply concerned" that the envisioned code would both constrain U.S. national security and infringe on congressional prerogatives. "Taken literally," Bolton and Yoo subsequently wrote in the *New York Times*, "it could limit freedom of action in space," including the development of space-based antiballistic missiles, the testing of antisatellite weapons, and the gathering of intelligence. "But the more far-reaching danger is that Mr. Obama is eroding American sovereignty on the sly" by seeking to bind the United States to an international arms control agreement without bothering with Senate approval. "American security must not be sacrificed for the false promise of global governance," they insisted.[63]

These concerns were overwrought. According to the Pentagon, nothing in the draft code would hinder either U.S. intelligence collection or missile defense. Moreover, most defense experts regarded a ban on space-based and antisatellite weapons as a reasonable concession to prevent an unpredictable arms race in outer space. Also, Bolton and Yoo's constitutional concerns were unwarranted, since voluntary adherence to a code of conduct is fully within the prerogative of the executive branch, and it could easily be reversed by a democratically elected successor. In sum, Bolton and Yoo played the sovereignty card both selectively and unpersuasively. Beyond their specious suggestion that a code would undermine U.S. sovereignty-as-authority, they ignored that its modest constraints on U.S. sovereignty-as-autonomy would advance U.S. sovereignty-as-influence by helping to stabilize an open outer space commons.

TECHNOLOGICAL CHANGE, SOVEREIGNTY, AND THE FUTURE OF VIOLENCE

In the decades to come, preserving national and global security will likely require the United States to cut even more sovereignty bargains. The primary driving forces will be the furious pace of technological change and the increasingly distributed nature of global threats.

Advances in technology have long driven global rule making. As new breakthroughs occur, governments naturally seek common standards to mitigate the risks of novel forms of interdependence.[64] But two things complicate the picture today. First, rapid technological change is leaving national governments and international organizations scrambling to regulate innovations with profound implications for global security, in areas from cyberspace to drones, robotics, nanotechnology, artificial intelligence, and synthetic biology. In each case, protecting American and international security will require the United States to cede some freedom of action for the promise of greater safety through international cooperation. Sovereignty-as-influence must trump sovereignty-as-autonomy. Second, contemporary global threats are distributed, emerging not just from the world's 200-odd sovereign states but increasingly from legions of nonstate actors able to acquire and exploit disruptive and potentially lethal technologies with or without the knowledge of government authorities. This trend raises profound challenges for the United States, among them how to hold private actors (as well as states) accountable for the cross-border consequences of actions they commit within foreign territorial jurisdictions.[65]

Cyberia

It may be in cyberspace where the need for and dilemmas of multilateral security cooperation are most acute. Because cyberspace transcends national jurisdictions and is (in principle) accessible to all, it is often grouped as one of the global commons. But unlike the maritime and outer space domains, it is of course a purely human construction—a digital world composed of interlocking information technology networks and infrastructures that permit massive data transmission through the Internet, telecommunications systems, computers, and mobile devices. In addition, its actual physical infrastructure (exchanges, servers, routers, etc.) is located primarily on sovereign territory and is owned by governments, corporations, or individuals. This leaves cyberspace especially susceptible to interference and fragmentation, even as it becomes ever more indispensable to global security, prosperity, and social interaction.[66] The dangers that an ungoverned cyberspace could pose to U.S. sovereignty were dramatically illustrated in 2016, when Russia orchestrated a massive effort to hack and influence the outcome of that year's U.S. presidential election.[67]

The United States, where the digital age began, remains the leading champion of an open, decentralized, and secure cyberdomain that remains largely in private hands. That vision is now under threat, however, as despotic regimes seek to restrict citizen use of the Internet, national governments prepare for cyberwars, criminals run rampant in the "dark web," and both public and private actors seek to distort truth to advance nefarious political agendas. Preserving an open, decentralized, and secure digital world will require enhanced multilateral agreement on rules to govern the Internet, mitigate cyberconflict, and crack down on cybercrime. It will also demand new norms to curtail outside interference in the electoral processes of sovereign countries, as well as standards for retaliation.

For decades, the primary regulatory institution "governing" cyberspace has been the Internet Corporation for Assigned Names and Numbers (ICANN), an independent nonprofit corporation licensed and loosely supervised, until September 30, 2016, by the U.S. Department of Commerce. The widespread perception of U.S. (and broader Western) "control" over the Internet has been a sore point for authoritarian and developing countries that would prefer to bring the Internet under intergovernmental purview.[68] Hoping to defuse global tensions in the wake of the 2013 revelations of America's massive, bulk surveillance of private global communications, President Obama announced in March 2014 that the United States would gradually relinquish U.S. stewardship of the Internet Assigned Numbers Authority (IANA), transferring responsibility for regulating the web's domain name system to the Internet's multistakeholder community. In taking this decision the administration was ceding symbolic sovereign autonomy to preserve the substance of an open global Internet.[69]

These steps outraged Republican lawmakers, who accused the Obama administration of "giv[ing] the Internet away to foreign governments," in the words of Senators Ted Cruz (Tex.), Mike Lee (Utah), and James Lankford (Okla.), and Representative Sean Duffy (Wisc.). The president, they said, had no right to unilaterally transfer (alleged) U.S. control of cyberspace to a murky, unaccountable organization. "I will continue to fight President Obama's irresponsible plan to surrender U.S. sovereignty of the Internet to the world's worst actors and to protect our Constitutional right to free speech," Duffy declared.[70] Of course, such statements ignored that the United States never actually "owned" the Internet. What the Obama administration did in engineering the IANA transfer was to enter into a sovereignty bargain: The United States ceded ICANN supervision to a body perceived as more neutral, so that it could preserve an invaluable international regime that retained a multistakeholder character, rather than risk the emergence of a heavy-handed, intergovernmental arrangement.

The United States confronts similar sovereignty trade-offs in its efforts to prevent cyberwarfare. In recent years dozens of governments, as well as the would-be Islamic State, have developed capabilities to infiltrate, disrupt, and even destroy critical digital infrastructure. Some governments, including Russia and North Korea, have launched or tacitly endorsed proxy attacks on adversaries. Such attacks are not easily deterred or punished, however, since it is often difficult to identify the perpetrators. And even when the attacker is known it may be unclear whether a state adversary orchestrated the attack—in which case it could be treated as an act of aggression—or it was the work of a private individual—and should be treated as a criminal act.

Beyond this attribution problem, the normative and legal framework governing cyberconflict has lagged. There is no global consensus on what constitutes a cyberattack, or on what targets are legitimate or responses permissible, including against ostensibly private entities operating in foreign jurisdictions. Countries continue to disagree over whether to extend existing laws of war to cover cyberwarfare, or how rules of cyberengagement should address the often fuzzy line between military and civilian targets. Should state-directed cyberinterference into another nation's electoral system and process, for example, be regarded as an act of war?

Mitigating cyberthreats requires greater multilateral cooperation—and innovative approaches to navigating cybersovereignty. High on the U.S. agenda must be negotiating new norms of state responsibility for offensive cyberoperations and cybercrime attacks launched from sovereign territory—as well as criteria for retaliation. States must build confidence by committing themselves to share information and manage crises jointly. They must also agree to preserve humanitarian fundamentals, for instance by not attacking the Internet's "root" servers or to conducting denial-of-service (DOS) attacks during cyberconflicts.[71]

Establishing new cyberspace rules is even more complicated when the threat emanates from malevolent nonstate actors operating from within the borders of other states. "As technologies of mass empowerment enable terrorism, cyberattacks, and other harmful acts from faraway lands," the legal scholars Benjamin Wittes and Gabriella Blum observe, "states' interests in reaching across their borders are becoming more, not less, pronounced."[72] The United States, for example, has a strong interest in going after foreign perpetrators of cybercrime and cyberterrorism. But there is no agreement on what responsibility "host" nations have to prevent attacks, or what jurisdictional right an aggrieved nation has to respond to them. Generally speaking, the international legal system remains skeptical of endorsing the unilateral, extraterritorial enforcement of one nation's laws in another country, without the consent of that second country. Moreover, purely punitive approaches ignore that even well-intentioned countries may lack the practical capacity to prevent their territory from being used as a base for cyberattacks.

Given these realities, U.S. and international efforts to combat cybercrime must include both incentives for national governments to take responsibility for policing their sovereign territory and capacity-building assistance to permit them to do so. One promising starting point might be to begin with informal arrangements, which are inherently less threatening from a sovereignty perspective, before moving on to treaty-based arrangements. For example, one might start with a multilateral body similar to the Financial Action Task Force, an informal, intergovernmental body created in 1989 to combat money laundering (and now terrorist financing). Under such an initiative, U.S. officials would start with like-minded governments, seeking to negotiate common national standards, regulations, and enforcement procedures regarding cybercrime. Ideally, the group would agree on a system of peer review and institute a process to "name and shame" noncooperating jurisdictions that fail to meet baseline commitments. Such a body could facilitate law enforcement cooperation in deterring and prosecuting cross-border cybercrime.[73]

Droning On

In other instances the United States has found itself at the cutting edge of the technological revolution in warfare, but must consider whether the weapons it is using (or developing) will ultimately undermine its own security, as other states and actors get ahold of them. Consider drones, which have become a preferred U.S. weapon in the battle against transnational terrorists in others' sovereign territories. The United States clearly values this freedom of action.

But it has struggled to develop a legal rationale for what are in essence assassinations by remotely controlled, pilotless aircraft. In the process, it has generated accusations that it is not only violating international humanitarian law and the laws of war but also courting international anarchy, as others will assuredly gain access to the same technology.[74] The solution is negotiating international norms, and eventually legal rules, even if these constrain some U.S. sovereign autonomy.

The rise of "killer robots," or fully autonomous lethal weapons, poses a similar predicament. While such systems may afford freedom of action, the inevitable diffusion of militarized robot technology to state and nonstate groups may well make the world, and Americans, less safe in the long run by lowering even more the threshold for violence. "Out of self-interest, then," as Denise Garcia argues, "the United States should want other countries to agree to preventively ban such weapons now."[75]

Finally, rapid advances in biotechnology could create catastrophic threats, by placing in the hands of private actors the capability to create new biological systems through the manipulation of existing—and the insertion of novel—genetic material. While the advent of synthetic biology brings enormous potential benefits for public health, it could also undermine global biosecurity by allowing rogue states and scientists to fabricate pathogens like smallpox. To mitigate these risks, the United States and other sovereign governments must work quickly to update the current patchwork of national and international regulations, including negotiating international codes of conduct.[76]

CONCLUSION

Today's complex global security environment challenges the long-standing U.S. desire to maximize its freedom of action in national security policy. The United States confronts a greater number of threats that are transnational in nature, requiring by definition multilateral responses that may constrain America's notional room for maneuver. To gain the benefits of cooperative security, the United States will need on occasion to accept some diminished sovereignty-as-autonomy (and, much more rarely, sovereign authority). At the same time, prudence requires that the United States retain certain sovereign prerogatives. The reality is that traditional geopolitical rivalries and regional dangers persist, and the United Nations, given its structural weaknesses, will not always protect vital U.S. national interests. Given its role as the guarantor of world order, the United States must retain the option of going it alone, or acting in narrow coalition, when its fundamental interests dictate.

This is especially true in matters involving the use of force. While the United States should work to win UN Security Council endorsement whenever possible, it should never make UNSC assent an absolute prerequisite for action. At the same time, the United States should beware of lowering the threshold for "preemptive" (actually "preventive") action.

When it comes to arms control and nonproliferation, the United States should remain open to making reasonable sovereignty bargains, where U.S. officials perceive that the anticipated gains of multilateral cooperation outweigh potential autonomy losses. Likewise, it should seek to expand cooperative security efforts in managing the global commons, and in new spheres of violent conflict in which the pace of technological change has outstripped the development of shared rules of the road. Finally, the United States ought to redouble its support for UN peacekeeping—an indispensable, if often flawed, instrument for mitigating violence in the world's most wretched places.

SIX

Stop the World, I Want to Get Off

Globalization and American Sovereignty

Senator Elizabeth Warren was in high dudgeon. The target of her animus was a February 2015 draft agreement for the Trans-Pacific Partnership (TPP), a proposed bloc of twelve trading nations, including the United States. Its most objectionable provision was the envisioned Investor-State Dispute Settlement (ISDS) mechanism. This mechanism would allow companies that believed they had gotten a raw deal from TPP governments to bring their complaints to an independent tribunal composed (in Warren's view) of well-paid corporate lawyers. "Agreeing to ISDS in this enormous new treaty would tilt the playing field in the United States further in favor of big multinational corporations," the Massachusetts Democrat complained in the *Washington Post*. "Worse, it would undermine U.S. sovereignty," she continued. "This isn't a partisan issue," the liberal icon insisted. "Conservatives who believe in U.S. sovereignty should be outraged that ISDS would shift power from American courts, whose authority is derived from our Constitution, to unaccountable international tribunals."[1]

Warren's rare appeal across the aisle proved superfluous. Since early 2015, growing numbers of conservatives like Rep. Dana Rohrabacher of California had joined liberals like Rep. Rosa DeLauro of Connecticut in opposing the blockbuster trade pact. That was bad news for President Obama, who had counted on strong GOP legislative support for TPP, the centerpiece of his trade agenda. As Tea Party Republicans skeptical of Wall Street and international organizations began making common cause with left-wing legislators, Senate majority leader Mitch McConnell and House speaker John A. Boehner were struggling to deliver the legislative majorities the president needed to secure TPP. All this tumult clearly tickled Vermont senator Bernie Sanders, an independent who caucused with the Democrats and would soon upend that party by declaring his candidacy for its presidential nomination. As he told the *New York Times*, "Some of my conservative friends are worried legitimately about the issue of sovereignty."[2]

Conservatives outside Congress were similarly split. The influential Club for Growth, a political action committee financed by major corporations, supported TPP. So did the Heritage Foundation, which argued that the "arbitration of freely accepted commitments . . . does not undermine national sovereignty." But the libertarian Cato Institute disagreed, depicting ISDS as both an unfair giveaway to foreign companies and a tool that those companies could use to challenge U.S. regulations. Elsewhere on the right, both the Eagle Forum and TheTeaParty.net "strongly opposed" the mega-trade deal.[3]

TPP had turned once-predictable U.S. trade politics topsy-turvy.[4] For several decades, Republicans had championed liberalization as an engine of growth and prosperity, the global accompaniment to deregulation and lower taxes at home; Democrats had been skeptical, warning of massive job losses and a regulatory "race to the bottom." Democrats charged Republicans with shilling for corporate America and indifference to the plight of American workers. Republicans accused Democrats of protectionist pandering to union bosses and tree huggers. Given these dynamics, a Democratic president seeking trade promotion (or "fast-track") authority needed to cobble together a legislative coalition reliant on GOP support to counterbalance opposition from his own party. Bill Clinton had used this approach to win passage of the North American Free Trade Agreement (NAFTA) and to secure U.S. entry into the World Trade Organization (WTO).

Believing that old rules still applied, President Obama had enlisted Republicans like Senator Orrin Hatch of Utah and Representative Paul Ryan of Wisconsin to help him secure trade promotion authority. But suddenly, outraged Tea Partiers and libertarians opposed to the ISDS risked upending his plans. Their complaint was not simply that companies could exploit binding arbitration to remedy allegedly unfair or discriminatory treatment. It was that the envisioned international panel would consist not of professional judges but independent lawyers, operating under rules established by the United Nations Commission on International Trade Law or the International Center for Settlement of Investment Disputes. "This is unconstitutional," declared

Americans for Limited Government, a conservative political action group. The resulting "trade pact . . . would constitute a judicial authority higher than even the U.S. Supreme Court that could overrule rulings applying U.S. law to foreign companies."[5]

In fact, ISDS provisions were nothing new. The United States was already party to fifty accords containing such clauses. But TPP was the first trade megadeal to include them, and critics predicted a torrent of ISDS complaints, as it empowered 9,000 foreign-owned firms to bring cases against U.S. federal, state, and local governments. Predictably, left-leaning groups denounced the ISDS provisions as a threat to U.S. employment and public health. Public Citizen warned that TPP "would grant foreign corporations extraordinary new powers to attack the laws we rely on for a clean environment, essential services, and healthy communities." Michael Froman, the U.S. trade representative, tried to dispel such fears. But he hurt his cause by keeping the emerging TPP text secret while consulting with U.S. corporations during its drafting.[6]

More unexpected were conservative doubts about TPP. As chapter 4 explained, right-leaning U.S. politicians and commentators have long rejected multilateral treaties in fields including human rights, the environment, and nuclear weapons as placing unacceptable constraints on the United States. But they had usually given trade agreements a pass. The TPP debate suggested that this historical era might be ending.

For progressive legislators, the growing sovereignty concerns of their GOP colleagues were a godsend; for President Obama, they were a nightmare. Most congressional Democrats already opposed TPP on the grounds that it would expose American workers to unfair competition from countries with cheap labor and inadequate human rights and environmental standards. Progressives outside government depicted TPP as a giveaway to multinational corporations. By March 2015, 150 of 188 House Democrats had signed a letter opposing "fast-track," forcing the president to lean overwhelmingly on a fragmenting Republican caucus—which had spent six years denying him any legislative victory—to get the 218 votes he needed in the House for trade promotion authority. The bogeyman of an unaccountable international tribunal able to rule on behalf of foreign corporations against U.S. federal, state, and local governments only added to the president's TPP woes. On May 12, 2015, the Senate handed Obama a stinging if temporary defeat, rejecting TPP by a vote of 52 to 48.[7]

The president eventually prevailed in a second Senate vote six weeks later, 60–38, after Republicans conceded to the Democrats' demands on enhanced trade adjustment assistance for displaced U.S. workers. Public Citizen denounced the result, citing "the inexcusable and anti-democratic veil of secrecy surrounding the TPP."[8] At first glance, the outcome suggested a return to business as usual. After all, GOP senators had lined up solidly behind trade liberalization, with a healthy minority of Democrats, to get the legislation over the hump.

In fact, the subsequent 2016 presidential election campaign suggested that U.S. trade politics had changed. On the Democratic side the insurgent candidate Bernie Sanders came close to capturing the nomination, buoyed by his relentless attacks on trade liberalization. He lost but pushed the eventual nominee, Hillary Clinton, to disavow her previous support for TPP.

But the real shock was on the Republican side, where real estate magnate Donald Trump surged to the nomination on the back of antiglobalization rhetoric. Trump's criticisms of "terrible" trade deals like NAFTA, the WTO, and TPP resonated with rank-and-file GOP voters, particularly economically vulnerable working-class whites persuaded that his protectionist policies (including punitive tariffs on Chinese goods) would revive the nation's fortunes—and their own. Indeed, polling documented an abrupt shift in public opinion on trade. In 2009, 57 percent of Republican-leaning voters had considered trade agreements a "good thing" (31 percent thought they were "bad"). By 2016 those figures had inverted, with 61 percent now considering trade agreements "bad" and only 32 percent "good." (Democrats' support for trade, meanwhile, had increased from 48 percent to 58 percent.)[9]

For the first time in decades, multilateral trade pacts had become a major target of Republican opposition. Senator Jeff Sessions (R-Ala.) explained why in a November 2015 radio interview with Stephen Bannon, then head of Breitbart Media. "We shouldn't be tying ourselves down like Gulliver in the land of Lilliputians with so many strings a guy can't move." That same month Bannon proposed a new approach to candidate Trump, whereby the United States would use its leverage to hammer out tough bilateral trade agreements, one deal at a time. Bannon had found his man. Throughout the 2016 campaign, Trump pledged to tear up trade deals he claimed had ravaged the U.S. economy, particularly the country's manufacturing sector. In place of multilateral deals that constrained U.S. commercial options and influence over trade rules, Trump proposed to negotiate one-on-one arrangements with specific trading partners.

Trump's election allowed him to advance this agenda. In his inaugural address the new president pledged to restore U.S. economic sovereignty through an unapologetic embrace of protectionism. "We must protect our borders from the ravages of other countries making our products, stealing our companies and destroying our jobs," he declared. "Protection will lead to great prosperity and strength."[10] One of the president's first acts was to withdraw the United States from TPP—a decision Bannon hailed as "one of the most pivotal moments in modern American history." The president's bold stroke "got us out of a trade deal and let our sovereignty come back to ourselves, the people." Henceforth the United States would experiment with "bilateral trading relationships . . . that will reposition America in the world as a . . . fair trading nation and start to bring . . . high-value-added manufacturing jobs back to the United States of America."[11] In March 2017 the Trump administration presented Congress with its new "Trade Policy Agenda." That strategy's first priority was "defending our national sovereignty over trade policy"—not least against the WTO.[12]

Two months later Michael Anton, adviser for strategic planning at the National Security Council, explained the Trump administration's thinking. "We want to put the brakes on globalization a little bit and reassert control over our country, our borders, our economic policy, our tax policy, with the recognition that, you know, the distinction of citizenship means something," he told NPR's Steve Inskeep. "There's a reason why there are countries and why there are borders and why some people are citizens of one country and not citizens of another country and that citizens of one country owe obligations to fellow citizens that they don't owe to non-citizens." This is what it meant to finally place America first.[13]

SOVEREIGNTY AND ANXIETY IN AN AGE OF GLOBALIZATION

In endorsing protectionism, Trump broke with eight decades of U.S. commitment to trade liberalization dating back to Cordell Hull's days as secretary of state. But his shift resonated with the public mood—namely, deepening anxiety about globalization. Many Americans, regardless of party affiliation, had come to believe that global economic integration was a sucker's game. It had placed the country's fate in the hands of foreigners and fickle international markets, endangering Americans' livelihoods, security, and even identity.

A defining attribute of sovereignty is the state's authority to determine what—as well as who—crosses its frontiers, and on what terms. All states insist on this prerogative, whatever their actual capacity to regulate and police cross-border flows. But globalization has made life harder for states. Yes, there have been previous episodes of globalization, notably at the end of the nineteenth century and the start of the twentieth. But thanks to technological change, today's globalization is "orders of magnitude different, with vast differences in kind, and not just degree, from that of a century ago."[14]

Since the 1980s, cross-border flows of money, goods, services, ideas, and people have surged, thanks to the liberalization of capital and trade and to revolutions in telecommunications and transportation (including the universal spread of the shipping container). Globalized production chains, capital markets, and commerce have generated unprecedented (if unevenly shared) wealth. Yet deeper economic integration has also tested long-standing social bargains within advanced market democracies, including those related to employment, while porous borders have sharpened domestic debates over the entry and assimilation of immigrants. The pressing question is not how to reverse globalization but how to manage it to better cope with the abrupt changes it has wrought.

Preserving a relatively open world economy will require persuading publics in the United States and elsewhere that globalization can benefit average citizens, not just the fortunate owners of capital. Rather than scapegoating globalization, as they often do, U.S. political leaders need to marshal America's considerable sovereign powers to tame its excesses by hammering out new international rules and making domestic policy adjustments that persuade U.S. citizens that their concerns are being heard. The United States must also recalibrate the balance among sovereignty-as-autonomy, sovereignty-as-authority, and sovereignty-as-influence, making the best use of available political authorities and policy space to craft new international bargains on trade, finance, employment, and migration. This chapter focuses on sovereignty concerns related to the world economy. Chapter 7 will turn to the fraught issue of immigration.

AMERICAN SOVEREIGNTY AND THE WORLD ECONOMY

The turbulent 2016 election cycle will be remembered for many things. But the populist tsunami that swept Trump to the GOP nomination and drove Bernie Sanders's impressive showing in the Democratic primaries reflected widespread anger that globalization was no longer working for many or even most Americans. Although the wave struck suddenly, surprising the political class, it had been building for decades, as successive U.S. administrations and Congresses failed to prepare the U.S. economy—and American workers and families—to adjust to the rigors of global economic competition.

All too often the debate over globalization had glossed over these domestic policy shortcomings, as politicians had found it easier to fault alleged external threats to U.S. "sovereignty"—including from other foreign governments, multilateral trade agreements, and intergovernmental bodies like the IMF, the World Bank, and the WTO.

The truth is that the economic insecurity and inequality that permeates contemporary American society owes less to any external commitments or constraints than to the repeated failures of U.S. elected officials of both major parties to make effective use of the sovereign powers and policy options at their disposal, such as expanded trade adjustment assistance and retraining programs, so as to make American workers, as well as firms, more competitive. As Edward Alden of the Council on Foreign Relations writes, "The problem is not globalization itself" but the "domestic political response to globalization, which in too many ways has been deeply irresponsible."[15]

American anxiety about globalization is ironic, in a way, for the modern world economy is a U.S. creation. The United States spearheaded the global market liberalization of the past several decades, just as it sponsored the major multilateral institutions that govern international economic relations. And yet contemporary unease also makes sense because, in pushing for hyperglobalization, successive U.S. administrations, both Republican and Democratic, gradually unwound a political compromise that had been the heart of the post-1945 international economic order: namely, the implicit pledge that the U.S. government (like its counterparts abroad) would temper the nation's integration into the global marketplace by pursuing domestic policies that promoted social welfare, inclusive growth, and other public policies. Rather than exercising the flexibility inherent in its sovereignty to help American workers and firms adjust to greater global competition, or negotiating and enforcing international rules to ensure a so-called level playing field, the United States became too enamored by the vision of an unfettered global market. That stance facilitated the emergence of a world economy that was too lightly regulated, overly tolerant of systemic risk, tilted toward global capital and multinational corporations, and too often inimical to the broader interests and social welfare of struggling citizens.

The roots of the current conundrum lie in part in the global victory of neoclassical economics in the early 1980s, under the political leadership of U.S. president Ronald Reagan and U.K. prime minister Margaret Thatcher. The Reagan-Thatcher revolution identified a set of policy reforms—including market liberalization, deregulation, capital mobility, and privatization—intended to eliminate obstacles to growth. This ideology came to dominate the thinking of national governments as well as the prescriptions of major international financial and economic institutions. But the mixture of policy reforms it recommended also undermined fundamental societal bargains.

The Compromise of Embedded Liberalism

The foundation of that postwar order, laid down at the Bretton Woods conference in 1944, had been what Harvard professor John Ruggie calls a "compromise of embedded liberalism."[16] This is a fancy way of saying that the major world economies, led at the time by the United States and Great Britain, had committed themselves to liberalizing postwar trade and financial relations, but on the understanding that external openness would be balanced and tempered by an allowance for state intervention in the domestic and global economy to boost employment and pursue other social welfare objectives. Their motivation was plain. With fresh memories of the Great Depression, Western governments were determined to control the terms and pace of their integration into the global economic system, rather than simply letting the free market rip. They thus insisted on retaining the leeway—the sovereign autonomy, if you will—to pursue domestic objectives like full employment, shared growth, price stability, and social security. This broad middle ground between economic nationalism and laissez-faire detachment allowed governments to manage global interdependence, so as to buffer certain sectors or cushion their citizens from being whipsawed by inevitable fluctuations in the world economy.[17] This mindset shaped U.S. attitudes toward postwar international trade and monetary relations until the underlying bargain came unstuck in the last decades of the twentieth century.

The Origins of the Postwar U.S. Trade and Monetary Policy

For most of American history, U.S. national sovereignty and trade policy had gone hand in hand. The first treaty the United States signed after declaring its independence was the Treaty of Amity and Commerce with France, on February 6, 1778. The signatories pledged "the most perfect equality and reciprocity" in the treatment of one another's imports, while noting that each remained "at liberty to make . . . those interior regulations which it shall find most convenient to itself."[18] In other words, external commercial openness would coexist with domestic regulatory autonomy.

Two decades later, in his farewell address, George Washington made a clear distinction between international political and economic relations. While counseling the United States to "steer clear of any permanent alliances," he endorsed "extending our commercial relations" with other countries on the basis of nondiscrimination and reciprocity.[19]

Consistent with Washington's advice, the United States over the next century and a half negotiated dozens of bilateral trade agreements with other countries based on the principles of nondiscrimination and reciprocity, while opposing mercantilist rules that denied equal treatment to U.S. exports. The nation agreed to extend bilateral tariff treaties to third nations, provided that they extend concessions to the United States equivalent to those offered by the first country. Still, this was a cumbersome way to liberalize trade, requiring interminable negotiations with many countries. Moreover, Congress controlled the setting of tariffs, which provided the primary source of federal government revenue.

A breakthrough in U.S. trade policy came in 1934, when Franklin D. Roosevelt secured passage of the Reciprocal Trade Agreements Act (RTAA). It contained two provisions that advanced the cause of global multilateral trade. First, it transferred leadership on trade liberalization to the president, who could now negotiate directly with trading partners, submitting the final package to Congress for an up-or-down vote. Second, the RTAA included automatic application of the most favored nation principle—meaning that third countries that did not discriminate against U.S. goods now enjoyed the same access.[20]

It was in the aftermath of World War II, though, that global trade liberalization began in earnest, through successive negotiating rounds of the General Agreement on Tariffs and Trade (GATT). The GATT was actually the fallback solution for the Truman administration, which had promoted the International Trade Organization (ITO) as a standing body to advance multilateral trade. But U.S. trading partners used these negotiations to push a panoply of illiberal provisions that U.S. business interests complained could discriminate against U.S. goods and investment. The National Foreign Trade Council objected that these clauses would "transform the free enterprise system of this country into a system of planned economy . . . threat[ening] . . . the free institutions and liberties of the American people." Equally bad, warned the U.S. Chamber of Commerce, the United States would be relegated to a "permanent minority position owing to [the ITO's] one vote one country voting procedure," thus "making it impossible for the United States to engage in an independent course of policy in favor of multilateral trade."[21] The costs for U.S. sovereign autonomy, in this view, were simply too onerous.

The death of the ITO was arguably a blessing. To be sure, the GATT contained numerous escape clauses, exceptions, and qualifications. It permitted discriminatory customs unions and tolerated imperial preferences, and it excluded entire sectors like agriculture, fisheries, services, and foreign investment. Yet, compared to the ITO, the GATT took a more pragmatic approach to trade liberalization, one sensitive to domestic political realities in trading nations. Its very informality, moreover, made it palatable to sovereignty-minded members of Congress. Between 1950 and 1995, the United States worked with partners to conclude several successive rounds of GATT negotiations, during which the volume of global exports expanded from $61.8 billion to nearly $5.18 trillion, a nearly eighty-fourfold increase.[22]

Alongside new rules to govern global trade, the post-1945 international economy would rest on a reformed global monetary system, underpinned by new international financial institutions—with the U.S. dollar as its centerpiece. Like the GATT, the postwar monetary order would seek to balance the need for international rules with the prerogatives of national sovereignty.

Inherent in sovereignty is the state's authority to issue a national currency in the denomination and supply of its choice and to insist that this money circulate freely and be treated as legal tender within its territory. To symbolize this link between political authority and economic exchange, coins and (more recently) paper currency have long featured the visages of rulers, past and present. Indeed, for centuries the English applied the word "sovereign" to gold coinage, beginning with a coin that appeared in 1489 with King Henry VII sitting on a throne. (The sovereign would become the gold coin standard throughout the British Isles and the American colonies.)[23]

Sovereign states, then, mint coins and print money. But they and their citizens also trade with foreigners, and such international commerce requires a way to settle accounts. This raises the question of exchange rates—or determining the par values of monies denominated in different currencies. During the heyday of the British Empire until the early 1930s, the global monetary system was based on the gold standard, with major national currencies being convertible to gold. That system broke down during the Great Depression, when it contributed to deflationary pressures that many experts believe prolonged the length and depth of the global economic crisis.

Toward the end of World War II, in August 1944, representatives of the allied nations met in New Hampshire to devise a postwar international monetary order intended to facilitate commerce while providing relief to national governments experiencing temporary balance-of-payments difficulties. The result, known as the Bretton Woods system, was founded on dollar-gold convertibility. The dollar was designated as the world's key currency, its value pegged to gold at $35 per troy ounce. All countries agreed to make their currencies freely convertible after a postwar transition period, and to buy and sell their currencies to maintain their dollar exchange rates (par values)—with an escape clause permitting devaluations in situations of "fundamental disequilibrium." The negotiators also created the IMF to assist countries experiencing temporary balance-of-payments difficulties and the International Bank for Reconstruction and Development (or World Bank) to furnish long-term loans, on commercial terms, to help countries meet their recovery and development objectives.

The U.S. Senate passed the Bretton Woods Agreements handily, though not without bellyaching from conservatives. Senate majority leader Robert Taft objected to devolving U.S. sovereignty to new global agencies in which the United States held a minority position and from which deficit countries could borrow freely, irrespective of their creditworthiness. To his mind, this constituted "pouring money down a rat hole."[24] The Ohio Republican rejected the proposition "that American money and American charity shall solve every problem." Despite Taft's misgivings, the Senate approved the accords, by a 61–16 vote, on July 18, 1945.

The Bretton Woods agreements, like the GATT, reflected a managed multilateralism that would temper market opening with ample scope for state intervention in the domestic economy. This approach treated regulation and the market not as alternatives but as complements. It recognized that the world economy would not be stable or sustainable if left in invisible hands. The global market needed rules of the road and institutions to enforce them at the international level, and it had to tolerate economic pluralism at the national level, allowing each country some maneuvering room to pursue unique policy choices tailored to national circumstances and societal values. Finally, it had to have safeguards, including provisions to protect vulnerable sectors and escape clauses in cases of fundamental disequilibrium. Such flexibility was essential to retain public support for trade liberalization—and even capitalism itself.

The Collapse of Bretton Woods and the Triumph of Neoclassical Economics

Unfortunately, the managed multilateral order created at Bretton Woods did not long endure. Its dollar exchange standard was predicated on the right of countries to exchange their dollars for gold, which the United States lacked in sufficient quantity to cover its worldwide dollar obligations. After periodic runs on the clearly overvalued dollar, the Nixon administration on August 13, 1971, abruptly closed the gold window. Less than two years later the United States and its European partners formally abandoned the fixed exchange rate system, inaugurating an era of floating exchange rates that continues to the present day.

The demise of Bretton Woods altered the balance between the state and the market, and the compromise of embedded liberalism came unglued. Taking its place would be a new model of turbocharged globalization, characterized by capital mobility, market integration, and the retreat of the state, widely regarded as an enemy of growth that had to be downsized. This economic program, which picked up global steam after the end of the Cold War, has been variously labeled "neoliberalism," "market fundamentalism," "neoclassical economics," or the "Washington Consensus." Whatever the moniker, it called on all nations to embrace lower taxes, tight fiscal policy, deregulation, liberalization, and privatization. Capital was liberated, the welfare state retreated, and organized labor continued its slow, steady decline.[25]

In hindsight, champions of neoliberalism exaggerated the benefits and downplayed the risks of commercial and financial globalization. This is not just the conclusion of left-wing critics. In 2016 former U.S. treasury secretary Lawrence Summers acknowledged that globalization had been oversold and prosperity too often unshared. In the same year the IMF published a self-critical report conceding that its neoliberal orthodoxy had exacerbated social inequality and dampened global growth.[26]

For states seeking to exercise sovereign autonomy, global market integration poses a major challenge. This is particularly true for developing countries, which are apt to find their policy space constrained by financial markets and, at times, by international financial institutions. "Globalization has entailed a loss of national sovereignty," claims Nobel laureate Joseph Stiglitz. "International organizations, imposing international agreements, have seized power. So have international capital markets, as they have been deregulated."[27] As Stiglitz, himself a former chief economist for the World Bank, explains,

Countries are effectively told that if they don't follow certain conditions, the capital markets or the IMF will refuse to lend them money. They are basically forced to give up part of their sovereignty, to let capricious capital markets, including the speculators whose only concerns are short-term rather than long-term growth of the country and the improvement of living standards, "discipline" them, telling them what they should and should not do.[28]

Stiglitz's critique is hyperbolic. With the exception of the weakest borrowers, state sovereignty is rarely so at bay. Still, global financial markets—and sometimes international financial institutions—do constrain policy choices, and not always to the benefit of developing countries.

Turbocharged global capitalism also magnified systemic risk within the world economy. This became clear in 2007–08, when unprecedented leverage resulted in the near implosion of the global financial system. The slow and uneven recovery from global recession, coupled with historic inequality in many economies, had by the mid-2010s exacerbated a populist backlash and stimulated demands for greater state intervention to make global economic integration subservient to national economic management (rather than vice versa).[29]

This was certainly true in the United States, and its resulting political implications were profound. Although the United States enjoyed decent if not robust growth from 2011 to 2016,[30] many U.S. workers and their families felt more vulnerable to dislocation, outsourcing, economic competition, and skill obsolescence. The political corollary to this economic malaise was a wave of angry populism on both the right and the left against a system that (in the words of both Trump and Sanders) seemed "rigged" against common people, to the benefit of corporations and well-connected elites. The crisis of globalization has become a crisis of Western democracy inasmuch as many citizens no longer believe their political system is capable of or even interested in responding to their complaints and desires. In the United States the "failure to adjust" meant that too many "Americans got left behind in the global economy."[31]

The political consequences of this disillusionment have been dramatic. In November 2016, Donald Trump triumphed in the U.S. presidential election, riding to power in part on the backs of those who had lost out from globalization, not least downwardly mobile white men who felt abandoned and expendable in the world economy. Trump's criticisms of "horrible" trade deals clearly resonated with anxious middle-class and blue-collar workers. In 1992 the "pitchfork populist" Patrick J. Buchanan had attracted less than 20 percent of the Republican electorate. Two dozen years later, his ideological heir was bound for the White House.[32]

If this global economic turbulence had a potential silver lining, it was in affording Americans an opportunity to demand that their government make full use of its ample sovereign powers to reduce their exposure to the excesses of globalization—and to provide U.S. firms and workers with the tools they need to compete in an international marketplace. Since the 1970s, two generations of U.S. policymakers have failed to take the policy steps needed to adjust to global economic integration, including by helping losers adapt to foreign competition. Too often, "globalization"—and its associated international organizations like the IMF, World Bank, or WTO—have been convenient scapegoats for U.S. politicians on the right or the left, as they try to deflect attention from their own failures to preserve domestic social safety nets.

As a way to restore U.S. economic sovereignty, President Trump came to office promising a new approach to trade negotiations, based not on the WTO or TPP-style mega-trade deals but by using the diplomatic leverage the United States enjoyed as the world's largest economy to strike better deals with weaker partners. The administration's goal was "to expand trade in a way that is freer and fairer for all Americans," the Office of the United States Trade Representative (USTR) explained. "We believe that these goals can be best accomplished by focusing on bilateral negotiations rather than multilateral negotiations—and by renegotiating and revising trade agreements when our goals are not being met."[33]

While this impulse was understandable, Trump's protectionist instincts and his threats of unilateral retaliation against trading partners risked being counterproductive if implemented. History suggests that the route to greater social welfare gains lies not in launching tit-for-tat protectionism or throwing up walls, but in working with multiple partners to recast the international trade regime to create greater opportunities for domestic interventions and adjustments, including by compensating the "losers" in globalization. There must be a middle ground, in other words, between giving free rein to international trade and finance and closing oneself off by adopting a mercantilistic stance or striking bilateral deals.

The most logical path forward would be to restore some balance among the state, the global marketplace, and the American people. As things stand today, all nations confront what the Harvard economist Dani Rodrik terms a "political trilemma." They are able to pursue only two of the following three options simultaneously: national sovereignty, democracy, and hyperglobalization (see figure 6-1). In recent years, the United States has pursued hyperglobalization—or extreme global integration—along with a barren conception of national sovereignty, but at the expense of democratic accountability (and, of late, democratic support). Rodrik refers to this approach as the "golden straitjacket": sovereign states have restricted democracy in the interests of market efficiency, at the long-term risk of populist reaction.

In principle there are two ways to democratize globalization. The first is to create supranational structures of global governance that are authoritative but democratically accountable, being empowered and constrained by a global citizenry. The problem with this theoretical option is that the world is too

FIGURE 6-1. The Political Trilemma of the World Economy

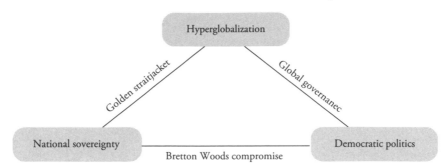

Source: Adapted from Dani Rodrik, *The Globalization Paradox: Democracy and the Future of the World Economy* (New York: W. W. Norton, 2011).

diverse—it has too many individual national political communities—for democracy to work on a global scale. It also runs roughshod over sovereignty-as-authority, making it inconceivable in a U.S. context. That leaves only a second option: "limit globalization, in the hope of building democratic legitimacy at home."[34]

Limiting globalization should not be confused with isolationism, mercantilism, or autarky. It does not imply rejecting the multilateral world economy. But it does suggest enhancing international regulation, as well as establishing employment-friendly norms and rules, so that the United States and other national governments can once again determine the pace and scope of their integration into the world economy, in accordance with the wishes of their citizens. This project would shift the world economy back toward the compromise of embedded liberalism that was at the heart of the Bretton Woods order.[35]

Two implications flow from this discussion. First, when it comes to managing globalization, advancing U.S. sovereignty-as-influence—in this case, fostering an open global economy—should not come at the expense of U.S. sovereignty-as-autonomy—in this case, ensuring sufficient national policy space to preserve the domestic social contract essential for democratic support for globalization. On the contrary, more effective international rules to protect citizens from dramatic global economic swings will require greater latitude for pluralism in domestic economic policy choices, rather than one-size-fits-all prescriptions. Second, the United States needs to make full use of the sovereign powers that it has available to it to help its citizens adjust to globalization. For too many decades U.S. officials paid only lip service to the need to invest in worker retraining, new infrastructure, secondary education, and unemployment insurance—all areas where the United States lags badly behind many of its peers in the wealthy democratic world.

Internationally, pressure to tame globalization will likely come not only from advanced market democracies but also from emerging countries. In its latest *Global Trends* report, the U.S. National Intelligence Council predicts that, over the next five years, "Great and middle powers alike will search for ways to keep the risks of global economic interdependence in check—with many tempted to exercise economic sovereignty, stepping back from global trade and finance as a way to manage risk."[36]

THE WORLD TRADE ORGANIZATION: A THREAT TO U.S. SOVEREIGNTY?

Globalization, then, poses dilemmas for U.S. sovereignty-as-autonomy and sovereignty-as-influence. Does it also pose challenges to U.S. sovereignty-as-authority? For those who believe it does, including President Trump and his senior advisers, exhibit A is the World Trade Organization. Critics contend that the WTO, created by the Marrakesh Treaty of 1994, undermines the U.S. Constitution by unfairly constraining U.S. sovereign authority over American trade policy.[37] The WTO does indeed possess greater powers than typical international organizations, notably a binding dispute resolution mechanism and the authority, in principle, to create new trade rules over the wishes of its members. However, these incursions on U.S. sovereign authorities are limited and likely to remain so. They are also a small price to pay for the benefits of a rule-bound international trading system that allows parties to resolve their differences peaceably.

Before Trump, as chapter 4 explained, the Republican Party had traditionally worried less about the sovereignty implications of international trade agreements than those of international human rights or environmental conventions. This equanimity reflected their faith in capitalism and markets. Most U.S. conservatives thus supported the creation of the WTO, into which the former GATT system was subsumed. They remained nonchalant despite the warnings of some sovereigntist scholars that the WTO marked a small but decisive shift toward unaccountable global governance (as well as of liberals who complained that it presaged a regulatory "race to the bottom").[38]

Similar sovereigntist concerns had arisen earlier during bilateral negotiations of the Canada-U.S. Free Trade Agreement (CUSFTA), as well as NAFTA, which succeeded it. The biggest novelty of CUSFTA was the introduction of a new system for resolving bilateral trade disagreements, through binding arbitration rather than conventional diplomacy. Canadian negotiators had insisted on such a quasi-judicial scheme to insulate bilateral commercial disputes from the power asymmetry inherent in the U.S.-Canada relationship, and specifically to prevent the U.S. Commerce Department from unilaterally slapping "countervailing duties" on Canadian products it believed were being dumped on U.S. markets. Ultimately, the George H. W. Bush administration agreed to submit trade disagreements to a binational panel of arbitrators and even to accept its decisions as final, with no recourse to appeal or any prospect of findings being overturned by U.S. courts.

The United States subsequently agreed to incorporate the same provision into NAFTA, a trilateral agreement with Canada and Mexico. Under NAFTA's general dispute settlement procedure, parties may refer disagreements to the good offices of the Free Trade Commission. If that consensual path fails, they may submit their dispute to a panel of five independent experts for ad hoc arbitration—the decisions of which are binding. NAFTA also provides a binational panel system to review antidumping and countervailing duties claims, with a 315-day window to make decisions. Should a ruling favor the complaining state, it is entitled to demand remedy and, if this is not forthcoming, to adopt retaliatory legislation or statutes.[39]

What the WTO did was extend this principle of binding arbitration to the global, multilateral level and embed it within a new framework for negotiating and enforcing international trade rules. The WTO differs from the GATT in multiple respects. Whereas the GATT was a negotiating forum with a modest secretariat, in which parties negotiated trade bargains, the WTO is a standing international organization, established by treaty and embedded in international law, that imposes formal legal obligations on its members. The GATT had permitted countries to opt out of certain provisions, whereas the WTO has an "all or nothing" aspect that requires members to buy into an entire package of agreements. Finally, their methods for resolving disputes are wholly different. Under the GATT, countries that complained about unfair treatment would seek a bilateral solution and, if dissatisfied, retaliate on a bilateral basis. In contrast, the WTO explicitly obliges all parties to submit all disputes falling under the treaty's "covered agreements" to the compulsory jurisdiction of its binding dispute settlement understanding (DSU).

From the perspective of political realism, the U.S. decision to join the WTO is mysterious. That body of thought—the dominant academic approach to world politics—suggests that powerful states will maintain independent authority and maximal freedom to pursue their material interests. In 1994 the United States enjoyed more relative power than it had in decades, standing as the sole superpower. Why would it push for a binding dispute resolution mechanism that constrained its capacity for international action? The most compelling answer is that senior U.S. officials in the administrations of George H. W. Bush and Bill Clinton understood that this "unipolar moment" was fleeting. They recognized that the WTO would consolidate the rules of the global trading system the United States had written decades before, reducing the possibility that other major economies would promote very different goals, including greater discrimination or redistributionist schemes, in the future. The U.S. goal was to lock in a set of favorable institutional arrangements, reinforced by a binding dispute resolution mechanism.[40]

From its earliest days, the WTO became the target of antiglobalization critics, primarily from the progressive left, who accused it of catering to business interests at the expense of workers' rights and the environment. Of more relevance to this book, many liberals and conservatives also accused the WTO of infringing on America's sovereignty-as-authority.

From a constitutional perspective, the U.S. decision to join the WTO was significant in two respects. First, it raised the possibility that the WTO might impose on the United States a new trade rule that elected U.S. leaders did not support. Sensitive to this risk, Clinton administration negotiators insisted on—and secured—a very high bar for any amendments to the WTO's legal instruments. Any amendment had to be approved by a three-fourths majority of member states. Moreover, if *any* member rejected the new rule, other WTO members had to muster an even higher threshold—seven-eighths of the entire WTO membership—to impose it on a recalcitrant party. These high hurdles made it extremely unlikely—though not impossible—that other states could impose a rule on the United States against its wishes.

An even greater source of sovereigntist anxiety was the WTO's mandatory DSU. The DSU gives the WTO exclusive jurisdiction to resolve trade disputes, a competence that potentially involves a vast array of commercial policy and regulatory issues. It requires that parties first attempt to resolve their differences amicably through bilateral consultations. If the disagreement persists, the two parties must request a ruling from a panel of independent experts. If one party disagrees with that decision, it may appeal to a panel of three judges drawn from the WTO's standing Appellate Body (AB). The AB's decisions are "final"—and thus not subject to appeal.[41]

The legality and finality of AB rulings bears scant resemblance to the GATT dispute resolution process, which was based on a more traditional model of intergovernmental diplomacy and ultimately consensus among independent sovereign states. Under the GATT, all contracting parties had to agree to rulings, meaning that any single state could obstruct them, as well as block authorization of sanctions for noncompliance. By contrast, the AB panel's rulings are binding and automatic, permitting no veto. All states must abide by them and change offending domestic statutes accordingly—or else accept the removal of trade concessions to which they are otherwise entitled. The DSU is charged with monitoring implementation of the AB's recommendations for negotiation of compensation. In effect, the WTO has created a "supreme court of world trade disputes." But unlike the U.S. Supreme Court, the AB is not anchored in any domestic legal system or grounded in any national constitution, meaning that its decisions lack a clear democratic basis of legitimacy. In addition, there is no democratic recourse for citizens (or firms) seeking redress against the AB's decisions.[42]

American sovereignty concerns nearly derailed U.S. entry into the WTO. During 1994, opposition emerged from across the political spectrum. This diverse coalition encompassed the consumer rights advocate Ralph Nader, the populist Patrick J. Buchanan, the independent presidential candidate H. Ross Perot, and conservative southern senators such as Strom Thurmond (R-S.C.) and Jesse Helms (R-N.C.). As the *New York Times* explained, "All of the pact's critics have contended that the new trade organization will effectively have the power to rule against any American laws—from environmental protections to laws against the purchase of goods made by child labor—that it judges to be a barrier to imported goods. The result, they argue, is a loss of sovereignty for the United States."[43]

Progressives claimed the WTO would gut important U.S. social, environmental, and other protections that American citizens supported and that their legislators had enacted into law. Nader blasted this as a threat to U.S. constitutional democracy. It "would . . . undermine citizen control and chill the ability of domestic democratic bodies to make decisions on a vast array of domestic policies from food safety to federal and state procurement to communications and investment policies." Fundamental decisions affecting Americans would now take place in secret in Geneva, resulting in "a practical erosion of our domestic sovereignty through an external layer of regulatory bureaucracy that pull standards down, but not up."[44]

Nader's resistance was predictable. More alarming for President Clinton, who backed U.S. entry, were the sovereignty concerns of Republican legislators, who also worried about the new body's power to override U.S. trade laws. Robert Dole (R-Kans.), the incoming Senate majority leader, insisted that the administration provide "stronger assurances that WTO panels would not infringe on American sovereignty by issuing arbitrary rulings against U.S.

laws." To mollify Dole, the White House proposed that the United States create a new U.S. commission composed of five federal appellate judges, charged with reviewing the fairness of any WTO decisions against the United States. Should the commission find the WTO guilty of three unreasonable rulings, Congress could initiate moves to withdraw from the body. This new "three strikes and you're out" rule reassured legislators that Congress would serve as the WTO's watchdog.[45]

Congress never established the envisioned commission, but the GOP continued to explore the issue of potential withdrawal. The House requested a General Accounting Office (GAO) study on the impact of the DSU on trade policy and U.S. national interests. The GAO's final report, delivered in June 2000, quieted debate. "Overall, our analysis shows that the United States has gained more than it has lost from the WTO dispute settlement system to date," the authors concluded. "WTO cases have resulted in a substantial number of changes in foreign trade practices, while their effect on U.S. laws and regulations has been minimal."[46] On June 21, 2000, the House handily rejected a resolution to withdraw the United States from the WTO, 365–56.[47]

To avoid raising sovereignty hackles, WTO officials themselves scrupulously avoided describing the DSU as a "judicial" process, or the AB as a "court" or "tribunal." Nevertheless, the AB quickly emerged as the most important international law tribunal. In its very first ruling, as Rabkin notes, the seven judges of the AB announced that "WTO agreements were now part of the general body of public international law and must be interpreted with reference to 'general principles of international law.'" The WTO's early ambitions elicited ire from Republicans, who charged that "the Appellate Body was exceeding its authority by 'judicial activism' and slanted treaty interpretation that inappropriately impinge upon the sovereignty of the United States."[48] The WTO also mobilized leftist antiglobalization critics, most famously in 1999, when violent protestors disrupted the body's ministerial meeting in Seattle, Washington.

At times, antiglobalization critiques of the right and left seemed to merge—nowhere more so than in the fiery rhetoric of Buchanan, in retrospect Donald Trump's intellectual godfather. In his 1998 broadside *The Great Betrayal: How American Sovereignty and Justice Are Being Sacrificed to the Gods of the Global Economy*, Buchanan wrote,

Like a shipwrecked, exhausted Gulliver on the beach of Lilliput, America is to be tied down by threads, strand by strand, until it cannot move when it awakens. "Piece by piece," our sovereignty is being surrendered. By accession to NAFTA, GATT, the UN, the WTO, the World Bank, and the IMF, America has ensnared itself in a web that restricts its freedom of action, diminishes its liberty, and siphons off its wealth.[49]

(Seventeen years later, as noted earlier, Alabama senator Jeff Sessions would invoke the same literary imagery in his interview with Breitbart's Stephen Bannon.)

In the first decade of the twenty-first century, the WTO faded as a lightning rod for U.S. sovereigntists, thanks in part to the generally high quality of its quasi-judicial outputs. At the same time, the DSU demonstrated its power to force changes in U.S. trade policy. The most prominent instance was the *Steel Safeguards* (2003) case, in which the AB invalidated tariffs that the George W. Bush administration had imposed to limit steel imports into the United States. The *New York Times* described this landmark ruling in historical terms, as "the rough equivalent of *Marbury vs. Madison*, the 1803 decision that established the Supreme Court as the final arbiter of the Constitution, able to force Congress and the executive branch to comply with its rulings."[50]

Such comparisons alarm constitutional traditionalists like Rabkin, who believe the AB "should be taken very seriously as a threat to [American] sovereignty." Sovereigntists worry that the WTO's rule-making function will increasingly unfold not through multilateral negotiating rounds among sovereign states but instead via the AB's judicial activism. Although the Marrakesh Treaty declares that the DSU mechanism must not expand or diminish obligations of WTO members, pressures and temptations will surely build for the AB to create new rules through adjudication. This risk has only risen, sovereigntists worry, given the failure to conclude the WTO's Doha Development Round of trade talks, launched in 2001. Such a trend would only add to the WTO's "democratic deficit," by removing rule creation even farther from the decisions of member states that are accountable to the will of their citizens.[51]

Shortly after taking office, the Trump administration highlighted another sovereigntist objection to the WTO: namely, that it placed unacceptable constraints on U.S. freedom to retaliate against perceived enemies of fair trade. A case in point was China, which the president claimed had been gaming the global economy through currency manipulation. In March 2017 the administration fired a shot over the WTO's bow, suggesting that the United States might unilaterally impose tariffs against countries it judged to have unfair trade practices. It also declared that future adverse WTO rulings would not automatically result in any change in U.S. laws and announced that it would ignore any rulings by the Appellate Body that the White House deemed to infringe on U.S. sovereignty.[52] The stage seemed set not only for a more confrontational relationship with China and other trading partners—who might well retaliate—but indeed for a potential showdown with the WTO itself.[53]

Writing in the *Wall Street Journal*, John Bolton defended the Trump administration's hard line, arguing that the WTO had locked the United States into an "unaccountable, legalistic morass into which free trade can all but disappear."[54] According to this narrative, WTO membership had infringed on U.S. sovereign authority and limited U.S. sovereign autonomy, without delivering to the United States any sovereign influence.

Such sovereigntist concerns deserve to be taken seriously, but they should not be blown out of proportion. Neither should the United States overlook the potential risks of destabilizing the WTO-led trade regime. To begin with the obvious point, the WTO has not seized sovereignty from the United States. The U.S. decision to join the WTO, pursue trade liberalization within it, and accept the jurisdiction of the AB were all sovereign choices ratified by the president and the Senate as representatives of the American people. WTO agreements are legally binding on the United States because Congress has said they are. The WTO remains an intergovernmental rather than supranational body, lacking an administrative organ that can independently issue new regulations.

The point here is not that the WTO is perfect—an impossible bar for any human institution. Its rulings will not always be wise, much less advance immediate U.S. interests. The AB will sometimes get it wrong—with certain WTO rulings on tax policies being a case in point, in the view of many trade lawyers. The AB can also foreclose certain steps that the U.S. government might want to take—such as the George W. Bush limits on steel imports to protect domestic production—by labeling them non-WTO-compliant.

Even when the United States loses in the WTO, however, it still preserves its sovereign right to retain its offending trade provisions, albeit in the knowledge that its aggrieved partners are justified in taking compensatory steps in retaliation. Alternatively, it may seek a bilateral remedy to satisfy the offended party. A case in point is the AB's finding against the United States in the *Cotton* case, which sided with Brazil in ruling that U.S. subsidies to domestic cotton producers were not WTO-compliant. The two countries thereupon negotiated a bilateral framework agreement that allowed the United States to maintain its discriminatory treatment while compensating Brazilian exporters.[55]

The WTO is also not a panacea for all forms of unfair competition the United States confronts, with currency manipulation being one example. Still, notwithstanding the constraints and setbacks it occasionally imposes, the WTO remains in the U.S. interest, helping to stabilize expectations among trading partners and establish important standards of behavior. In choosing to join the WTO, elected U.S. officials rightly calculated that some constraints on America's sovereign autonomy (in its trade policy space) and more modestly on its sovereign authority (including through the DSU) were acceptable prices to pay for a predictable system of international trade governed by rules that embody multilateral principles of nondiscrimination and reciprocity. In sum, what the trade expert Robert Z. Lawrence wrote a decade ago remains true today: "The [WTO] dispute settlement system reflects a delicate balance between toughness and respect for sovereignty; rather than criticizing the result, U.S. policymakers and legislators should invest more energy in defending it."[56]

At the same time, the United States must remember that the global trading regime is inherently fragile. By attacking the WTO's legitimacy in early 2017, President Trump increased the likelihood that U.S. trading partners would also play the sovereignty card, refusing to comply with AB rulings that they find inconvenient. For precisely this reason Senator Sander Levin (D-Mich.) in March 2017 cautioned the Trump administration against such a strategy. "Too often 'sovereignty' is used as a red herring by others to avoid changing their laws, which are blocking U.S. exports or disadvantaging U.S. workers," Levin told *Politico*. "We insist on reasonable changes to other nations' intellectual property protections, regulations that unjustifiably discriminate against U.S. products in foreign markets, and labor laws, to name just a few, and we would never accept the argument that a country in a trading arrangement with us won't act because their sovereignty is being impinged."[57]

Were other governments to assert similar "sovereign" privileges, the result could well be a downward cycle of tit-for-tat protectionism, undermining a global institution that remains valuable to the United States.

The U.S. goal should be to formulate a national trade policy that complements, rather than shoves aside, the WTO. Within that body Washington should press for better, more comprehensive international trade rules geared toward eliminating rampant market distortions, including those "caused by government subsidies, discriminatory regulations, intellectual property theft, and location incentives" (which encourage firms to relocate). In parallel, the U.S. government should be more aggressive in enforcing its own existing trade rules by pressuring trading partners to end discrimination against U.S. exports, in accordance with WTO rules that "permit governments to 'self-initiate' either anti-dumping or countervailing duty cases on their own."[58]

It is true that the WTO's membership can in principle create new trade rules that are binding on nonconsenting partners. As Rabkin observes, this is, "in effect, a delegation of treaty-making powers from the president and the Senate to a body of foreign officials."[59] At the same time, the United States is well protected against this risk, thanks to the high hurdles implied by a seven-eighths majority of member states. It is highly unlikely (though admittedly not impossible) that the United States could come out on the losing end of such a vote.

Of greater concern for sovereigntists is the prospect that the AB may gradually impinge on U.S. treaty power more indirectly, including by reinterpreting WTO agreements and obligations in more activist ways, as well as depicting WTO commitments not merely as contracts but as binding obligations of public international law.[60] To date, however, these dangers remain almost entirely hypothetical. More than twenty years after the U.S. accession to the WTO there is little evidence of such dynamics.

In the end, the United States retains an ultimate safeguard to protect its sovereign authority. Should senior U.S. officials conclude that the AB has overstepped its mandate by making decisions that violate U.S. constitutional authorities, the United States can always exercise its "exit" option, either by deciding not to comply with specific rulings or, in the extreme, by renouncing membership in the WTO and associated treaty obligations (something that candidate Trump's campaign rhetoric suggested was a possibility).[61] To be sure, the United States would incur heavy costs by invoking this ultimate safeguard. But these would likely be temporary costs of adjustment, associated with the transition to a less formal trading arrangement with other WTO members. In sum, the United States has agreed to trade off a measure of sovereignty autonomy, and a slice of sovereign authority, for greater sovereign influence over its destiny.

SEVEN

Good Fences Make Good Neighbors

Immigration and Border Security

O n June 16, 2015, Donald Trump convened his supporters and the media in the lobby of his eponymous tower in midtown Manhattan. His ostensible purpose was to declare that he would seek the presidency of the United States. But what made headlines was not that long-anticipated announcement but rather his vow to crack down on illegal immigration. As the mogul explained, "When Mexico sends its people, they're not sending their best. . . . They're sending people that have lots of problems. . . . They're bringing drugs. They're bringing crime. They're rapists. And some, I assume, are good people." Trump had spoken to U.S. border guards, and their message to him was clear: the United States had lost control of its southern frontier, resulting in a flood of illegal immigrants. Some might even be Middle Eastern terrorists, he speculated. "But we don't know. Because we have no protection and we have no competence, [so] we don't know what's happening. And it's got to stop and it's got to stop fast." Fortunately, the newly minted candidate had a solution: "I will build a great, great wall on our southern border," he promised. "And I will have Mexico pay for that wall."[1]

Trump's pledge galvanized many Americans frustrated by years of broken promises from politicians to "solve" the crisis of illegal immigration. By October 2015, some 73 percent of Republicans surveyed, as well as 43 percent of independents (and 29 percent of Democrats), endorsed Trump's proposal. Not only was the concept of a wall easy to communicate, it also resonated with commonsense concepts of national sovereignty.[2]

Trump did not retreat from this pledge after securing the GOP nomination, despite the risk of alienating Hispanic and moderate, college-educated swing voters. Indeed, he doubled down. On August 31, 2016, the candidate traveled to Mexico City for private discussions with Mexican president Enrique Peña Nieto. In the subsequent press conference, Trump suggested the two had reached a fundamental agreement: "Having a secure border is a sovereign right and mutually beneficial," he declared. "We recognize and respect the right of any country to build a physical barrier or wall on any of its borders to stop the illegal movement of people, drugs, and weapons."[3]

Back on U.S. soil in Phoenix that evening, Trump delivered a hardline speech on curbing illegal immigration. "It's our right, as a sovereign nation, to choose immigrants that we think are the likeliest to thrive and flourish and love us," he began. The first item in his ten-point plan was his signature pledge: "On day one [of my administration], we will begin working on a tangible, physical, tall, powerful, beautiful southern border wall." Trump also promised to end the "catch and release" of illegal immigrants, expand America's deportation force, shut down the "jobs and benefits magnet" attracting illegal immigrants, and conduct "extreme vetting" of all aspiring migrants. "And if people don't like it, we've got to have a country folks. Got to have a country."[4]

Trump campaigned as a demagogue and a xenophobe. But he successfully tapped into widespread anxieties that the United States had lost control over its borders, with potentially catastrophic long-term consequences for U.S. prosperity, security, and societal cohesion. Trump was hardly the first American populist to amplify nativist prejudices and insecurities. Concerns that permissive immigration policies would permit entry of "undesirables" date from at least the mid-nineteenth century, when waves of Irish fleeing the potato famine began to alter the country's demographic makeup. Later in that century the Chinese Exclusion Act of 1882 barred immigrants from China. Following a massive wave of arrivals from southern and eastern Europe in the first two decades of the twentieth century, the United States passed the Immigration Act of 1924, the most restrictive such law in U.S. history.

Seven decades later, anti-immigrant nativism featured prominently in the failed 1992 presidential bid of GOP conservative firebrand Patrick J. Buchanan, as well as in the successful 1994 reelection of California's Republican governor Pete Wilson, who narrowly won by vocally supporting Proposition 187. That state ballot initiative (christened "Save our State" or SOS) established a citizenship screening system to deny illegal aliens public services, including access to education and nonemergency health care.

In promising to plug the country's leaky borders, Trump was also exploiting public anxiety about terrorism, a specter that had hovered over Americans' heads since 9/11. Those events revealed the nation's vulnerability to a sudden, devastating attack from even lightly armed individuals. They also offered nativists new opportunities to defame entire religious and ethnic communities. Trump fell squarely in this camp with a second outrageous proposal, which he delivered on December 6, 2015, in the wake of a massacre perpetrated by radical American Islamists in San Bernardino, California. The candidate called for "a total and complete shutdown of Muslims entering the United States until our country's representatives can figure out what the hell is going on."[5]

Trump's language was bombastic and his "solution" extreme. But it was also savvy, given growing public unease about transnational terrorism, a concern that merged with worries about uncontrolled immigration and leaky borders. On Capitol Hill, Republicans had already rejected President Obama's plan to admit modest numbers of Syrian refugees to the United States, warning that terrorists might well find cover in the flood of people fleeing dictator Bashar al-Assad. As Representative Michael McCaul (R-Tex.), chair of the House Homeland Security Committee, explained, "I am worried that [the Islamic State] could exploit this effort in order to deploy operatives to America via a federally-funded jihadi pipeline."[6]

On the basis of any rational risk assessment, this was a hysterical overreaction. A formal request by a refugee for asylum is among the most demanding of the many possible ways to enter the United States. Applicants must undergo extensive background and security checks, biometric screening, and (if accepted), a lengthy, often years-long delay before resettlement in America. According to a 2015 study by the libertarian Cato Institute, of the 859,629 refugees admitted to the United States since 2001, *none* had launched a domestic terrorist attack, and only three had been convicted of planning one abroad. Indeed, Cato scholar Alex Nowrasteh estimated the odds of an American being killed by a terrorist attack perpetrated by a refugee at 1 in 3.64 billion. By contrast, some 15,696 Americans were murdered in 2015 alone.[7] Nevertheless, the argument resonated strongly with Trump supporters, 77 percent of whom in a June 2016 poll opposed the United States' accepting refugees from Middle East conflict zones, even after screening for security risks.[8]

Much of Trump's political appeal as a candidate was his promise to restore the sanctity of U.S. national frontiers. And as president he was determined to follow through. In his first week in office he issued a series of controversial executive orders. One, which he announced at the Department of Homeland Security, directed the immediate construction of his wall along the border with Mexico. As Trump explained, "A nation without borders is not a nation."[9] Another halted all refugee admissions. And a third (initially stayed by federal courts) suspended the entry of citizens from seven Muslim-majority nations.[10] As Trump consigliere Stephen Bannon explained to the Conservative Political Action Conference in February 2017, "Protecting the sovereignty of the United States, putting a wall on the southern border, making sure that criminals are not part of our [immigration] process. These are all things that 80 percent of Americans agree with, and these are all things that President Trump is doing within 30 days." The president's message, Bannon continued, was that henceforth the "rule of law is going to exist when you talk about our sovereignty and you talk about immigration."[11]

In the view of the Trump White House, fortifying U.S. borders was the single most important step the country could take to end illegal immigration, crack down on transnational crime, and combat the terrorist threat posed by jihadist networks. The administration's determination to reassert border control, however, overlooked important realities. To begin with, illegal immigration, transnational crime, and jihadist terrorism are inherently different problems that require tailored approaches well beyond simply tighter policing of America's frontiers. In addition, the president's focus on an imposing physical barrier on the southern border was a simplistic response to illegal immigration, one that failed to address underlying economic incentives driving domestic demand for migrant labor and, accordingly, was unlikely to have a significant impact on illegal immigration. Finally, the Trump administration ignored that a critical precondition for improving U.S. border security was to strike "sovereignty bargains" with important international partners, particularly Mexico. In his quest to reassert U.S. sovereignty-as-authority and sovereignty-as-autonomy, the president risked forfeiting an opportunity to expand U.S. sovereignty-as-influence—in this case, by taking more practical steps to address the border crisis.

BORDER CONTROL, SOVEREIGNTY, AND IMMIGRATION

Much like a monopoly on the use of force, the state's authority and ability to control flows across its borders is today considered a core attribute—and yardstick—of sovereignty.[12] But whereas countries have long enjoyed full authority to police their frontiers, their practical ability to do so has always been incomplete. No country has achieved perfect border control—and none likely ever will.

By one estimate, the world possesses more than 220,000 kilometers of land borders (in addition to extensive maritime frontiers). Most of these boundaries are uncontested by other states. But their permeability varies dramatically, depending (among other variables) on the terrain, local traditions, and capabilities of the relevant governments. In much of the postcolonial world, such as the African Sahel, the neat lines that nineteenth-century imperialists demarcated on maps are crisscrossed daily by bandits, herders, merchants, migrants, nomads, rebels, smugglers, and traffickers. And even when ruling regimes aspire to control these borders rather than look the other way, their ability to do so is often negligible.[13]

But even wealthy world governments strain to prevent illicit entry of people and contraband, despite possessing extensive bureaucracies, surveillance technologies, and professional border guards. Consider the ill-fated "war on drugs," which President Richard Nixon first declared in 1971. Despite many tens of billions spent on interdiction and source-country eradication, the United States has failed to stanch the inward flow of narcotics. In 2015, according to Drug Enforcement Agency (DEA) estimates, Americans consumed approximately 300 metric tons of imported cocaine with a street value of $7.32 billion. Meanwhile, U.S. seizures of heroin (a small fraction of the total American consumption of that drug) amounted to 6,722 kilograms, valued at $3.36 billion.[14] Viewed dispassionately, the drug war's main accomplishments appear to have been twofold: inflating the profits enjoyed by foreign producers and traffickers ingenious enough to evade the U.S. prohibition regime, and contributing to soaring rates of violence in the transit countries of Mexico and Central America.[15]

Notwithstanding such daily violations, international law treats national frontiers as sacrosanct, recognizing the sovereign right of each nation-state to secure them. Here is another example of the "organized hypocrisy" that (as Stephen Krasner notes) infuses the concept and practice of sovereignty.[16] The reason is clear enough: all states live in glass houses, and they have a mutual interest in recognizing their sole authority to police their respective boundaries and territories, regardless of their actual capacity to do so.

Globally, there is a widespread perception that states are struggling as never before to control their borders, not least from illegal entry by economic migrants and refugees.[17] In 2015 an estimated 244 million people—or 3.3 percent of the planet's inhabitants—lived outside the country in which they were born.[18] Although most migrants use regular channels, millions also arrive illegally each year, after desperate journeys, having enlisted smugglers to secure passage on rickety boats or through remote frontier regions. Too often the result is tragedy, as documented in disturbing images like a drowned

Syrian toddler washed up on a Greek beach or a Central American mother dead of thirst in the Sonoran desert.

Migration is nothing new, of course. What is different today is its global scope. Virtually every nation, rich and poor alike, is now both a source and destination country. Revolutions in transportation and telecommunications have lowered travel costs, exposed populations to the allure of better lives in distant lands, and facilitated the emergence of licit infrastructures and illicit networks to deliver migrants to new destinations. Growing economic inequality within and between nations encourages more workers to seek fortunes abroad, including as migrant laborers who send remittances back to their families. Finally, many migrants today leave involuntarily as victims of complex humanitarian emergencies. In 2016 some 65.6 million people were designated as displaced, the largest number since World War II. These included 22.5 million refugees (those who had crossed national borders) and 2.8 million asylum seekers.[19]

At times, massive, uncontrolled, and undocumented population flows can overwhelm nations, as Greece discovered when hundreds of thousands of refugees and migrants suddenly landed on its doorstep in 2015. Beyond challenging national governments' claims to supreme authority over demarcated territories and populations, the sudden entry of large number of foreigners can create economic dislocation. But it also poses subtler challenges. Many citizens in receiving countries fear that migrants will undermine social cohesion and national identity, as host societies strain to absorb and assimilate new ethnic, cultural, and religious groups with different values, customs, and allegiances.[20]

The United States is hardly immune to such pressures. For decades the U.S. government has struggled to deliver on promises to restrict inflows of illegal immigrants, especially across the nation's southern border. This failure is a function not only of the daunting complexity of that task but also of the continued dependence of American businesses on unskilled immigrant labor for employment in agriculture and other economic sectors. This governance lapse understandably frustrates American citizens, who overwhelmingly oppose illegal immigration, perceiving it as a threat to their livelihoods, their security, and (in many cases) their culture.

MIGRATION IN U.S. HISTORY

From a sovereignty perspective, immigration (both legal and illegal) is an even more sensitive and vexing issue than trade policy. This is because immigration touches on fundamental questions of national identity. The very concept of popular sovereignty, after all, presupposes that there exists an identifiable "people" who, through democratic processes of self-determination, are able to translate their aspirations into political preferences and to provide guidance to political agents they elect to act on their behalf. But who exactly are the "people"?

As heirs to the Enlightenment, Americans are predisposed to define "the people" as individual citizens—and to assume that anyone can become "American," regardless of his or her country of origin. This ethos distinguishes the United States from other countries—Germany, for example—that have historically defined the people (*Volk*) along ethno-nationalist lines, based on shared ties of blood and soil. Most of America's Founders were confident that foreign-born arrivals would imbibe the liberal elixir at the heart of the American project and come to embrace the principles of individual liberty and self-government. George Washington was certainly among them. "America is open to receive not only the Opulent and respectable Stranger, but the oppressed and persecuted of all Nations and Religions," he declared in 1783.[21]

The United States remains the quintessential land of immigrants, and immigrant narratives are at the core of its national mythology. And yet for all of that, Americans tend to celebrate *their own* immigrant pasts far more than they do recent trends and arrivals. And it is hard to blame them entirely, since sustained, large-scale immigration brings not only benefits but also potential headaches. It can test the nation's control over its borders and territory, upend established industries, weaken employment prospects, strain social services, and challenge cultural norms. The issue of immigration also reveals tensions within political liberalism itself—notably, between the universalist ideal of open borders, on the one hand, and the conviction that democratic self-determination and the exercise of popular sovereignty are only possible within the confines of a bounded civic community, on the other.[22]

Periodically through U.S. history, moreover, immigration has exposed illiberal strains lurking below the surface of liberal America. Despite its ideological commitment to radical individualism, the United States has repeatedly succumbed to ugly, nativist nationalism based on ethnic or racist stereotypes. The targets of these chauvinist outbursts have shifted over time, from Germans in the late 1700s to Irish in the mid-nineteenth century, to Chinese and Japanese decades later, to southern and eastern Europeans (as well as Jews) in the early twentieth century, to Mexicans since the 1980s, and to Muslims and Arabs today. But the underlying motivations have remained constant: a determination to safeguard status hierarchies, defend cultural homogeneity, and preserve economic livelihoods against new groups deemed "alien" on racial, ethnic, linguistic, religious, or other grounds.

American ambivalence toward immigration has been reflected in alternating eras of openness and closure, intervals punctuated by major federal legislation.[23] Over the past century and a half, the United States has tended to embrace openness at moments of high confidence in globalization and to restrict entry during times of economic downturn, national insecurity, and cultural anxiety, particularly when recent immigration (legal and illegal) has approached historical highs.

Until the late 1800s the United States made virtually no effort to police its national frontiers—and neither did other Western countries. This nonchalance reflected a liberal conviction that open borders were the handmaiden of economic expansion, as well as a perceived complementarity between the sources of and destinations for migrant labor. In the United States the need for a growing population to settle, tame, and develop America's enormous territory made massive immigration the logical course.

Accordingly, from 1790 to 1875 the U.S. government placed no restrictions on immigration. Individuals from anywhere could enter the country without travel documents and with the right to work upon arrival. America's long northern and southern borders were unguarded, and the forts along its expanding western frontier existed primarily to protect settlers from and conduct punitive expeditions against Native American tribes. What border controls existed were concentrated in seaports and devoted to collecting customs duties, on which the federal government depended for an overwhelming share of its revenue before World War I.[24]

It was only in the late nineteenth and early twentieth centuries that the U.S. government and its European counterparts began to establish a uniform international system to regulate the cross-border movement of people, a shift symbolized by, among other things, the "universal adoption of the passport."[25] The growing power of nationalism and the gradual emergence of the welfare state underpinned this regulatory impulse. The nationality principle suggested that a state's borders should be coterminous with (even restricted to) the "nation"—increasingly conceived as an identifiable ethnolinguistic community with deep historical roots. Simultaneously, industrialization and urbanization placed pressure on governments to provide their citizens (and *only* their citizens) with basic social protections. The right to control entry of nonnationals, and to restrict "alien" races and cultures, became an inherent attribute of sovereignty.[26] Henceforth, good fences would make good neighbors.

The U.S. Congress passed its first legislation to restrict immigration in 1875, when the Immigration Act barred the entry of prostitutes and criminals. Far more significant was the Chinese Exclusion Act (1882). This prohibited admission of Chinese laborers, whose numbers had surged in California and other western states during the mining and railroad building booms of the previous three decades, breeding a racist backlash among the region's white population. Nine years later Congress passed a new Immigration Act, marking the first time that the United States began to deport illegal immigrants, a "category at the time limited principally to Chinese workers as well as felons, paupers, and the insane."[27]

These U.S. efforts had little impact on overall immigration, however. In the first decade of the twentieth century more than 8 million immigrants arrived in the country, most through Ellis Island. By 1910 the foreign-born had reached 15 percent of the total U.S. population—the highest level since the mid-1850s. The new arrivals, who hailed disproportionately from southern and eastern Europe, encountered hostility from other, more established white Americans hailing from western and northern Europe.

Seeking to turn off the spigot, American nativists made common cause with Progressive-era advocates of government activism. Their victories included an extension of the Chinese Exclusion Act, as well as the Gentlemen's Agreement to limit Japanese labor immigration into the United States. But their bigger triumph came in 1921, on the heels of the "Red Scare" and during the heyday of the pseudo-science of eugenics, when Congress passed the highly restrictive National Quota Act. It established annual immigration allocations for each nationality, pegged to 3 percent of their share of the U.S. population in 1910. Three years later Congress shut the gate even tighter: the National Origins Act reduced annual national quotas to only 2 percent of their share of the U.S. population *in 1890*.

Such draconian restrictions enjoyed broad support within "respectable" American society, including the two debaters introduced at the beginning of this book, Henry Cabot Lodge and A. Lawrence Lowell. "If a nation cannot say without appeal who shall come within its gates and become part of its citizenship it has ceased to be a sovereign nation," the Massachusetts senator declared in their 1919 face-off.[28] The Harvard president concurred. The United States must resist "the influx in great numbers of a widely different race."[29] In their view, the survival of liberal democracy depended on racial and ethnic homogeneity.

The 1921 and 1924 acts closed the "front door" to the United States by strictly curtailing legal overseas immigration from Europe and Asia. But there remained plenty of "back door" immigration, much of it illegal, across the nation's largely uncontrolled land borders with Canada and Mexico. The result, as immigration historian Daniel J. Tichenor explains, was a "two-tier regulatory regime." Despite the creation of the U.S. Border Patrol in 1924 (intended to enforce the 1924 National Origins Act, as well as the Eighteenth Amendment prohibiting the production, transport, and sale of alcohol in the United States), U.S. officials turned a blind eye to Mexican immigration—much of it seasonal agricultural labor—upon which U.S. farmers depended. And in 1942, during World War II, the United States negotiated with the Mexican government to establish the Bracero guest worker program, which lasted until 1964.[30]

The national origins system, meanwhile, would persist for another forty-one years, until President Lyndon B. Johnson secured passage of the Immigration Act of 1965. That legislation dramatically reshaped U.S. demographics by reducing European quotas and expanding the share of new arrivals from Asia and Latin America. Unfortunately but unsurprisingly, this shifting immigrant composition generated a growing political reaction, spearheaded by anti-immigration groups like the Federation for American Immigration Reform (FAIR) and the Center for Immigration Studies (CIS). Nevertheless, legal immigration continued to soar through the 1980s and 1990s. Presidents Reagan, George H. W. Bush, and Clinton adopted expansive immigration policies as a natural extension of their free-market, proglobalization orientation, even as a majority of U.S. citizens favored reductions in legal admissions.[31]

But it was illegal immigration, particularly from Mexico, that engendered growing public outrage. The 1965 act had opened up new pathways for legal immigration to the United States, but it also terminated Mexican guest worker programs that had facilitated a circular, seasonal flow of labor to and from the United States. As a result, increasing numbers of Mexicans began to sneak into the United States—and to remain once they arrived. Seeking to regain control of the border, Congress in 1986 passed the Immigration Reform and Control Act (IRCA). It provided one-time amnesty to Mexicans who had resided illegally in the United States for four years, while imposing new border controls and sanctions for employers who hired undocumented workers. As it happened, the amnesty provision was the only part of the law that succeeded, and the stream of illegal aliens continued unabated, at approximately 300,000 arrivals per year.[32] To get around border controls, greater numbers of illegal immigrants contracted the services of organized criminal organizations.

BORDER SECURITY IN THE AGE OF TERROR

During the Cold War, efforts to secure the U.S. border focused primarily on national defense—specifically, deterring potential military threats posed by the Soviet Union. As the communist threat receded and then collapsed, however, the rationale for American border security shifted to countering illegal immigration and narcotics trafficking. Indeed, the United States invested a healthy share of its post–Cold War "peace dividend" in border law enforcement, in an effort to secure the nation's southern frontier and maritime approaches to it. Between 1995 and 2001 alone, the U.S. Immigration and Naturalization Service budget for border enforcement tripled, topping $2.5 billion in fiscal year 2002.[33]

But it was the terrorist attacks of September 11, 2001, that made U.S. border control a central element in what became known as "homeland security." The global war on terrorism would be fought in multiple theaters, but it was at the border where the overseas and home fronts met. Increasingly, U.S. officials and the American public perceived the threats of terrorism, transnational crime, and illegal immigration not as distinct challenges, each with its own causal dynamics and potential solutions, but as intertwined dangers amenable to the same course of treatment.

The immediate U.S. response to 9/11 was to tighten the American border, previously among the world's most open. American homeland security officials faced daunting challenges. Chief among them was "monitoring the $1 trillion in goods and 493 million vehicles and people that were to cross over the 7,500 miles of U.S. land borders and through nearly 130 airports and seaports" each year.[34] The George W. Bush administration ramped up border inspections, initially bringing land traffic and trade with Canada and Mexico to a virtual standstill. It also imposed stringent screening and vetting for visa applicants from Arab and Muslim-majority nations and adopted a highly restrictive system—known as the National Security Entry-Exit Registration System (NSEERS)—to register citizens from those countries. The result was a public relations and diplomatic nightmare for the United States, as well as a major dip in overseas students coming to study at U.S. universities.[35]

These early responses showed just how hard it was to secure the nation's frontiers without bringing globalization—based on lengthy supply chains and just-in-time deliveries—to a halt. By walling itself off, the United States also risked losing one of its most valuable attributes, and an important pillar of its economic vitality, diplomatic strength, and indeed national security—namely, its openness.[36]

Over time, through often painful trial and error, the Bush administration adopted a more balanced, technocratic approach to securing the U.S. border. This risk management method, which the Obama administration would continue, recognized that perfect security was a mirage—and that the costs of pursuing it, in terms of lost opportunities from globalization, would be extraordinary. Given its scarce resources, the United States had to prioritize threats according their probability, as well as consequences. To secure its borders adequately, without cutting off the free flow of goods and people on which its prosperity depended, the United States had to adopt a "smart border" approach based on a combination of high technology, intelligence sharing, and big data collection. Border security also had to become "layered"—that is, extending out from the U.S. frontier—so that American officials would have a sense of what and who was headed the nation's way well before cargo or persons entered the United States.

Between fiscal year 2003 and fiscal year 2017, U.S. spending on border security surged 73.6 percent, from $11 billion to $19.1 billion.[37] Much of this expenditure was devoted to improving surveillance of human movement. Important innovations included exploiting massive databases and new biometric technologies, enhancing visa and identification requirements, screening prospective entrants outside of the country, and monitoring all passengers, including citizens (albeit softened by innovations like "trusted traveler" programs).[38]

The story was not all positive, however. One of the biggest flaws in the post-9/11 U.S. approach to homeland security was to combine counterterrorism efforts with combating illegal immigration.[39] On the surface, the decision to merge these two tasks seemed reasonable. After all, how could the nation protect itself from terrorist attacks if U.S. officials had no idea who was traversing the (mostly southern) border, and when more than 10 million illegal immigrants already lived in the United States? But as experience would teach, these two border security challenges were—and remain—fundamentally different.

Every year hundreds of thousands of illegal migrants stream across the U.S. border. And yet at the time of this writing, not a single terrorist suspect arrested in the United States had entered from Mexico. Transnational terrorists remain a tiny, distinct group of people who are unlikely to be caught through better enforcement of immigration laws.

Despite this reality, the Obama administration, like its predecessor, continued to allocate the lion's share of U.S. homeland security funds to trying to control the border with Mexico—a pattern that continues today.[40] Indeed, by 2017 the distinct challenges of terrorism and illegal immigration, as well as the separate problem of drug trafficking, had become hopelessly conflated in U.S. political discourse. The predictable result was a warped, one-size-fits-all border security policy.

Illegal Immigration and U.S. Politics

Long before Donald Trump began seeking the U.S. presidential nomination, conservative politicians and commentators depicted lax control of the U.S. border as a multipronged threat to U.S. sovereignty that endangered American jobs, security, and identity. In economic terms, a flood of undocumented, unskilled labor threatened to depress domestic wages and raise U.S. unemployment. Porous borders, they said, also facilitated the entry of drugs, criminals, and other ne'er-do-wells. Finally, many citizens, particularly of European descent, feared that uncontrolled migration would dramatically change the U.S. demographic and ethnic makeup, driving the nation toward a multicultural future that forever altered what it meant to be "American."[41]

In 1984 President Ronald Reagan warned, "The simple truth is that we've lost control of our borders, and no nation can do that and survive."[42] A decade later, California governor Pete Wilson's reelection campaign produced a brutally effective television spot featuring blurred footage of "illegals" evading U.S. border controls, as the narrator intoned, "They keep coming, and coming." In the first decade of the twenty-first century, Joe Arpaio, the tough-talking sheriff of Maricopa County, Arizona, became a conservative folk hero and talk radio darling for his hardline stance against illegal aliens, as well as criminals, in Phoenix and its environs.[43]

By 2014, according to the U.S. Census Bureau, 42.3 million foreign-born immigrants lived in the United States, amounting to 13.3 percent of the U.S. population. Of these, an estimated 11–12 million—perhaps 27 percent of that total—were unauthorized immigrants, with 70 percent of them hailing from Mexico and Central America.[44] These percentages were high by historical standards, but not unprecedented. As figure 7-1 shows, since the 1860s the immigrant proportion of the U.S. population has waxed and waned, cresting at about 15 percent around 1890, and again in 1910, declining to about 5 percent around 1970, and rising steadily since.

What is unprecedented, however, is the proportion of arrivals who have entered the United States in recent years from the same country (Mexico), speaking the same language (Spanish). This is significant because it has increased the salience of ethnic identity considerations in how many Americans (not least among the country's still-white majority) conceive of U.S. national sovereignty—and its vulnerability.

Such concerns gained new prominence in summer 2014, thanks to a surge of undocumented migrants and asylum seekers—many of them unaccompanied minors fleeing violence in Central America—across the U.S. southern

FIGURE 7-1. Immigrants as Share of U.S. Population, 1850–2014

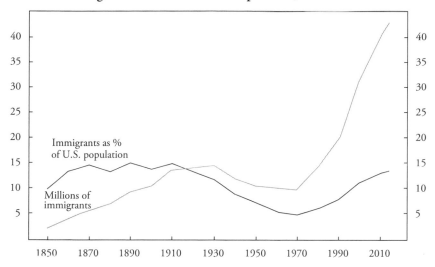

Source: Migration Policy Institute tabulations of the U.S. Census Bureau's 2010–15 American Community Surveys and 1970, 1990, and 2000 census data. All other data are from Campbell Gibson and Emily Lennon, "Historical Census Statistics on the Foreign-Born Population of the United States: 1850 to 1990," Working Paper No. 29, U.S. Census Bureau (Government Printing Office, 1999).

border. On Capitol Hill, Republican legislators attacked President Obama's failure to impose order and his plans to offer "amnesty" to illegal immigrants. One of the most prominent was Senator Jeff Sessions of Alabama, whom three years later Donald Trump would name to be his attorney general. "Our border is not secure; it is in crisis. . . . Our communities are not safe . . . and our sovereignty is not protected," railed Sessions. That same year Daryl Metcalfe, a Republican member of Pennsylvania's House of Representatives, complained that "our federal government has been AWOL for decades in . . . defending our nation from illegal alien invaders." The calamitous results had included "homicide, rape, property theft, serious infectious diseases, drug running, gang violence, human trafficking, terrorism, stolen jobs and growing cost to taxpayers."[45]

Conservative media commentators agreed. "A nation that encourages foreigners to enter its territory illegally can hardly be considered a sovereign nation," Howard Foster opined in the *National Interest*. Robert Merry, writing in the same journal, concurred. "Most Americans . . . have an interest in their country's sovereignty," he declared. "They understand that a country that can't control its borders is, to that extent, a diminished country; and that citizenship in such a country is of diminished value."[46]

On the fringes of American society, meanwhile, anxiety that the United States had lost control over its borders quickly merged with broader fears that U.S. sovereignty was besieged by alien global forces that threatened the nation's destiny and indeed the liberties of its citizens. One response to this alarm has been the emergence of a paramilitary "militia" movement in the American Southwest, composed of armed U.S. citizens who have deputized themselves to defend the country's remote frontier regions. Its members seem quite certain of the dangers confronting the United States. As one militiaman told an undercover reporter for *Mother Jones* in 2016, "I see a time comin' when there will be blue hats [UN troops] patrolling our streets. Cuz [Obama] wants to make the world government. He wants to subject the US to international law and submissiveness. UN control. World government control. Just to make the US another satellite nation. Do away with sovereignty."[47]

No doubt some Americans' discomfort with recent immigration trends reflects racism pure and simple. But that is not the entire story. Equally salient is the purported threat that immigrants—legal as well as illegal—pose to the nation's civic and cultural fabric. American public discourse on immigration is heated precisely because it touches on these societal dimensions of sovereignty. That is, when many Americans speak of a potential loss of U.S. sovereignty, they are conceiving not only of the territorially bounded political unit known as the United States but of an American nation whose identity is at stake, thanks to rapid and unsettling changes in its demographic and cultural makeup.

The fact that much of this migration is illegal only fuels these anxieties. As Roxanne Doty explains, "When it is no longer clear who makes up the nation, a state's internal sovereignty and the existence of the state itself is threatened."[48] In a July 2014 poll, 70 percent of respondents agreed that undocumented immigrants threatened traditional U.S. beliefs and customs. For many of these citizens, the stakes in border control transcend worries about crime and employment to include the survival of the American way of life. And any move to provide such illegal aliens with a pathway to citizenship, in the words of former representative Ron Paul (R-Tex.), "sells out our sovereignty."[49]

And this sentiment is not restricted to *illegal* immigrants. Many Americans perceive recent arrivals as less supportive of national values and more resistant to assimilation than previous generations. Such worries are hardly unique to the United States, of course. Anti-immigrant sentiments are even stronger in some European societies that lack America's experience with multiculturalism. But whereas national identity in many other countries is based heavily on long-standing kinship and territorial ties, the United States is a nation of immigrants, in which citizenship is not a birthright but—at least in theory—a political commitment.

This makes American national identity and societal cohesion uniquely reliant on the willingness of U.S. inhabitants to embrace common political principles. And that, according to many conservatives, is no longer happening. The Hudson Institute, for instance, finds "a large 'patriotic gap' . . . between native born citizens and immigrant citizens." Another conservative outfit, the Bradley Foundation, finds that "immigrant citizens [are] less likely than native-born citizens to emphasize the uniqueness of America and American identity."[50] In a Breitbart interview in March 2016, Stephen Bannon, who would become the senior strategist in the Trump White House, put the question plainly: "Don't we have a problem with legal immigration?" he asked. "Twenty percent of this country is immigrants. Is that not the beating heart of this problem?"[51]

Donald Trump tapped into these growing anxieties and grievances during his presidential campaign, when he repeatedly decried a U.S. border "out of control" and a nation overwhelmed by immigrants that did not share and indeed imperiled American values. Consistent with their nominee, the Republican Party included in its 2016 platform a commitment to walling off America's frontier with Mexico:

> In a time of terrorism, drug cartels, human trafficking, and criminal gangs, the presence of millions of unidentified individuals in this country poses grave risks to the safety and sovereignty of the United States. Our highest priority, therefore, must be to secure our borders and all ports of entry and to enforce our immigration laws. That is why we support building a wall along our southern border and protecting all ports of entry. The border wall must cover the entirety of the southern border and must be sufficient to stop both vehicular and pedestrian traffic.[52]

Ironically, Trump pushed for his impenetrable physical barrier at a time when illegal migration from Mexico had declined to its lowest level in years—and when more Mexicans were leaving the United States than entering it—thanks to improving economic conditions in that country and the Obama administration's own massive investments in U.S. border security.[53] From 2009 to 2015 the United States deported record numbers of undocumented individuals, in the process antagonizing human rights groups for "treating women and children fleeing violence in Central America as economic migrants rather than refugees."[54] As a result of U.S. efforts and changing economic conditions in Mexico, a million fewer undocumented Mexicans lived in the United States in 2015 than in 2007.

Nevertheless, perceptions remained widespread that the U.S. immigration system was hapless and the southern border leaky. Many Americans seethed at the thought of 11–12 million undocumented foreigners residing illegally in the United States, taking their jobs, contributing to wage stagnation, and freeloading on U.S. generosity. The fact that undocumented migrants could be framed not simply as lawbreakers and economic competitors but also as potential terrorists and other threats to U.S. national security merely increased political outrage, which Trump was happy to stoke and exploit. According to an October 2016 poll by the Chicago Council on Global Affairs, taken just weeks before the election, two-thirds of Republicans viewed illegal immigration as a "critical threat" to the United States and believed that controlling it should be "a very important goal" of U.S. foreign policy.[55]

To be sure, the desire to regain control of porous national borders is hardly restricted to the United States: In Mexico itself, 60 percent of respondents surveyed in a 2014 poll supported building a wall along their country's *own* southern border (with Guatemala) to stanch the inflow of Central American migrants. The following year the European Union nearly blew apart as it coped with the challenge of absorbing more than a million refugees and migrants from Syria, as well as Afghanistan, Somalia, Eritrea, and other conflict zones. In response to the latter crisis, European states suspended the Schengen Agreement allowing free movement of peoples among twenty-six countries, as well as the Dublin Regulations requiring refugee applications to be processed in the first EU country of entry. European governments hastily erected fences and closed borders in an unedifying game of "pass the migrant," and they rejected a proposal from Brussels that they adopt a bloc-wide quota system to equitably share the refugee burden.[56] (And in June 2016, discontent with the migration crisis helped the "Leave" camp secure victory in the referendum on "Brexit"—a British exit from the EU.)

Migration, Border Control, and Sovereignty Bargains

To secure the gains of global integration, the United States must remain open to beneficial cross-border transactions while regulating this traffic and securing its frontiers against unwanted flows. The trade-off between openness and sovereignty is especially fraught when it comes to illegal immigration, which remains one of the most contentious issues in contemporary American politics.

There is an understandable temptation to frame the policy solution as a simple matter of erecting physical (and other) barriers to the entry of undocumented individuals, as well as arresting and deporting those already in the United States. Such a strategy has a visceral appeal, particularly for Americans who perceive "illegal aliens" not only as lawbreakers but indeed as unfamiliar "others" who threaten the societal cohesion on which popular sovereignty ultimately rests. To his supporters, Donald Trump's pledge to crack down on illegal immigration was a promise to restore the nation's sovereignty-as-authority (framed as "the rule of law") and to make full use of the nation's sovereignty-as-autonomy (in employing all the tools at the state's disposal), regardless of reactions of countries like Mexico or the politically correct sensitivities of more liberal U.S. citizens.

As an approach to border security, however, Trump's diagnosis of the problem and his proposed solution were misguided on several levels. To begin with, the claim that the United States had "lost control" of its borders was both ahistorical and exaggerated. Contemporary critiques about the porosity of the nation's frontiers reflect misplaced nostalgia for a time when the federal government wielded absolute power to control its borders. In truth, no such era ever existed. Smuggling was rampant in the earliest days of the American republic—to the degree that the United States can be said to have been built on illicit commerce.[57] Likewise, until a century ago the United States took little interest in controlling immigration. Since that time, the United States has experienced periodic waves of migration, both legal and illegal. As a percentage of the population, the number of illegal immigrants from Mexico to the United States peaked in 2007. Since then, the number of migrants in the United States has remained high but it is not unprecedented.[58]

Second, contrary to what Trump alleged as a candidate, the United States had hardly remained passive in its efforts to improve its border security. Far from throwing in the towel, the federal government under President Obama adopted more sophisticated, layered strategies to police U.S. borders and became more zealous in its effort to remove undocumented migrants. This included erecting more physical barriers as well as using fleets of drones and remote sensors to detect illegal transit, dispatching aircraft and coast guard vessels to interdict migrant smugglers at sea, augmenting and arming border control agents, constructing massive detention centers, and expanding "third border" initiatives by placing U.S. immigration officers at foreign airports and other points of embarkation.[59] Thanks to these diverse initiatives, by the time Trump took office the United States possessed an extensive border-protection-industrial-complex and had reduced annual flows of illegal immigrants.

Third, Trump conflated the border security problems of illegal immigration, drug trafficking, and terrorism, ignoring that distinct challenges are driven by different dynamics and are best addressed through tailored strategies. Combating terrorism, for instance, requires above all close bilateral and multilateral intelligence coordination and information sharing among governments to identify and screen small numbers of dangerous individuals and interdict them before they have an opportunity to cross the border, much less to strike their targets. Counternarcotics efforts, meanwhile, rely on a combination of intelligence and law enforcement cooperation among source, transit, and destination countries; domestic demand (and harm) reduction policies; and targeted interdiction efforts outside, at, and within U.S. borders. Combatting illegal immigration, finally, entails addressing the economic incentives behind both the supply and demand for migrant labor. Any successful policy will likely require negotiation with Mexico and other source countries of bilateral guest worker programs that permit a circular flow of labor, effective sanctions against U.S. firms that knowingly hire illegal aliens, and some legal pathway to regularize the status of aliens already in the United States.[60]

Fourth, the vision of a completely secure U.S. border—as Trump implied when he proposed an "impenetrable" wall—is a mirage. The United States will never achieve 100 percent control over its borders. Not only is that goal impossible, but the cost of attempting to approach that objective would be crippling. "Trying to turn every port and crossing into a little Maginot Line is a losing strategy," James Jay Carafano of the Heritage Foundation has written. "Like the French defenses for World War II, this approach would be both very expensive and likely to fail because an innovative enemy will find a way around the defenses."[61] Exhaustive screening of every individual (or, as some would like, every bit of cargo entering the United States) would impede the smooth flow of people and goods required for international commerce and American economic prosperity.

One indicator of the potential costs came more than three decades ago, in 1985, in the aftermath of the kidnapping of U.S. DEA agent Enrique "Kiki" Camarena by a Mexican drug cartel. Furious at perceived Mexican government foot-dragging, William von Raab, commissioner of the U.S. Customs Service, abruptly ordered U.S. inspectors to search *every* passenger vehicle and commercial truck entering the United States at all fifteen official U.S.-Mexico border crossings. "Operation Camarena" brought cross-border transportation and commerce to a standstill.

The challenge for the United States is to hit the sweet spot between closing itself off from the world by constructing imposing physical barriers and issu-

ing draconian travel bans, on the one hand, and leaving its frontiers unregulated and undefended, on the other. The solution to this conundrum will be
found not in heavy-handed border control efforts, but in a risk management
approach to human mobility that allows the United States to focus its security efforts on the greatest dangers while still benefiting from globalization.[62]
This is in effect the approach that the United States has adopted for shipping
containers, only 3–4 percent of which undergo physical inspection upon entering the country. At first glance, that number seems awfully small. But U.S.
officials can reduce the risk significantly by targeting specific containers based
on the latest intelligence, their knowledge of the relevant supply chain, and
their confidence in security protocols at the port of origin and transit points.

A risk management approach recognizes that borders are more usefully
conceived not as impenetrable "walls" but as (semipermeable) "membranes"
that—as in living cells—mediate the relationship between internal and external spaces. National borders can be configured (and reconfigured) to facilitate
or restrict particular flows between the outside world and a nation's autonomous political and legal space.[63] Already the United States employs elements
of this approach in its policies for granting visas to individuals for both short-
and long-term stays. The resulting system tends to privilege legal entry for the
affluent, entrepreneurs, and highly skilled workers, while shutting out those
designated as potential threats to national security, economic prosperity, and
sociocultural cohesion.[64]

Finally, taming illegal immigration will require the United States to cooperate with Mexico and other source and transit countries for illegal immigration, in the process striking sovereignty bargains in which America trades off
autonomy for influence. In principle, of course, the United States could simply
try to end illegal border crossings unilaterally, as well as dramatically expand
its deportation policies. The associated diplomatic and economic costs, however, would be heavy. A more effective strategy would be to work closely with
governments in Mexico and Central America, which retain significant leverage
to discourage emigration, by deploying incentives that could alter the calculations of potential emigrants. These countries will also be essential partners in
any guest worker arrangement Washington may seek to negotiate to restore a
circular flow of migrant labor to and from the United States.

Reviving hemispheric cooperation on illegal immigration would imply entering into new sovereignty bargains—specifically, relinquishing some freedom of action (sovereignty-as-autonomy) in return for the anticipated benefits
of collaboration (sovereignty-as-influence) with other nations on the challenge
of illegal immigration. This collective approach to managing interdependence—

in this case regulating the flow of people across borders—may require some psychological adjustments on the part of Americans. "As two distinct components of state sovereignty," explains migration scholar Fiona Adamson, "autonomy and capacity are often viewed as going hand-in-hand." But globalization tests this traditional conception of state effectiveness, since "to manage cross-border challenges, state capacity is enhanced, rather than threatened, by increased cooperation with other states in areas such as the formulation and enforcement of migration policy." Specifically, international migration "create[s] incentives for states to selectively relinquish dimensions of their autonomy so as to increase their capacity to control their borders."[65]

For the United States, restoring control over migration is likely to require greater bilateral and multilateral cooperation. This will include new arrangements that increase the collective capacity of the United States and its partners to stem illegal flows of people, interdict illicit goods, and expand their ability to enforce laws within their borders. A central element of any effective U.S. approach to illegal immigration is likely to be a bilateral deal with Mexico, focused on registered guest workers, and involving social protections for them while they remain in the United States.

Even so, migration will always be a trickier cooperation problem than other globalization challenges, like trade, for the simple reason that it touches directly on concepts of national identity. In the case of the WTO, the United States has found it (relatively) straightforward to exchange some sovereign autonomy (and even some sovereign authority under the DSU) for the promise of trade benefits. Migration is a tougher nut to crack because the border itself helps to distinguish "us" from "them," defining who is included within (or excluded from) the nation. And as Christopher Rudolph explains, "When societal dimensions of sovereignty are included in the analysis, 'sovereignty bargains' are far more complex than 'trading' one dimension of sovereignty for another."[66] Accordingly, the first instinct of national authorities, when confronted with uncontrolled population flows, is typically to harden the shell of the state. Experience has shown, however, that hardening America's frontiers is at best a partial solution to the problem of illegal immigration. A comprehensive response must acknowledge the underlying incentives driving the demand for (and supply of) migrant labor and create legitimate channels for that flow to occur through legal means.

EIGHT

Don't Tread on Me

The United States and International Organizations

B oris Johnson, the mop-haired former mayor of London, was incredulous. It was mid-April 2016. President Barack Obama had just inserted himself into the most momentous political decision to confront the United Kingdom in decades: whether to leave the European Union. Johnson, a leader of the "Leave" campaign, found it "absolutely bizarre" to be "lectured by the Americans about giving up our sovereignty," and he scoffed at Obama's plan to deliver his plea in person just two months before Britain held its pivotal referendum. "I don't know what he's going to say," Johnson told the BBC, "but if that is the American argument then it is nakedly hypocritical." After all, "the Americans won't even sign up to the international convention on the law of the seas, let alone the International Criminal Court."[1]

One week later Obama stood beside U.K. prime minister David Cameron, himself a champion of the "Remain" camp. The president made it clear where he stood. Leaving the bloc would carry enormous risks, he warned, and also place Britain "at the back of the queue" in negotiations to enter the planned Transatlantic Trade and Investment Partnership (TTIP). "A strong Europe is not a threat to Britain's global leadership; it enhances Britain's global leadership," the president elaborated in the *Telegraph* the next day. "In today's world, even as we all cherish our sovereignty, the nations who wield their influence most effectively are the nations that do it through the collective action that today's challenges demand."[2]

Many others made similar pleas, including officials from the Bank of England, the City of London, the International Monetary Fund, and the Organization for Economic Cooperation and Development, as well as leading academics. In the end, none of it mattered. On June 23, 2016, British voters handed the Leave campaign a shocking if narrow victory, choosing by 52 percent to 48 percent to depart the EU. Johnson heralded it as Britain's "Independence Day."[3]

The result threw the EU into turmoil. The bloc had long suffered from deficits of both democracy and affection, of course. "Brussels"—where most EU institutions are located—had become shorthand for officious, unaccountable Eurocrats meddling in everything from national fisheries policies to the proper shape of bananas.[4] For too many of its 500 million citizens, the EU seemed distant, opaque, and unresponsive. Now it faced a real possibility of unraveling were other members to join the United Kingdom in the departure lounge.

In the past European leaders had seized on crises to deepen integration, depicting "more Europe" as the only solution. That dynamic seemed to have run its course. From its origins as a tight bloc of six members, the EU had grown into an unwieldy, continent-spanning behemoth encompassing twenty-eight heterogeneous nations. Stuck in an unmanagable halfway house between a confederation of sovereign states and a federal political union, the EU seemed less likely to achieve the "ever-closer union" envisioned in its Lisbon Treaty (2009) than a looser, multi-speed arrangement that allowed members greater flexibility to opt into (or out of) particular provisions and initiatives.[5]

The Brexit vote reverberated across the Atlantic. Donald Trump, by then the presumptive Republican presidential nominee, lauded Britons for their "brave and brilliant" decision to "take back their independence." He promised to help Americans do the same. "Come November, the American people will have the chance to re-declare their independence. . . . They will have the chance to reject today's rule by the global elite and to embrace real change that delivers a government of, by and for the people."[6]

BREXIT'S RELEVANCE FOR U.S. SOVEREIGNTY DEBATES

The U.S. media depicted Brexit as part of a populist storm surge inundating Western democracies, one propelled by the economic anxiety and political alienation felt by globalization's "losers." What united Johnson and Trump, in this narrative, was their ability to tap into voter discontent and class resentment.[7]

This was at best a partial explanation, and it is worthwhile exploring the other major impetus for Brexit, since it bears on contemporary U.S. sovereignty debates. It turns out that the "Leave" camp was animated not merely by anti-globalization sentiments but also by prosovereignty convictions. Many Britons were angry that critical matters like immigration had been handed to supranational institutions beyond the control of their Parliament.

Proponents of "Remain" protested that these concerns were overblown. Shortly before the referendum, Robin Niblett, director of the London think tank Chatham House, dismissed what he termed "the sovereignty myth." The United Kingdom had transferred only limited powers to the European Commission (EC), he insisted. These included the authority to negotiate trade agreements, to set common standards and regulations for products and services, to develop rules for the common market, and to liberalize intra-EU migration and employment. Moreover, any EU policies still had to be approved by the European Council, an intergovernmental body composed of officials from member states, as well as the European Parliament, to which the citizens of each EU country elected national representatives. The bottom line, Niblett argued, was the United Kingdom was "still largely sovereign."[8]

Other advocates of "Remain" depicted the United Kingdom's effort to take back control as illusory. Even outside of the EU, *The Economist* opined, the United Kingdom would remain "at the mercy of [the same] economic forces and the members of the Union it had spurned."[9] To regain access to EU markets, it would still need to accept almost all of the EU's regulations. Only now it would have no influence in drafting and approving them.

Such subtleties were lost in the Brexit debate, which focused on those powers that Britain *had* ceded to Brussels. Brexit advocates were convinced "that the EU is run by unaccountable bureaucrats who trample on Britain's sovereignty as they plot a superstate," *The Economist* reported. "Quitting the sclerotic, undemocratic EU, the Brexiteers say, would set Britain free to reclaim its sovereign destiny as an outward-looking power."[10] Writing in the *New York Times* on June 14, 2016, Douglas Carswell of the U.K. Independence Party framed Britain's choice in a way Americans might understand. "The European Commission . . . is the only European Union body that can propose laws, and it is unelected—an arrangement George III might have admired," he noted. "We're voting for reclaiming the principle of democratic self-determination on which the United States was founded." Given America's own history, Boris Johnson added, it was "a piece of outrageous and exorbitant hypocrisy" for the Obama administration to sing the EU's praises. "They sometimes seem to forget that we are quite fond of liberty, too."[11]

Brexit's champions may have been shortsighted and undiplomatic. But their critique of U.S. hypocrisy hit the mark: Americans who counseled the United Kingdom to remain in the EU were indeed asking Brits to accept infringements on their sovereignty-as-authority that few U.S. citizens would countenance. And this was nothing new: Since the Marshall Plan, both Republican and Democratic administrations had championed European integration. They did so even as U.S. elected officials and American citizens rejected any supranational authority over themselves as a threat to U.S. popular sovereignty, as embodied in the Constitution.

To appreciate just how different the post-1945 American and European experiences with sovereignty have been, consider the following passage from a landmark 1964 ruling by the European Court of Justice, in *Costa v. ENEL*. That decision, reached less than two decades after World War II, spelled out the degree to which the members of the (then) European Community had already transferred sovereignty to continental institutions, in ways unimaginable to Americans:

> By creating a Community of unlimited duration, having its own institutions, its own personality, its own legal capacity and capacity of representation on the international plane and, more particularly, real powers stemming from a limitation of sovereignty or a transfer of powers from the States to the Community, the Member States have limited their sovereign rights, albeit within limited fields, and have thus created a body of law which binds both their nationals and themselves. . . . The transfer by the States from their domestic legal system to the Community legal system of their rights and obligations arising under the Treaty carries with it a permanent limitation of their sovereign rights, against which a subsequent unilateral act incompatible with the concept of the Community cannot prevail.[12]

In the more than five decades following the *Costa v. ENEL* ruling, a growing number of European nations had delegated tangible state authorities to supranational institutions in Brussels, as well as accepted pooled decisionmaking within intergovernmental EU bodies.

The one area where European states had clawed back power was insisting on the right to withdraw from the EU (a right that *Costa v. ENEL* had not recognized). The Lisbon Treaty of 2009—while declaring EU members' intent to pursue "ever closer union"—explicitly acknowledged this prerogative in its Article 50: "Any Member State may decide to withdraw from the Union in accordance with its own constitutional requirements." In October 2016, Theresa May, the United Kingdom's first post-Brexit prime minister, announced that the government would soon begin formal negotiations to do just that. "We are leaving [the EU] to become, once more, a fully sovereign and independent country," she explained.[13] On March 29, 2017, May triggered Article 50, starting the two-year timetable for the United Kingdom's divorce from the EU.

THE UNITED STATES AND THE UNITED NATIONS

The purpose in recounting the Brexit decision is to underscore how different the U.S. experience with international organizations has been from membership in the EU, particularly when it comes to ceding sovereignty. In contrast with Europe's post-1945 experience, the United States has resisted submitting to the political authority of any supranational body. Nearly two and a half centuries after the nation's founding, this stance remains a bedrock of U.S. constitutionalism and a neuralgic foreign policy reflex, limiting America's willingness to delegate powers to and pool decisionmaking within international institutions.

Of the many purported threats to American sovereignty, no international organization generates as much political controversy as the United Nations. Thanks to its universal membership, broad mandate, and binding Charter, the UN lies at the heart of the contemporary multilateral system. This very centrality has made the world body from its earliest days a lightning rod for American sovereigntists. In 1952 Representative John Travers Wood (R-Idaho) worried that the new United Nations Educational, Scientific and Cultural Organization (UNESCO) would teach American children to revere not "our country and its beautiful Star-Spangled Banner," but instead "a world government and the spider web banner of the United Nations." Two decades later, Representative John R. Rarick (D-La.) proposed legislation "to remove the United States from the UN and the UN from the United States, thus freeing our people from the ever-tightening yoke of international controls and the erosion of national sovereignty and constitutional government."[14]

One might have expected such sovereigntist vigilance to wane after the Cold War's end, which left the United States as the world's unchallenged superpower. Not so. Sovereigntist anxieties waxed. This emerged most starkly in armed "militia" movements on the right-wing fringe of American politics. But a number of conservative intellectuals beat a similar drum, insisting that the

United States rein in international organizations. "It is extremely important that Americans and/or the US government *not* come to think or speak as if it regarded the UN as the ultimate source of legitimacy," Jeanne Kirkpatrick, former U.S. envoy to the United Nations, testified before Congress in 1996. "Our Declaration of Independence and Constitution identify very different sources of legitimacy. The Declaration of Independence says clearly: 'To protect these rights governments are instituted among men deriving their *just powers* (that is, their legitimacy) from the consent of the governed.'"[15]

This determination to protect U.S. sovereignty has occasionally elicited head-scratching behavior from U.S. political leaders. Consider the American Land Sovereignty Protection Act, which Representative Don Young (R-Alaska) introduced in the House in 1997. That legislation would have mandated congressional approval before UNESCO could designate any portion of U.S. territory as a Biosphere Reserve or World Heritage Site. In the previous quarter century such designations had been commonplace and uncontroversial— in part because UNESCO could only consider locations that a U.S. president had explicitly nominated. That safeguard was apparently no longer enough for Young, who introduced his bill to underscore "our congressional duty to keep international commitments from abridging traditional constitutional constraints." As he reminded his colleagues, "We are not a one-world group. We are the sovereign Nation of the United States of America."[16]

In response, President Clinton threatened to veto the bill, arguing that it "would unduly restrict" the executive's ability to nominate such lands. The White House also disputed the congressman's implication "that international conservation agreements and programs infringe upon the national sovereignty of the United States." In the end, Young's legislation failed to advance, as did a Senate version introduced in 2002 by Senator Bob Smith (R-N.H.).[17]

Senator Helms Goes to New York

When it comes to defending U.S. sovereignty in Congress, few individuals took to the task with as much relish as Jesse Helms, a five-term (1973–2003) Republican senator from North Carolina and bête noire of U.S. liberal internationalists. The main target of Helms's animus—at least after the demise of the Soviet Union—was the United Nations, which he regarded as corrupt, inefficient, and irretrievably anti-American. In the 1990s, Helms led a campaign to impose reform on and reduce U.S. financial obligations to the world body. This included demanding that the UN agree to zero nominal budget growth and meet specific reform "benchmarks."

Under Helms's leadership, Congress also began withholding payments of U.S. contributions to the UN's regular and peacekeeping budgets as a way to increase U.S. leverage over UN reform. Beyond poisoning the diplomatic atmosphere in New York, the steady accumulation of U.S. arrears precipitated a UN financial crisis. This controversy was finally resolved in 1999 thanks to Richard Holbrooke, U.S. envoy to the UN, an indefatigable diplomat who cajoled and browbeat other member states until they agreed to reduce America's annual dues.

With that crisis resolved, Holbrooke hoped to put U.S.-UN relations on a more secure footing. To that end he arranged in January 2000 for Helms, then chair of the Senate Foreign Relations Committee, to be granted an unprecedented audience before the fifteen-nation UN Security Council, as well as ambassadors from another 100-odd member states. The courtly but cagey senator used the occasion to fire a shot across the UN's bow.[18] Helms opened by apologizing for his "Southern" drawl and "blunt" language. "I am not a diplomat and thus not fully conversant in the elegant and rarified language of the diplomatic trade," he explained. "I am an elected official, with something of a reputation for saying what I mean and meaning what I say."

What he had to say was plenty. The American people were willing to work with a UN that knew its place and stuck to its knitting by focusing on "core tasks" like delivering humanitarian aid, conducting peacekeeping missions, carrying out weapons inspections, and helping member states form "coalitions of the willing." What they would *not* tolerate was a United Nations that aspired "to establish itself as the central authority of a new international order of global laws and global governance," he declared. "This is an international order the American people will not countenance."

> The U.N. must respect national sovereignty. The U.N. serves nation-states, not the other way around. This principle is central to the legitimacy and ultimate survival of the United Nations, and it is a principle that must be respected. . . .
>
> The American people do not want the United Nations to become an "entangling alliance." That is why Americans look with alarm at U.N. claims to a monopoly on international moral legitimacy. They see this as a threat to the God-given freedoms of the American people, a claim of political authority over America and its elected leaders without their consent. . . . There is only one source of legitimacy of the American government's policies—and that is the consent of the American people.

If the United Nations is to survive into the 21st century, it must recognize its limitations. The demands of the United States have not changed much since Henry Cabot Lodge laid out his conditions for joining the League of Nations 80 years ago: Americans want to ensure that the United States of America remains the sole judge of its own internal affairs, that the United Nations is not allowed to restrict the individual rights of U.S. citizens, and that the United States retains sole authority over the deployment of United States forces around the world.

Helms closed with what he had promised—a blunt warning: "If the United Nations respects the sovereign rights of the American people, and serves them as an effective tool of diplomacy, it will earn and deserve their respect and support," he declared. "But a United Nations that seeks to impose its presumed authority on the American people without their consent begs for confrontation and, I want to be candid with you, eventual withdrawal."[19]

Helms's broadside annoyed even U.S. allies. France's UN ambassador, Alain Dejammet, rejected the implication that the U.S. Congress could dictate the UN's future. "We hear you, but the idea in this house is that others must be heard as well," he sniffed. "The United Nations is not a separate organ to which we turn, like a fire service," Britain's Sir Jeremy Greenstock reminded the senator. "It is the member states, and the United States owns 25 percent of the power and the resources of the United Nations. What it does well, the U.S. gets credit for. What it does badly, the U.S. must bear some responsibility for." Frustration with collective decisionmaking was simply part of life at the UN, Greenstock continued. "We have to do things here democratically because we all have national sovereignties," he said, repeating, "We all have national sovereignties." The very purpose of the UN was to try to reconcile these independent perspectives for the common good. And, "in a globalizing world, there is such a thing as the international collective interest."[20]

Helms's extraordinary audience may have improved mutual understanding—if not affection—between Capitol Hill and Turtle Bay (the Manhattan location of UN headquarters). But it also exposed how the separation of powers complicates coherence in U.S. foreign policy. Just four days after Helms had addressed the Council, it was Secretary of State Madeleine Albright's turn. "Only the President and the Executive Branch can speak for the United States," she underscored. "Today, on behalf of the President, let me say that the Administration, and I believe most Americans, see our role in the world, and our relationship to this organization, quite differently than does Senator Helms."[21]

The crafty North Carolinian has long departed this world. But legions of "new sovereigntists" have picked up his standard to warn the nation that the expanding number, complexity, and scope of international organizations threatens U.S. freedom of action and constitutional liberties, portending the rise of an oppressive world government.[22] "I have said for years that we ought to get the U.S. out of the U.N. and the U.N. out of the U.S.," Representative Paul Broun (R-Ga.) declared in 2009, at the launch of the Congressional Sovereignty Caucus. "I'll do everything I can in the Congress to maintain the U.S. as a sovereign nation, subservient to no one but the almighty God."[23] The Sovereignty Caucus is "not a paranoiacs association," Danielle Pletka of the neoconservative American Enterprise Institute insisted. "Its members see real risks in ceding more and more constitutional prerogatives to supranational institutions that have no accountability to the American voter, signing up to treaties that have no prospect of entry into force."[24]

For critics of the United Nations and other international organizations, the risks are clear. Gradually but inexorably, such bodies are expanding their activities, with little or no oversight by their sovereign state creators. They "have slipped their restraints and now run amok," like "institutional Frankensteins terrorizing the global countryside."[25]

Coming to Terms with the United Nations

The UN is front and center in this critique. "The fact that the U.S. continues to contribute billions of taxpayer dollars every year to an unaccountable, unreformed UN is no laughing matter," Representative Ileana Ros-Lehtinen (R-Fla.) told *The Hill* in early 2011. She pledged to use her position as the incoming chair of the House Foreign Affairs Committee to rein in the world body. Such concerns were not simply about reported waste, incompetence, and inefficiency. They were also about the alleged threat that the United Nations poses to American sovereignty. Reflecting such concerns, the Republican Party chose as the title of the UN plank in its June 2016 platform "Sovereign American Leadership in International Organizations."[26]

To other UN member states, the very idea that the United Nations poses a serious threat to American sovereignty is risible. After all, the United States is by far the UN's most influential actor, and the world body depends on U.S. political and material support for its relevance and, arguably, its very existence.

Contrary to what many Americans believe, moreover, the size of the UN is modest. For 2016–17 its annual regular budget was only $5.4 billion—slightly more than that of the New York City Police Department ($4.9 billion) and less than double the 2015 lobbying expenditures ($3.6 billion) of the National Rifle Association—and the United States paid only 22 percent of that total.[27] This figure does not include expenditures for UN peacekeeping, the U.S. share of which amounted to roughly $2.5 billion in 2016, or voluntary U.S. contributions to multiple UN agencies (particularly for humanitarian purposes), which totaled approximately $5 billion in that same year.[28] Adding up all these sums, U.S. spending on the UN and its activities in fiscal year 2016 was slightly less than $8 billion—or about 0.2 percent of the federal budget (much of it channeled through budgets of U.S. agencies).

Despite its relatively modest scale, the UN has indeed expanded on multiple fronts since 1945, from the size of its membership to the number of its agencies to the scope of its activities. All this expansion—approved by member states—can feed misperceptions of a UN global power grab. The UN Charter established only a handful of UN central organs. These included the office of the UN secretary general, conceived as its chief administrative officer; the Security Council, responsible for maintenance of international peace and security; the General Assembly, composed of all member states; the Economic and Social Council (ECOSOC), designed to advance development; the International Court of Justice; and the Trusteeship Council, intended to assist decolonization. Over more than seven decades the UN has grown both upward and outward. António Gutteres, the former Portuguese prime minister elected the ninth secretary general in 2016, presides over a Secretariat that now includes twenty separate departments and offices. The Security Council has also established multiple subsidiary bodies, among these the Counterterrorism Committee, the Peacebuilding Commission, and committees to monitor specific countries under sanction. Peacekeeping—something that the Charter did not even envision—has become one of the organization's core activities.

Meanwhile, the United Nations General Assembly (UNGA) and ECOSOC have used their authority to establish more than seventy specialized agencies, bodies, commissions, funds, and programs, from the Economic Commission for Latin America to the Human Rights Council, the World Health Organization (WHO), and the UN Environmental Program. Farther afield, the UN family encompasses other bodies, such as the International Atomic Energy Agency (IAEA) and the Intergovernmental Panel on Climate Change (IPCC), to monitor the implementation of international commitments (in

FIGURE 8-1. Increase in UN Multilateral Bodies by Decade

Number of multilateral bodies

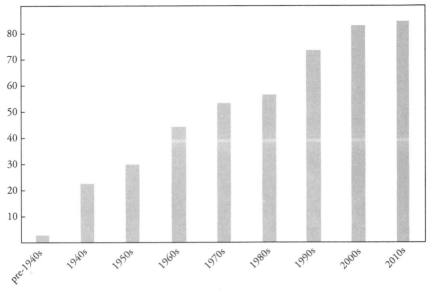

these cases, the NPT and the United Nations Framework Convention on Climate Change [UNFCCC]). Figure 8-1 shows how UN multilateral bodies have proliferated since the 1940s.

The overall result—euphemistically known as the "United Nations System"—is a tangle of multilateral organs reporting to diverse authorities and dependent on diverse funding streams (figure 8-2). This institutional labyrinth provides a target-rich environment for critics to blast the UN as opaque, unaccountable, inefficient, and (frequently) un-American. Such critiques are sometimes on the mark, particularly as they relate to management within the UN Secretariat, deliberations within UNGA and ECOSOC, and the performance of many subsidiary bodies. Across the UN system, overlapping authorities and mandates create redundancy and hinder coherent policies. Despite repeated reform efforts, the UN's organs and overseas operations still lack sufficient transparency, monitoring, and accountability.

Much of this dysfunction is of course the fault of member states, whose diverse preferences and incompatible interests often undercut UN performance and produce negative outcomes.[29] To begin with, member states can sidetrack agencies by pursuing narrowly self-interested motives, or indeed seek to sabotage their functioning. A case in point is the Human Rights Council, to which human rights abusers often seek election precisely to undercut its purposes.

FIGURE 8-2. The United Nations System

Secretariat

Departments and Offices

EOSG Executive Office of the
Secretary-General

DESA Department of Economic and
Social Affairs

DFS Department of Field Support

DGACM Department for General
Assembly and Conference Management

DM Department of Management

DPA Department of Political Affairs

DPI Department of Public Information

DPKO Department of Peacekeeping
Operations

DSS Department of Safety and Security

OCHA Office for the Coordination of
Humanitarian Affairs

OHCHR Office of the United Nations
High Commissioner for Human
Rights

OIOS Office of Internal Oversight
Services

OLA Office of Legal Affairs

OSAA Office of the Special Adviser
on Africa

PBSO Peacebuilding Support Office

SRSG/CAAC Office of the Special
Representative of the Secretary-
General for Children and Armed
Conflict

SRSG/SVC Office of the Special
Representative of the Secretary-
General on Sexual Violence in
Conflict

UNISDR United Nations Office for
Disaster Risk Reduction

UNODA United Nations Office for
Disarmament Affairs

UNODC[a] United Nations Office on
Drugs and Crime

UNOG United Nations Office at Geneva

UN-OHRLLS Office of the High
Representative for the Least Developed
Countries, Landlocked Developing
Countries and Small Island Developing
States

UNON United Nations Office at Nairobi

UNOP[b] United Nations Office for
Partnerships

UNOV United Nations Office at Vienna

Security Council

Subsidiary Organs

Counterterrorism committees

International Criminal Tribunal for
Rwanda (ICTR)

International Criminal Tribunal for the
former Yugoslavia (ICTY)

Mechanism for International Criminal
Tribunals (MICT)

Military Staff Committee

Peacekeeping operations and political
missions

Sanctions committees (ad hoc)

Standing committees and ad hoc bodies

General Assembly

Subsidiary Organs

Main and other sessional committees

Disarmament Commission

Human Rights Council

International Law Commission

Standing committees and ad hoc bodies

Funds and Programmes[a] ■

UNDP United Nations
Development Programme

UNCDF United Nations
Capital Development
Fund

FIGURE 8-2. *(continued)*

UNV United Nations Volunteers

UNEP[c] United Nations Environment Programme

UNFPA United Nations Population Fund

UN-HABITAT[c] United Nations Human Settlements Programme

UNICEF United Nations Children's Fund

WFP World Food Programme (UN/FAO)

Research and Training ■

UNIDIR United Nations Institute for Disarmament Research

UNITAR United Nations Institute for Training and Research

UNSSC United Nations System Staff College

UNU United Nations University

Other Entities ■

ITC International Trade Centre (UN/WTO)

UNCTAD[a,c] United Nations Conference on Trade and Development

UNHCR[a] Office of the United Nations High Commissioner for Refugees

UNOPS United Nations Office for Project Services

UNRWA[a] United Nations Relief and Works Agency for Palestine Refugees in the Near East

UN-Women[a] United Nations Entity for Gender Equality and the Empowerment of Women

Related Organizations ●

CTBTO Preparatory Commission Preparatory Commission for the Comprehensive Nuclear-Test-Ban Treaty Organization

IAEA[a,d] International Atomic Energy Agency

ICC International Criminal Court

ISA International Seabed Authority

ITLOS International Tribunal for the Law of the Sea

OPCW[d] Organisation for the Prohibition of Chemical Weapons

WTO[a,e] World Trade Organization

Advisory Subsidiary Body ●
Peacebuilding Commission

HLPF High-level Political Forum on Sustainable Development ■

Economic and Social Council

Functional Commissions

Crime Prevention and Criminal Justice

Narcotic Drugs

Population and Development

Science and Technology for Development

Social Development

Statistics

Status of Women

United Nations Forum on Forests

Regional Commissions[c] ▲

ECA Economic Commission for Africa

ECE Economic Commission for Europe

ECLAC Economic Commission for Latin America and the Caribbean

ESCAP Economic and Social Commission for Asia and the Pacific

ESCWA Economic and Social Commission for Western Asia

Other Bodies

Committee for Development Policy

Committee of Experts on Public Administration

Committee on Non-Governmental Organizations

Permanent Forum on Indigenous Issues

UNAIDS Joint United Nations Programme on HIV/AIDS

UNGEGN United Nations Group of Experts on Geographical Names

Research and Training

UNICRI United Nations Interregional Crime and Justice Research Institute

UNRISD United Nations Research Institute for Social Development

(continued)

FIGURE 8-2. *(continued)*

Specialized Agencies[a,f]
  FAO Food and Agriculture Organization
    of the United Nations
  ICAO International Civil Aviation
    Organization
  IFAD International Fund for Agricultural
    Development
  ILO International Labour Organization
  IMF International Monetary Fund
  IMO International Maritime
    Organization
  ITU International Telecommunication
    Union
  UNESCO United Nations Educational,
    Scientific and Cultural Organization

UNIDO United Nations Industrial
    Development Organization
  UNWTO World Tourism Organization
  UPU Universal Postal Union
  WHO World Health Organization
  WIPO World Intellectual Property
    Organization
  WMO World Meteorological
    Organization
  World Bank Group[g]
    IBRD International Bank for
      Reconstruction and Development
    IDA International Development
      Association
    IFC International Finance Corporation

International Court of Justice

Trusteeship Council[h]

---

a. All members of the United Nations System Chief Executives Board for Coordination (CEB).

b. UNOP is the UN's focal point vis-à-vis the United Nations Foundation, Inc.

c. The secretariats of these organs are part of the UN Secretariat.

d. IAEA and OPCW report to the Security Council and the GA.

e. WTO has no reporting obligation to the GA, but contributes on an ad hoc basis to GA and Economic and Social Council (ECOSOC) work on, inter alia, finance and development issues.

f. Specialized agencies are autonomous organizations whose work is coordinated through ECOSOC (intergovernmental level) and CEB (inter-secretariat level).

g. International Centre for Settlement of Investment Disputes (ICSID) and Multilateral

Investment Guarantee Agency (MIGA) are not specialized agencies but are part of the World Bank Group in accordance with Articles 57 and 63 of the Charter.

h. The Trusteeship Council suspended operation on 1 November 1994, as on 1 October 1994 Palau, the last United Nations Trust Territory, became independent.

This chart is a reflection of the functional organization of the United Nations System and for informational purposes only. It does not include all offices or entities of the United Nations System.

Source: United Nations, 2015.

■ General Assembly / Economic and Social Council

● General Assembly / Security Council

▲ Economic and Social Council / Secretariat

The suspicion that foxes too often guard the proverbial UN henhouse is a constant complaint of sovereigntists.

The pursuit of narrow self-interest by member states is hardly confined to the United Nations, of course, but extends to other international organizations. The World Bank, for instance, is charged with alleviating poverty. But its lending decisions are ultimately determined by an executive board dominated by powerful member states that may be preoccupied with short-term geopolitical or commercial goals. (In the years after September 11, for instance, the United States itself worked on the World Bank board to channel huge resources to Pakistan and other "front-line states" in the global struggle against terrorism, often at the expense of traditional development objectives and standards.)

Second, member states often use international organizations to engage in political theater. This is most problematic in larger bodies like the 193-nation General Assembly or the 54-nation ECOSOC, where the United States frequently finds itself on the defensive, as developing country and authoritarian governments seek to score ideological points against the West, or to block scrutiny of their own human rights records. (Such dynamics led Daniel Patrick Moynihan to title the memoir of his 1970s tenure as America's UN envoy *A Dangerous Place*.) The fact that many UN member states are ruled by dictators understandably discourages U.S. officials from granting them the same moral standing as democracies, despite the UN principle of sovereign equality.[30]

Third, member states themselves are often to blame for institutional mission creep, particularly when they expand an organization's mandate without providing adequate financial, personnel, or other resources. Since 1990, for example, the UN Security Council (with full U.S. support) has repeatedly added new mission elements to UN peace operations, in often dangerous environments, without equipping the UN Department of Peacekeeping Operations to handle these new requirements, and thus setting it up for failure.[31] Likewise, after 2000 the World Health Assembly saddled WHO headquarters in Geneva with new responsibilities, while cutting its overall budget and continuing to grant nearly complete autonomy to the WHO's several regional offices. These budgetary woes and institutional design flaws contributed to the WHO's flailing response to the 2014 ebola crisis in West Africa.[32]

Finally, many governments treat the UN's Secretariat, programs, and agencies essentially as a spoils system to provide sinecures for well-connected, though not necessarily competent or honest, citizens.

But the pathologies of the UN and other large global bodies are not simply a function of interstate maneuvering to advance national power, interests, or values. Such organizations are more than intergovernmental settings; they are also actors in their own right that enjoy legitimacy, and a degree of freedom of action, thanks to their international legal status and their possession of specialized technical expertise and information. They can use these attributes to become "autonomous sites of authority," capable of influencing the global agenda, championing new norms and standards, and shaping international rules. These roles can be beneficial. But they can also produce dysfunction.

Like the sorcerer's apprentice, they sometimes behave in ways that diverge from the interests of their creators and ostensible masters.[33]

Two inherent features of international organizations allow them to dilute the sovereign authority of their member states—including the United States. First, these bodies typically require members to *delegate* some authority to an independent secretariat, which may then take actions contrary to any given state's preferences. Second, member states must *pool* some measure of sovereignty within the boards or councils they create to govern international organizations. Together, "delegation" and "pooling" make it harder for U.S. officials to hold international organizations accountable to U.S. citizens, in whom American sovereignty ultimately resides. Over time, such incremental incursions can chip away at U.S. democratic sovereignty as well as produce outcomes contrary to U.S. interests.

THE DILEMMAS OF DELEGATION

All contractual relationships—such as between an investor and her broker, a client and his lawyer, or a town and its snow removal service—involve "a conditional grant of authority from a *principal* to an *agent* that empowers the latter to act on behalf of the former."[34] This grant of authority is known as delegation. It occurs in domestic political relationships, as when Congress, on behalf of the American people, authorizes the Food and Drug Administration to determine the safety and efficacy of antidepressant medications, or when the U.S. Agency for International Development (USAID) contracts with the U.S.-based NGO World Vision to implement a rural education project in Tanzania.

Inherent in delegation is uncertainty about whether the agent can be trusted. Will the agent uphold its end of the bargain? Or will it pursue its own interests rather than those of its principal? Deviant behavior (known as *agency slack*) can take two forms. One is *shirking*, in which the agent fails to deliver on commitments to its principal. The other is *slippage*, in which the agent takes actions divergent from the principal's preferences. Both are costly, giving the principal an incentive to monitor and control its agents. Agents, meanwhile, try to conceal deviant behavior by hiding their actions and relevant information.[35]

Even in a domestic context, it can be hard to hold agents accountable. The White House and cabinet secretaries try to provide clear direction to federal agencies, for example, and congressional paymasters seek to exercise legislative oversight, but civil servants may pursue their own agendas, obstruct reform

FIGURE 8-3. The Delegation Chain for an International Organization (IO)

The People ———▶ President and Congress ———▶ Intergovernmental Board ———▶ IO Secretariat

efforts, and defend turf. Elected leaders come and go. Meanwhile, "bureaucracy does its thing."[36]

This so-called principal-agent problem is even tougher at the global level, where the United States and other national governments try to hold international organizations accountable. Chains of delegation tend to be longer, making it harder to monitor the relevant agent.[37] Under the U.S. constitutional system, the American people delegate to their elected federal officials various authorities, including the authority to ratify treaties establishing international organizations, as well as to nominate and confirm U.S. ambassadors to represent them on any intergovernmental board or council charged with supervising that organization's secretariat.

As figure 8-3 shows, the chain of accountability for international organizations includes *at least* three separate principal-agent relationships, complicated by the division of labor between the executive branch and Congress. And the number of links increases as global organizations create subsidiary bodies.

The danger inherent in this scenario is that the secretariat of an international organization may behave in ways that diverge widely from the preferences of the American people, who are likely to be "rationally ignorant of most of its activities" or, if dissatisfied with its performance, "lack the power to impose their will" on that body.[38] Typically, U.S. citizens pay more attention to (and better understand) public policy debates on topics closer to their daily lives—like how their mayor is doing or where school district boundaries should be drawn. They have fewer obvious opportunities or incentives to familiarize themselves with multilateral deliberations, particularly when these involve technical topics and occur behind closed doors.

As trustees of the people's sovereignty, the U.S. executive and legislative branches (and at times the Supreme Court) have a fiduciary responsibility to hold UN agencies and other international organizations to account. But a host of practical, political, and structural hurdles can get in the way. These include heavy demands on officials' time, toxic partisan divisions, competing national priorities, and the bluntness of tools available to discipline or impose reform on wayward, freelancing, or spendthrift international organizations.

Intuitively, Americans understand that distance complicates accountability. That is why Americans, even if multilaterally inclined, often regard "international institutions . . . as runaway trains whose conductors have lost contact with the station and drive on [to] a destination of their own choosing without regard for their passengers or freight."[39]

When the secretariats of multilateral bodies are well insulated from external influence, they have more leeway to shirk responsibilities, strike out on their own, or go down paths (or rabbit holes) against the wishes of member states. They can commit a host of bureaucratic sins. These include "kicking the can" down the road, ignoring "wrongheaded" guidance from governing boards, sugar-coating annual reports, "stonewalling" rather than producing damaging information, and promoting their own pet causes or norms.[40]

At a grander level of deviance, the same secretariats may act beyond their legitimate power (or *ultra vires*, in lawyerly Latin). During the early 1990s, many critics in the United States chastised then-UN secretary general Boutros Boutros-Ghali for claiming to speak on behalf of the "world community" rather than acting as the diffident servant of UN member states. Global bodies can also divert their power from its true purpose (*détournement de pouvoir*, in French legalese), by taking actions unnecessary to advance outside the scope of their mandate.[41]

Suspicion that international institutions are serving their own (or others') interests makes them a fat target for sovereignty-minded U.S. politicians and commentators. In 1995, during his ultimately unsuccessful campaign for the presidency, Senator Robert Dole (R-Kans.) took aim at what he viewed as President Bill Clinton's imprudent faith in the United Nations, declaring, "U.S. sovereignty must be defended, not delegated." Two decades later, the conservative commentator Andrew Quinlan took to the pages of the *Washington Times* to castigate the OECD—a standard-setting body uniting the world's advanced market democracies—for "wandering beyond its initial mandate" to "pursue an agenda opposed to the interests of most Americans."[42]

One of the biggest bugaboos of American sovereigntists is the fear that the UN and other international organizations will gain unwarranted independence by securing funding streams that are outside of state control. Prominent economists have contributed to these anxieties by proposing innovative revenue-generating schemes (such as modest charges on foreign exchange transactions) that would allow the UN and other parts of the "international community" to pay for "global public goods."[43] In their jeremiad, *Here Come the Black Helicopters! UN Global Governance and the Loss of Freedom*, the husband-and-wife team of pundits Dick Morris and Eileen McGann declare that UN taxes are just around the corner. Unlike normal UN dues approved by Congress, Morris and McGann warn, these will "be mandatory levies imposed by treaty on American citizens."[44] On this matter, at least, there is little to fear. Both Republican and Democratic parties remain loath to grant the UN and its agencies any independent source of revenue.

Problems with Pooling

The second potential threat to U.S. sovereign authority arises from the need for member states to establish organs of collective decisionmaking to govern international organizations. Such pooling of sovereignty requires national governments to reconcile their diverse preferences, and it inevitably dilutes each nation's influence over multilateral organizations.[45]

Things are a lot simpler when the U.S. government delegates a task to a U.S. agency. In this domestic scenario, the president and Congress are responsible for aggregating and deciding among the diverse preferences of U.S. citizens, translating these into policy, and contracting with U.S. agencies to implement relevant programs. But international organizations require a second process of aggregating preferences, at the global level. The U.S. government and its foreign counterparts must reconcile their own nationally generated preferences, hammer out what powers to delegate to the new organization, and agree on decisionmaking rules for its governing board.

Such collective decisionmaking inevitably attenuates the ability of any one country—including the United States—to influence (much less determine) the organization's behavior.[46] Indeed, this is *the very purpose* of multilateral cooperation: to force states to reciprocally adjust their domestic preferences so that they all gain, even if they do not gain everything that they want. It is the only way to manage globalization in a world of pluralism. The dilemma inherent in pooling is navigating the trade-offs between the benefits of international cooperation and the natural desire to control the organization. Where possible, the United States prefers decisionmaking systems based on weighted voting, as in the executive boards of the World Bank and the IMF, or that provide it with an effective veto, as in the UN Security Council. But many multilateral organizations lack these attributes.[47]

This predicament sharpens as membership grows. More encompassing bodies imply more states, and each additional player can undercut the organization's performance or redirect its activities. Most problematic are multilateral bodies like the UN General Assembly or the UN Committee on Disarmament, which are anchored in the ideal of sovereign equality and make decisions on a one-state-one-vote basis. As blockages rise, members may be tempted to delegate more authority to the organization's secretariat. But that too carries risks, since a secretariat with many masters can play its principals against one another—bobbing and weaving among competing preferences to advance its own institutional interests, which may deviate from its ostensible mandate.

Large memberships also make it harder to sanction secretariats that underperform, particularly when some member states support shirking or slippage. The United States often finds itself in "damage-control" mode, working to prevent ideological constituencies like the Non-Aligned Movement or the Group of 77 (G-77) coalition of developing countries, encrusted regional groupings, and coalitions of bad actors from (in the U.S. view) hijacking the global agenda.[48]

These twin realities—elongated accountability chains and collective governance by multiple principals—help explain why multilateral bodies proliferate and persist. International organizations are indeed adept at reproducing: more than half of those that have emerged since 1945 are spin-offs from preexisting organizations. And in most cases it has been senior officials within existing bodies that provided the impetus for new ones.[49]

Principal-agent dynamics also enable international organizations, unlike milk, to survive well beyond their "sell-by" dates. As Vaubel observes, "It is easier to found [one] than to abolish it."[50] Institutions create vested interests among beneficiaries, contractors, and advocacy groups. They also evolve with the times, changing their mandates and activities both with and without member state guidance.

Consider the Bank for International Settlements (BIS). Created in 1930 to facilitate the payment of German reparations required by the Treaty of Versailles, the BIS survives as a "bank for central banks," helping set capital account requirements and encourage reserve transparency among its more than sixty members. Or take the OECD. First established in 1947 as a European-only organization (the Organization for European Economic Cooperation, OEEC) to coordinate Marshall Plan aid, it has since become a leading source of standard setting and data sharing for its advanced market democracy members. Likewise, the International Energy Agency (IEA), created in the mid-1970s in the wake of the Arab oil embargo to ensure that OECD members had sufficient oil stockpiles, has expanded its energy security mandate to promote "green" technologies and reach out to emerging economies like China and India. The apparent lesson is that "international institutions may change their names or lose their function but they never die."[51]

So Why Join?

Given these common pathologies, why would the United States agree to delegate authorities and pool decisionmaking within international organizations?[52] After all, powerful states can often accomplish a lot unilaterally, and none is mightier than the United States. And even when cooperation is required, it can sometimes be accomplished through informal "coalitions of the willing" or via simple multilateral agreement to take specific policy steps, as in the 2015 Paris Agreement on climate change.

In some circumstances, though, a formal organization just makes sense. First, some enduring challenges require the clear mandate, technical expertise, predictable resources, and staying power that only a standing institution possesses. Global development is a case in point. The field is crowded with donors, but the World Bank is unequaled as a repository of relevant knowledge and public financial resources. Second, standing international organizations help sovereign countries surmount collective action problems. They make it easier to agree on common standards, like how to divide the electromagnetic spectrum or assign orbital slots for satellites. They can also overcome free-rider dilemmas—for example, by ensuring that all countries meet their trade obligations. And they help nations make credible commitments, allowing other governments to monitor and verify follow-through on pledges to (say) destroy chemical weapons.

Third, standing organizations can offer a neutral setting to help nations solve disputes, including through arbitration, as with the WTO's dispute settlement mechanism. Fourth, of particular value to the United States, international organizations can help "lock in" favorable institutional arrangements (such as weighted voting in the IMF or veto power in the Security Council) in the face of long-term uncertainties about the trajectory of the nation's relative power.

Finally, international institutions can advance important U.S. interests in situations where the United States cannot or prefers not to do everything itself. By supporting UN agencies like the WHO, the UN High Commissioner for Refugees (UNHCR), the IAEA, and the International Civil Aviation Organization (ICAO), the United States can leverage the resources of other member states to (respectively) respond to emerging infectious diseases, provide humanitarian relief, monitor compliance with nuclear disarmament, and improve the safety of civil aviation. In this regard, UN peacekeeping merits special mention. At the start of 2017 the UN Department of Peacekeeping Operations managed sixteen missions involving 100,000 soldiers and 20,000 police and other civilians—making "blue helmets" the largest globally deployed military force in the world.[53] These missions helped reduce violence and instability in nations such as the Democratic Republic of the Congo and South Sudan, countries where the United States has humanitarian interests but little appetite to assume all the costs and risks of trying to end violence.

The World Health Organization as a Case Study

The field of global health illustrates how deepening global interdependence can create incentives for national governments, including the United States, to sacrifice some sovereign autonomy—and even modest sovereign authority— for the benefits of international cooperation. This is most obvious in the powers granted to the WHO to combat dangerous infectious diseases. Over the past three decades the world has experienced a surge of new and reemerging infectious diseases, as economic development in previously remote regions increases human exposure to zoonotic pathogens and as revolutions in transportation and travel make formerly distant populations more epidemiologically interdependent. Faced with the specter of global pandemics, national authorities have granted the WHO unprecedented powers, notably through the revised International Health Regulations (IHR), which came into force in 2005.

The first iteration of the IHR, adopted in 1969, was limited out of respect for the sovereignty of WHO member states. They applied to only three diseases (cholera, plague, and yellow fever), and even then afflicted member states, worried about political and economic repercussions, failed to reliably notify the WHO of disease outbreaks. (Their fears were often justified, since other member states frequently imposed restrictions on travel to and trade with outbreak-affected countries.) In another bow to sovereignty, states forbade the WHO from using information about outbreaks provided by nongovernmental sources.[54] These weaknesses were thrown into sharp relief in the 1980s and 1990s, as the WHO—and the world—struggled to cope with both a resurgence of known diseases (such as cholera in South America and plague in India) and the appearance of novel ones (including HIV/AIDS and ebola) that threated international public health. As globalization accelerated and the world became more microbially interconnected, it became obvious that the legal foundation of global public health was no longer fit for its purpose.

With strong U.S. support, the World Health Organization in 1995 adopted a resolution calling for the revision of the IHR. Negotiating the updated regulations took ten years, however, as sovereignty concerns slowed acceptance of two radical WHO proposals. One was that the new IHR adopt a broader, more flexible approach to infectious diseases, so that they could cover all "public health emergencies of international concern" (PHEICs). The second was that WHO be allowed to use nongovernmental information sources, since states could not always be trusted to self-report. Both proposals won growing support after the 2003 outbreak of severe acute respiratory syndrome (SARS), which the Chinese government initially tried to cover up and, subsequently, to downplay. In the end, as David Fidler notes, China's efforts to "play the sovereignty card" proved futile.[55]

It was in this context that the revised IHR were formulated and adopted in 2005. The new regulations struck a balance between sovereign prerogatives and obligations. They explicitly recognized that "States have . . . the sovereign right to legislate and to implement legislation in pursuit of their health policies" (Article 3.4). But they required national governments to report to the WHO on potential PHEICs in a timely manner and to refrain from imposing unnecessary trade and travel restrictions. They also permitted the WHO to use information from nongovernmental sources, to request verification about diseases from the relevant government, and to share this information with other WHO member states. Most dramatically, the revised IHR granted the WHO the right to name and shame countries that failed to comply with their reporting obligations (Article 10.4). Although the WHO was not given formal enforcement mechanisms, such as sanctions, its new authority to declare states noncompliant carried potential economic as well as reputational costs. Last, the revised IHR granted the WHO director-general unprecedented power to coordinate global epidemic response, including the authority to independently designate an epidemic as a PHEIC. As Fidler and Lawrence Gostin write, "In short, the information and verification provisions privilege global health governance over state sovereignty."[56]

The major ebola outbreak in West Africa in 2014–15 revived the debate on the IHR and, more generally, on the meaning of sovereignty in a world in which pathogens easily hop borders and continents. The crisis underscored the failure of many countries to implement their minimum core capacity requirements under the IHR and exposed the tendency of member states to impose excessive travel and trade restrictions against affected countries. It also revealed a WHO director-general, Margaret Chan, who was hesitant to declare a PHEIC in deference to the wishes of ebola-affected West African countries—thus undercutting the principle that state sovereignty must be balanced with the goal of global health. The Report of the Ebola Interim Assessment Panel—an independent review panel appointed by Chan herself—cited these failures in making the case for "shared sovereignty," as follows:

> Whereas health is considered the sovereign responsibility of coun-
> tries, the means to fulfill this responsibility are increasingly global, and
> require international collective action and effective and efficient gover-
> nance of the global health system. . . . This Panel suggests that in the
> interests of protecting global health, countries must have a notion of
> "shared sovereignty." Through the International Health Regulations
> (2005), Member States recognized that there are limits to national sov-
> ereignty when health crises reach across borders.[57]

The report's conclusions echoed the prescient words of Secretary of State
Dean Rusk, who had testified to Congress in 1965, "There are no such things
as sovereignty with respect to epidemic diseases . . . because disease does not
recognize political borders."[58]

Whether the goal is managing cross-border financial flows, combating
transnational terrorism, preventing catastrophic greenhouse gas emissions, or
stemming the next pandemic, advancing the domestic public good more frequently requires some delegation of sovereignty to international organizations.
As Robert Keohane, Stephen Macedo, and Andrew Moravcsik write, "The
choice, therefore, is not between international cooperation and domestic autonomy, but between complementary activities of international and domestic
institutions, on the one hand, and uncoordinated state action, on the other."[59]

REMEDIES FOR PATHOLOGIES IN INTERNATIONAL ORGANIZATIONS

The lesson of this chapter is that international organizations are both mad-
dening and imperative. The goal for the United States is to tame these sometimes unwieldy creatures. It is to ensure that they can advance their global
mandates, as well as narrower U.S. national interests, at acceptable costs to
U.S. sovereign authority and freedom of action. In joining any formal body,
the United States must decide what if any sovereign authority it is willing to
transfer to the organization's secretariat, or to pool within any collective intergovernmental board or council set up to direct and supervise the work of that
body. Generally speaking, the most appropriate U.S. approach is a posture of
tough love that balances constructive and sustained U.S. leadership with con-
tinuous vigilance and a commitment to reform. The option of leaving always
remains, but it should remain a last resort.

With respect to the United Nations, specifically, it is imperative to recognize that there are multiple "UNs," and that these unique institutional com-

ponents merit different strategic approaches.[60] Given the centrality of the UN Security Council for global peace and security, as well as the veto the United States enjoys as a permanent member, America should work vigorously through the Council whenever possible. With respect to the Secretariat, the United States should take the position of a friendly critic, supporting its work but insisting always on reform. America should engage UN specialized agencies and programs selectively, working closely with and channeling extra resources toward islands of excellence (such as UNHCR), while marginalizing those that are beyond salvage, have outlived their purpose, or have poor records of achievement, such as the United Nations Industrial Development Organization (UNIDO). As for the UNGA and ECOSOC, the United States must continue its effort to break down encrusted and outdated regional and ideological blocs, while recognizing that America's practical challenge will often be one of damage control.

In confronting international organizations generally, the United States has multiple mechanisms at its disposal to improve performance and reduce slack in bodies to which it has delegated authority, as well as to discipline those that go off track. It also has options to overcome some (albeit not all) of the downsides of pooling sovereignty.[61]

The best way to manage dilemmas of delegation is to keep organizations on a relatively short leash. This is admittedly easier to accomplish when an institution is first being designed rather than already operating. Potential steps include limiting the discretion granted to its senior officials and specifying in detail the rules that the organization (as the agent of its member states) must observe. As institutional performance varies, the United States can loosen or tighten the leash. To be sure, the effectiveness of this strategy will depend on how many other state principals share U.S. assessments of the agent's performance, and indeed U.S. goals. For instance, authoritarian members of the Human Rights Council strenuously resist the appointment of rapporteurs to investigate human rights situations in specific countries, which takes place under the Council's "special procedures."

Second, the United States might also insist, in setting up an organization and mandating the functions of its subagencies, that the body and its activities be time-limited, or at least subject to periodic review and reauthorization by the board. Part of the success of the United Nations Relief and Rehabilitation Agency (UNRRA), founded in 1943 to help meet the needs of those displaced by World War II and shuttered in 1947, can be attributed to its limited duration, which was planned from the outset.[62] Too few international organizations today have "sunset provisions" that anticipate that their initiatives or indeed the multilateral body itself will cease after a given time frame.

Third, the United States can bolster accountability by insisting on regular, stringent reporting requirements.[63] As with any bureaucracy, of course, a generic challenge remains: how to ensure that reports to member states and intergovernmental boards contain honest appraisals and meaningful information so that principals can accurately gauge how well the organization is fulfilling the terms of its contractual relationship. Lakhdar Brahimi, an experienced Algerian diplomat and UN troubleshooter, made this case in presenting his eponymously named report on UN peacekeeping in 2000: "The Secretariat must tell the Security Council what it needs to know, not what it wants to hear."[64] Beyond self-reporting by UN and other multilateral agencies, and direct monitoring by executive boards, the United States should also promote third-party monitoring, which can expose hidden information and action. Outside watchdog groups like Transparency International, as well as investigative journalists and global action networks like Principles for Responsible Investment, can complement U.S. and intergovernmental efforts to hold international organizations' feet to the fire.[65]

Fourth, the governing boards of international organizations can increase the likelihood of consistency with their aims by requiring rigorous personnel screening and selection procedures for both senior leadership and staff. Alas, state shareholders are often AWOL in this effort, more intent on preserving country-specific slots and privileges than in appointing the most qualified agency heads or recruiting knowledgeable and competent civil servants. A glaring example is the U.S. and European insistence on maintaining their informal prerogative to choose the World Bank president and the IMF managing director, respectively. The uncontested reappointment of the American Jim Young Kim as president of the World Bank in 2016 mocked the executive board's pledge of an "open and transparent" selection process, confirming suspicions that the United States is more interested in retaining its historical privileges than in submitting its candidate to real competition.[66]

The situation is only slightly better with respect to the selection of the UN secretary general. Although that choice ultimately remains in the hands of the Security Council, the 2016 nomination and selection process was markedly more open, consultative, and inclusive than the closed-door deliberations that had chosen António Gutteres's eight predecessors. Unfortunately, at the staff level, UN management reform remains hamstrung by an outdated, barnacled, and sclerotic personnel system that prevents managers from hiring the best performers and firing those who underperform or are guilty of misconduct.[67]

Fifth, the United States and other nations can discourage opportunistic behavior within an international organization by inserting checks and balances within the body itself. These may include decentralization to avoid a concentration of power at the center, as well as the establishment of divisions with some competitive overlap. Once again, such engineering is more easily accomplished in the architectural design phase than through subsequent structural remodeling. Moreover, even well-intentioned efforts can create new problems. Overlapping mandates can create inefficient redundancies, while decentralization can hamper agile responses (as the WHO experience suggests).

In the end, the most important check on organizational slack may be insistence on an independent inspector general capable of auditing performance. Unfortunately, international organizations (and some member states) typically resist creating and giving real power to internal watchdogs. A case in point is the UN's Office of Internal Oversight Services (OIOS) created under Ban Ki Moon's tenure, which has too often failed to hold staff to account or to offer protection to whistle-blowers. Going forward, the United States must work with other like-minded member states and the secretary general to change deeply ingrained UN habits. Priorities must include strengthening the OIOS, mandating more flexible human resource policies, reforming the UN's opaque procurement system, reviewing any UN mandates older than five years, and bolstering the UN ethics office, whistle-blower protections, and financial disclosure requirements. Success will require the United States to cultivate common approaches with moderate developing countries that have an inherent stake in a smoothly functioning United Nations. Dogged diplomacy, not righteous indignation, must rule the day.

It's All about the Money

Financial leverage offers another, albeit problematic, avenue for the United States to signal its displeasure with international bodies that go off track. The United States has occasionally withheld (or threatened to withhold) contributions to the UN, as well as the World Bank and other entities, to press for reform. Where U.S. contributions are voluntary, this action may raise political but not legal hackles. The same cannot be said of assessed contributions, such as those that the United States owes for the UN's regular and peacekeeping budgets. While opinion is not universal, most international lawyers consider it a violation of treaty obligations to withhold assessed contributions.[68]

Despite such qualms, during the 1990s the GOP-controlled Congress repeatedly withheld annual U.S. assessments to the UN in a unilateral effort to impose reform on and reduce U.S. support for the world body. In 1999, as discussed earlier, the Clinton administration negotiated a partial settlement of the arrears crisis. Consistent with the Helms-Biden agreement—a compromise between Senators Jesse Helms and Joseph Biden (D.-Del.), the chair and ranking member (respectively) of the Senate Foreign Relations Committee— the United States persuaded other member states to lower its contributions to the UN's regular budget (from 25 to 22 percent) and the UN peacekeeping budget (from 30 to 26.5 percent), linked to benchmarks in UN performance.

The discount came at a price, however. The U.S. carrot-and-stick approach magnified the UN's chronic budgetary woes, hobbled UN peacekeeping, distracted the attention of the U.S. mission to the UN from the global security agenda, alienated U.S. allies and potential partners in New York and member state capitals, and undercut America's reputation for enlightened global leadership. The episode suggested the limits of trying to micromanage UN reform from the U.S. Congress.[69] While there may be occasions when the U.S. separation of powers allows a U.S. administration to secure goals at the UN by playing "good cop" to Congress's "bad cop," the United States must beware of overplaying its hand.

More evidence that financial withholding is a blunt and counterproductive instrument came in 2011, when UNESCO members voted to admit the Palestinian Authority (PA). That step triggered a provision of the U.S. Code prohibiting U.S. funding of any UN organ that accorded Palestine member state status. The State Department immediately suspended its payment of annual assessments to the organization (22 percent of the agency's budget). In so doing, the United States violated its treaty obligations and lost its seat on the UNESCO governing body. Obama administration officials suddenly faced the real prospect that the PA might dramatically complicate matters for Washington by trying to join up to twenty other UN agencies, forcing the United States to suspend payments to the WHO, World Intellectual Property Organization, IMF, and IAEA, among other bodies. Legislative constraints, in other words, could force the United States to cut off its nose to spite its face.[70] Fortunately for the the United States, the PA ultimately agreed not to go down this route—for now.

Given these lessons, it was worrisome when the Trump administration in early 2017 suggested that the United States might unilaterally abandon any formal legal obligation to support the UN's regular and peacekeeping budgets and henceforth treat all U.S. contributions to the United Nations as voluntary. This has long been a dream of UN skeptics, including Representative Ros-Lehtinen who, as chair of the House Foreign Affairs Committee, introduced a bill in 2015 that would do just that, as well as John Bolton, who recommended a similar step shortly after Trump's election.[71]

In his first week in office, President Trump commissioned the drafting of an executive order, "Auditing and Reducing U.S. Funding of International Organizations." Beyond envisioning a 40 percent cut in annual U.S. voluntary contributions to UN agencies and programs, it endorsed transforming U.S. assessed contributions to the UN and other international organizations into purely voluntary rather than legally binding commitments. Such a strategy would be irresponsible and shortsighted. Beyond wreaking havoc on the UN budget, this rash move would undermine U.S. diplomatic influence at the UN, reducing Washington's ability to shape the UN agenda. It would also set a terrible precedent, since other countries would surely follow suit, cherry-picking among their own preferred UN activities. Finally, such a unilateral step would violate America's solemn legal obligations under the UN Charter.[72]

If All Else Fails

Short of cutting off finances, the United States has two final options for reining in organizations that have gone rogue. The first is to object persistently to acts and decisions that U.S. officials believe violate the mandate and objectives of the body in question. Signaling displeasure can have legal significance, since it repudiates any notion that the United States has "consented" to new, objectionable norms or rules being promoted by the organization (and thus accepts them as "custom"). While adopting such a "persistent objector" stance would not "necessarily prevent the formation of a norm of customary international law," it would exempt the United States from being bound by the practice.[73]

In the end, there remains the ultimate option: renouncing U.S. membership in an organization that U.S. officials believe has abused or exceeded the authorities delegated to it. As the political theorist Albert Hirschman pointed out in his 1970 treatise *Exit, Voice, and Loyalty*, there are essentially two choices available to any dissatisfied member of an organization—expressing one's displeasure or departing. When the United States has made its feelings known but has seen no change of behavior, it may choose to leave, either by suspending or (more provocatively) by terminating its membership. This is an extreme step. Nevertheless, the founding treaties of many international organizations explicitly grant states parties the right to withdraw unilaterally.[74] And the United States has occasionally done so, including from UNESCO in the 1980s, in response to that organization's anti-Western bias.

To be meaningful from the perspective of sovereignty, of course, the option of "exit" must be *plausible*. A state may have the notional authority to leave an international arrangement, but true sovereignty depends on its ability to credibly do so (or threaten to do so). Many American conservatives worry that when push comes to shove the United States will be so enmeshed in international bodies, such as the UN or the WTO, that the cost of exit is too onerous to constitute a real choice. Such concerns were often heard in the debate over Brexit, with some British advocates of "Remain" arguing that the costs of breaking with the EU were so exorbitant that even those leading the "Leave" campaign would inevitably be forced to lead their constituents on the path back to Europe.[75]

Leaving an international organization is not a step to be undertaken lightly. Beyond the international stigma that may attach to it, withdrawal would deprive the United States of the opportunity to shape the norms, objectives, and activities of the relevant body. It would shift the sovereignty bargain to increase autonomy at the expense of influence, in the face of challenges that do not respect borders. Still, it could in some rare circumstances be necessary.

What is dangerous, however, is any notion that the United States can as a blanket matter back away from multilateral institutions like the United Nations without damaging its own interests. The UN Human Rights Council is a case in point. Critics of that body correctly note that it is a flawed institution whose members include human rights violators. But, as defenders of U.S. membership point out, a U.S. departure would only create a vacuum of influence that would be filled by problematic actors like China and Pakistan, who would seek to curtail debate on human rights issues. The experience of the Obama administration suggests that the United States has more to gain by remaining and bringing U.S. diplomatic influence to bear within the Human Rights Council, so that it can restrain that body's worst excesses and—more positively—shine a spotlight on the world's worst abusers.[76]

More generally, there is a powerful strategic rationale for the United States to reinforce long-standing international institutions, rather than seek to dismantle them entirely. As a globally dominant power facing relative (though not absolute) decline, at least in its share of the world economy, the United States has a natural incentive to try to preserve the norms, rules, and standards in existing institutions that it has helped to establish since 1945, rather than back away from them. In this regard, the Trump administration's initial instinct to dismantle and renegotiate existing international arrangements was deeply problematic, since there was little guarantee that any new arrangements would be as favorable to U.S. interests and preferences as those frameworks that had been negotiated at the height of U.S. power.

THE FANTASY OF WORLD GOVERNMENT

In their search for more effective and accountable international organizations, the one direction in which Americans should *not* look is toward the ultimate goal of world government. There is admittedly little public appetite for such an objective. American nationalism is vigorous, as is popular support for U.S. sovereignty. Still, the prospect of a world state is one that generates attention at both extremes of the U.S. political spectrum—and as such it deserves scrutiny.

On the hard right, conservative nationalists regularly warn that U.S. concessions to or compromises within an international organization are misguided steps on the slippery slope toward global government.[77] On the utopian left, world federalists offer the gauzy vision of a pacific and just world that has moved "beyond sovereignty." In fact, both views are incorrect: world government is nowhere on the horizon.

Although arguments for world government come in many guises, its advocates typically envision a shift in global authority whereby the members of the (so-called) United Nations become truly "united" within a single polity, in the form of a planetary state. This argument—that a world state is imperative, that it is desirable, and that it is inevitable—is not new. It has been a staple of Western political thought for centuries, visible in the writings of William Penn, among others.[78]

Advocates of world government plead their case on grounds of necessity, functionality, morality, and legitimacy. Some argue that the sheer brutishness of world politics, and the inability of independent sovereign units to control destructive technologies or respect ecological boundaries, compels the creation of a supranational authority. Functionalists, meanwhile, predict that economic integration will create a "world polity," and that individual nation-states will coalesce into ever larger political units, ultimately culminating in a world state. Ethicists argue that only a universal state can deliver true global justice. Finally, advocates of cosmopolitan democracy argue that the legitimacy of global bodies depends on whether they give direct political voice to individuals, proposing various processes of "global constitutionalism" to move beyond the nation-state.[79]

Today, talk of "world government" is a fringe preoccupation, to which few scholars and even fewer policymakers give serious consideration. Such discussions occur at the margins of U.S. political discourse, among members of the visionary left and in some corners of academia.[80] This was not always the case. As UN expert Thomas G. Weiss notes, the possibility of world government was a common, serious topic of debate in the United States during the 1940s. On March 5, 1942, the Commission to Study the Bases of a Just and Durable Peace—chaired by John Foster Dulles no less—endorsed the formation of a nascent world government possessing a world parliament, an international court, and international agencies with the power to regulate trade, settle disputes, and control military power.[81]

By the end of World War II, a surprising number of American intellectuals, politicians, and ordinary citizens envisioned a postsovereign world. Some were motivated by the immense destructive power unleashed by the atomic bomb. In October 1945 Albert Einstein signed a letter in the *New York Times* predicting that the new United Nations would fail because it was based on "the absolute sovereignty of rival nation-states." What was needed, he wrote, was a "Federal Constitution of the world, a working worldwide legal order, if we hope to prevent atomic war."[82]

The early postwar years were the heyday of the United World Federalists, founded in 1947. And they were not alone. As Weiss writes, "Throughout the 1940s, it was impossible in the United States to read periodicals, listen to the radio, or watch newsreels and not encounter the idea of world government." In the late 1940s, thirty of the (then) forty-eight U.S. state legislatures passed resolutions supporting "a U.S. response to growing interdependence and instability that would pool American sovereignty with that of other countries."[83]

Testifying before the House of Representatives in 1948, Dulles asserted, "Our great Nation is ready to take the lead in surrendering its sovereignty to the extent necessary to establish peace through the ordering of just law." The following year, 111 members of the House of Representatives supported Concurrent Resolution 64, declaring that it should be "a fundamental objective of the foreign policy of the United States to support and strengthen the United Nations and to see its development into a world federation." Even Hans Morgenthau, a prominent Cold War realist, would write, "There can be no permanent international peace without a state coextensive with the confines of the political world. The question to which we must now direct our attention concerns the manner in which a world state can be created."[84]

By the early 1950s, though, such one-worldism was in retreat, overwhelmed by anticommunist obsessions, the rise of McCarthyism, anticolonial struggles, and the requirements of containment. Today, despite globalization, discussion of world government has vanished from the U.S. public sphere. And its objective seems as distant and unreal as the fictional "noplace" described by Sir Thomas More in his 1516 work *Utopia*.

And we are fortunate this is the case, because a global state is a terrible idea. The case for it rests on three dubious propositions: that world government is needed, that it is desirable, and that it is achievable. To begin with, a world state is unnecessary. Sovereign states are often seen as obstacles to managing global problems and, indeed, as generating such problems. And yet the international system is capable of at least incremental change, and of muddling through.[85] Though deeply imperfect, existing frameworks of multilateral cooperation have enjoyed some limited success in addressing pressing global problems, including global poverty, nuclear proliferation, and global financial instability. If there is an area in which the sovereign state system has not delivered, it is in the ecological realm, particularly in dealing with climate change. Nevertheless, there is no guarantee that a world state would manage these problems any better.

Second, a world state is undesirable because it is likely to produce bad outcomes. Advocates of world government regard sovereignty as the ultimate source of war, inasmuch as independent states that recognize no supreme global authority are inherently competitive, insecure, and prone to violence. Where they go astray is in presuming that a global Leviathan would be an inherently peaceful, even benevolent, world empire, rather than a despotic one. This is an astonishing leap of faith, given the violent internal history of many large states, as well as the human tendency to transform concentrated power into tyranny.

In fact, one can make a powerful ethical argument that the sovereign state is the best possible approach to world order on a planet of diverse political communities. If all the world's many peoples conceived of themselves as sharing a common identity, the case for a single global political unit would be strong. Without such solidarity, a supranational authority would inevitably run roughshod over distinctive national aspirations. For this reason even Immanuel Kant based his vision of perpetual peace not on a single world state but on a confederation of independent liberal republics. Modern political theorists like Michael Walzer have expanded on this theme, arguing that sovereign states are morally privileged entities, since the obligations that individuals owe to fellow citizens outweigh their real but lesser obligations to humanity at large. This argument is especially persuasive in democracies, which have a legitimate claim to represent the popular will of their citizens.[86]

Third, even if a world state were necessary and desirable, it remains an implausible political project even over the medium term—say, within the next century. And the main reason is that national governments remain deeply attached to sovereignty. To be sure, "world government" could take various forms, including a fairly loose arrangement analogous to the U.S. Articles of Confederation, which (as chapter 2 explained) left many powers in the hands of the thirteen former colonies. But such a framework would still imply a common, superior political authority, a prospect few nations are prepared to contemplate. Notwithstanding the proliferation of international, regional, and subregional organizations, as well as new doctrines of "contingent" sovereignty, the dominant global trend is for states to *reassert* rather than subordinate or pool sovereign privileges. This is a trend that unites many of the world's leading powers, both established (such as the United States, Britain, Japan, Russia) and emerging (China, India, Brazil, South Africa) alike. This attachment to sovereignty also helps account for the rise of flexible forms of multilateral cooperation (such as ad hoc coalitions) rather than more formal international organizations and binding treaty regimes.

There is nothing eternal about the sovereign state, of course. It is a historical artifact and as such will presumably be replaced someday. Still, its disappearance would be a world-historical transformation, akin to the transition from the medieval to the modern world associated with the Peace of Westphalia in 1648. In its most complete manifestation, a postsovereign world would imply the state's loss of exclusive and supreme political authority (and monopoly on legitimate use of armed force) within its territory, its surrender of policy autonomy, its cessation of control over cross-border flows, and its loss of juridical independence to a global supranational organization.

It is difficult to conceive how such a wholesale shift—which would involve the creation not just of a universal system of collective security but a single supranational authority above all component units—could occur without an apocalyptic crisis confronting humanity. The interests of the great powers, the forces of nationalism, and political tendencies toward fragmentation are simply too great.

On the other hand, the rise of existential threats does suggest that the preservation of democratic sovereignty will depend on more intensive forms of international cooperation. The U.S. domestic reaction to 9/11 demonstrated that traditional constitutional liberties can be overwhelmed by an acute sense of vulnerability, as society demands security. The world today has enough plutonium to make 400,000 weapons of the type used to destroy Hiroshima. In the aftermath of even one use in an American city, the United States would surely risk becoming a garrison state. (Global climate change presents a similar, if more gradual, threat of a Hobbesian world.)

Greater multilateral cooperation is frequently depicted as a slippery step toward a global federal union. But rather than "stepping stones," Daniel Deudney suggests, international bodies and agreements might better be viewed as capstones or a ceiling.[87] Indeed, the UN Charter implicitly rejects the notion of a world state, in focusing on the sovereignty of nation-states. To avoid either the hardening of the nation-state, at the expense of democracy and liberty, or the temptation of a supranational world state, the answer is for greater multilateral cooperation among sovereign state units.

NINE

Conclusion

American Sovereignty and International Cooperation

A century after Lodge and Lowell squared off in Boston over the United States' membership in the League of Nations, the country faces the same enduring dilemma: How can it reconcile its defense of national sovereignty with the imperative of international cooperation? This predicament has only grown since 1919, as the problems of an increasingly interdependent globe collide with an America that often seeks to chart its own course, unencumbered by the outside world.

The ascent of Donald J. Trump to the White House brought these long-simmering U.S. sovereignty concerns to a boil. During the president's first few months, journalists documented repeated clashes between "nationalists" and "globalists" within the administration.[1] As often as not, the former emerged victorious. The most prominent example was Trump's fateful decision on June 1, 2017, to pull the United States out of the Paris Climate Accord—the most important multilateral agreement of the twenty-first century. This step was necessary, the president insisted, to defend the foundations of American democracy. "Foreign leaders in Europe, Asia, and across the world should not have more say with respect to the U.S. economy than our own citizens and their elected representatives," Trump told his Rose Garden audience. "Thus, our withdrawal from the agreement represents a reassertion of America's sovereignty." As he explained, "Our constitution is unique among all nations of the world. And it is my highest obligation and greatest honor to protect it."[2]

This was a red herring if ever there was one. The Paris agreement is a purely voluntary arrangement among its 195 state parties. It is not a legally binding treaty but a collection of "intended, nationally determined contributions." Rather than adopting a one-size-fits-all approach, each country chooses for itself what it will bring to the climate change fight, tailoring these commitments to its unique national circumstances. Indeed, the Obama administration had insisted on such an approach precisely to avoid raising sovereignty hackles in the U.S. Senate. Perhaps aware of the thin ice on which he was skating, Trump also offered up that all-purpose justification beloved of self-styled defenders of U.S. sovereignty—the slippery slope. Sure, the Paris Accord might be voluntary. But who knows where it could lead? "The risks grow as historically these agreements only tend to become more and more ambitious over time," he warned. "In other words, the Paris Framework is a starting point—as bad as it is—not an end point. And exiting the agreement protects the United States from future intrusions on the United States' sovereignty."[3]

Trump's slippery slope thesis was alarmist and, if taken seriously, would rule out U.S. participation in virtually any international agreement. It also ignored the multiple avenues the United States possessed to prevent nonbinding commitments from acquiring the status of international law—much less allowing foreign governments and international organizations to meddle in U.S. constitutional processes. But if Trump's argument was a canard, it was also savvy. By playing the sovereignty card, the president hoped to short-circuit more sober-minded discussion of the actual balance of costs and benefits of the Paris Accord, both for U.S. competitiveness and for the survival of the planet. By invoking this sacred touchstone, Trump was reassuring the public that the best way to keep America free, prosperous, and "great" was through complete freedom of action.[4] The president wagered that his argument would resonate with many Americans.

Whether his bet would pay off over the long term was unclear, for the contemporary American public is actually more internationalist than the president assumed. To be sure, as this book has argued, a reverence for sovereignty is deeply rooted in U.S. political culture. It dates from the nation's origins as the first modern republic based on the consent of the governed, a principle anchored in the U.S. Constitution. As Tocqueville wrote in the 1830s, "If there is a country in the world where the doctrine of the sovereignty of the people can be fairly appreciated, where it can be studied in its application to the affairs of society, and where its dangers and its advantages may be judged, that country is assuredly America."[5] The powerful myth of American exceptionalism likewise depicts the United States as an inherently righteous nation, possessing a special destiny. To serve as the hope of the world, the United States must be vigilant in preserving its precious liberties at home and its room for maneuver abroad.

And yet despite these inherited instincts and its complicated political system, the United States emerged in the mid-twentieth century as history's most prolific architect of global institutions. The genius of U.S. leaders in the Roosevelt and Truman administrations lay in persuading a majority of their fellow citizens that the United States—a traditionally inward-looking nation—should embrace an internationalist vocation and lead the creation of an open, rule-bound international system. America established an array of international organizations and committed itself to a panoply of multilateral treaties that narrowed its range of action and imposed certain external obligations. Admittedly, the U.S. conversion to internationalism was partial and incomplete. The United States often chafed at the real and imagined constraints to its constitutional authorities and freedom of action, and it often insisted on opting out of rules that were binding on others or obtaining special treatment to preserve its prerogatives.[6] But the overall trend was clear: Thanks to U.S. exertions, a latticework of international cooperation arose to govern—or at least shape—virtually every field of international activity.

Today, the open, rule-bound international order that the United States helped to create is deeply vulnerable. Rapid geopolitical shifts and clashing preferences among major world powers are partly to blame. But an even more important factor is domestic: growing skepticism in some quarters of the United States that the liberal global order that America built is compatible with the U.S. Constitution, national security, domestic prosperity, and popular sovereignty. These anxieties helped propel Trump, who promised once again to place "America first," to the White House. And they are likely to persist long after he departs the scene.

At the same time, one should beware of overgeneralizing from a closely fought election in which the winning candidate got fewer votes than the loser. Based on Trump's victory, it is tempting to conclude that the entire U.S. electorate favors isolationist, protectionist, and unilateralist policies; is resistant to international commitments and anxious to throw up walls; and is determined to preserve absolute U.S. freedom of action. In reality, polling data suggests that most Americans are less obsessed than their leaders with matters of national sovereignty and more comfortable than U.S. elites with national participation in robust international organizations and treaties.

Two months after Trump's election, in January 2017, the Program for Public Consultation released a major poll that "found no evidence that the American public has tired of international engagement and is going through a phase of isolationism." Fewer than one in ten Americans endorsed "withdrawal from most efforts to solve international problems," while 82 percent wanted the United States to "play a shared leadership role." Moreover, respondents agreed overwhelmingly with the proposition that the United States should "look beyond its own interests and do what's best for the world as a whole" when formulating and conducting its foreign policy.[7]

While pollsters have not asked the public about U.S. "sovereignty" directly, their surveys on related topics are telling. Americans by large majorities support a global order based on international law, believe that the nation should abide by international law even when it conflicts with U.S. national interests, and are prepared to contribute U.S. military force to uphold it. Americans strongly support U.S. collective security obligations under the UN Charter, want the United States to work through the UN more than it does, and, indeed, endorse giving the UN *expanded* powers.[8] In sum, U.S. citizens support multilateral cooperation as a realistic means to mitigate transnational threats, resolve global challenges, and achieve shared aims.[9]

At the same time, Americans want the United States to play a less dominant (or hegemonic) global role than it has since 1945, one that involves other countries doing their fair share. In an April 2016 poll by the Pew Research Center, 57 percent of respondents wanted the United States "to deal with its own problems and let other countries deal with their own problems as best they can."[10] This sentiment should not be confused with isolationism, however. After years of war overseas, Americans are understandably tired of being the world's policeman, and they have little appetite for invading and trying to rebuild other nations. But they remain committed to internationalism and multilateral cooperation, provided that other countries are prepared to share the burden of global leadership in a more balanced fashion.

One logical conclusion to draw from polling data is that self-appointed defenders of U.S. popular sovereignty are out of step with what American citizens actually think.[11] None of this is to say that public opinion is always coherent or correct in its judgments, or that determined leaders cannot shape these attitudes. But it does suggest that internationally minded U.S. leaders should not buy into the notion of an isolationist citizenry or believe that they are more constrained than they are. There is no sovereignty-obsessed American majority (though vocal minorities may be). And while elites often fear the public as an irrational force, its opinions on global affairs have tended to be more rational and less volatile than the dramatic policy shifts we have seen over the past two and a half decades across the administrations of Bill Clinton, George W. Bush, Barack Obama, and Donald Trump. Intuitively, the American public seems to understand that sometimes it makes sense to trade some U.S. freedom of action (and on rare occasions even a bit of authority) for the prospect of effective global influence.

That intuition complements the thesis of this book, which has argued that the trade-off between sovereignty and cooperation is not as zero-sum as is often imagined—and that multilateralism is frequently the best avenue for expressing U.S. sovereignty and advancing U.S. interests. This becomes clear once we recognize that sovereignty has three different dimensions. The first is supreme political authority, including the right to make decisions about the nation's international obligations. The second is autonomy, or freedom of action in pursuing foreign and domestic policies. The third is influence, or the nation's ability to shape its destiny, by achieving outcomes consistent with its interests and preferences.

Once we disaggregate sovereignty, we can see that there is both less and more at stake in the sovereignty debate than one would glean from contemporary discourse. It is sovereignty's first dimension that generates the most heated polemics. Self-proclaimed defenders of American sovereignty protest that the United States, by entering into international treaties and multilateral organizations, risks sacrificing its constitutional authority on the altar of global governance. This alarmist view is not credible. As previous chapters have demonstrated, the United States remains adept at resisting encroachments on the U.S. Constitution. Prominent strategies include placing conditions on U.S. treaty ratification, insisting on the ultimate right to use military force unilaterally, and remaining alert to freelancing international organizations.

There is no reason to imagine that this vigilance will decline in the future. In rare but important instances—as in the WTO—the United States may decide to offer limited grants of sovereign authority to an international organization in exchange for the benefits of a rule-bound international system within which it can prosper. But critics of international organizations must do a better job distinguishing between actual and imaginary incursions on U.S. sovereign authority, lest the United States forsake the benefits of multilateral cooperation for specious reasons. In sum, constitutional authority is rarely at stake in the nation's multilateral engagements.

By barking up the wrong tree, would-be defenders of U.S. sovereign authority distract us from a far more common, and real, trade-off that pits sovereignty's other two dimensions against each other. Autonomy and influence often work at cross-purposes in managing globalization. To get what it wants—from stemming nuclear proliferation to expanding global trade—the United States often must make commitments, enter into treaties, or support multilateral bodies that simultaneously constrain its options and also promise the United States greater influence over outcomes than it could ever achieve on its own. The need for such sovereignty bargains is clear in a globalized world. After all, there is no purely unilateral (or bilateral) approach to stabilizing volatile financial markets, containing global pandemics, curtailing the spread of WMD technology, or reducing greenhouse gas emissions to sustainable levels. Not all problems can be solved multilaterally, of course, but even fewer can be solved by going it alone.

The dilemma for the United States is that international cooperation requires sacrificing some notional (though often impractical or ineffectual) freedom of action for the hoped-for benefits of a multilateral approach. It is often hard for U.S. political leaders, so steeped in a political culture of self-reliance and insistence on maintaining a free hand, to envision America becoming a more "normal" country in this fashion. It can be more tempting to hunker down, taking unilateral steps to insulate the United States from the pressures and incursions of globalization, than to embrace collective approaches to shared challenges because these limit its room for maneuver.

To be fair, though, the hurdles to this adjustment are not simply psychological. They are also practical. As chapter 8 described, formal international organizations are vulnerable to recurrent pathologies. Too often, global bodies are hard to monitor and hold to account. They frequently take refuge in lowest-common-denominator policymaking. They sometimes pursue agendas at odds with the preferences of their sovereign state masters. And they resist reforming their memberships, governance, and mandates, even in the face of sweeping global change. The limitations of international organizations can generate frustration and impose costs on the United States.

"MULTILATERALISM À LA CARTE" AS A SOLUTION?

Fortunately, the United States can avoid many of the pathologies of formal bodies and treaties by making greater use of more flexible forms of international cooperation. Besides permitting more nimble responses to many transnational challenges, ad hoc arrangements preserve the supremacy of the U.S. Constitution (sovereign authority) and expand U.S. freedom of action (sovereign autonomy), while still holding out the promise of achieving U.S. objectives (sovereign influence).[12] The good news is that the United States is no stranger to this form of cooperation—and indeed has pioneered it in the early twenty-first century. Frustrated by inefficiencies in current international organizations, U.S. policymakers and their counterparts abroad have since 2000 begun adopting a messier form of multilateralism that also happens to be sovereignty-friendly.[13]

This à la carte approach to multilateralism, as Richard N. Haass has christened it, has three distinctive aspects.[14] The first is a growing U.S. reliance on flexible, often purpose-built coalitions of the interested, capable, or like-minded. During the Obama years, pundits debated whether we lived in a G-2 (United States–China), G-8, G-20, or even G-zero world. In truth, ours is a G-x world in which the identity and number of parties at the head table (that is, x) varies by issue area and situation.[15]

Consider global economic coordination. In the depths of the global financial crisis, in November 2008, the leaders of the world's major economies met for the first time in Washington to create the Group of 20 (G-20). Within a year, they had designated the G-20 as the world's premier forum for macroeconomic coordination. But contrary to expectations, the preexisting Group of 8 (G-8) did not wither away. It actually gained a new lease on life as the United States became disillusioned with the diverse and unwieldy G-20. Indeed, the body became even more important to the United States when the G-8 members suspended Russia after its seizure of Crimea in 2014. The resulting Group of 7 (G-7) offered Washington a narrower grouping whose members shared broadly similar values, strategic interests, and major policy preferences, as well as assets to deploy in the service of these convictions.

At other times, informal "minilateral" groupings can create strange bedfellows. For example, the multinational armada that emerged around 2010 to combat Somali piracy in the Indian Ocean included vessels not only from the United States and traditional U.S. treaty allies (including NATO, Japan, and South Korea) but also from countries with which the United States has more complicated relations, including China, India, Indonesia, Malaysia, Russia, Saudi Arabia, and Yemen.

A second aspect of the new multilateralism is a preference for voluntary codes of conduct over binding conventions. After two decades of fruitless negotiations over a treaty to succeed the Kyoto Protocol, for instance, parties to the UN Framework Convention on Climate Change (UNFCCC) adopted a looser "pledge and review" system. As noted earlier, the historic December 2015 Paris Accord left it to the sovereign discretion of each national government to determine how it would contribute to global emissions reductions. The Obama administration's biennial Nuclear Security Summit process involved something similar, with governments expected to arrive with "gift baskets" enumerating separate national commitments to lock down the world's stockpiles of nuclear weapons and fissile materials.[16] We are likely to see greater American reliance on voluntary commitments in the years ahead.

The third noteworthy aspect of the new multilateralism is the search for piecemeal rather than comprehensive approaches to international challenges. Instead of trying to solve a complicated global puzzle like climate change in one fell swoop, as if it were a Rubik's Cube, the United States and other governments are more often pursuing "global governance in pieces," breaking complex problems down into their component parts.[17] Given the WTO's moribund Doha Round of trade negotiations, any future breakthroughs in global liberalization will likely also be disaggregated, taking the form of so-called plurilateral agreements—or sector-specific accords among a subset of WTO members who opt in to (or out of) commitments in areas like public procurement or investment rules. American negotiators may well pursue similar approaches in cyberspace, with different institutions tailored to specific issues like cybercrime, data protection, cyberwarfare, technical standards, and Internet governance.[18] In addition to making global challenges more tractable, thus expanding U.S. sovereignty-as-influence, this approach poses a less frontal assault on U.S. sovereignty-as-autonomy.

To be sure, other aspects of the "new" multilateralism can test traditional models of state sovereignty. One is a shift away from purely intergovernmental negotiations among foreign ministries toward new forms of networked cooperation. Faced with complex globalization challenges, for instance, U.S. national regulators and technical experts are becoming more likely to engage their counterparts abroad directly, on an ongoing basis. A case in point is the U.S. Food and Drug Administration, which during the Obama administration spearheaded the creation of an informal "global coalition of medicines regulators" intended to ensure the safety and reliability of medicines in an era of complex supply chains and major new producers like China and India.[19] Such technocratic networks can expand U.S. freedom of action (sovereign autonomy) in dealing with complicated threats, allowing the United States to better shape its own destiny (in this case, sovereign influence over public health). At the same time, such arrangements could in principle undermine U.S. sovereign authority if Congress fails to oversee and scrutinize the commitments made by U.S. technocrats and their foreign partners.

International cooperation is also more often multilevel, involving substate political units, notably in the growing global activism of cities. As humanity urbanizes, networks of cities are emerging as vibrant centers of policy innovation. Among the most dynamic forces in combating climate change today is the so-called C40 coalition, a global confederation of cities founded in 2012 by then-mayor Michael Bloomberg of New York and foreign counterparts to combat pollution and sustain green growth. More recently, in September 2016 the Global Parliament of Mayors met for the first time, agreeing to collaborate on two issues that disproportionately affect urban populations: climate change and migration.[20] Meanwhile, in the wake of Trump's withdrawal from the Paris Accord, individual U.S. states like California and New York are sidestepping the federal government to pursue their own climate change diplomacy.[21]

Finally, effective international cooperation today depends on innovative partnerships among national governments, private companies, and civil society that leverage the capabilities of different stakeholders.[22] Perhaps the most well-known arrangement is the Internet Corporation for Assigned Names and Numbers (ICANN), an independent, nonprofit entity. But private actors play a prominent role in other regulatory and standard-setting bodies, such as the Extractive Industries Transparency Initiative (EITI). The challenge for the United States is to expand its sovereignty-as-influence by drawing on the expertise, resources, and leverage that such nonstate actors provide, without allowing U.S. sovereignty-as-authority (namely, the will of the American people, as expressed through elected representatives) from being distorted or hijacked in the process.

Overall, à la carte multilateralism has a lot going for it. It imposes few costs on U.S. sovereignty-as-authority and widens U.S. sovereignty-as-autonomy. It also implies speed and flexibility. Rather than engaging in painstaking, drawn-out negotiations within formal, binding, universal (or large-membership) organizations, the United States can design nimble coalitions of nations (and other actors) that matter. Another benefit is modularity. Instead of trying to digest an entire complex global problem, like mitigating greenhouse gas emissions, governments can bite off manageable chunks, such as reforestation or controls on methane. Yet another advantage is discrimination: purpose-built frameworks may help the United States compartmentalize its bilateral relationships so that it can cooperate with geopolitical rivals like China and Russia in some forums to advance common security and economic or ecological or other interests—even as it competes in other arenas. Finally, diverse forms of collective action can in principle allow the United States to experiment with and glean lessons from alternative design solutions to cooperation problems (much as it was assumed the fifty U.S. states provide distinct "laboratories of democracy," in the famous formulation of the Supreme Court justice Louis Brandeis).[23]

At first blush, a world of à la carte options seems tailor-made for the United States, allowing it to maximize its sovereign freedom of action and domestic policy autonomy by picking and choosing among diverse international institutions, as its situational interests warrant. The "G-x" world, after all, rewards nations well positioned to play simultaneously on different chess boards and in different groupings, thanks to their military, economic, diplomatic, and technological weight, as well as the vitality of their private sector, civil society, and universities. On all these criteria, the United States reigns supreme.[24]

For all its advantages, however, ad hoc multilateralism is no panacea. Although an à la carte approach can protect U.S. sovereign authority and expand U.S. sovereign autonomy, its implications for American sovereignty-as-influence cannot be taken for granted. There is no guarantee that such institutional workarounds will actually deliver what formal organizations cannot.

Putting aside for the moment the U.S. withdrawal, the jury is out on whether the voluntary national pledges on climate change made at the 2015 Paris Climate Conference will amount to much, since the agreement lacks any credible enforcement mechanism. And even if fully implemented, it would still almost certainly fall well short of the scope of international effort required to stave off the dangers identified by the Intergovernmental Panel on Climate Change.

Moreover, flexible minilateralism is unlikely to resolve tough cooperation problems that pit great powers against one another. À la carte arrangements are most promising when participants' interests and preferences are broadly congruent, but more encompassing bodies are blocked. If interests diverge significantly—as in the clashes between Russia and the West over Syria or Crimea, or between China and its neighbors in the South China Sea—simply shifting forums may make little difference.

A second concern is that ad hoc-ism, if carried too far, could undermine formal organizations whose legitimacy, resources, and technical capacity the United States and its partners need over the long haul and cannot easily replace. The hope, of course, is that the opposite will be true. In 2005 the international law scholar Ruth Wedgwood argued that it was "time to give the UN a little competition." Experimenting with alternative forms of collective action, she implied, might give the UN an incentive to raise its game.[25] Proponents of preferential trade agreements likewise argue that they might actually spur the WTO to make greater progress on liberalization. But skeptics warn just as vigorously that the proliferation of minilateral arrangements will create a fragmented system of redundant institutions that are stumbling blocks (rather than building blocks) to global cooperation, as well as undercut the capabilities, credibility, and legitimacy of standing international organizations.[26]

The evidence is mixed. At times, informal multilateral frameworks can re-invigorate formal institutions, helping them to adapt to new conditions. A case in point is the G-20. During its first two, activist years (2008–10) the G-20 engineered the replacement of the weak Financial Stability Forum with the stronger Financial Stability Board. It also revitalized, increased funding for, and negotiated governance changes to the IMF and the World Bank. At other times, however, the rise of alternative institutions has reflected less a desire for partnership than antagonism: specifically, the conscious decision by a coalition of dissatisfied states to challenge the mandates, rules, and practices of established international institutions, and to try to shift the setting for multilateral deliberation and policymaking to an alternative existing institu-tion whose mandate and decision rules they find more congenial.[27]

This brings us to the third potential downside. A world of à la carte multi-lateralism lends itself to rampant forum shopping—and not just by the United States.[28] Emerging powers are moving swiftly to sponsor alternative institu-tions of their own, ranging from the Shanghai Cooperation Organization to the BRICS Bank, the BRICS Contingency Fund, and—most dramatically— the Beijing-led Asian Infrastructure Investment Bank (AIIB). The inability of the Obama administration in 2015 to dissuade even its closest European allies from joining the AIIB as founding members offered a stark lesson that others can play this game too. The U.S. defeat was rich in symbolism, suggest-ing how quickly the center of gravity of international economic cooperation could shift.[29]

The AIIB episode also signaled what might be called the limits of Ameri-can "exemptionalism." Particularly since the end of the Cold War, the United States has adopted an ambivalent and selective attitude toward formal multi-lateral commitments, particularly treaty obligations. The U.S. attitude has been one of the main driving forces behind the trend toward minilateral coop-eration. While this stance has brought some external freedom of action and domestic policy autonomy, the United States is discovering that it is not the only nation capable of cherry-picking among international commitments. If the United States is unwilling and unable to revitalize the institutions it founded to accommodate new players, other countries will build new ones in their place. More recently, the Trump administration's repudiation of the TPP mega-trade deal has cleared the field for China to push forward with its alter-native vision of a Regional Comprehensive Economic Partnership that excludes the United States. As major non-Western players learn to play the game of flexible multilateralism, the risk increases that the world could fragment into competing, self-contained, and discriminatory blocs.

In sum, enthusiasm for flexible multilateralism should not blind the United States to the potential risks of overreliance on ad hoc solutions. To persist, a rule-bound international order is likely to depend not only on flexible coalitions of the moment, tailored to particular exigencies and issues, but also on revitalized, formal, international bodies grounded in international law.

The trick for the United States is to combine the best of both strategies, designing à la carte mechanisms that complement and reinvigorate, rather than undermine and marginalize, the prix fixe menu of formal international organizations on which the world continues to depend. The first step is to think more soberly about the comparative advantages and trade-offs of these alternative forms of collective action, not least for American sovereignty. Coalitions bring the benefits of flexibility, agility, and exclusivity. They are most compelling when standing bodies do not exist or are paralyzed by divisions, or when bureaucracy slows responses to immediate threats. But they typically lack the capacity, legitimacy, and legal status of formal, permanent organizations like the UN (or NATO, for that matter). The UN can offer distinct advantages when the challenge is enduring and requires protracted burden sharing, specialized technical capacities, and broad international legitimacy. Going forward, the United States should align its forays into minilateralism with parallel diplomacy at the United Nations and World Bank, as well as within NATO and other standing alliances.

AMERICA AT HOME IN THE WORLD

A century after World War I, the struggle to reconcile American sovereignty with the demands of international cooperation persists. The sovereignty wars are a battle between two very different conceptions of the United States—and of the U.S. global role. The first, suspicious and inward-looking, regards international commitments with mistrust, as threats to America's beloved Constitution and unwarranted infringements on U.S. freedom of action. The second, more optimistic and outward-looking, envisions an America at home in the world. It recognizes that international institutions and law pose little threat to America's sovereign authorities. It also understands that shaping America's destiny will frequently require sovereignty bargains, whereby the United States judiciously trades off some notional autonomy for the promise of effective multilateral action.

The sovereignty wars will no doubt persist, for they are a struggle for the heart and soul of America, drawing sustenance from the nation's identity, ideals, institutions, and experiences. In the face of a complicated and some-times dangerous world, the United States will face constant temptations to strike out on its own, to wall itself off, and to hunker down in pursuit of na-tional greatness. Meanwhile the world will keep moving and the planet will keep getting smaller. The future will belong to a confident America—and confident Americans—who are prepared to lead, rather than retreat from, the world.

Notes

CHAPTER 1

1. John Lenger, "The Great Debate," *Harvard University Gazette*, March 18, 2004.

2. "Lodge vs. Lowell: A Joint Debate on the Covenant of the League of Nations," Symphony Hall, Boston, March 19, 1919, reprinted from the *Boston Evening Transcript*, March 19, 1919.

3. Ibid. (Subsequent debate quotations come from the same document.)

4. John Milton Cooper Jr., *Breaking the Heart of the World: Woodrow Wilson and the Fight for the League of Nations* (Cambridge University Press, 2001), pp. 74–84.

5. Dean Rusk is cited in Edward C. Luck, *Mixed Messages: American Politics and International Organization, 1919–1999* (Brookings Institution Press, 1999), p. 61.

6. John Fonte, *Sovereignty or Submission: Will Americans Rule Themselves or Be Ruled by Others?* (New York: Encounter, 2011); John Bolton, "The Coming War on Sovereignty," *Commentary*, March 1, 2009; Steven Groves, "The Importance of Protecting National Sovereignty," Heritage Foundation, December 8, 2010.

7. The Congressional Sovereignty Caucus was formed in June 2009 by Representatives Doug Lamborn (R-Colo.), Scott Garrett (R-N.J.), and Thaddeus McCotter (R-Mich.). David Weigel, "GOP 'Sovereignty Caucus' Battles Obama on Major Treaties," *Washington Independent*, July 1, 2009, http://lamborn.house.gov/news/doc

umentsingle.aspx?DocumentID=1093; John Gizzi, "House 'Sovereignty Caucus' Aimed at Koh," *Human Events*, July 13, 2010, http://lamborn.house.gov/news/doc umentsingle.aspx?DocumentID=1094; Oliver North, "What 'Sovereignty' Really Means," Fox News, June 26, 2009, www.foxnews.com/story/2009/06/26/what -overeignty-really-means.html.

8. Julian Hattem, "Trump Outlines 'America First' Foreign Policy," *The Hill*, April 27, 2016, http://thehill.com/policy/national-security/277854-trump-outlines -america-first-foreign-policy.

9. Transcript of Trump's acceptance speech at Cleveland Republican Convention, July 21, 2016, www.politico.com/story/2016/07/full-transcript-donald-trump -nomination-acceptance-speech-at-rnc-225974.

10. "Every decision on trade, on taxes, on immigration, on foreign affairs will be made to benefit American workers and American families," Trump said in his inauguration speech: www.cnbc.com/2017/01/20/transcript-of-president-trumps-inaug uration-speech.html.

11. Miriam Valverde, "Here's What Trump Did in His First Week as President of the United States," *Politifact*, January 27, 2017; Max Fisher, "Trump Prepares Executive Orders Aiming at Global Funding and Treaties," *New York Times*, January 25, 2017.

12. Frances Stead Sellers and David A. Farenthold, "Why Let 'Em In? Understanding Bannon's Worldview and the Policies that Follow," *Washington Post*, January 31, 2017.

13. See Council for America, www.councilforamerica.org/; WorldNet Daily, www.wnd.com/. See also American Sovereignty PAC, www.americansovereignty pac.org.

14. On General Jack D. Ripper, see www.imdb.com/character/ch0003297/quotes. See also Richard Hofstadter, *The Paranoid Style in American Politics and Other Essays* (Harvard University Press, 1964).

15. Stewart Patrick, "Don't Tread on Me: July 4th and U.S. Sovereignty," *The Internationalist* (blog), Council on Foreign Relations, July 1, 2001, http://blogs.cfr.org /patrick/2011/07/01/dont-tread-on-me-july-4th-and-u-s-sovereignty/.

16. On this important insight, see Christopher Rudolph, "Sovereignty and Territorial Borders in a Global Age," *International Studies Review* 7, no. 1 (March 2005), pp. 1–20.

17. See Gerard M. Gallucci, "Time to Begin Thinking about World Government?," March 18, 2014, posted on the website of the Democratic World Federalists, www .dwfed.org/; Thomas G. Weiss, "What Happened to the Idea of World Government?," *International Studies Quarterly* 53 (2009), pp. 253–71.

18. My thinking on "sovereignty bargains" draws inspiration from Karen T. Liftin, "Sovereignty in World Ecopolitics," *Mershon International Studies Review* (1997), pp. 167–294. See also Bruce Byers, "Ecoregions, State Sovereignty and Conflict," *Bulletin of Peace Proposals* 22, no. 1 (1991), pp. 65–76.

19. For a similar argument with respect to environmental agreements, see Robert O. Keohane, Peter M. Haas, and Marc A. Levy, eds., *Institutions for the Earth: Sources of Effective International Environmental Protection* (MIT Press, 1993).

20. Thomas C. Heller and Abraham D. Sofaer, "Sovereignty: A Practitioner's Perspective," in *Problematic Sovereignty: Contested Rules and Political Possibilities*, edited by Stephen D. Krasner (Columbia University Press, 2001), p. 25; Alan James, *Sovereign Statehood: The Basis of International Society* (London: Allen and Unwin, 1986), pp. 186–92.

21. Liftin, "Sovereignty in World Ecopolitics."

22. For earlier versions of this argument, see Abram Chayes and Antonia Handler Chayes, *The New Sovereignty: Compliance with International Regulatory Agreements* (Harvard University Press, 1998); Anne-Marie Slaughter, *A New World Order* (Princeton University Press, 2004).

23. Adriana Sinclair and Michael Byers, "When U.S. Scholars Speak of 'Sovereignty,' What Do They Mean?," *Political Studies* 55 (2007), pp. 318–40.

24. For more details, see Stewart Patrick, *The Best Laid Plans: The Origins of American Multilateralism and the Dawn of the Cold War* (Lanham, Md.: Rowman and Littlefield, 2009).

25. Michael John Garcia, *International Law and Its Effect upon U.S. Law*, CRS Report for Congress, March 1, 2013.

26. John Kyl, Douglas J. Feith, and John Fonte, "The War of Law: How New International Law Undermines Democratic Sovereignty," *Foreign Affairs*, July/August 2013, pp. 115–25.

27. For more details, see Stewart Patrick, "Conflict and Cooperation in the Global Commons," in *Managing Conflict in a World Adrift*, edited by Chester Crocker, Fen Osler Hampson, and Pamela Aall (Washington: United States Institute of Peace Press, 2015), pp. 101–22.

CHAPTER 2

1. The subtitle of this chapter, and some of its inspiration, is drawn from Jeffrey Legro, "Sovereignty American Style: Protecting Apple Pie, Fixing Foreign Recipes," in *America, China, and the Struggle for World Order: Ideas, Traditions, Legacies, and Global Visions*, edited by G. John Ikenberry, Zhu Feng, and Wang Jisi (New York: Palgrave Macmillan, 2015), pp. 19–42.

2. John Bolton, "The Coming War on Sovereignty," *Commentary*, March 1, 2009, www.commentarymagazine.com/articles/the-coming-war-on-sovereignty/.

3. Global Governance Watch is now run entirely by the Federalist Society for Law and Public Policy Studies, www.globalgovernancewatch.org/about/.

4. Peter Spiro, "The New Sovereigntists: American Exceptionalism and Its False Prophets," *Foreign Affairs*, November/December 2000, pp. 9–15; Josh Rogin, "Kyl Warns about the War on American Sovereignty," *Foreign Policy*, March 10, 2011, http://foreignpolicy.com/2011/03/10/kyl-warns-about-the-war-on-american

-sovereignty/; "Senator Kyl to Address 'American Sovereignty and Transnational Law' at Pedrik Lecture," February 12, 2012, Arizona State University website, https://asunow.asu.edu/content/sen-kyl-address-american-sovereignty-and-trans national-law-pedrik-lecture.

5. American Sovereignty Restoration Act of 2017, H.R. 193, 115th Congress (2017–18), www.congress.gov/bill/115th-congress/house-bill/193.

6. Remarks by President Trump at the Conservative Political Action Conference, February 24, 2017, www.whitehouse.gov/the-press-office/2017/02/24/remarks-presi dent-trump-conservative-political-action-conference.

7. For more on this, see Stewart Patrick: "Multilateralism and Its Discontents: The Causes and Consequences of U.S. Ambivalence," in *Multilateralism and U.S. Foreign Policy: Ambivalent Engagement*, edited by Stewart Patrick and Shepard Forman (Boulder, Colo.: Lynne Rienner, 2002), pp. 1–44.

8. Adriana Sinclair and Michael Byers, "When U.S. Scholars Speak of 'Sovereignty,' What Do They Mean?," *Political Studies* 55, no. 2 (2007), pp. 318–40.

9. The English word derives from the Latin *superanus*, by way of the French *souveraineté*. Jean Bethke Elshtain, *Sovereignty: God, State, and Self* (New York: Basic Books, 2008), pp. 1–3, 63; Howard M. Hensel, "Theocentric Natural Law and the Norms of the Global Community," in *Sovereignty and the Global Community: The Quest for Order in the International System*, edited by Howard M. Hensel (Aldershot, U.K.: Ashgate, 2004), p. 37.

10. Robert Jackson, *Sovereignty: The Evolution of an Idea* (Cambridge: Polity Press, 2007), pp. 24–36; Hendrik Spruyt, *The Sovereign State and Its Competitors* (Princeton University Press, 1994), pp. 3–7, 11–21.

11. Elshtain, *Sovereignty*, pp. 12, 29.

12. The new order was captured by the phrases *rex est imperator in regno suo* (the king is emperor in his own realm); *rex superiorem non-recognoscens* (the king recognizes no superior); and *cuius regio, eius religio* (whose realm, his religion). Elshtain, *Sovereignty*, p. 86; Jackson, *Sovereignty*, pp. 44–47.

13. Jackson, *Sovereignty*, pp. 51–52. See also Andreas Osiander, "Sovereignty, International Relations, and the Westphalian Myth," *International Organization* 55, no. 2 (March 2001), pp. 251–87.

14. Cited in Martin Van Creveld, *The Rise and Decline of the State* (Cambridge University Press, 1999), p. 87.

15. Hedley Bull, *The Anarchical Society: A Study of Order in World Politics* (London: Macmillan, 1977).

16. Alfred Cobban, *The Nation State and Self-Determination* (New York: Harper-Collins, 1969); Isaiah Berlin, "Nationalism: Past Neglect and Present Power," in *Against the Current: Essays on the History of Ideas*, edited by Isaiah Berlin (New York: Viking, 1980), pp. 333–55; Benedict Anderson, *Imagined Communities: Reflections on the Origin and Spread of Nationalism* (London: Verso, 1983).

17. Jackson, *Sovereignty*, p. x.

18. Thomas Hobbes, *Leviathan* (1651).

19. Alan James, *Sovereign Statehood: The Basis of International Society* (London: Allen and Unwin, 1986), pp. 39, 203–34; David Jason Karp, "The Utopia and Reality of Sovereignty: Social Reality, Normative IR, and 'Organized Hypocrisy,'" *Review of International Studies* 34 (2008), pp. 313–35.

20. Jackson, *Sovereignty*, p. 9.

21. Stephen D. Krasner refers to this dimension as "interdependence sovereignty," in *Sovereignty: Organized Hypocrisy* (Princeton University Press, 1999), pp. 12–14.

22. See chapter 1 of Stewart Patrick, *Weak Links: Fragile States, Global Threats, and International Security* (Oxford University Press, 2011).

23. John D. Montgomery, "Sovereignty in Transition," in *Sovereignty under Challenge*, edited by John D. Montgomery and Nathan Glazer (New Brunswick, N.J.: Transaction, 2002), pp. 3–32.

24. Janice E. Thomson, "State Sovereignty in International Relations: Bridging the Gap between Theory and Empirical Research," *International Studies Quarterly* 39, no. 2 (June 1995), pp. 213–33; Alan James, "The Practice of Sovereign Statehood in Contemporary International Society, *Political Studies* 47, no. 3 (1999), pp. 457–73; Thomas J. Biersteker and Cynthia Weber, "State Sovereignty," in *State Sovereignty as a Social Construct*, edited by Thomas J. Biersteker and Cynthia Weber (Cambridge University Press, 1996), p. 5.

25. Booth is cited in Christopher J. Bickerton, Philip Cunliffe, and Alexander Gourevitch, "Introduction: The Unholy Alliance against Sovereignty," in *Politics without Sovereignty*, edited by Christopher J. Bickerton, Philip Cunliffe, and Alexander Gourevitch (University College London, 2007), pp. 4–5.

26. Ian Goldin, *Divided Nations: Why Global Governance Is Failing, and What We Can Do about It* (Oxford University Press, 2013), p. 107; Simona Tituanu, *Towards Global Justice: Sovereignty in an Interdependent World* (The Hague: Springer, 2013), p. 29; Daniel Deudney, "Omniviolence, Arms Control, and Limited Government," in *The Limits of Constitutionalism*, edited by J. Tulis and S. Macedo (Princeton University Press, 2007), pp. 297–316; Alfred von Staden, "The Erosion of State Sovereignty: Towards a Post-Territorial World?," in *State, Sovereignty, and International Governance*, edited by Gerard Kreijen and others (Oxford University Press, 2002); Christopher Rudolph, "Sovereignty and Territorial Borders in a Global Age," *International Studies Review* 7, no. 1 (March 2005), pp. 1–20.

27. Such claims have a long pedigree. See Raymond Vernon, *Sovereignty at Bay: The Multinational Spread of U.S. Enterprises* (New York: Basic Books, 1971).

28. Krasner, *Sovereignty*, p. 239; Stephen D. Krasner, "Think Again: Sovereignty," *Foreign Policy*, January/February 2001, p. 20; Karp, "The Utopia and Reality of Sovereignty."

29. Bickerton, Cunliffe, and Gourevitch, "Introduction," pp. 11–14.

30. Statistics from the Union of International Associations, Yearbook of International Organizations, www.uia.org/sites/uia.org/files/misc_pdfs/stats/Historical_overview_of_number_of_international_organizations_by_type_1909-2013.pdf.

31. Margaret E. Keck and Kathryn Sikkink, *Activists beyond Borders: Advocacy Networks in International Politics* (Cornell University Press, 1998); Ken Abbott and Duncan Snidal, "The Governance Triangle: Regulatory Standards Institutions and the Shadow of the State," March 1, 2008, https://ec.europa.eu/digital-single-market/en/content/governance-triangle-regulatory-standards-institutions-and-shadow-state.

32. Stephen D. Krasner, "Sovereignty: An Institutional Perspective," *Comparative Political Studies* 21, no. 1 (April 1988), p. 76.

33. Jackson, *Sovereignty*, pp. 145–48.

34. World Bank, "Private Capital Flows in Historical Perspective," *Global Development Finance* (Washington, 2000), p. 121, http://siteresources.worldbank.org/INTGDF2000/Resources/CH6--118-139.pdf; Krasner, *Sovereignty*, p. 13; Institute of Medicine (U.S.) Forum on Microbial Threats, "The Threat of Pandemic Influenza: Are We Ready?," Workshop Summary, www.ncbi.nlm.nih.gov/books/NBK22148/.

35. Thomson, "State Sovereignty in International Relations," pp. 215–19; Stephen D. Krasner, "Abiding Sovereignty," *International Political Science Review* 22, no. 3 (2001), pp. 229–51.

36. John Gerard Ruggie, "International Regimes, Transactions, and Change: Embedded Liberalism in the Postwar Economic Order," *International Organization* 36, no. 2 (Spring 1982), pp. 379–419; Krasner, "Think Again," p. 20.

37. Edward A. Alden, *Failure to Adjust: How Americans Got Left Behind in the Global Economy* (Lanham, Md.: Rowman and Littlefield, 2017).

38. "16th Summit of Heads of State or Government of the Non-Aligned Movement," Tehran, Islamic Republic of Iran, August 26–31, 2012, http://cns.miis.edu/nam/documents/Official_Document/16thSummitFinalDocument(NAM2012-Doc.1-Rev.2).pdf.

39. "Putin Blasts West in State of Nation Address," *USA Today*, December 4, 2014, www.usatoday.com/story/news/world/2014/12/04/russia-putin-foreign-policy/19878441/.

40. Gerrit W. Gong, "China's Entry into International Society," in *The Expansion of International Society*, edited by Hedley Bull and Adam Watson (Oxford: Clarendon Press, 1984), pp. 171–83.

41. Fei-Ling Wang, "From *Tianxia* to Westphalia: The Evolving Chinese Conception of Sovereignty and World Order," in Ikenberry, Feng, and Jisi, *America, China, and the Struggle for World Order*, p. 52; Alistair Ian Johnstone, "How New and Assertive Is China's New Assertiveness?," *International Security* 37, no. 4 (Spring 2013), pp. 7–48; Yuan-kang Wang, "The Myth of Chinese Exceptionalism," *Foreign Policy*, March 6, 2012, http://foreignpolicy.com/2012/03/06/the-myth-of-chinese-exceptionalism/.

42. Preamble to the Indian Constitution, http://indiacode.nic.in/coiweb/coifiles/preamble.htm; Iain Atak, "Gandhi in Political Theory: Truth, Law and Experi-

ment," *Contemporary Political Theory* 15, no. 2 (May 2016), pp. e4–e7, https://link
.springer.com/article/10.1057/cpt.2015.36.

43. Gopal Krishna, "India and the International Order—Retreat from Idealism,"
in Bull and Watson, *The Expansion of International Society*, pp. 272–74.

44. Madhan Mohan Jaganathan and Gerrit Kurtz, "Singing the Tune of Sovereignty? India and the Responsibility to Protect," *Conflict, Security and Development*
14, no. 4 (June 2014), pp. 461–87, www.tandfonline.com/doi/pdf/10.1080/14678802
.2014.930591?needAccess=true&; Rajen Harshe, "India's Non-Alignment: An Attempt at Conceptual Reconstruction," *Economic and Political Weekly* 25, no. 7/8
(February 17–24, 1990), pp. 399–405, www.jstor.org/stable/pdf/4395968.pdf?seq
=1#page_scan_tab_contents; Kallol Bhattacherjee, "Respect Territorial Sovereignty,
India Tells China," *The Hindu*, January 18, 2017, www.thehindu.com/news/national
/Respect-territorial-sovereignty-India-tells-China/article17054467.ece; Summit
Ganguly and Eswaran Sridharan, "The End of India's Sovereignty Hawks?," *Foreign
Policy*, November 7, 2013, http://foreignpolicy.com/2013/11/07/the-end-of-indias
-sovereignty-hawks/.

45. Walter Russell Mead, *Special Providence: American Foreign Policy and How It
Changed the World* (New York: Knopf, 2001); Tony Smith, *America's Mission: The
United States and the Worldwide Struggle for Democracy in the Twentieth Century*
(Princeton University Press, 1994).

46. *The Political Thought of Benjamin Franklin*, edited by Frank Ketcham (India-
napolis: Hackett, 2003), p. 398; Jackson, *Sovereignty*, pp. 78–79; Christian G. Fritz,
*American Sovereigns: The People and America's Constitutional Tradition before the Civil
War* (Cambridge University Press, 2008).

47. *Chisholm v. Georgia*, 2 U.S. 419 (1793).

48. *Hamlet*, act I, scene 4, and King James Bible are cited in Elshtain, *Sovereignty*,
pp. 66, 95–96; Jean Bodin, *Les Six Livres de la République* (1576), www.amazon.fr/six
-livres-R%C3%A9publique-Jean-Bodin/dp/2253063541.

49. Ernst Kantorowicz, *The King's Two Bodies: A Study in Medieval Political Theol-
ogy* (Princeton University Press, 1958); Elshtain, *Sovereignty*, pp. 63–64; Jackson,
Sovereignty, pp. 57–60.

50. Edmund S. Morgan, *Inventing the People: The Rise of Popular Sovereignty in
England and America* (New York: W. W. Norton, 1988), pp. 78, 117–120.

51. Elshtain, *Sovereignty*, pp. 120–24; Morgan, *Inventing the People*, p. 105.

52. Morgan, *Inventing the People*, pp. 123–43, 231, 239–41.

53. Gordon Wood, *The Idea of America: Reflections on the Birth of the United States*
(New York: Penguin, 2011), pp. 173–74; Fritz, *American Sovereigns*, pp. 1–15.

54. Jean-Jacques Rousseau, *Du Contrat Social, ou Principes du Droit Politique*
(1762).

55. French Constitution of 1791, Title 3 ("Public Powers"), Art. 1, https://
worldhistoryproject.org/1791/9/3/french-constitution-of-1791; Jackson, *Sovereignty*,
pp. 94–98.

56. Daniel Deudney, "Binding Sovereigns: Authorities, Structures, and Geopolitics in Philadelphian Systems," in Biersteker and Weber, *State Sovereignty as a Social Construct*, pp. 190–223.

57. Fritz, *American Sovereigns*, pp. 1–7; Wood, *The Idea of America*, pp. 178–85, 305.

58. Alexis de Tocqueville, *Democracy in America*, vol. 1 (1835), chapter 4 ("The Principle of the Sovereignty of the People of America"), archived online at http://xroads.virginia.edu/~hyper/DETOC/1_ch04.htm.

59. Robert W. Johannsen, *The Frontier, the Union, and Stephen A. Douglas* (University of Illinois Press, 1989), pp. 95–96; Stephen Douglas, "Popular Sovereignty in the Territories," *Harper's Magazine*, September 1859, http://harpers.org/sponsor/balvenie/stephen-douglas.1.html.

60. *The Schooner Exchange v. McFaddon*, 11 U.S. (7 Cranch) 116 (1812), www.casebriefs.com/blog/law/international-law/international-law-keyed-to-damrosche/chapter-12/the-schooner-exchange-v-mcfaddon/.

61. John Bolton, "The First Post-American President and American Sovereignty," remarks at the Heritage Foundation, May 18, 2010, www.aei.org/publication/the-first-post-american-president-and-american-sovereignty/; John R. Bolton and John Yoo, "Restore the Senate's Treaty Power," *New York Times*, January 4, 2009.

62. Stewart Patrick, "Global Governance Reform: An American View of U.S. Leadership," Stanley Foundation Policy Analysis Brief (Muscatine, Iowa, February 2010), www.stanleyfoundation.org/publications/pab/PatrickPAB210.pdf.

63. Adam Lupel, *Globalization and Popular Sovereignty: Democracy's Transnational Dilemma* (New York: Routledge, 2009).

64. Louis Hartz, *The Liberal Tradition in America: An Interpretation of American Political Thought since the Revolution* (New York: Harcourt, Brace, and World, 1955), p. 6; Anderson, *Imagined Communities*; Christopher Thorne, "American Political Culture and the End of the Cold War," *Journal of American Studies* 26, no. 3 (1993), pp. 303–30; Wood, *The Idea of America*, pp. 321–22.

65. Tocqueville, *Democracy in America*, vol. 1; Hartz, *The Liberal Tradition in America*, pp. 6, 11; Seymour Martin Lipset, *American Exceptionalism: A Double-Edged Sword* (New York: W. W. Norton, 1996), pp. 25–26.

66. Wood, *The Idea of America*, pp. 275–77, 322; Thomas Paine, *Common Sense* (1776), www.constitution.org/tp/comsense.htm; Dean Acheson, *Present at the Creation: My Years at the State Department* (New York: W. W. Norton, 1969).

67. Herman Melville, *White Jacket, or the World on a Man of War* (1850), chapter 16, www.online-literature.com/melville/white-jacket/36/.

68. Stanley R. Sloan, *The U.S. Role in a New World Order: Prospects for George Bush's Global Vision* (Washington: Congressional Research Service, 1991). On NBC's *Today* show on February 19, 1998, Albright famously stated: "We are America; we are the indispensable nation. We stand tall and we see further than other countries into the future, and we see the danger here to all of us."

69. Pew Research Center on Religion and Public Life, "U.S. Public Becoming Less Religious," November 3, 2015, www.pewforum.org/2015/11/03/u-s-public -becoming-less-religious/.

70. The White House, "News Conference by President Obama 4/04/09," www .whitehouse.gov/the-press-office/news-conference-president-obama-4042009; John Bolton, *How Barack Obama Is Endangering Our National Sovereignty*, Encounter Broadside no. 11 (New York: Encounter Books, 2010).

71. Republican Party Platform of 2016, p. 1, www.gop.com/the-2016-republican -party-platform/.

72. Ron Fournier, "Obama's New American Exceptionalism," *The Atlantic*, July 28, 2016; Sahil Kapur, "Democrats Emphasize American Exceptionalism at Convention, Blurring Party Lines," Bloomberg.com, July 29, 2016, www.bloomberg .com/politics/articles/2016-07-29/democrats-emphasize-american-exceptionalism -at-convention.

73. Samuel Huntington, "America's Ideals versus America's Institutions," *Political Science Quarterly* 97, no. 1 (Spring 1982), pp. 1–37; Stephen Walt, "The Myth of American Exceptionalism," *Foreign Policy*, October 11, 2011.

74. Paine is cited in Henry Kissinger, *Diplomacy* (New York: Simon and Schuster, 1994), pp. 32–33; David M. Fitzsimmons, "Tom Paine's New World Order: Idealistic Internationalism in the Ideology of Early American Foreign Relations," *Diplomatic History* 19 (1995), pp. 569–82.

75. Jeremy A. Rabkin, *Law without Nations? Why Constitutional Government Requires Sovereign States* (Princeton University Press, 2005), p. 233.

76. Nick Bryant, "Donald Trump and the End of American Exceptionalism," BBC, March 2, 2017, www.bbc.com/news/world-us-canada-39133677; Jelani Cobb, "Donald Trump and the Death of American Exceptionalism," *New Yorker*, November 4, 2016; Peter Beinart, "How Donald Trump Wants to Make America Exceptional Again," *The Atlantic*, February 2, 2017.

77. Sophie Tatum, "Trump Defends Putin: 'You Think Our Country's So Innocent?,'" *CNN*, February 6, 2017, www.cnn.com/2017/02/04/politics/donald-trump -vladimir-putin/index.html.

78. Spiro, "The New Sovereigntists."

79. Anton DePorte, *Europe between the Superpowers: The Enduring Balance* (Yale University Press, 1986), p. 80; John Gerard Ruggie, "The Past as Prologue: Interests, Identity, and American Foreign Policy," *International Security* 21, no. 4 (1997), pp. 89–125; Stewart Patrick, *The Best Laid Plans: The Origins of American Multilateralism and the Dawn of the Cold War* (Lanham, Md.: Rowman and Littlefield, 2009).

80. Cordell Hull, *The Memoirs of Cordell Hull* (New York: Macmillan, 1948), p. 1731.

81. The British official is cited in Christopher Thorne, *Allies of a Kind: The United States, Britain, and the War against Japan* (Oxford University Press, 1978), p. 138.

82. Eric Kleefeld, "Congressional Sovereignty Caucus Launching Next Week," *Talking Points Memo*, June 19, 2009, http://talkingpointsmemo.com/dc/congressional -sovereignty-caucus-launching-next-week.

83. Robert Kagan, *The World America Made* (New York: Knopf, 2012); John Gerard Ruggie, "American Exceptionalism, Exemptionalism, and Human Rights," in *American Exceptionalism and Human Rights*, edited by Michael Ignatieff (Princeton University Press, 2005); Anatol Lieven, *America Right or Wrong: An Anatomy of American Nationalism*, 2nd ed. (Oxford University Press, 2012), p. 9.

84. Fritz, *American Sovereigns*, pp. 1–7; Morgan, *Inventing the People*, p. 249.

85. Fritz, *American Sovereigns*, pp. 32–42, 117–28; see also James Madison, "Federalist No. 10," November 22, 1787, in *The Essential Federalist and Anti-Federalist Papers* (New York: Classic Books, 2009), pp. 46–52.

86. Articles of Confederation, https://memory.loc.gov/cgi-bin/ampage?collId =llsl&fileName=001/llsl001.db&recNum=127.

87. Walter A. MacDougal, *Promised Land, Crusader State: The American Encounter with the World since 1776* (New York: Houghton Mifflin, 1997), pp. 36–41, 71–72.

88. James Madison, "Vices of the Political System of the United States," April 1787, compiled in *The Founders' Constitution*, vol. 1, chapter 5, document 16, edited by Philip B. Kurland and Ralph Lerner, http://press-pubs.uchicago.edu/founders/documents /v1ch5s16.html; Wood, *The Idea of America*, pp. 235–37.

89. Rabkin, *Law without Nations?*, pp. 62–64; James Madison, "Federalist No. 44," January 25, 1788, in *The Essential Federalist*, pp. 201–07.

90. Daniel H. Deudney, "The Philadelphian System: Sovereignty, Arms Control, and the Balance of Power in the America States-Union, Circa 1787–1861," *International Organization* 49, no. 2 (Spring 1995), pp. 191–228; Elshtain, *Sovereignty*, pp. 152–58; *Cohens v. Virginia*, 19 U.S. 264 (1821), www.vlib.us/amdocs/texts/cohens.htm.

91. Daniel Deudney, *Bounding Power: Republican Security Theory from the Polis to the Global Village* (Princeton University Press, 2007), p. 177.

92. *U.S. Term Limits, Inc., v. Thornton* (93-1456), 514 U.S. 779 (1995), www.law .cornell.edu/supct/html/93-1456.ZC.html; James Madison, "Federalist No. 62," in *The Essential Federalist*, p. 276.

93. Deudney, "Binding Sovereigns," pp. 210–11; Fritz, *American Sovereigns*, pp. 25–29; David C. Hendrickson, "Three Governing Systems in American History: Philadelphia, Appomattox, Washington," paper presented at annual meetings of the International Studies Association, Chicago, February 2001, p. 7.

94. "Declaration of the Immediate Causes Which Induce and Justify the Secession of South Carolina from the Federal Union," December 24, 1860, http://avalon .law.yale.edu/19th_century/csa_scarsec.asp.

95. Cited in Rabkin, *Law without Nations?*, p. 67.

96. Joseph P. Kalt and Joseph William Singer, "Myths and Realities of Tribal Sovereignty: The Law and Economics of Indian Self-Rule," Faculty Research Working Paper Series (Harvard University JFK School of Government, March 2004),

www.mynafsa.org/wp-content/uploads/2011/10/Myths-and-Realities-of-Tribal
-Sovereignty.pdf.

97. Peter d'Errico, "Sovereignty: A Brief History in the Context of U.S. 'Indian Law,'" in *The Encyclopedia of Minorities in American Politics*, edited by Jeffrey D. Schultz, Kerry L. Haynie, Anne M. McColloch, and Andrew Aoki (Phoenix: Oryx Press, 2000), pp. 691–93, www.umass.edu/legal/derrico/sovereignty.html; Philip J. Prygoski, "From Marshall to Marshall: The Supreme Court's Changing Stance on Tribal Sovereignty," www.americanbar.org/content/newsletter/publications/gp_solo _magazine_home/gp_solo_magazine_index/marshall.html.

98. Keynes is cited in Randall Bennett Woods, *A Changing of the Guard: Anglo-American Relations, 1941–1946* (University of North Carolina Press, 1990), pp. 55–56.

CHAPTER 3

1. Portions of this chapter draw on Stewart Patrick, "The United States and Collective Security: Exploring the Deep Sources of American Conduct," in *America, China, and the Struggle for World Order*, edited by G. John Ikenberry, Zhu Feng, and Wang Jisi (New York: Palgrave Macmillan, 2015).

2. Gordon Wood, *The Idea of America: Reflections on the Birth of the United States* (New York: Penguin, 2011), p. 274.

3. Alexander Hamilton, "Federalist No. 6," p. 29; Hamilton, "Federalist No. 7," p. 35; and Hamilton, "Federalist No. 8," pp. 38–42, all in *The Essential Federalist and Anti-Federalist Papers* (New York: Classic Books, 2009); David C. Hendrickson, *Peace Pact: The Lost World of the American Founding* (University of Kansas Press, 2003); Daniel Deudney, "Binding Sovereigns: Authorities, Structures, and Geopolitics in Philadelphian Systems," in *State Sovereignty as a Social Construct*, edited by Thomas J. Biersteker and Cynthia Weber (Cambridge University Press, 1996), pp. 200–02.

4. Adams is cited in Charles Kupchan, *The End of the American Era: U.S. Foreign Policy after the Cold War* (New York: Alfred Knopf, 2002), p. 165.

5. Jeremy A. Rabkin, *Law without Nations? Why Constitutional Government Requires Sovereign States* (Princeton University Press, 2005), pp. 89–90; Daniel George Lang, *Foreign Policy in the Early Republic: The Law of Nations and the Balance of Power* (Louisiana State University Press, 1985); Peter Onuf and Nicholas Onuf, *Federal Union, Modern World: The Law of Nations in an Age of Revolutions, 1776–1814* (Madison, Wisc.: Madison House, 1993).

6. Washington's Farewell Address, September 19, 1796, http://avalon.law.yale .edu/18th_century/washing.asp.

7. Hamilton, "Federalist No. 11," in *The Essential Federalist*, pp. 52–57; Thomas Jefferson, First Inaugural Address, March 4, 1801, http://avalon.law.yale.edu/19th _century/jefinau1.asp.

8. Mlada Bukovansky, "American Identity and Neutral Rights from Independence to the War of 1812," *International Organization* 51 (1997), pp. 209–43.

9. Address by John Quincy Adams, July 4, 1821, www.theamericanconservative
.com/repository/she-goes-not-abroad-in-search-of-monsters-to-destroy/.

10. Monroe Doctrine, December 2, 1823, http://avalon.law.yale.edu/19th_century
/monroe.asp.

11. Monroe to Congress, May 4, 1822, cited in James D. Richardson, *A Compilation of the Messages and Papers of the Presidents 1789–1897*, vol. 2 (Washington: Government Printing Office, 1896), p. 178.

12. Inaugural Address of James K. Polk, March 4, 1845, www.presidency.ucsb
.edu/ws/index.php?pid=25814.

13. George B. Young, "Intervention under the Monroe Doctrine: The Olney Corollary," *Political Science Quarterly* 57, no. 2 (June 1942), pp. 247–80.

14. Barbara Salazar Torreon, *Instances of Use of United States Armed Forces Abroad, 1798 2016*, CRS Report for Congress, October 6, 2016, https://fas.org/sgp
/crs/natsec/R42738.pdf; Global Policy Forum, "U.S. Military and Clandestine Operations in Foreign Countries, 1798–Present," 2005, www.globalpolicy.org/us
-westward-expansion/26024.html.

15. Stewart Patrick, *The Best Laid Plans: The Origins of American Multilateralism and the Dawn of the Cold War* (Lanham, Md.: Rowman and Littlefield, 2009), pp. 7–18. Roosevelt had added his own, eponymous corollary to the Monroe Doctrine in December 1904, insisting on the U.S. right to "exercise international police power in 'flagrant cases of such wrongdoing or impotence'" in neighboring states. See "Roosevelt Corollary to the Monroe Doctrine, 1904," Department of State, Office of the Historian, https://history.state.gov/milestones/1899-1913/roosevelt-and
-monroe-doctrine.

16. Roosevelt is cited in Thomas J. Knock, *To End All Wars: Woodrow Wilson and the Quest for a New World Order* (Oxford University Press, 1992), p. 48; Henry Kissinger, *Diplomacy* (New York: Simon and Schuster, 1994), pp. 43–44.

17. Taft is cited in John Milton Cooper Jr., *Breaking the Heart of the World: Woodrow Wilson and the Fight for the League of Nations* (Cambridge University Press, 2001), p. 13; Lodge is cited in David C. Hendrickson, "Three Governing Systems in American History: Philadephia, Appomattox, Washington," paper presented at the annual meetings of the International Studies Association, Chicago, February 2001, p. 25.

18. Woodrow Wilson, "American Principles," address delivered at the First Annual Assemblage of the League to Enforce Peace, May 27, 1916, www.presidency.ucsb.edu
/ws/?pid=65391.

19. Ibid.

20. Wilson's "Peace without Victory" speech to Congress, January 22, 1917, http://mtholyoke.edu/acad/intrel/ww15htm.

21. Cooper, *Breaking the Heart of the World*, pp. 19–22.

22. President Wilson's War Message to Congress, April 2, 1917, www.lib.byu.edu
/index.php/Wilson%27s_; Wilson's Fourteen Points speech is cited in H. W. V. Temperley, ed., *A History of the Peace Conference of Paris* (Oxford University Press,

1920), pp. 192–96; Wilson's "Five Particulars" speech is cited in Knock, *To End All Wars*, p. 163.

23. Patrick, *The Best Laid Plans*, pp. 16–24.

24. Theodore Roosevelt, Knox, Borah, and Root are cited in Cooper, *Breaking the Heart of the World*, pp. 40–41, 60–65.

25. Taft is cited in Edward C. Luck, *Mixed Messages: American Politics and International Organization, 1919–1999* (Brookings Institution Press, 1999), p. 68.

26. Luck, *Mixed Messages*, p. 69.

27. Knock, *To End All Wars*, p. 71; Cooper, *Breaking the Heart of the World*, pp. 133–37.

28. Wilson's speeches in Los Angeles and in Pueblo, Colorado, are cited in Cooper, *Breaking the Heart of the World*, p. 182, and in Knock, *To End All Wars*, pp. 206–07.

29. Lodge is cited in Knock, *To End All Wars*, p. 266.

30. Patrick, *The Best Laid Plans*, p. 23.

31. Harding, message to a joint session of Congress, April 12, 1921; Harding is cited in Cooper, *Breaking the Heart of the World*, pp. 383–89.

32. Calvin Coolidge, First Annual Message to Congress, December 6, 1923, www.presidency.ucsb.edu/ws/?pid=29564.

33. Borah is cited in Walter A. McDougall, *Promised Land, Crusader State: The American Encounter with the World since 1776* (New York: Houghton Mifflin Harcourt, 1997), pp. 149–50.

34. Kissinger, *Diplomacy*, pp. 385–89; McDougall, *Promised Land, Crusader State*, pp. 217–18.

35. Vandenberg is cited in Joseph Marion Jones, *The Fifteen Weeks (February 21–June 5, 1947)* (New York: Viking, 1955), p. 122.

36. Jeffrey Legro, *Rethinking the World: Great Power Strategies and International Order* (Cornell University Press, 2005), pp. 76–77; Paul Kennedy, *The Rise and Fall of the Great Powers: Economic Change and Military Conflict from 1500 to 2000* (New York: Random House, 1987), pp. 198–203.

37. Legro, "Whence American Internationalism?," *International Organization* 54, no. 2 (April 2000), pp. 253–89; Patrick, *The Best Laid Plans*, pp. 49–55, 110–11.

38. Jeffrey W. Legro, "Sovereignty American Style: Protecting Apple Pie, Fixing Foreign Recipes," in Ikenberry, Feng, and Jisi, *America, China, and the Struggle for World Order*, p. 27.

39. Patrick, *The Best Laid Plans*, pp. 105–40.

40. Harley Notter, *Postwar Foreign Policy Preparation* (Washington: Department of State, 1950), pp. 103, 113, 126–28.

41. Hendrickson, "Three Governing Systems in American History"; Patrick, *The Best Laid Plans*, p. 54.

42. State Department document is cited in Townsend Hoopes and Douglas Brinkley, *FDR and the Creation of the UN* (Yale University Press, 1997), p. 113.

43. Robert A. Divine, *Second Chance: The Triumph of Liberal Internationalism in America during World War II* (New York: Atheneum, 1967), p. 130.

44. Mundt and Reynolds cited in Divine, *Second Chance*, pp. 143, 147–48; Hoopes and Brinkley, *FDR and the Creation of the UN*, p. 86.

45. Cordell Hull, *The Memoirs of Cordell Hull* (New York: Macmillan, 1948), pp. 1688–689.

46. Divine, *Second Chance*, pp. 182–90, 204–05.

47. Hoopes and Brinkley, *FDR and the Creation of the UN*, p. 197; Hull, *The Memoirs of Cordell Hull*, pp. 1662–664.

48. Divine, *Second Chance*, pp. 238–41.

49. Charter of the United Nations, www.un.org/en/charter-united-nations/index .html.

50. Robert C. Hilderbrand, *Dumbarton Oaks: The Origins of the United Nations and the Search for Postwar Security* (University of North Carolina Press, 1990), pp. 140–45.

51. Willkie is cited in Divine, *Second Chance*, pp. 236–37.

52. The full film is available online at https://media.dlib.indiana.edu/media _objects/avalon:3533.

53. Stettinius is cited in Divine, *Second Chance*, pp. 246–47; Truman is cited in Stephen C. Schlesinger, *Act of Creation: The Founding of the United Nations* (Boulder, Colo.: Westview, 2003), p. 7; Joseph Grew, "Pioneering the Peace," *Department of State Bulletin*, February 18, 1945, pp. 223–24.

54. Franklin D. Roosevelt, address to Congress on the Yalta Conference, March 1, 1945, www.presidency.ucsb.edu/ws/?pid=16591.

55. Harry S. Truman, address at the closing session of the San Francisco conference on the United Nations, June 26, 1945, www.presidency.ucsb.edu/ws/index .php?pid=12188; *New York Times* article cited in Schlesinger, *Act of Creation*, pp. 261–62.

56. Connally is cited in Schlesinger, *Act of Creation*, p. 271; Vandenberg is cited in McDougall, *Promised Land, Crusader State*, p. 153.

57. Connally is cited in Rabkin, *Law without Nations?*, p. 123.

58. Patrick, *The Best Laid Plans*, pp. 213–30.

59. Charles Bohlen, August 30, 1947, in *Foreign Relations of the United States*, vol. 1 (Washington: U.S. Government Printing Office, 1947), pp. 763–64.

60. George Kennan, *Memoirs 1925–1950* (London: Hutchinson, 1967), pp. 407–09; Steve Weber, "Shaping the Postwar Balance of Power: Multilateralism in NATO," in *Multilateralism Matters: The Theory and Praxis of an Institutional Form*, edited by John Gerard Ruggie (Columbia University Press, 1993), pp. 233–92.

61. Jeremy Diamond, "Trump Scolds NATO Allies over Defense Spending," *CNN*, May 25, 2017, www.cnn.com/2017/05/25/politics/trump-nato-financial-pay ments/.

62. Patrick, *The Best Laid Plans*, pp. 271–74.

63. G. John Ikenberry, *After Victory: Institutions, Strategic Restraint, and the Rebuilding of Order after Major Wars* (Princeton University Press, 2001), pp. 205–10; Weber, "Shaping the Postwar Balance of Power," pp. 233–92.

64. Thomas Risse-Kappen, "Collective Identity in a Democratic Community: The Case of NATO," in *The Culture of National Security*, edited by Peter J. Katzenstein (Columbia University Press, 1996), pp. 356–71.

65. Timothy P. Ireland, *Creating the Entangling Alliance: The Origins of the North Atlantic Treaty Organization* (Westport, Conn.: Greenwood Press, 1981), pp. 89–93; Patrick, *The Best Laid Plans*, pp. 274–82.

66. John Gerard Ruggie, *Winning the Peace: America and World Order in the New Era* (New York: Twentieth Century Fund, 1996), p. 45; Ireland, *Creating the Entangling Alliance*, pp. 142–46.

67. Weber, "Shaping the Postwar Balance of Power"; Charles S. Maier, "Alliance and Autonomy: European Identity and U.S. Foreign Policy Objectives in the Truman Years," in *The Truman Presidency*, edited by Michel J. Lacey (Cambridge University Press, 1989), pp. 273–98.

68. William Reitzel, Morton A. Kaplan, and Constance G. Coblenz, *United States Foreign Policy 1945–1955* (Brookings Institution Press, 1956), pp. 244–45; Arnold Wolfers, "Collective Defense versus Collective Security," in *Alliance Politics in the Cold War*, edited by Arnold Wolfers (Johns Hopkins University Press, 1959).

69. Charles Krauthammer, "The Unipolar Moment," *Foreign Affairs* 70, no. 1 (1990/1991), pp. 23–33.

70. The White House, *A National Security Strategy of Engagement and Enlargement* (Washington, 1994).

71. Eric Schmidt, "Senate Kills Test Ban Treaty in Crushing Loss for Clinton: Evokes Versailles Defeat," *New York Times*, October 14, 1999; Stewart Patrick, "Multilateralism and the U.S. National Interest," in *Power and Responsibility in World Affairs: Reformation versus Transformation*, edited by Cathal J. Nolan (Westport, Conn.: Praeger, 2004), pp. 165–213.

72. Larry Korb, "Force Is the Issue," Govexec.com, January 1, 2000, www.govexec.com/features/0100/0100s6.htm; Ruth Wedgwood, "Unilateral Action in a Multilateral World," in *Multilateralism and U.S. Foreign Policy*, edited by Stewart Patrick and Shepard Forman (Boulder, Colo.: Lynne Rienner, 2002), pp. 167–89.

73. Stewart Patrick, "Global Governance Reform: An American View of US Leadership," Stanley Foundation, Policy Analysis Brief, February 2010, www.stanleyfoundation.org/publications/pab/PatrickPAB210.pdf.

74. Address to the United Nations Security Council by U.S. senator Jesse Helms, chairman of the Senate Foreign Relations Committee, January 29, 2000, www.101bananas.com/library2/helms.html; Walter Russell Mead, "Why the World Is Better for Jesse Helms," *New York Times*, April 22, 2001.

75. Stewart Patrick, "Don't Fence Me In: The Perils of Going It Alone," *World Policy Journal* 18, no. 3 (2001), pp. 2–14.

76. Ivo Daalder and James Lindsay, *America Unbound: The Bush Revolution in U.S. Foreign Policy* (Brookings Institution Press, 2003).

77. Patrick, "Global Governance Reform."

78. Stewart Patrick, "'The Mission Determines the Coalition': The United States and Multilateral Security Cooperation after 9/11," in *Cooperating for Peace and Security: Evolving Institutions and Arrangements in the Context of Changing U.S. Security Policy*, edited by Bruce D. Jones, Shepard Forman, and Richard Gowan (Cambridge University Press, 2010), pp. 20–44.

79. Richard N. Haass, as State Department director of policy planning, introduced the concept of "à la carte" multilateralism in 2001; Thom Shanker, "White House Says the United States Not a Loner, Just Choosy," *New York Times*, January 31, 2001; Stewart Patrick, "Prix Fixe *and* à la Carte: Avoiding False Multilateral Choices," *Washington Quarterly* (Fall 2009).

80. Secretary of Defense Donald Rumsfeld, interview with Larry King, CNN, December 5, 2001, http://transcripts.cnn.com/TRANSCRIPTS/0112/05/lkl.00 .html; Steven Erlanger, "Europe Seethes as the U.S. Flies Solo in World Affairs," *New York Times*, February 22, 2002; Stewart Patrick, "Beyond Coalitions of the Willing: Assessing U.S. Multilateralism," *Ethics and International Affairs* 17, no. 1 (March 2003), pp. 37–54.

81. The White House, *National Security Strategy of the United States* (Washington, 2002); Ivo Daalder and Robert Kagan, "America and the Use of Force: Sources of Legitimacy," in *Bridging the Foreign Policy Divide*, edited by Derek Chollet, Tod Lindborg, and David Shorr (Muscatine, Iowa: Stanley Foundation, June 2007), p. 5.

82. Stewart Patrick, "A Return to Realism? The United States and Global Peace Operations Since 9/11," in *U.S. Peace Operations Policy: A Double-Edged Sword?*, edited by Ian Johnstone (New York: Routledge, 2009), pp. 116–31.

83. Guy Dinmore, "U.S. Sees Coalition of the Willing as Best Ally," *Financial Times*, January 4, 2006.

84. John Bolton, "An All-Out War on Proliferation," *Financial Times*, September 7, 2004; Patrick, "Prix Fize *and* à la Carte."

85. Patrick, "The United States and Collective Security," p. 92; Patrick, "The Mission Determines the Coalition."

86. Remarks of Senator Barack Obama to the Chicago Council on Global Affairs, April 23, 2007, https://en.wikisource.org/wiki/Remarks_of_Senator_Barack_Obama _to_the_Chicago_Council_on_Global_Affairs; Barack Obama, "Renewing American Leadership," *Foreign Affairs*, July/August 2007, pp. 2–16.

87. The White House, *National Security Strategy of the United States of America* (Washington, 2010). These paragraphs draw on Stewart Patrick, "The New 'New Multilateralism': Minilateral Cooperation, but at What Cost?," *Global Summitry* 1, no. 2 (2015), and also Patrick, "Prix Fixe *and* à la Carte."

88. Patrick, "The New 'New Multilateralism.'"

89. Walter Russell Mead, "The Return of Geopolitics: The Revenge of the Revisionist Powers," *Foreign Affairs*, May/June 2014, pp. 69–79.

90. Stewart Patrick, "Surface Tension: Chinese Aggression Roils Southeast Asian Waters," *The Internationalist* (blog), Council on Foreign Relations, April 12, 2016, http://blogs.cfr.org/patrick/2016/04/12/surface-tension-chinese-aggression-roils-southeast-asian-waters/.

91. Stewart Patrick, "United Nations, Divided World: Obama, Putin, and World Order," *The Internationalist* (blog), Council on Foreign Relations, September 28, 2015, http://blogs.cfr.org/patrick/2015/09/28/united-nations-divided-world-obama-putin-and-world-order/.

92. Richard N. Haass, "The Case for Messy Multilateralism," *Financial Times*, January 5, 2010.

93. This paragraph draws on Patrick, "The New 'New Multilateralism.'"

94. Ibid.

95. Blake Hounsell, "Trump vs. the Globalists," *Politico*, February 13, 2017.

CHAPTER 4

1. *Roper v. Simmons* (03-633), 543 U.S. 551 (2005), www.law.cornell.edu/supct/html/03-633.ZD1.html.

2. Ibid.

3. Ibid.

4. Catherine Powell, "A Missed Opportunity to Lead by Example," *New York Times*, December 6, 2012.

5. David Kopel, "The U.S. Is Right to Be Skeptical," *New York Times*, December 6, 2012.

6. Dana Milbank, "Santorum's New Cause: Opposing the Disabled," *Washington Post*, November 26, 2012; Julian Pecquet, "UN Disabilities Treaty Expected to Fail in Senate amid GOP Opposition," *The Hill*, December 4, 2012, http://thehill.com/policy/international/270729-un-disabilities-treaty-expected-to-fail-in-senate-; Office of Senator Inhofe, "Inhofe Praises Senate Rejection of CRPD," December 4, 2012, www.inhofe.senate.gov/newsroom/press-releases/inhofe-praises-senate-rejection-of-crpd; Home School Legal Defense Association, "Reject the CRPD," www.hslda.org/landingpages/crpd/default.aspx; Sean Lengell, "Senate Rejects U.N. Disabilities Treaty," *Washington Times*, December 4, 2012.

7. Pecquet, "UN Treaty on Disabilities."

8. Office of Senator Orin Hatch, "Hatch: UN Disabilities Treaty a Threat to American Sovereignty and Self-Government," July 10, 2013, www.hatch.senate.gov/public/index.cfm/2013/7/hatch-u-n-disabilites-treaty-a-threat-to-american-sovereignty-and-self-government.

9. Jenny Martinez, "There Are Two Ways to Look at Sovereignty," *New York Times*, December 6, 2012. For a paradigmatic example of the sovereigntist stance, see John

Kyl, Douglas J. Feith, and John Fonte, "The War of Law: How New International Law Undermines Democratic Sovereignty," *Foreign Affairs*, July/August 2013, pp. 115–25.

10. Adapted from J. L. Brierly, *The Law of Nations*, 6th ed. (Oxford University Press, 1963). While the classical definition of international law pertained to relations among states, more modern definitions (reflecting the human rights revolution) include rules binding on states with regard to individuals.

11. Morgenthau, cited in *State Sovereignty as a Social Construct*, edited by Thomas J. Biersteker and Cynthia Weber (Cambridge University Press, 1996), p. 4.

12. Noah Feldman, "When Judges Make Foreign Policy," *New York Times Magazine*, September 25, 2008, www.nytimes.com/2008/09/28/magazine/28law-t.html.

13. Their leading authority was the Swiss legal positivist Emerich de Vattel, whose *The Law of Nations* (1758) applied universal legal principles to relations among states.

14. Jay is cited in Detlev F. Vagts, "The United States and Its Treaties: Observation and Breach," *American Journal of International Law* 95 (2001), pp. 313–21; *Murray v. Schooner Charming Betsy*, 6 U.S. 64, 2 L.Ed.208 (1804).

15. Michael John Garcia, *International Law and Agreements: Their Effect upon U.S. Law*, CRS Report for Congress, February 18, 2015, https://fas.org/sgp/crs/misc /RL32528.pdf.

16. United States Treaties and International Agreements, 1776–1949, Library of Congress, www.loc.gov/law/help/us-treaties/bevans.php; U.S. Treaties and Agreements Library, HEIN Online, http://bit.ly/2gu8M6v.

17. Nico Krisch, "Weak as Constraint, Strong as Tool: The Place of International Law in U.S. Foreign Policy," in *Unilateralism and U.S. Foreign Policy*, edited by David Malone and Yuen Foong Khong (Boulder, Colo.: Lynne Rienner, 2003), pp. 41–70. Consider, in this regard, the standard reservation that Senator Jesse Helms (R-N.C.) insisted accompany Senate treaty resolutions. Nothing in the relevant treaty, it read, "requires or authorizes legislation or other action by the United States of America that is prohibited by the Constitution of the United States." Tellingly, Helms phrased the language as not as a universal but as *applicable only to the United States*—suggesting that it alone could subordinate international law to its national constitution.

18. Steven G. Calabresi, "A Shining City on a Hill: American Exceptionalism and the Supreme Court's Practice of Relying on Foreign Law," Northwestern Public Law Research Paper 892585 (June 20, 2006), https://papers.ssrn.com/sol3/papers.cfm ?abstract_id=892585; Paul W. Kahn, "American Exceptionalism, Popular Sovereignty, and the Rule of Law," in *American Exceptionalism and Human Rights*, edited by Michael Ignatieff (Princeton University Press, 2005), pp. 198–222; Adriana Sinclair and Michael Byers, "When U.S. Scholars Speak of 'Sovereignty,' What Do They Mean?," *Political Studies* 55, no. 2 (2007), pp. 318–40.

19. Congressional Research Service, *Treaties and Other International Agreements: The Role of the United States Senate* (2001), p. 212.

20. Segregationist sentiments were not limited to discrimination against blacks. In 1950 the California state appeals court ignited a national firestorm when it struck

down the state's discriminatory Alien Land Act (1913), which targeted Asians. Conservatives were incensed that the judges based their decision not on the Fourteenth Amendment's equal protection clause but on the UN Charter, which committed all member states to "promoting and encouraging respect for human rights and for fundamental freedoms for all, without distinction as to race, sex, language, or religion." The provocative implication—that the Charter had the status of domestic law—reverberated nationally. Representative Paul Shafer (R-Mich.) denounced the ruling on the House floor, explaining, "Our sovereignty is too sacred to be tossed away for a mess of international pottage." Mark Philip Bradley, "The Ambiguities of Sovereignty: The United States and the Global Rights Cases of the 1940s and 1950s," in *The State of Sovereignty: Territories, Laws, Populations*, edited by Douglas Howland and Luise White (Indiana University Press, 2008), pp. 124–47. On *Fujii v. California*, see http://encyclopedia.densho.org/Fujii_v._California/.

21. John Gerard Ruggie, "American Exceptionalism, Exemptionalism, and Global Governance," in Ignatieff, *American Exceptionalism*, pp. 323–24.

22. Jack L. Goldsmith and Eric A. Posner, *The Limits of International Law* (Oxford University Press, 2006); Michael J. Glennon, "Why the UN Security Council Failed," *Foreign Affairs*, May/June 2003, pp. 16–35.

23. Sinclair and Byers, "When U.S. Scholars Speak of Sovereignty," pp. 332–35; Kal Raustiala, "Refining the Limits of International Law," www2.law.ucla.edu /raustiala/publications/Raustiala%20page%20proof%20feb%2014.pdf; Eric A. Posner, *The Perils of Global Legalism* (University of Chicago Press, 2009).

24. In a November 17, 1997, op-ed in the *Wall Street Journal*, John Bolton wrote, "In their international operation, treaties are simply political obligations," and "become law only for U.S. domestic purposes" when Congress passes relevant implementing legislation. See John McGinnis and Ilya Somin, "Democracy and International Human Rights Law," *Notre Dame Law Review* 84, no. 4 (May 2009), pp. 1739–798.

25. Louis Henkin, *How Nations Behave* (Columbia University Press, 1968); Thomas M. Franck, *The Power of Legitimacy among Nations* (Oxford University Press, 1990).

26. Harold Hongju Koh, "On American Exceptionalism," *Stanford Law Review* 55, no. 5 (May 2003), pp. 1479–1527.

27. Ruggie, "American Exceptionalism."

28. John Bolton, "The Coming War on Sovereignty," *Commentary*, March 2009.

29. David Rivkin and Lee Casey, "The Rocky Shoals of International Law," *National Interest* (Winter 2000/2001); John Fonte, *Sovereignty or Submission: Will Americans Rule Themselves or Be Ruled by Others?* (New York: Encounter Books, 2011); Steven Groves, "Why Does Sovereignty Matter to America?," *American Founders*, December 3, 2012.

30. Kyl, Feith, and Fonte, "The War of Law."

31. Josh Rogin, "Kyl Warns about the War on American Sovereignty," *Foreign Policy*, March 10, 2011, http://foreignpolicy.com/2011/03/10/kyl-warns-about-the

-war-on-american-sovereignty/. Kyl is also quoted in Sohrab Ahmari, "American Sovereignty and Its Enemies," *Wall Street Journal*, July 19, 2013.

32. Fonte, *Sovereignty or Submission*, pp. 341–69.

33. Stewart Patrick, "Don't Tread on Me: July 4 and U.S. Sovereignty," *The Internationalist* (blog), July 4, 2011, http://blogs.cfr.org/patrick/2011/07/01/dont-tread -on-me-july-4th-and-u-s-sovereignty/; Fonte, *Sovereignty or Submission*, pp. 121–58; John Bolton, "Should We Take Global Governance Seriously?," *Chicago Journal of International Law* 1, no. 2 (September 1, 2000), pp. 220–21.

34. Ulrich Haltern, "Pathos and Patina: The Failure and Promise of Constitutionalism in the European Imagination," *European Law Journal* 9, no. 1 (February 2003), pp. 14–44, http://onlinelibrary.wiley.com/doi/10.1111/1468-0386.00168 /abstract.

35. Kyl is cited in Ahmari, "American Sovereignty and Its Enemies"; Jeremy A. Rabkin, *The Case for Sovereignty: Why the World Should Welcome American Independence* (Washington: AEI Press, 2004), p. 43.

36. Walter Russell Mead, "Nuking Westphalia: Obama's Deep Convictions Point to War with Iran," *American Interest Online*, July 16, 2010, www.the-american-interest .com/2010/07/16/nuking-westphalia-obamas-deep-convictions-point-to-war-with -iran/; William W. Burke-White and Anne-Marie Slaughter, "The Future of International Law Is Domestic (or, The European Way of Law)," *Harvard International Law Journal* 47, no. 2 (2006), p. 332; Julian Ku and John Yoo, *Taming Globalization: International Law, the U.S. Constitution, and the New World Order* (Oxford University Press, 2012), p. 44.

37. For more details, see Stewart Patrick, "An Ever-Looser Union? Can Europe Survive Its Current Crisis?," *Foreign Affairs*, March 29, 2016, www.foreignaffairs.com /articles/europe/2016-03-29/ever-looser-union.

38. Georg Nolte, "The United States and the International Criminal Court," in Malone and Khong, *Unilateralism and U.S. Foreign Policy*, pp. 71–94, 82–85.

39. Brian Urquhart, "One Angry Man," *New York Review of Books*, March 6, 2008, www.nybooks.com/articles/2008/03/06/one-angry-man/.

40. American Servicemembers' Protection Act of 2002, http://legcounsel.house .gov/Comps/aspa02.pdf; Emily C. Barber and Matthew C. Weed, *The International Criminal Court (ICC): Jurisdiction, Extradition, and U.S. Policy*, CRS Report for Congress, March 16, 2010, www.fas.org/sgp/crs/row/R41116.pdf; Sense of Congress Resolution, April 21, 2010, http://bit.ly/2gcsPIP.

41. David Scheffer, "America's Embrace of the International Criminal Court," *Jurist*, July 2, 2012, http://jurist.org/forum/2012/07/dan-scheffer-us-icc.php.

42. Harold Hongju Koh, "Why Transnational Law Matters," *Penn State International Law Review* 24, no. 745 (2006), http://digitalcommons.law.yale.edu/fss_papers /1793/.

43. Steven Groves and Theodore R. Bromund, "The Ottawa Mine Ban Convention: Unacceptable on Substance and Process," Heritage Foundation Backgrounder

no. 2496 on International Law (Washington, December 13, 2010), www.heritage.org /research/reports/2010/12/the-ottawa-mine-ban-convention-unacceptable-on -substance-and-process#_ftn57; Fonte, *Sovereignty or Submission*, pp. 3–9; Bolton, "Should We Take Global Governance Seriously?," pp. 215–21.

44. Fonte, *Sovereignty or Submission*; Sinclair and Byers, "When U.S. Scholars Speak of Sovereignty," pp. 326–28.

45. Anne-Marie Slaughter, *A New World Order* (Princeton University Press, 2004).

46. Anne-Marie Slaughter, "The Real New World Order," *Foreign Affairs*, September/October 1997, pp. 183–97.

47. *Paquete Habana*, 175 U.S. 677, 700 (1900), Restatement 102(2).

48. Kyl, Feith, and Fonte, "The War of Law," pp. 123–24.

49. Curtis A. Bradley and Jack L. Goldsmith, "Customary International Law as Federal Common Law: A Critique of the Modern Position," *Harvard Law Review* 110 (1997), pp. 815, 839.

50. Ruggie, "American Exceptionalism," p. 327.

51. Republican Party Platform of 2016, p. 10, www.gop.com/the-2016-republican -party-platform/.

52. Trump administration's draft of the executive order on treaties, http://apps .washingtonpost.com/g/documents/world/read-the-trump-administrations-draft-of -the-executive-order-on-treaties/2307/.

53. John Bellinger, comments in an online briefing, "The Future of International Agreements," American Society of International Law Panel discussion on International Law and the Trump Administration, February 1, 2017, www.asil.org/100part1.

54. As John Bolton writes, "For virtually every arena of public policy, there is a globalist proposal, consistent with the overall objective of reducing individual nation-state autonomy, particularly that of the United States." Bolton, "Should We Take Global Governance Seriously?," p. 220.

55. U.S. Department of State, *List of Treaties in Force as of January 1, 2016*, www .state.gov/s/l/treaty/tif/index.htm; Congressional Research Service, *Treaties and Other International Agreements*, p. 42.

56. Karen DeYoung and Philip Rucker, "Trump Lays Groundwork to Change U.S. Role in the World," *Washington Post*, January 26, 2017.

57. Rusk is cited in Edward C. Luck, *Mixed Messages: American Politics and International Organization, 1919–1999* (Brookings Institution Press, 1999), p. 61.

58. Julie E. Fischer, Rebecca Katz, and Sarah Kornblet, *The International Health Regulations (2005): Surveillance and Response in an Era of Globalization* (Washington: Henry L. Stimson Center, 2011), www.stimson.org/images/uploads/The_International _Health_Regulations_White_Paper_Final.pdf.

59. James M. Inhofe and Jim DeMint, "UN Treaties Mean Lost U.S. Sovereignty: Liberals Intent on Imposing Backdoor Globalism," *Washington Times*, July 25, 2012.

60. Theodore Bromund, "UN Arms Treaty Will Be Menace to US for Years to Come," Fox News, September 25, 2013, www.foxnews.com/opinion/2013/09/25/un -arms-treaty-will-be-menace-to-us-for-years-to-come.html.

61. W. Michael Reisman, "Sovereignty and Human Rights in Contemporary international Law," *American Journal of International Law* 84 (1990), p. 866.

62. See Michael Ignatieff, "Introduction: American Exceptionalism and Human Rights"; Harold Hongju Koh, "America's Jekyll and Hyde Exceptionalism," pp. 114–15; and Andrew Moravcsik, "The Paradox of U.S. Human Rights Policy," pp. 148–49, all in Ignatieff, *American Exceptionalism*.

63. A *reservation* is a unilateral statement that purports to exclude or modify the legal affect of particular treaty provisions. A *declaration*, for its part, is a Senate statement of position or opinion on regarding issues raised by the treaty, as opposed to its specific provisions. *Understandings*, meanwhile, are "interpretive statements that clarify or elaborate provisions but do not alter them."

64. The United States repeatedly denied requests from the Human Rights Council's special rapporteur on torture to visit the U.S. detention center in Guantanamo Bay, Cuba. "Report of the Special Rapporteur on torture and other cruel, inhuman or degrading treatment or punishment, Juan E. Mendez," Human Rights Council, Twenty-Eighth session, March 5, 2015, www.refworld.org/pdfid/550824454 .pdf.

65. Moravcsik, "Paradox," pp. 150–51.

66. Kim R. Holmes, "How Should Americans Think about Human Rights?," Heritage Foundation (Washington, June 13, 2011), www.heritage.org/research/reports /2011/06/how-should-america-think-about-human-rights; Cass R. Sunstein, "Why Does the American Constitution Lack Social and Economic Guarantees?," in Ignatieff, *American Exceptionalism*, pp. 90–110; Moravcsik, "Paradox," p. 162.

67. James B. Risch, "Treaties Must Not Harm America's Sovereignty," Office of Senator Risch, November 30, 2012, www.risch.senate.gov/public/index.cfm/editorials ?ID=B1C5C571-DC3D-41EC-B80B-790253F34333&IsTextOnly=True.

68. Sohrab Ahmari, describing Kyl's reaction, in Ahmari, "American Sovereignty and Its Enemies."

69. Frederick Schauer, "The Exceptional First Amendment," in Ignatieff, *American Exceptionalism*, pp. 29–56; Moravcsik, "Paradox," pp. 172–73.

70. Moravcsik, "Paradox," pp. 184–85.

71. Bricker is cited in Mark Philip Bradley, "The Ambiguities of Sovereignty: The United States and the Global Rights Cases of the 1940s and 1950s," in *The State of Sovereignty: Territories, Laws, Populations*, edited by Douglas Howland and Luise White (Indiana University Press, 2008), p. 137.

72. Republican Party Platform of 2016, p. 53.

73. Moravcsik, "Paradox," pp. 181–83; "20 Things You Need to Know about the UN Convention on the Rights of the Child," www.parentalrights.org/index.asp?SEC ={550447B1-E2C1-4B55-87F1-610A9E601E45.

74. U.S. Department of State, *Treaty Priority List*, www.gc.noaa.gov/documents /gcil_bd_2009TreatyPriorityList.pdf.

75. This paragraph and the two that follow draw on Stewart Patrick, "More Treaty Gridlock: Another Impact of GOP Senate Takeover," *The Internationalist* (blog), November 10, 2014, http://blogs.cfr.org/patrick/2014/11/10/more-treaty-gridlock -another-impact-of-gop-senate-takeover/.

76. John B. Bellinger III, "Obama's Weakness on Treaties," *New York Times*, December 18, 2012; Jeffrey S. Peake, "The Domestic Politics of International Agreements during the Obama Administration: Presidential Unilateralism and Senate Obstruction," APSA 2013 Annual Meeting Paper, https://papers.ssrn.com/sol3/papers.cfm?abstract _id=2300380; John Bellinger, "Senate Approves Two More Treaties, Bringing Obama Administration's Treaty Record to Fifteen," *Lawfare* (blog), www.lawfareblog.com/senate -approves-two-more-treaties-bringing-obama-administrations-treaty-record-fifteen.

77. "Inhofe and DeMint: UN Treaties Mean LOST U.S. Sovereignty," *Washington Times*, July 25, 2012; Julian Ku, "What Are the U.S. Objections to the Law of the Sea Treaty?," *Opinio Juris*, September 19, 2011, http://opiniojuris.org/2011/09/19 /what-are-the-u-s-objections-to-the-law-of-the-sea-treaty/; Larry Bell, "Will U.S. Sovereignty Be LOST at Sea? Obama Supports UN Treaty that Redistributes Drilling Revenues," *Forbes*, May 20, 2012.

78. Scott G. Borgerson, *The National Interest and the Law of the Sea*, Council Special Report no. 46 (Washington: Council on Foreign Relations, May 2009).

79. Thomas Wright, "Outlaw of the Sea: The Senate Republicans' UNCLOS Blunder," *Foreign Affairs*, August 7, 2012, www.foreignaffairs.com/articles/oceans /2012-08-07/outlaw-sea.

80. David Kaye, "Stealth Multilateralism," *Foreign Affairs*, September/October 2013, pp. 113–24.

81. Oona Hathaway, "Treaties' End: The Past, Present, and Future of International Law-Making in the United States," *Yale Law Journal* 117, no. 8 (March 2008), https:// papers.ssrn.com/sol3/papers.cfm?abstract_id=1108065; Congressional Research Service, *Treaties and Other Agreements*, p. 42.

82. Republican Party Platform of 2016, pp. 26–27; John R. Bolton and John Yoo, "Restore the Senate's Treaty Power," *New York Times*, January 4, 2009; Bolton, *How Barack Obama Is Endangering Our National Sovereignty* (New York: Encounter Books, 2010).

83. Kaye, "Stealth Multilateralism"; Stewart Patrick, "The New 'New Multilateralism': Minilateral Cooperation, but at What Cost?," *Global Summitry* 1, no. 2 (2015), pp. 115–34.

84. Krisch, "Weak as Constraint, Strong as Tool," p. 62.

85. Ku and Yoo, *Taming Globalization*, pp. 87–112; Alexander Hamilton, "Federalist No. 75," in *The Essential Federalist and Anti-Federalist Papers* (New York: Classic Books, 2009), pp. 332–35.

86. *Thirty Hogsheads of Sugar* v. *Boyle*, 13 U.S. (9 Cranch) 191, 198 (1815), Restatement 112 b.

87. Feldman, "When Judges Make Foreign Policy"; Republican Party Platform of 2016, p. 10.

88. Norman Dorsen, "The Relevance of Foreign Legal Materials in U.S. Constitutional Cases: A Conversation between Justice Antonin Scalia and Justice Stephen Breyer," *International Journal of Constitutional Law* 3, no. 4 (2005), pp. 519–41.

89. Ibid., p. 526.

90. Ibid., pp. 522–23.

91. Ganesh Sitaraman, "The Use and Abuse of Foreign Law in Constitutional Interpretation," *Harvard Journal of Law and Public Policy* 32, no. 653 (2009), pp. 655–93.

92. Garrett Epps, "Constitutional Myth #10: International Law Is a Threat to the Constitution," *The Atlantic*, July 28, 2011.

93. Frank I. Michelman, "Integrity-Anxiety," in Ignatieff, *American Exceptionalism*, pp. 241–76.

94. Ibid.; Charles Fried, "Scholars and Judges: Reason and Power," *Harvard Journal of Law and Public Policy* 23 (2000), pp. 807–32.

95. Sandra Day O'Connor, Keynote Address, *Proceedings of the American Society of International Law* 96 (2002), pp. 348, 350.

96. Feldman, "When Judges Make Foreign Policy."

97. Adam Liptak, "U.S. Court, a Longtime Beacon, Is Now Guiding Fewer Nations," *New York Times*, September 18, 2008.

98. Slaughter, "A Brave New Judicial World," pp. 295–96.

99. *Trop v. Dulles*, 356 U.S. 86 (1958), www.law.cornell.edu/supremecourt/text/356/86.

100. Sitaraman, "The Use and Abuse of Foreign Law."

101. *Stanford v. Kentucky*, 492 U.S. 361 (1989), www.law.cornell.edu/supremecourt/text/492/361; *Knight v. Florida* (98-9741), www.law.cornell.edu/supct/html/98-9741.ZD.html.

102. *Bowers v. Hardwick* (85-140), 478 U.S. 186 (1986), www.law.cornell.edu/supremecourt/text/478/186.

103. *Roper v. Simmons* (03-633), 543 U.S. 551 (2005), www.law.cornell.edu/supct/html/03-633.ZS.html.

104. H.R. 372, www.congress.gov/bill/110th-congress/house-resolution/372.

105. Charles Stimson and Jonathan Levy, "The Mysterious Disappearance of International Law Arguments from Juvenile Sentencing in *Miller v. Alabama*," legal memorandum no. 85 (Washington: Heritage Foundation, August 22, 2012), www.heritage.org/research/reports/2012/08/mysterious-disappearance-of-international-law-arguments-from-juvenile-sentencing-in-miller-v-alabama.

106. Stephen Breyer, *The Court and the World: American Law and the New Global Realities* (New York: Knopf, 2015), pp. 244–45.

107. *New York v. United States*, 505 U.S. 144 (1992).

108. Alexis de Tocqueville, *Democracy in America*, vol. 1 (1835), chapter 5 ("Necessity of Examining the Condition of the States—Part I"), archived online at www.gutenberg.org/files/815/815-h/815-h.htm.

109. Kirk Johnson, "Negotiated at The Hague, a Child Support Treaty Falters in Boise," *New York Times*, April 21, 2015. The treaty was the Hague Convention on the International Recovery of Child Support and Other Forms of Family Maintenance.

110. Julie Turkewitz, "Idaho Approves Child Bill Support, Removing Treaty Roadblock," *New York Times*, May 18, 2015.

111. *Missouri v. Holland*, 252 U.S. 416 (1920).

112. "Avena and Other Mexican Nationals (*Mexico v. United States*)," International Court of Justice, press release, www.icj-cij.org/docket/index.php?pr=605&p1=3&p2=3&p3=6&case=128; U.S. Department of State, "President's Determination (Feb. 28, 2005) Regarding U.S. Response to the Avena Decision in the ICJ," www.state.gov/s/l/2005/87181.htm.

113. Feldman, "When Judges Make Foreign Policy."

114. Ronald J. Bettauer, "Supreme Court May Consider How Broadly the 'Necessary and Proper' Clause of the Constitution Authorizes Legislation to Implement Treaties," *ASIL Insights*, March 11, 2013, www.asil.org/sites/default/files/insight130311.pdf.

115. Oona A. Hathaway, Sabria McElroy, and Sara Aronchick Solow, "International Law at Home: Enforcing Treaties in U.S. Courts," *Yale Journal of International Law* 37, no. 1 (2012), http://digitalcommons.law.yale.edu/fss_papers/3851/; John Bellinger, "John Bellinger Comments on International Law at Home," *Opinio Juris*, February 24, 2012, http://opiniojuris.com.org/2012/02/24/john-bellinger-comments-on-international-law-at-home/; Ted Cruz, "Defending U.S. Sovereignty, Separation of Powers, and Federalism in *Medellin v. Texas*," *Harvard Journal of Law and Public Policy* 33, no. 1 (2009), pp. 25–35.

116. Ted Cruz, "Limits on the Treaty Power," *Harvard Law Review* (January 8, 2014), http://harvardlawreview.org/2014/01/limits-on-the-treaty-power/.

117. Ku and Yoo, *Taming Globalization*, pp. 151–76; Kristina Daugirdas, "Review of Taming Globalization: International Law, the U.S. Constitution, and the New World Order," *American Journal of International Law* 108, no. 3 (2014), pp. 568–75.

118. Abram Chayes and Antonia Handler Chayes, *The New Sovereignty: Compliance with International Regulatory Agreements* (Harvard University Press, 1998), p. 26; Anne-Marie Slaughter, "Sovereignty and Power in a Networked World Order," *Stanford Journal of International Law* 40 (2004), pp. 283–327.

CHAPTER 5

1. Commission on Presidential Debates, "September 30, 2004 Debate Transcript," www.debates.org/index.php?page=september-30-2004-debate-transcript.

2. Dana Milbank, "Bush Says Kerry Will Allow Foreign Vetoes," *Washington Post*, October 3, 2004.

3. "Kerry Dismisses Criticism of 'Global Test' Remark as 'Pathetic,'" CNN, October 5, 2004, www.cnn.com/2004/ALLPOLITICS/10/04/kerry.global/; "Kerry Forced to Explain 'Global Test' of Legitimacy," *Washington Times*, October 5, 2004; Richard W. Stevenson, "Bush Says Kerry's Remarks Show Weakness on Security," *New York Times*, October 3, 2004.

4. Commission on Presidential Debates, "October 8, 2004 Debate Transcript," www.debates.org/index.php?page=october-8-2004-debate-transcript.

5. "Obama's U.N. First Gambit," *Wall Street Journal*, July 20, 2015.

6. "Our Rulers in the United Nations Now Make America's Treaties," *Investor's Business Daily*, July 21, 2015, www.investors.com/politics/editorials/un-iran-vote -will-be-used-politically-against-congress/.

7. Bryan is cited in Edward C. Luck, *Mixed Messages: American Politics and International Organization, 1919–1999* (Brookings Institution Press, 1999), p. 186.

8. Both Richard N. Haass and Bruce Jentleson have used this analogy.

9. Charles Krauthammer, "As the 'International Community' Is a Fiction, the United States Must Go It Alone," *Pittsburgh Post-Gazette*, December 27, 1997.

10. Stewart Patrick, "Trump and World Order: The Return of Self-Help," *Foreign Affairs*, March/April 2017, pp. 52–59.

11. Bruce W. Jentleson, "Tough Love Multilateralism," *Washington Quarterly* 27, no. 1 (Winter 2003–2004), p. 9.

12. Kenneth Anderson, *Living with the UN: American Responsibilities and International Order* (Stanford, Calif.: Hoover Institution Press, 2012), pp. 85–109.

13. For more on this, see Stewart Patrick, "Prix Fixe *and* à La Carte: Avoiding False Multilateral Choices," *Washington Quarterly* 32, no. 4 (2009), pp. 77–95.

14. Barbara Salazar Torreon, "Instances of Use of United States Armed Forces Abroad, 1798–2015," Congressional Research Service, October 7, 2016, www.fas.org /sgp/crs/natsec/R42738.pdf.

15. Barbara Starr and Jeremy Diamond, "Trump Launches Military Strike against Syria," CNN, April 7, 2017, www.cnn.com/2017/04/06/politics/donald-trump-syria -military/.

16. Erik Voeten, "The Political Origins of the UN Security Council's Ability to Legitimize the Use of Force," *International Organization* 59 (Summer 2005), pp. 527–28.

17. CFR and World Public Opinion, *Public Opinion on Global Issues*, chapter 11: "U.S. Opinion on Violent Conflict" (August 28, 2012), www.cfr.org/backgrounder /us-opinion-violent-conflict.

18. Thomas Stilson, "Former UN Ambassador John Bolton Talks U.S. Sovereignty at the Law School," *Stanford Review*, May 1, 2009, https://stanfordreview.org /former-un-ambassador-john-bolton-talks-us-sovereignty-at-law-school -94a95cf8c91b; Jeremy A. Rabkin, *The Case for Sovereignty: Why the World Should Welcome American Independence* (Washington: AEI Press, 2004), pp. 11, 72, 175–77.

19. George H. W. Bush and Brent Scowcroft, *A World Transformed* (New York: Alfred A. Knopf, 1998), p. 491.

20. "Press Briefing by Ari Fleischer," March 10, 2003, The American Presidency Project, www.presidency.ucsb.edu/ws/index.php?pid=61052.

21. Bush and Scowcroft, *A World Transformed*, p. 491. Also see Edward Luck, "The U.S., International Organization, and the Quest for Legitimacy," in *Multilateralism and U.S. Foreign Policy: Ambivalent Engagement*, edited by Stewart Patrick and Shepard Forman (Boulder, Colo.: Lynne Rienner, 2002), p. 59.

22. James B. Steinberg, "Force and Legitimacy in the Post-9/11 Era: What Principles Should Guide the United States?," in *Power and Superpower: Global Leadership and Exceptionalism in the 21st Century*, edited by Morton H. Halperin, Jeffrey Laurenti, Peter Rundlet, and Spencer P. Boyer (Washington: Century Foundation, 2007), p. 139.

23. Sarah Kreps, *Coalitions of Convenience: United States Military Interventions after the Cold War* (Oxford University Press, 2011).

24. Ibid., pp. 5–10.

25. Richard N. Haass, "Sovereignty: Existing Rights, Evolving Responsibilities," remarks at Mortara Institute at Georgetown University, January 14, 2013, https://2001 -2009.state.gov/s/p/rem/2003/16648.htm; Stewart Patrick, "The Evolving Structure of World Politics, 1991–2011," in *International Relations since the End of the Cold War: New and Old Dimensions*, edited by Geir Lundestad (Oxford University Press, 2013), pp. 16–41.

26. Kofi Annan, "Two Concepts of Sovereignty," *The Economist*, September 16, 1999; International Commission on Intervention and State Sovereignty, *The Responsibility to Protect* (December 2001), http://responsibilitytoprotect.org/ICISS%20 Report.pdf.

27. Micah Zenko, "Obama's Drone Warfare Legacy," *Politics, Power, and Preventive Action* (blog), Council on Foreign Relations, January 12, 2016, http://blogs.cfr .org/zenko/2016/01/12/obamas-drone-warfare-legacy/.

28. Clinton is cited in Stewart Patrick, "Libya and the Future of Humanitarian Intervention," *Foreign Affairs*, August 26, 2011, www.foreignaffairs.com/articles /libya/2011-08-26/libya-and-future-humanitarian-intervention; see also Stewart Patrick, "R2P on Life Support: Humanitarian Norms vs. Practical Realities in Syria," *The Internationalist* (blog), Council on Foreign Relations, June 12, 2013, http://blogs.cfr .org/patrick/2013/06/12/r2p-on-life-support-humanitarian-norms-vs-practical -realities-in-syria/.

29. Patrick, *The Best Laid Plans: The Origins of American Multilateralism and the Dawn of the Cold War* (Lanham, Md.: Rowman and Littlefield, 2009), p. 76; Luck, *Mixed Messages*, p. 188.

30. Bush and Scowcroft, *A World Transformed*.

31. Edward F. Bruner and Nina M. Serafino, *Peacekeeping: Military Command and Control Issues*, CRS Report for Congress, updated November 1, 2001, p. 2, https://file.wikileaks.org/file/crs/RL31120.pdf.

32. Bruner and Serafino, *Peacekeeping*, p. 4.

33. The White House, "U.S. Policy on Reforming Multilateral Peace Operations," May 3, 1994, http://nsarchive.gwu.edu/NSAEBB/NSAEBB53/rw050394.pdf; Victoria K. Holt and Michael G. MacKinnon, "The Origins and Evolution of US Policy Towards Peace Operations," in *U.S. Peace Operations Policy: A Double-Edged Sword?*, edited by Ian Johnstone (New York: Routledge, 2009), pp. 1–17.

34. Republican Party Contract with America, www.nationalcenter.org/Contract withAmerica.html.

35. Luck, *Mixed Messages*, pp. 184–85; Bruner and Serafino, *Peacekeeping*, p. 5.

36. American Sovereignty Restoration Act of 2015, H.R. 1205, www.govtrack.us /congress/bills/114/hr1205/text/ih.

37. Statistics from the UN Department of Peacekeeping Operations (UND-PKO), www.un.org/en/peacekeeping/contributors/2016/apr16_2.pdf.

38. Jeffrey Lewis, "What a Real Liberal Foreign Policy Would Look Like," *Foreign Policy*, June 26, 2015, http://foreignpolicy.com/2015/06/26/what-a-real-liberal-for eign-policy-would-look-like-obama-democrats/.

39. President John F. Kennedy, Address before the 18th General Assembly of the United Nations, September 20, 1963, www.jfklibrary.org/Research/Research-Aids /JFK-Speeches/United-Nations_19630920.aspx.

40. Mika Nishimura, "Constraints in the Chemical Weapons Convention from the Perspective of International Law," in *Sovereignty and the Global Community: The Quest for Order in the International System*, edited by H. M. Hensel (Aldershot, U.K.: Ashgate, 2004), p. 59.

41. Treaty on the Non-Proliferation of Nuclear Weapons, www.state.gov/t/isn /trty/16281.htm; Nishimura, "Constraints," p. 59.

42. According to the Federation of American Scientists, the exact figure is 4,571. See https://fas.org/blogs/security/2016/05/hiroshima-stockpile/; and Department of Defense data set from 2015, hosted on "DoD Open Government" at http://open.defense .gov/Portals/23/Documents/frddwg/2015_Tables_UNCLASS.pdf. Israel, India, and Pakistan, which remain outside the NPT regime, also possess weapons programs.

43. U.S. Customs and Border Protection, "CSI: Container Security Initiative," June 26, 2016, www.cbp.gov/border-security/ports-entry/cargo-security/csi/csi-brief; U.S. Customs and Border Protection, "Container Security Initiative Office of Field Operations: Operational Ports," February 2014, www.cbp.gov/sites/default/files /documents/CSI%20Ports%20Map%201%20page%20062614.pdf.

44. U.S. Department of State, "Container Security Initiative Expands Operations in Japan," August 5, 2004, http://iipdigital.usembassy.gov/st/english/texttrans /2004/08/20040805160752ajesrom0.8979303.html#axzz4RWHuoGqn.

45. Organization for the Prohibition of Chemical Weapons, "Chemical Weapons Convention," www.opcw.org/chemical-weapons-convention/.

46. Nishimura, "Constraints," pp. 60–65.

47. Julian Ku and John Yoo, *Taming Globalization: International Law, the U.S. Constitution, and the New World Order* (Oxford University Press, 2012), pp. 64–65.

48. Amy E. Smithson, "The Chemical Weapons Convention," in *Multilateralism and U.S. Foreign Policy: Ambivalent Engagement*, edited by Stewart Patrick and Shepard Forman (Boulder, Colo.: Lynne Rienner, 2002), pp. 247–65.

49. Haass, "Sovereignty."

50. Stewart Patrick, "The 2013 Nobel Message: Hold the Line against Chemical Weapons," *The Internationalist* (blog), October 11, 2013, http://blogs.cfr.org/patrick/2013/10/11/the-2013-nobel-message-hold-the-line-against-chemical-weapons/.

51. John Yoo and John R. Bolton, "The Senate Should Block an End Run on Nuclear Arms," *Wall Street Journal*, December 27, 2012.

52. Theodore R. Bromund, "The Risks the Arms Trade Treaty Poses to the Sovereignty of the United States," Heritage Foundation Issue Brief no. 3622 (Washington, June 4, 2012), www.heritage.org/research/reports/2012/06/arms-trade-treaty-and-the-sovereignty-of-the-united-states.

53. Letter to President Obama from Rep. Michael Kelly and colleagues, October 15, 2013, http://kelly.house.gov/sites/kelly.house.gov/files/Kelly%20Member%20Letter%20to%20Obama%20on%20UN%20Arms%20Trade%20Treaty%20FINAL%2010-15-2013.pdf; Steven Edwards, "UN Arms Treaty Could Put U.S. Gun Owners in Foreign Sights, Say Critics," Fox News, July 11, 2012, www.foxnews.com/world/2012/07/11/un-arms-treaty-could-put-us-gun-owners-in-foreign-sights-say-critics/.

54. Robert Wright, "America's Sovereignty in a New World," *New York Times*, September 24, 2001.

55. Bruce Jones, Carlos Pascual, and Stephen John Stedman, *Power and Responsibility: Building International Order in an Era of Transnational Threats* (Brookings Institution Press, 2009), p. 9.

56. Richard N. Haass, "World Order 2.0: The Case for Sovereign Obligation," *Foreign Affairs*, January/February 2017, pp. 2–9.

57. Michael Chertoff, "The Responsibility to Contain," *Foreign Affairs*, January/February 2009, pp. 130–47.

58. Stewart Patrick, "Conflict and Cooperation in the Global Commons," in *Managing Conflict in a World Adrift*, edited by Chester A. Crocker, Fen Osler Hampson, and Pamela Aall (Washington: USIP, 2015), pp. 101–22.

59. Stewart Patrick, "Surface Tension: Chinese Aggression Roils Southeast Asian Waters," *The Internationalist* (blog), April 12, 2016, http://blogs.cfr.org/patrick/2016/04/12/surface-tension-chinese-aggression-roils-southeast-asian-waters/.

60. George Soroka, "Putin's Arctic Ambitions," *Foreign Affairs*, May 5, 2016, www.foreignaffairs.com/articles/russia-fsu/2016-05-05/putins-arctic-ambitions.

61. Scott G. Borgerson, *The National Interest and the Law of the Sea*, Council Special Report no. 46 (Washington: Council on Foreign Relations, May 2009).

62. Patrick, "Conflict and Cooperation in the Global Commons," pp. 102–06.

63. John R. Bolton and John C. Yoo, "Hands Off the Heavens," *New York Times*, March 8, 2012.

64. Stewart Patrick, "Technological Change and the Frontiers of Global Governance," *The Internationalist* (blog), Council on Foreign Relations, March 14, 2013, http://blogs.cfr.org/patrick/2013/03/14/technological-change-and-the-frontiers-of -global-governance/.

65. Benjamin Wittes and Gabriella Blum, *The Future of Violence: Robots and Germs, Hackers and Drones—Confronting a New Age of Threat* (New York: Basic Books, 2015), p. 235.

66. Patrick, "Conflict and Cooperation," pp. 111–16.

67. Kathy Gilsinian and Krishnadev Calamur, "Did Putin Direct Russian Hacking? And Other Big Questions," *The Atlantic*, January 6, 2017.

68. For more on this, see Stewart Patrick, "The Obama Administration Must Act Fast to Avoid the Internet's Fragmentation," *The Internationalist* (blog), February 26, 2014, http://blogs.cfr.org/patrick/2014/02/26/the-obama-administration-must-act -fast-to-prevent-the-internets-fragmentation/.

69. Statement from U.S. Secretary of Commerce Penny Pritzker on IANA Stewardship Transition, June 9, 2016, www.commerce.gov/news/press-releases/2016/06 /statement-us-secretary-commerce-penny-pritzker-iana-stewardship.

70. Office of Senator Ted Cruz (R-Tex.), "Obama Administration Preparations to Give Away the Internet Violate Federal Law," June 9, 2016, www.cruz.senate.gov/?p =press_release&id=2675; "Sen. Cruz and Rep. Duffy Introduce the Protecting Internet Freedom Act," June 8, 2016, www.cruz.senate.gov/?p=press_release&id=2669.

71. Patrick, "Conflict and Cooperation," p. 116.

72. Wittes and Blum, *The Future of Violence*, pp. 156, 172–73.

73. Robert K. Knake, *Internet Governance in an Age of Cyber-Insecurity*, Council Special Report no. 56 (Washington: Council on Foreign Relations, September 2010), pp. 18–19.

74. John F. Burns, "UN Panel to Investigate Rise in Drone Strikes," *New York Times*, January 24, 2013.

75. Denise Garcia, "The Case against Killer Robots," *Foreign Affairs*, May 10, 2014, www.foreignaffairs.com/articles/united-states/2014-05-10/case-against-killer -robots.

76. Laurie Garrett, "The Bioterrorist Next Door," *Foreign Policy*, December 15, 2011, http://foreignpolicy.com/2011/12/15/the-bioterrorist-next-door/.

CHAPTER 6

1. Elizabeth Warren, "The Trans-Pacific Partnership Clause Everyone Should Oppose," *Washington Post*, February 25, 2016.

2. Jonathan Weisman, "Left and Right Align in Fighting Obama's Trade Agenda," *New York Times*, February 9, 2015.

3. Ted Bromund, James M. Roberts, and Riddhi Dasgupta, "Investor-State Dispute Settlement (ISDS) Mechanisms: An Important Feature of High-Quality Trade

Agreements," Issue Brief no. 4351 (Washington: Heritage Foundation, February 20, 2015),www.heritage.org/research/reports/2015/02/investor-state-dispute-settlement -isds-mechanisms-an-important-feature-of-high-quality-trade-agreements; Daniel J. Ikenson, "A Compromise to Advance the Trade Agenda: Purge Negotiations of Investor-State Dispute Settlement," *Free Trade Bulletin* no. 57, Cato Institute, March 4, 2014, www.cato.org/publications/free-trade-bulletin/compromise-advance-trade-agenda -purge-negotiations-investor-state; Weisman, "Left and Right Align."

4. These paragraphs describing the ISDS aspects of the TPP debate draw on Stewart Patrick, "The Odd Couple: Democrats, Republicans, and the New Politics of Trade," *The Internationalist* (blog), April 1, 2015, http://blogs.cfr.org/patrick/2015 /04/01/the-odd-couple-democrats-republicans-and-the-new-politics-of-trade/.

5. William Mauldin, "Dispute-Resolution System Fuels Criticism of Pacific Trade Pact," *Wall Street Journal*, March 2, 2015; Jonathan Weisman, "Trans-Pacific Partnership Seen as Door to Foreign Suits against the United States," *New York Times*, March 25, 2015; Americans for Limited Government, "Leaked Pacific Trade Pact Exempts Foreign Firms from U.S. Law?," http://getliberty.org/leaked-pacific -trade-pact-exempts-foreign-firms-from-u-s-law/?utm_source=The+Trans-Pacific+ Partnership+Would+Destroy+our+National+Sovereignty&utm_campaign=Trans -Pacific+Partnership&utm_medium=email.

6. "Don't Buy the Trade Deal Alarmism," *Washington Post*, March 11, 2015; Weisman, "Trans-Pacific Partnership Seen as Door to Foreign Suits"; Public Citizen, "The Trans-Pacific Partnership: Empowering Corporations to Attack Citizens," www .citizen.org/tppinvestment; Katrina van den Heuvel, "Transpacific Partnership Treaty Will Help Neither Workers nor Consumers," *Washington Post*, March 31, 2015.

7. Jonathan Weisman, "Senate Democrats Foil Obama on Asia Trade Deal," *New York Times*, May 12, 2015.

8. Alexander Bolton, "Senate Approves Fast-Track, Sending Trade Bill to White House," *The Hill*, June 24, 2016, http://thehill.com/homenews/senate/246035-senate -approves-fast-track-sending-trade-bill-to-white-house; Carter Dougherty and Angela Greiling Keane, "Obama, Democrats, Suit Up for Latest Tussle on Trade," *Bloomberg*, June 25, 2015.

9. Scott Clement and Jim Tankersley, "Even If Trump Loses, This Poll Shows Why Hard-Line Immigration Positions Are Here to Stay," *Washington Post*, October 6, 2016.

10. Frances Stead Sellers and David A. Fahrenthold, "Why Even Let 'Em In? Understanding Bannon's Worldview and the Policies That Follow," *Washington Post*, January 31, 2017.

11. Aaron Blake, "Stephen Bannon's Nationalist Call to Arms, Annotated," *Washington Post*, February 23, 2017.

12. Office of the United States Trade Representative (USTR), *2017 Trade Policy Agenda and 2016 Annual Report* (Washington, March 2017), pp. 1–2, https://ustr .gov/sites/default/files/files/reports/2017/AnnualReport/AnnualReport2017.pdf.

13. "President Trump's Worldview Puts the Brakes on Globalization," NPR, May 2, 2017, www.npr.org/templates/transcript/transcript.php?storyId=526386332.

14. John H. Jackson, *Sovereignty, the WTO, and Changing Fundamentals of International Law* (Cambridge University Press, 2006), p. 10.

15. For a sophisticated treatment, see Edward Alden, *Failure to Adjust: How Americans Got Left Behind in the Global Economy* (Lanham, Md.: Rowman and Littlefield, 2016), p. 8.

16. John Gerard Ruggie, "International Regimes, Transactions, and Change: Embedded Liberalism in the Postwar Political Order," *International Organization* 36 (Spring 1982), pp. 379–415.

17. For more on this, see Stewart Patrick, *The Best Laid Plans: The Origins of American Multilateralism and the Dawn of the Cold War* (Lanham, Md.: Rowman and Littlefield, 2009), pp. 127–28.

18. Treaty of Amity and Commerce between The United States and France, February 6, 1778, http://avalon.law.yale.edu/18th_century/fr1788-1.asp. The two nations also signed the Treaty of Alliance that same day.

19. George Washington's Farewell Address, September 19, 1796, http://avalon.law.yale.edu/18th_century/washing.asp.

20. Judith Goldstein, "The Impact of Ideas on Trade Policy: The Origins of U.S. Agricultural and Manufacturing Policies," *International Organization* 43, no. 1 (Winter 1989), pp. 31–71; Stephan Haggard, "The Institutional Foundations of Hegemony: Explaining the Reciprical Trade Agreements Act of 1934," *International Organization* 42, no. 1 (Winter 1988), pp. 91–119.

21. NFTC cited in E. Brett, "The Post-war Political Settlement," in *Global Politics: Block IV: A Global Economy?* (Milton Keynes: Open University, 1990), p. 10. Chamber of Commerce cited in Richard N. Gardner, *Sterling-Dollar Diplomacy: Anglo-American Collaboration in the Reconstruction of Multilateral Trade* (Oxford: Clarendon Press, 1956), p. 378.

22. "Trends in Global Export Volume of Trade in Goods from 1950 to 2015," *Statista*, www.statista.com/statistics/264682/worldwide-export-volume-in-the-trade-since-1950/.

23. Anna Pukas, "The Sovereign Coin Is Steeped in History and Still Being Made at the Royal Mint Today," *Daily Express*, November 21, 2013, www.express.co.uk/news/royal/444252/The-Sovereign-coin-is-steeped-in-history-and-still-today-being-made-at-the-Royal-Mint.

24. Taft is cited in Gardner, *Sterling-Dollar Diplomacy*, pp. 129–32.

25. Thomas Biersteker, "The 'Triumph' of Neoclassical Economic Thinking in the Developing World: Ideas, Interests and Institutions in the Construction of a New International Division of Labor," in *Governance without Government: Order and Change in World Politics*, edited by James N. Rosenau and Ernst-Otto Czempiel (Cambridge University Press, 1991), pp. 102–31.

26. Dani Rodrik, *The Globalization Paradox: Democracy and the Future of the World Economy* (New York: W. W. Norton, 2011); Lawrence Summers, "What's behind the Revolt against Globalization," *Washington Post*, April 10, 2016; Jonathan D. Ostry, Prakash Loungani, and David Furceri, "Neoliberalism Oversold?," *Finance and Development* 53, no. 2 (June 2016), www.imf.org/external/pubs/ft/fandd/2016/06/ostry.htm.

27. Joseph E. Stiglitz, "The Overselling of Globalization," in *Globalization: What's New?*, edited by Michael M. Weinstein (New York: Columbia University Press, 2000), p. 235.

28. Joseph E. Stiglitz, *Globalization and Its Discontents* (New York: W. W. Norton, 2003), p. 247.

29. Rodrik, *The Globalization Paradox*, pp. 74–75; Thomas Pikkety, *Capital in the Twenty-First Century* (Harvard University Press, 2014).

30. "GDP Growth Rate," Trading Economics, www.tradingeconomics.com /united-states/gdp-growth.

31. Alden, *Failure to Adjust*.

32. Matthew Boyle, "Exclusive—Donald Trump: 'Disaster' Trade Deal Empowers America's Enemies, Another Sign Country Is Going to Hell," Breitbart, May 8, 2015, www.breitbart.com/big-government/2015/05/08/exclusive-donald-trump-disaster -trade-deal-empowers-americas-enemies-another-sign-country-is-going-to-hell/.

33. USTR, *2017 Trade Policy Agenda*, pp. 1–2.

34. Rodrik, *The Globalization Paradox*, pp. 200–03.

35. Daniel Deudney and G. John Ikenberry, "Democratic Internationalism: An American Grand Strategy for a Post-Exceptionalist Era," Council on Foreign Relations Working Paper (Washington, November 2012), www.cfr.org/grand-strategy/demo cratic-internationalism-american-grand-strategy-post-exceptionalist-era/p29417.

36. National Intelligence Council, *Global Trends: Paradox of Progress* (Washington, 2017).

37. John Bolton, "Trump, Trade, and American Sovereignty," *Wall Street Journal*, March 8, 2017.

38. Jackson, *Sovereignty, the WTO, and Changing Fundamentals*.

39. Jeremy A. Rabkin, *Law without Nations? Why Constitutional Government Requires Sovereign States* (Princeton University Press, 2005), pp. 211–17; Project on International Courts and Tribunals, www.pict-pcti.org/courts/NAFTA.html.

40. For the premier explanation of such behavior by a dominant state, see G. John Ikenberry, *After Victory: Institutions, Strategic Restraint, and the Rebuilding of Order after Major Wars* (Princeton University Press, 2001).

41. Rabkin, *Law without Nations?*, pp. 217–24; Jeremy Rabkin, *The Case for Sovereignty: Why the World Should Welcome American Independence* (Washington: AEI Press, 2004), p. 150.

42. Rabkin, *Law without Nations?*, pp. 224–32; Jackson, *Sovereignty, the WTO, and Changing Fundamentals*, pp. 152–59.

43. David E. Sanger, "Dole and Clinton Strike a Deal on World Trade Pact," *New York Times*, November 24, 1994.

44. Nader to House Small Business Committee in April 1994, cited in Jackson, *Sovereignty, the WTO, and Changing Fundamentals*, pp. 70–71; Robert Weissman, "GATT: The Final Act," *Multinational Monitor*, October 1994, www.multinational monitor.org/hyper/issues/1994/10/mm1094_04.html.

45. John Jackson, "The Great 1994 Sovereignty Debate: United States Acceptance and Implementation of the Uruguay Round Results," *Columbia Journal of Transnational Law* 36, no. 157 (1997); Peter Behr, "Dole's Concerns about GATT Seem to Be Easing, Clinton Officials Say," *Washington Post*, November 23, 1994.

46. U.S. General Accounting Office, "World Trade Organization: U.S. Experience to Date in Dispute Settlement System," June 14, 2000; Dan Sarooshi, *International Organizations and Their Sovereign Powers* (Oxford University Press, 2005), pp. 96–97.

47. Vladimir M. Pregelj, *Seeking Withdrawal of Congressional Approval of the WTO Agreement*, CRS Report for Congress, updated June 9, 2005, http://congressionalresearch.com/RL32700/document.php?.

48. Rabkin, *Law without Nations?*, p. 219; Jackson, *Sovereignty, the WTO, and Changing Fundamentals*, pp. 135–36, 162.

49. Patrick J. Buchanan, *The Great Betrayal: How American Sovereignty and Social Justice Are Being Sacrificed to the Gods of the Global Economy* (New York: Little, Brown, 1998).

50. David E. Sanger, "A Blink from the Bush Administration," *New York Times*, December 5, 2003; WTO, "United States—Definitive Safeguard Measures on Imports of Certain Steel Products," www.wto.org/english/tratop_e/dispu_e/cases_e/ds252_e.htm; Eliza Patterson, "WTO Rules against U.S. Safeguard Measures on Steel," *ASIL Insights* 8, no. 26 (2003), www.asil.org/insights/volume/8/issue/26/wto-rules-against-us-safeguard-measures-steel.

51. Rabkin, *The Case for Sovereignty*, p. 157; Claude E. Barfield, *Free Trade, Sovereignty, Democracy: The Future of the World Trade Organization* (Washington: AEI Press, 2001), pp. 7, 42.

52. Bryce Baschuk, "Trump Trade Team Signals Aggressive Posture toward WTO," *Bloomberg BNA*, March 2, 2017, www.bna.com/trump-trade-team-n57982084668/.

53. Damian Paletta and Ana Swanson, "Trump Suggests Ignoring World Trade Organization in Major Policy Shift," *Washington Post*, March 1, 2017.

54. Bolton, "Trump, Trade, and American Sovereignty."

55. U.S. Department of Agriculture, "United States and Brazil Reach Agreement to End WTO Cotton Dispute," October 1, 2014, www.usda.gov/media/press-releases/2014/10/01/united-states-and-brazil-reach-agreement-end-wto-cotton-dispute.

56. Robert Z. Lawrence, *The United States and the WTO Dispute Settlement System*, Council on Foreign Relations Special Report (Washington, 2007).

57. Megan Cassella, "Trump's Trade Agenda Short on Solutions," *Politico*, March 2, 2017, www.politico.com/tipsheets/morning-trade/2017/03/democrats-trumps-trade -agenda-short-on-solutions-219010.

58. Alden, *Failure to Adjust*, pp. 192, 197.

59. Rabkin, *Law without Nations?*, p. 227.

60. Rabkin, *The Case for Sovereignty*, pp. 157–58.

61. Indeed, Article XV of the Marrakesh Treaty, which established the WTO, permits members to leave the organization with six months' notice.

CHAPTER 7

1. "Full Text: Donald Trump Announces a Presidential Bid," *Washington Post*, June 16, 2015.

2. Pew Research Center, "On Immigration Policy, Wider Partisan Divide over Border Fence Than Path to Legal Status," October 8, 2015, www.people-press.org /2015/10/08/on-immigration-policy-wider-partisan-divide-over-border-fence-than -path-to-legal-status/.

3. Associated Press, "Trump in Mexico: Border Security Is a Sovereign Right," *Tucson.com*, August 31, 2016, http://tucson.com/news/local/trump-in-mexico-bor der-security-is-sovereign-right/article_fb46fea6-6fbb-11e6-8f82-7fa6d8f0f194 .html.

4. "Transcript: Donald Trump's Full Immigration Speech, Annotated," *Los Angeles Times*, August 31, 2016.

5. Jeremy Diamond, "Donald Trump: Ban All Muslim Travel to U.S.," CNN, December 8, 2015, www.cnn.com/2015/12/07/politics/donald-trump-muslim-ban -immigration/index.html.

6. Martin Matishak, "Republican Fears U.S. Has Created 'Federally-Funded Jihadi Pipeline,'" *The Hill*, February 11, 2015, http://thehill.com/policy/defense /232526-republican-fears-us-is-creating-federally-funded-jihadi-pipeline.

7. Alex Nowrasteh, "Syrian Refugees Don't Pose a Serious Security Threat" (Washington: Cato Institute, November 18, 2015); "Latest Crime Statistics Released," FBI, September 26, 2016, www.fbi.gov/news/stories/latest-crime-statistics-released.

8. Shibley Telhami, "American Attitudes on Refugees from the Middle East" (Brookings Institution, June 13, 2016), www.brookings.edu/research/american-attitudes-on -refugees-from-the-middle-east/.

9. Bill Chappell, Tamara Keith, and Merrit Kennedy, "'A Nation without Borders Is Not a Nation': Trump Moves Forward with U.S.-Mexico Wall," *NPR*, January 25, 2017, www.npr.org/sections/thetwo-way/2017/01/25/511565740/trump-expected-to -order-building-of-u-s-mexico-wall-wednesday.

10. Mark Berman and Matt Zapotosky, "Acting Attorney General Declares Justice Department Won't Defend Trump's Immigration Order," *Washington Post*, January 30, 2017.

11. Aaron Blake, "Stephen Bannon's Nationalist Call to Arms, Annotated," *Washington Post*, February 23, 2017.

12. Willem van Schendel, "Spaces of Engagement: How Borderlands, Illegal Flows, and Territorial States Interlock," in *Illicit Flows and Criminal Things: States, Borders, and the Other Side of Globalization*, edited by Willem van Schendel and Itty Abraham (Indiana University Press, 2005), p. 59.

13. Ibid., p. 46; Stewart Patrick, *Weak Links: Fragile States, Global Threats, and International Security* (Oxford University Press, 2011), pp. 144–45.

14. According to the Drug Enforcement Agency, in 2015 cocaine sold for $244/gram and heroin for $500/gram. See "2016 National Drug Threat Assessment Summary," www.dea.gov/resource-center/2016%20NDTA%20Summary.pdf, and "National Heroin Threat Assessment Summary," www.dea.gov/divisions/hq/2016/hq062716_attach.pdf.

15. For more on this, see Stewart Patrick, "The War on Drugs: Time for an Honest Conversation," *The Internationalist* (blog), April 20, 2012, http://blogs.cfr.org/patrick/2012/04/20/the-war-on-drugs-time-for-an-honest-conversation/.

16. Stephen Krasner, *Sovereignty: Organized Hypocrisy* (Princeton University Press, 1999).

17. Raymond Michalowski, "Security and Peace in the U.S.-Mexico Borderlands," in *Rethinking Border Control for a Globalizing World*, edited by Leanne Weber (New York: Routledge, 2015), p. 47.

18. International Organization for Migration, "Global Migration Trends Factsheet," http://gmdac.iom.int/global-migration-trends-factsheet; Christopher Joyner, *International Law in the Twenty-First Century: Rules for Global Governance* (Lanham, Md.: Rowman and Littlefield, 2005), p. 290.

19. The remainder, some 40.3 million, were internally displaced persons (IDPs). United Nations High Commission for Refugees, "Global Trends: Forced Displacement in 2016," www.unhcr.org/5943e8a34.

20. Christopher Rudolph, "Sovereignty and Territorial Borders in a Global Age," *International Studies Review* 7, no 1 (March 2005), pp. 9–11.

21. Daniel Tichenor, *Dividing Lines: The Politics of Immigration Control in America* (Princeton University Press, 2002), pp. 50–52.

22. Ibid., pp. 289–90.

23. Tichenor provides an excellent overview of major U.S. immigration legislation (ibid., esp. pp. 3–5).

24. Alex Nowrasteh, "National Sovereignty and Free Immigration Are Compatible," *Cato at Liberty* (blog), April 28, 2014, www.cato.org/blog/national-sovereignty-free-immigration-are-compatible; Karl Jacoby, "When Mexicans Feared American Immigration," *Politico*, June 5, 2016.

25. Galina Cornelisse, "State Borders, Human Mobility and Social Equality: From Blueprints to Pathways," in Weber, *Rethinking Border Control*; John Torpey, *The Invention of the Passport* (Cambridge University Press, 2000).

26. David Kyle and Christina A. Siracusa, "Seeing the State Like a Migrant: Why So Many Non-Criminals Break Immigration Laws," in Schendel and Abraham, *Illicit Flows and Criminal Things*, pp. 153–55.

27. Peter Andreas, "Redrawing the Line: Borders and Security in the Twenty-First Century," *International Security* 28, no. 2 (Fall 2003), p. 86.

28. Lodge is cited in Jeremy A. Rabkin, *Law without Nations? Why Constitutional Government Requires Sovereign States* (Princeton University Press, 2005), p. 120.

29. Lowell is cited in Tichenor, *Dividing Lines*, p. 38.

30. Andreas, "Redrawing the Line," p. 86.

31. Tichenor, *Dividing Lines*, pp. 244–46.

32. Edward Alden, *The Closing of the American Border* (New York: HarperCollins, 2008), pp. 69–72.

33. Andreas, "Redrawing the Line," pp. 86–88.

34. Alden, *The Closing of the American Border*, p. 26.

35. Some 650,000 enter the United States legally each day, 85 percent across land borders with Canada and Mexico. Bureau of Transportation Statistics, "Border Crossing/Entry Data," https://transborder.bts.gov/programs/international/trans border/TBDR_BC/TBDR_BCQ.html.

36. Alden, *The Closing of the American Border*.

37. The first post-9/11 budget increased homeland security spending from $19.5 to $37.7 billion. President George W. Bush, "Securing the Homeland, Strengthening the Nation," p. 17, www.dhs.gov/sites/default/files/publications/homeland_security _book.pdf. Border security rose from $11 billion requested in FY03 to $19.1 billion in FY17, including $13.9 billion for Customs and Border Protection (CBP) and $6.2 billion for Immigration and Customs Enforcement (ICE). Department of Homeland Security, "Budget in Brief 2017," www.dhs.gov/sites/default/files/publications /FY2017_BIB-MASTER.pdf.

38. Valsamis Mitsilegas, "The Law of the Border and the Borders of Law: Rethinking Border Control from the Perspective of the Individual," in Weber, *Rethinking Border Control*, pp. 15–16; Andreas, "Redrawing the Line," pp. 91–93.

39. Susan Ginsburg, *Securing Human Mobility in the Age of Risk: New Challenges for Travel, Migration, and Borders* (Washington: Migration Policy Institute, 2010), pp. 18–21.

40. Alden, *The Closing of the American Border*, p. 292.

41. Trump's election raised hopes among conservatives for a more "nationalist" approach to immigration. John Fonte and John O'Sullivan, "The Return of American Nationalism," *National Review*, November 18, 2016.

42. Reagan is cited in Michalowski, "Security and Peace in the U.S.-Mexico Borderlands," pp. 48–49.

43. "Pete Wilson 1994 Campaign Ad on Illegal Immigration" (video), www .youtube.com/watch?v=lLIzzs2HHgY; William Finnegan, "Sheriff Joe," *New Yorker*, July 20, 2009.

44. Migration Policy Institute, "Frequently Requested Statistics," www.migrationpolicy .org/article/frequently-requested-statistics-immigrants-and-immigration-united -states#Unauthorized Immigrants.

45. Office of Jeff Sessions, "Sessions Says Congress Must Fight Executive Amnesty: 'This Cannot Stand. It Will Not Stand,'" July 31, 2014, www.sessions.senate .gov/public/index.cfm/2014/7/sessions-says-congress-must-fight-executive-amnesty -this-cannot-stand-it-will-not-stand; Office of Daryl Metcalfe, "National Security Begins at Home," www.repmetcalfe.com/Immigration.aspx.

46. Howard W. Foster, "Why More Immigration Is Bad for America," *National Interest*, September 4, 2015, http://nationalinterest.org/blog/the-buzz/why-more -immigration-bad-america-11210?page=2; Robert W. Merry, "Why America's Immigration Crisis Matters," *National Interest*, July 21, 2014, http://nationalinterest .org/feature/why-americas-immigration-crisis-matters-10917.

47. Shane Bauer, "Undercover with a Border Militia," *Mother Jones*, November/ December 2016, www.motherjones.com/politics/2016/10/undercover-border-militia -immigration-bauer.

48. Doty is cited in Rudolph, "Sovereignty and Territorial Borders," p. 13.

49. Alistair Bell, "Americans Worry That Illegal Immigrants Threaten Way of Life, Economy," Reuters, August 7, 2014, www.reuters.com/article/us-usa-immigration -worries-idUSKBN0G70BE20140807. Paul's comments in 2007 are cited in Michalowski, "Security and Peace," pp. 48–49.

50. John Fonte and Althea Nagai, "America's Patriotic Assimilation System Is Broken," Culture and Society Briefing Paper (Hudson Institute, April 2013), www.hudson .org/content/researchattachments/attachment/1101/final04-05.pdf. Bradley Foundation findings are described in John Fonte, "Jack Kemp's Huddled Masses—Idealists Forget That Immigration Needs Assimilation," *National Review*, November 11, 2013, www.nationalreview.com/nrd/articles/362058/jack-kemps-huddled-masses.

51. Breitbart News Daily—Stephen Miller, March 9, 2016, https://soundcloud .com/breitbart/breitbart-news-daily-stephen-miller-march-9-2016.

52. Republican Party Platform of 2016, p. 26, www.gop.com/the-2016-republican -party-platform/.

53. Miriam Jordan, "Mexican Immigration to U.S. Reverses," *Wall Street Journal*, November 19, 2015; Jens Manuel Krogstad, Jeffrey S. Passel, and D'Vera Cohn, "Five Facts about Illegal Immigration to the United States," Pew Research Center, November 3, 2016, www.pewresearch.org/fact-tank/2016/11/03/5-facts-about-illegal -immigration-in-the-u-s/; Aaron Terrazas, "Mexican Immigrants in the United States," Spotlight (Washington: Migration Policy Institute, February 22, 2010), www .migrationpolicy.org/article/mexican-immigrants-united-states-2#24.

54. U.S. Immigration and Customs Enforcement, "FY2015 ICE Immigration Removals," www.ice.gov/removal-statistics; James Traub, "To Stay Open, Europe Needs to Close Its Doors," *Foreign Policy*, June 20, 2016, http://foreignpolicy.com/2016/06 /20/to-stay-open-europe-needs-to-close-its-doors/.

55. Some 68 percent and 67 percent of Republicans agreed with these two statements, respectively, in comparison with only 27 percent and 32 percent of Democrats. Scott Clement and Jim Tankersley, "Even If Trump Loses, This Poll Shows Why Hard-Line Immigration Positions Are Here to Stay," *Washington Post*, October 6, 2016.

56. Stewart Patrick, "The EU's Migration Crisis: When Solidarity and Sovereignty Collide," *The Internationalist* (blog), September 9, 2015, http://blogs.cfr.org/patrick/2015/09/09/the-eus-migration-crisis-when-solidarity-and-sovereignty-collide/; "Joint Statement of the Heads of Government of the Visegrad Group Countries," Prague, September 4, 2015, www.visegradgroup.eu/calendar/2015/joint-statement-of-the-150904.

57. Peter Andreas, *Smuggler Nation: How Illicit Trade Made America* (Oxford University Press, 2013).

58. Krogstad, Passel, and Cohn, "Five Facts"; Jordan, "Mexican Immigration to U.S. Reverses."

59. Leanne Weber, "Peace at the Border: A Thought Experiment," in Weber, *Rethinking Border Control*.

60. This paragraph builds on Alden, *The Closing of the American Border*, p. 296.

61. James Jay Carafano, "Safeguarding America's Sovereignty: A 'System of Systems' Approach to Border Security," Backgrounder no. 1898 (Washington: Heritage Foundation, November 28, 2005).

62. Susan Ginsberg, *Securing Human Mobility in the Age of Risk* (Washington: Migration Policy Institute, 2010).

63. Rainer Bauböck, "Rethinking Borders as Membranes," in Weber, *Rethinking Border Control*.

64. Weber, "Peace at the Border," p. 3.

65. Fiona Adamson, "Crossing Borders: International Migration and National Security," *International Security* 31, no. 1 (Summer 2006), pp. 180, 197.

66. Rudolph, "Sovereignty and Territorial Borders," p. 15.

CHAPTER 8

1. Arnaud Busquets Guàrdia, "Boris Johnson Accuses Barack Obama of Hypocrisy," *Politico*, April 16, 2016, www.politico.eu/article/boris-johnson-accuses-barack-obama-of-brexit-hypocrisy-uk-eu-referendum-date-june-23/.

2. Laura Hughes, "Barack Obama: Britain Would Go to the Back of the Queue When It Comes to US Trade Deals If It Leaves the EU," *The Telegraph*, April 22, 2016; "Barack Obama: As Your Friend, Let Me Say That the EU Makes Britain Even Greater," *New York Times*, April 23, 2016.

3. Tom McTague and Alex Spence, "Boris Johnson Makes Final Pitch for Britain's 'Independence Day,'" *Politico*, June 23, 2016, www.politico.eu/blogs/on-media/2016/06/boris-johnson-makes-final-pitch-for-british-independence-day-brexit-debate-wembley-sadiq-khan-ruth-davidson/.

4. Jon Swaine, "Bent Banana and Curved Cucumber Rules Dropped," *The Telegraph*, July 24, 2008.

5. Stewart Patrick, "The EU's Migration Crisis: When Solidarity and Sovereignty Collide," *The Internationalist* (blog), September 9, 2015, http://blogs.cfr.org/patrick /2015/09/09/the-eus-migration-crisis-when-solidarity-and-sovereignty-collide/; Stewart Patrick, "An Ever Looser Union: Can Europe Survive Its Current Crisis?," *Foreign Affairs*, March 29, 2016, www.foreignaffairs.com/articles/europe/2016-03 -29/ever-looser-union.

6. Heather Saul, "Donald Trump Praises 'Brave and Brilliant' Brexit Vote: 'They Took Back Control of Their Country,'" *The Independent*, June 24, 2016, www .independent.co.uk/news/people/donald-trump-praises-brexit-they-took-back -control-of-their-country-a7100201.html.

7. John Cassidy, "What Do the Brexit Movement and Donald Trump Have in Common?," *New Yorker*, June 23, 2016.

8. Robin Niblett, "Britain, the EU, and the Sovereignty Myth" (London: Chatham House, May 2016), pp. 4–6, www.chathamhouse.org/sites/files/chathamhouse /publications/research/2016-05-09-britain-eu-sovereignty-myth-niblett-final.pdf.

9. "Brexit: What If?," *The Economist*, June 18, 2016.

10. "Britain's EU Referendum: Divided We Fall," *The Economist*, June 18, 2016.

11. Douglas Carswell, "Britain's Coming Independence Day," *New York Times*, June 14, 2016; "Boris Johnson: Americans Would Never Accept EU Restrictions—So Why Should We?," *The Telegraph*, March 16, 2016.

12. *Costa* v. *Enel* (1964), http://eur-lex.europa.eu/legal-content/EN/TXT/?uri =CELEX%3A61964CJ0006.

13. "Theresa May's Keynote Speech at Tory Conference in Full," *The Independent*, October 5, 2016, www.independent.co.uk/news/uk/politics/theresa-may-speech-tory -conference-2016-in-full-transcript-a7346171.html.

14. Wood and Rarick are cited in Edward C. Luck, *Mixed Messages: American Politics and International Organization, 1919–1999* (Brookings Institution Press, 1999), pp. 56, 45.

15. Kirkpatrick is cited in ibid., p. 30.

16. American Land Sovereignty Protection Act, H. Rept. 105–245, 105th Congress, www.congress.gov/congressional-report/105th-congress/house-report/245/1; Luck, *Mixed Messages*, p. 126.

17. American Land Sovereignty Protection Act, Statement of Administration Policy: H.R. 883, May 19, 1999, www.govtrack.us/congress/bills/107/s2575/text.

18. Robert McMahon, "UN: U.S. Official Stresses Sovereignty over Engagement," Radio Free Europe/Radio Liberty, January 21, 2000, www.rferl.org/a/1093130.html.

19. "Address to the United Nations Security Council, by U.S. Senator Jesse Helms, Chairman of the Senate Foreign Relations Committee, 1/29/2000," www.101bananas .com/library2/helms.html; see also Barbara Crossette, "Helms, in Visit to UN, Offers a Harsh Message," *New York Times*, January 21, 2000.

20. Dejammet and Greenstock are cited in "Helms Lectures UN about Its Treatment of U.S.," *Baltimore Sun*, January 21, 2000, http://articles.baltimoresun.com /2000-01-21/news/0001210098_1_helms-united-nations-security-council. See also Tony Caron, "Why UN Got an Earful from Jesse Helms," *Time*, January 20, 2000.

21. Albright is cited in Sean Murphy, *United States Practice in International Law*, vol. 1, *1999–2001* (Cambridge University Press, 2003), p. 7.

22. Prominent members include Kenneth Anderson, Curtis Bradley, Lee Casey, John Fonte, Frank Gaffney, Jack Goldsmith, William Hawkins, David Horowitz, James Kelly, Herbert London, Andrew McCarthy, John O'Sullivan, Daniel Pipes, Jeremy Rabkin, and David Rivkin.

23. David Weigel, "GOP 'Sovereignty Caucus' Battles Obama on Major Treaties," *Washington Independent*, July 1, 2009, http://washingtonindependent.com/49312 /gop-sovereignty-caucus-battles-obama-on-treaties.

24. Danielle Pletka, "Senate Sovereignty Caucus Not a Paranoiacs Association," American Enterprise Institute Commentary (Washington, July 1, 2009), www.aei .org/publication/senate-sovereignty-caucus-not-a-paranoiacs-association/.

25. David A. Lake and Mathew D. McCubbins, "The Logic of Delegation to International Organizations," in *Delegation and Agency in International Organizations*, edited by Darren G. Hawkins and others (Cambridge University Press, 2006), p. 4.

26. Brett D. Schaefer, ed., *ConUNdrum: The United Nations and the Search for Alternatives* (Lanham, Md.: Rowman and Littlefield, 2009); "The World from The Hill: U.N. Funding an Early Target for House Republicans," *The Hill*, January 23, 2011, http:// thehill.com/news-by-subject/foreign-policy/139563-the-world-from-the-hill-un-funding -an-early-target-for-house-republicans; "United Nations Corruption and the Need for Reform" (Washington: Foundation for Defense of Democracies, March 2013), www .defenddemocracy.org/united-nations-corruption-and-the-need-for-reform/; Republican Party Platform of 2016, p. 51, www.gop.com/the-2016-republican-party-platform/.

27. United Nations press office, www.un.org/press/en/2015/gaab4185.doc.htm; Finance Division of New York City Council, http://council.nyc.gov/html/budget /2016/ex/nypd.pdf; Center for Responsive Politics, www.opensecrets.org/lobby /clientsum.php?id=D000000082.

28. U.S. Department of State, *United States Contributions to International Organizations* (2016), www.state.gov/documents/organization/267550.pdf.

29. Katherine V. Bryant, "Agency and Autonomy in International Organizations: Political Control and the Effectiveness of Multilateral Aid," unpublished paper, September 30, 2015, p. 2, http://wp.peio.me/wp-content/uploads/PEIO9/102_80 _1443656227537_KatherineBryant30092015.pdf.

30. Daniel Patrick Moynihan, *A Dangerous Place* (Boston: Little, Brown, 1978); Kenneth Anderson, *Living with the UN: American Responsibilities and International Order* (Stanford, Calif.: Hoover Institution Press, 2012), pp. 229–32.

31. Victoria K. Holt and Tobias C. Berman, *The Impossible Mandate? Military Preparedness, the Responsibility to Protect and Modern Peace Operations* (Washington:

Henry L. Stimson Center, 2006); Stewart M. Patrick, "President Obama Tackles UN Peacekeeping," *The Internationalist* (blog), September 25, 2015, http://blogs.cfr .org/patrick/2015/09/25/president-obama-tackles-un-peacekeeping/.

32. Stewart M. Patrick and Daniel Chardell, "Course Correction: WHO Reform after Ebola," *The Internationalist* (blog), January 27, 2015, http://blogs.cfr.org/patrick /2015/01/27/course-correction-who-reform-after-ebola/.

33. Michael N. Barnett and Martha Finnemore, "The Politics, Power, and Pathologies of International Organizations," *International Organization* 53, no. 4 (Autumn 1999), pp. 699, 705.

34. Darren G. Hawkins and others, "Delegation under Anarchy: State, International Organizations, and Principal-Agent Theory," in *Delegation and Agency*, edited by Darren G. Hawkins and others (Cambridge University Press, 2006), p. 7.

35. Daniel P. Carpenter, *The Forging of Bureaucratic Autonomy* (Princeton University Press, 2001); Mathew D. McCubbins and Talbot Page, "A Theory of Congressional Delegation," in *Congress: Structure and Policy*, edited by Mathew D. McCubbins (Cambridge University Press, 1987), pp. 409–25.

36. Robert W. Komer, *Bureaucracy Does Its Thing: Institutional Constraints on U.S.-GVN Performance in Vietnam* (Santa Monica, Calif.: Rand, 1972), www.rand .org/pubs/reports/R967.html.

37. Roland Vaubel, "Principal-Agent Problems in International Organizations," *Review of International Organizations* 1 (2006), pp. 125–38.

38. Ibid., pp. 126–27.

39. Carmen Pavel, *Divided Sovereignty: International Institutions and the Limits of State Authority* (Oxford University Press, 2015), p. 44. See also "2014 Chicago Council Survey of American Public Opinion and U.S. Foreign Policy Shows Public Support for 'Active' Role in World Affairs," Chicago Council on Global Affairs, September 15, 2014, www.thechicagocouncil.org/press-release/2014-chicago-council-survey-american -public-opinion-and-us-foreign-policy-shows-public.

40. Michael Barnett and Martha Finnemore, *Rules for the World: International Organizations in Global Politics* (Cornell University Press, 2004), pp. 27–29; Tana Johnson, *Organizational Progeny: Why Governments Are Losing Control over the Proliferating Structures of Global Governance* (Oxford University Press, 2014), pp. 1–15.

41. Dan Sarooshi, *International Organizations and Their Exercise of Sovereign Powers* (Oxford University Press, 2005), pp. 108n2, 117.

42. Robert Dole, "Shaping America's Global Future," *Foreign Policy* 98 (1995), p. 36; Andrew Quinlan, "International Organizations Poised to Impact Presidential Race," *Washington Times*, May 4, 2015.

43. The most celebrated is the "Tobin tax," named for Nobel laureate James Tobin, which would impose a modest charge on foreign exchange transactions. Although Tobin envisioned the tax as a way to reduce the financial volatility associated with currency speculation, others argue that such mechanisms could generate revenues for the United Nations or efforts to combat climate change.

44. Dick Morris and Eileen McGann, *Here Come the Black Helicopters! UN Global Governance and the Loss of Freedom* (New York: Broadside Books, 2012).

45. Liesbet Hooghe and Gary Marks, "Delegation and Pooling in International Organizations," *Review of International Organizations* 10, no. 3 (September 2015), pp. 305–28.

46. Julian Ku and John Yoo, "Globalization and Sovereignty," *Berkeley Journal of International Law* 31, no. 1 (2013), pp. 210–34, http://scholarship.law.berkeley.edu /cgi/viewcontent.cgi?article=1437&context=bjil.

47. Andrew Moravcsik, "The Paradox of U.S. Human Rights Policy," in *American Exceptionalism and Human Rights*, edited by Michael Ignatieff (Princeton University Press, 2005), pp. 167–68; Hooghe and Marks, "Delegation," p. 4.

48. Bryant, "Agency and Autonomy," p. 15; Mona M. Lyne, Daniel L. Nielson, and Michael J. Tierney, "Who Delegates? Alternative Models of Principals in Development Aid," in Hawkins and others, *Delegation and Agency*, pp. 41–76; Lake and McCubbins, "The Logic of Delegation to International Organizations," in Hawkins and others, *Delegation and Agency*, pp. 365–67.

49. Johnson, *Organizational Progeny*, pp. 6–10.

50. Vaubel, "Principal-Agent Problems," p. 127.

51. Ibid.; Stewart Patrick and Naomi Egel, "The International Energy Agency's Hybrid Model," *Foreign Affairs*, August 9, 2016, www.foreignaffairs.com/articles/2016-08 -09/international-energy-agencys-hybrid-model; Stewart Patrick and Naomi Egel, "Economic Coalition of the Willing: The OECD Reinvents Itself," *Foreign Affairs*, March 11, 2015, www.foreignaffairs.com/articles/2015-03-11/economic-coalition -willing; Gottfried Haberler, *Economic Growth and Stability: An Analysis of Economic Change and Policies* (Los Angeles: Nash, 1974), p. 156.

52. Brett Schaeffer, "How Should Americans Think about International Organizations?," Heritage Foundation report no. 12UA (Washington, October 26, 2011), www.heritage.org/Research/Reports/2011/10/How-Should-Americans-Think -About-International-Organizations.

53. Statistics from UN Department of Peacekeeping Operations, www.un.org/en /peacekeeping/operations/current.shtml.

54. David P. Fidler, "Revision of the World Health Organization's International Health Regulations," *ASIL Insights* 8, no. 8 (2004), www.asil.org/insights/volume/8 /issue/8/revision-world-health-organizations-international-health-regulations.

55. David P. Fidler, "SARS: Political Pathology of the First Post-Westphalian Pathogen," *Journal of Law, Medicine, and Ethics* 31 (2003), pp. 485–505.

56. David P. Fidler and Lawrence O. Gostin, "The New International Health Regulations: An Historic Development for International Law and Public Health," *Journal of Law, Medicine, and Ethics* 34, no. 1 (2006), p. 90, http://onlinelibrary.wiley .com/doi/10.1111/j.1748-720X.2006.00011.x/abstract. See also Julie E. Fischer, Sarah Kornblet, and Rebecca Katz, "The International Health Regulations (2005): Surveillance and Response in an Era of Globalization" (Washington: Henry L. Stimson Center,

2011), www.stimson.org/content/international-health-regulations-2005-surveillance-and -response-era-globalization.

57. World Health Organization, *Report of the Ebola Interim Assessment Panel* (July 2015), www.who.int/csr/resources/publications/ebola/report-by-panel.pdf?ua=1.

58. Dean Rusk's 1965 testimony is cited in Luck, *Mixed Messages*, p. 61.

59. Robert O. Keohane, Stephen Macedo, and Andrew Moravcsik, "Democracy-Enhancing Multilateralism," *International Organization* 63 (Winter 2009), p. 23.

60. For a more conservative take on this general argument, see Anderson, *Living with the UN*, p. 18.

61. Hawkins and others, "Delegation under Anarchy," pp. 26–31.

62. Ely Karetny and Thomas G. Weiss, "UNRRA's Operational Genius and Institutional Design," in *Wartime Origins and the Future of the United Nations,* edited by Dan Plesch and Thomas G. Weiss (New York: Routledge, 2015), pp. 110–13.

63. Mathew D. McCubbins and Thomas Schwartz, "Congressional Oversight Overlooked: Police Patrols versus Fire Alarms," *American Journal of Political Science* 2, no. 1 (1984), pp. 165–79.

64. *Report of the Panel on United Nations Peace Operations* (Brahimi Report), Executive Summary, p. 3, www.un.org/en/events/pastevents/pdfs/Brahimi_Report _Exec_Summary.pdf.

65. Steve Waddell, *Global Action Networks: Creating Our Future Together* (New York: Palgrave, 2011).

66. "Lucky Jim," *The Economist*, September 17, 2016; Michael Clemens, "World Bank's U.S. Dependency Has to End," *Politico*, September 13, 2016, www.politico.eu /article/world-bank-president-elections-us-jim-yong-kim/.

67. Megan Roberts, "The UN's Ninth Secretary-General Is António Gutteres," *The Internationalist* (blog), October 13, 2016, http://blogs.cfr.org/patrick/2016/10 /13/the-uns-ninth-secretary-general-is-antonio-guterres/?utm_source =feedburner&utm_medium=feed&utm_campaign=Feed%3A+spatrick+ %28Stewart+M.+Patrick%3A+The+Internationalist%29; Anthony Banbury, "I Love the UN, but It Is Failing," *New York Times*, March 18, 2016.

68. F. Francioni, "Multilateralism à la Carte: The Limits of Unilateral Withhold-ings of Assessed Contributions to the UN Budget," *European Journal of International Law* 11, no. 1 (2000), pp. 43–59.

69. Margaret P. Karns and Karen A. Mingst, "The United States as 'Deadbeat'? U.S. Policy and the UN Financial Crisis," in *Multilateralism and U.S. Foreign Policy: Ambivalent Engagement*, edited by Stewart Patrick and Shepard Forman (Boulder, Colo.: Lynne Rienner, 2002), pp. 287–89.

70. Pub.L. 101-246, Title IV, § 414, February 16, 1990, https://graphics8.nytimes .com/packages/pdf/world/PLO-UN-legislation.pdf; Tim Wirth, "Let U.S. Lead," *Huffington Post*, November 3, 2011, www.huffingtonpost.com/timothy-wirth/let-us -lead_b_1066999.html.

71. For the Ros-Lehtinen legislation, see United Nations Transparency, Reform, and Accountability Act of 2015, H.R. 3667, www.govtrack.us/congress/bills/114 /hr3667. For the Bolton proposal, see John Bolton, "The New Order Is Our Chance to Keep Up in Fast Changing World," *Times of London*, November 15, 2016, www .thetimes.co.uk/article/the-new-order-is-our-chance-to-keep-up-in-fast-changing -world-ntnp2j3n3.

72. For text of draft executive order, see Noah Schactman, Erin Gloria Ryan, and Asawin Suebsaeng, "Trump Draft Executive Order: No Funding for UN Abortions," *The Daily Beast*, January 26, 2017, www.thedailybeast.com/trump-draft-executive -order-no-funding-for-un-abortions; Stewart Patrick, "Trump's UN Executive Order Would Cut Off America's Nose to Spite Its Face," *The Internationalist* (blog), January 26, 2017, http://blogs.cfr.org/patrick/2017/01/26/trumps-uns-executive-order -would-cut-off-americas-nose-to-spite-its-face/.

73. Sarooshi, *International Organizations*, p. 116.

74. Albert O. Hirschman, *Exit, Voice, and Loyalty: Responses to Decline in Firms, Organizations, and States* (Harvard University Press, 1970); Sarooshi, *International Organizations*, p. 55.

75. Andrew Moravcsik, "The Great Brexit Kabuki—a Masterclass in Political Theatre," *Financial Times*, April 8, 2016.

76. Mark P. Lagon and Ryan Kaminski, "Bolstering the UN Human Rights Council's Effectiveness," Council on Foreign Relations Discussion Paper, January 3, 2017, www.cfr.org/report/bolstering-un-human-rights-councils-effectiveness.

77. Anderson, *Living with the UN*, pp. 16, 36–38.

78. F. H. Hinsley, *Power and the Pursuit of Peace* (Cambridge University Press, 1963); Strobe Talbott, *The Great Experiment: The Story of Ancient Empires, Modern States, and the Quest for a Global Nation* (New York: Simon and Schuster, 2008); Mark Mazower, *Governing the World: The History of an Idea* (New York: Penguin, 2012).

79. Andrew Hurrell, *On Global Order: Power, Values, and the Constitution of International Society* (Oxford University Press, 2007), pp. 91–94; Daniel Deudney, "Regrounding Realism: Anarchy, Security, and Changing Material Contexts," *Security Studies* 10, no. 1 (September 2000), pp. 1–42; Christopher Chase-Dunn, "World State Formation: Historical Processes and Emergent Necessity," *Political Geography Quarterly* 9, no. 2 (1996), pp. 108–30; David Held, *Democracy and Global Order* (Stanford University Press, 1995); David Held and others, *Global Transformations* (Stanford University Press, 1999); Danielle Archibugi, *The Global Commonwealth of Citizens: Toward Cosmopolitan Democracy* (Princeton University Press, 2008).

80. Alexander Wendt, "Why a World State Is Inevitable," *European Journal of International Relations* 9, no. 4 (2003), pp. 491–92; Luis Cabrera, *Political Theory of Global Justice: A Cosmopolitan Case for the World State* (New York: Routledge, 2004); W. E. Scheuerman, *The Realist Case for Global Reform* (Cambridge: Polity Press, 2011).

81. Thomas G. Weiss, "What Happened to the Idea of World Government?," *International Studies Quarterly* 53, no. 2 (2009), pp. 253–71; Townsend Hoopes and

Douglas Brinkley, *FDR and the Creation of the UN* (Yale University Press, 1997), p. 56.

82. Einstein is cited in Mazower, *Governing the World*, p. 231.

83. Weiss, "What Happened?," pp. 259–60.

84. Hans Morgenthau, *Politics among Nations: The Struggle for Power and Peace* (New York: Knopf, 1959), p. 477; Weiss, "What Happened?," p. 259.

85. Stewart Patrick, "The Unruled World: The Case for Good Enough Global Governance," *Foreign Affairs*, January/February 2014, pp. 58–73.

86. Michael Walzer, *Spheres of Justice: A Defense of Pluralism and Equality* (New York: Basic Books, 1983); Andrew Linklater, *Men and Citizens in the Theory of International Relations* (London: Palgrave Macmillan, 1982).

87. Daniel Deudney, *Bounding Power: Republican Security Theory from the Polis to the Global Village* (Princeton University Press, 2007), pp. 275–77.

CHAPTER 9

1. Chuck Todd, Mark Murray, and Carrie Dann, "West Wing Battle Brews between Nationalists and Globalists," *NBC News*, April 6, 2017, www.nbcnews.com /politics/first-read/west-wing-battle-brews-between-nationalists-globalists-n743271.

2. The White House, "Statement by President Trump on the Paris Climate Change Accord," June 1, 2017, www.whitehouse.gov/the-press-office/2017/06/01/statement -president-trump-paris-climate-accord.

3. Ibid.

4. Stewart Patrick, "Trump's Sovereignty Canard," *U.S. News and World Report*, June 6, 2017, www.usnews.com/opinion/op-ed/articles/2017-06-06/donald-trump -is-wrong-to-say-the-paris-accord-threatens-us-sovereignty.

5. Alexis de Tocqueville, *Democracy in America*, vol. 1 (1835), chapter 4 ("The Principle of the Sovereignty of the People of America"), archived online at http:// xroads.virginia.edu/~hyper/DETOC/1_ch04.htm.

6. Edward C. Luck, *Mixed Messages: American Politics and International Organization, 1919–1999* (Brookings Institution Press, 1999); Stewart Patrick and Shepard Forman, eds., *Multilateralism and U.S. Foreign Policy: Ambivalent Engagement* (Boulder, Colo.: Lynne Rienner, 2002).

7. "Americans on the U.S. Role in the World: A Study of U.S. Public Attitudes," Program for Public Consultation, January 2017, www.publicconsultation.org/wp -content/uploads/2017/01/PPC_Role_in_World_Report.pdf.

8. These include: to maintain a standing peacekeeping force that the UN trains and commands, investigate human rights violations in other countries, create an international marshals service to arrest leaders responsible for genocide, regulate the international arms trade, monitor elections, and intervene with military force to deliver urgent humanitarian aid if a government tries to block it. "Review of Polling Finds International and American Support for World Order Based on Law, Stronger UN," WorldPublicOpinion.org, December 15, 2011, http://worldpublicopinion.net

/review-of-polling-finds-international-and-american-support-for-world-order-based
-on-international-law-stronger-un/.

9. "New Poll Finds 88 Percent of Americans Support Active Engagement at the United Nations," Better World Campaign, January 4, 2017, https://betterworld campaign.org/news-room/press-releases/new-poll-finds-88-percent-of-americans -support-active-engagement-at-the-united-nations/.

10. "Public Uncertain, Divided over America's Place in the World," Pew Research Center, May 6, 2016, www.people-press.org/2016/05/05/public-uncertain-divided -over-americas-place-in-the-world/.

11. Joshua Busby and others, "How the Elite Misjudge the U.S. Electorate on International Engagement," *RealClear World*, November 7, 2016, www.realclearworld .com/articles/2016/11/07/how_the_elite_misjudge_the_us_electorate_on _international_engagement_112112.html.

12. These paragraphs draw on Stewart Patrick, "The New 'New Multilateralism': Minilateral Cooperation, but at What Cost?," *Global Summitry* 1, no. 2 (2015), pp. 115–34.

13. Richard N. Haass, "The Case for Messy Multilateralism," *Financial Times*, January 2, 2010.

14. Haass first used this term in a 2001 interview. See Thom Shanker, "White House Says the U.S. Is Not a Loner, Just Choosy," *New York Times*, July 31, 2001.

15. Alan Alexandroff, "Challenges in Global Governance: Opportunities for G-x Leadership," Stanley Foundation, Policy Analysis Brief (Muscatine, Iowa, March 2010), www.stanleyfoundation.org/publications/pab/AlexandroffPAB310.pdf.

16. For more on this, see "Nuclear Security Summit at a Glance," Arms Control Association, March 2016, www.armscontrol.org/factsheets/NuclearSecuritySummit.

17. See also Stewart Patrick, "The Unruled World: The Case for 'Good Enough' Global Governance," *Foreign Affairs*, January/February 2014, pp. 58–73.

18. Joseph S. Nye, "The Regime Complex for Managing Cyber Activities," Belfer Center for Science and International Affairs, Harvard University (Cambridge, Mass., November 2014), http://belfercenter.hks.harvard.edu/publication/24797 /regime_complex_for_managing_global_cyber_activities.html?breadcrumb =%2Fexperts%2F3%2Fjoseph_s_nye.

19. Stewart M. Patrick and Jeffrey A. Wright, "Designing a Global Coalition of Medicines Regulators," Policy Innovation Memorandum no. 48 (Washington: Council on Foreign Relations, August 20, 2014), www.cfr.org/pharmaceuticals-and -vaccines/designing-global-coalition-medicines-regulators/p33100.

20. Benjamin R. Barber, "A Governance Alternative to Faltering Nation-States," *CityLab*, December 5, 2016, www.citylab.com/politics/2016/12/a-governance-alternative -to-faltering-nation-states/509612/.

21. Office of Governor Edmund G. Brown Jr., "CA Governor Brown, NY Governor Cuomo and WA Governor Inslee Announce Formation of U.S. Climate Alliance," *CA.gov*, June 1, 2017, www.gov.ca.gov/news.php?id=19818.

22. Kenneth W. Abbott and Duncan Snidal, "The Governance Triangle: Regulatory Standards Institutions and the Shadow of the State," in *The Politics of Global Regulation*, edited by Walter Mattli and Ngaire Woods (Princeton University Press, 2009), pp. 40–88.

23. *New State Ice Co. v. Liebman*, 285 U.S. 262 (1932), https://supreme.justia.com /cases/federal/us/285/262/.

24. Stewart Patrick, "Multilateralism à la Carte: The New World of Global Governance," Valdai Paper no. 22 (August 7, 2015), http://valdaiclub.com/a/valdai -papers/valdai_paper_22_multilateralism_la_carte_the_new_world_of_global _governance/?sphrase_id=5711.

25. Ruth Wedgwood, "Give the United Nations a Little Competition," *New York Times*, December 5, 2005.

26. Jagdish Bhagwati, *Termites in the Trading System* (Oxford University Press, 2008); Thomas Weiss, "Is Good Enough Global Governance Good Enough?," International Relations and Security Network, February 4, 2014, www.isn.ethz.ch /Digital-Library/Articles/Detail/?lng=en&id=176222.

27. Julia C. Morse and Robert O. Keohane, "Contested Multilateralism," *Review of International Organizations*, March 23, 2014, http://link.springer.com/article/10 .1007/s11558-014-9188-2.

28. Mark L. Busch, "Overlapping Institutions, Forum Shopping, and Dispute Settlement in International Trade," *International Organization* 61 (Fall 2007), pp. 735–61.

29. Stewart Patrick, "Present at the Creation, Beijing-Style," *The Internationalist* (blog), March 20, 2015, http://blogs.cfr.org/patrick/2015/03/20/present-at-the -creation-beijing-style/.

Index

Abortion, 98, 127

Acheson, Dean, 48, 82, 91

Activism: American exceptionalism as, 51; of cities, 259–60; international law as, 21, 29, 106, 116; judicial, 98, 132, 191, 192; non-alignment as, 41; WTO treaty reinterpretation for, 195

ADA (Americans with Disabilities Act, 1990), 98

Adams, John, 53, 61

Adams, John Quincy, 50, 62–63

Adamson, Fiona, 216

Advocacy groups. *See* Nongovernmental organizations (NGOs); Transnational organizations

AEI (American Enterprise Institute), 29

Afghanistan: refugees from, 212; war on terrorism in, 88–89, 146

Africa, border permeability in, 200. *See also specific countries*

African Union, criticism of Libya conflict, 152

Agency slack, 232–34, 243

AIIB (Asian Infrastructure Investment Bank), 262

Alarmism: foreign law vs. constitutional law, 134; human rights treaties, 127–28; international law, 108, 256; slippery slope thesis applied to treaties, 253; sovereignty, loss of, 10–11, 37; world government fears, 210, 221, 225, 247

Albright, Madeleine, 49, 84, 224–25

Alden, Edward, 178

Alito, Samuel, 140

al Qaeda terrorist network, 88, 146, 151

America First movement, 71

America First rhetoric of 2016 presidential campaign, 9, 23, 95, 176, 254

American Indians, sovereign rights of, 56–57

American Land Sovereignty Protection Act (1997), 222

American Revolution: exceptionalism concept, 50; foreign command of U.S. troops during, 153; international law, recognition of, 62; popular sovereignty concept, 34, 42–46; unique destiny concept, 48; vulnerability of sovereignty during, 61. *See also* Founding fathers

American Servicemembers' Protection Act (2002), 112

Americans for Limited Government, 173–74

Americans for Sovereignty, 10

American Sovereignty Restoration Act (2017), 29–30, 155

Americans with Disabilities Act (ADA, 1990), 98

Annan, Kofi, 151

Anti-Ballistic Missile Treaty (1972), 85

Anti-Federalists, 53–54

Anton, Michael, 176

Appellate Body (AB) of WTO, 189–95

Arbitration for country disputes, 4, 187–88

Arctic Ocean, claim on, 163–64

Aristocracy of United States, 53

Arizona, immigration policy, 208

Arms control: Committee on Disarmament of UN, 236; international cooperation in, 22–23, 162; for international security, 155–60; League of Nations and disarmament, 4; opposition to, 160–62; outer space code of conduct, 165; Proliferation Security Initiative for, 88–89; sovereignty, reconciling, 162–63, 171; treaties for, 41, 120, 124, 131, 155–59; UN resolution on, 89

Arms races: maritime commons, 163–64; outer space commons, 165; preventing, 71

Arms Trade Treaty (ATT), 124, 161

Arpaio, Joe, 208

Articles of Confederation (1778), 54–55, 60, 250

Asian Infrastructure Investment Bank (AIIB), 262

al-Assad, Bashar, 93, 148, 160, 198

Assistance Mission in Afghanistan (UN), 89

Asylum seekers, 201, 208–09

Atlantic Charter (1941), 124

Authority: delegation of, 26, 232–40; as dimension of sovereignty, 8, 12–14, 256; as historical attribute of sovereignty, 33–35; influence vs., 134–35; informal networks undermining, 115; political and military self-reliance for, 61. *See also* Sovereignty bargains

Autonomy: as dimension of sovereignty, 8, 12–14, 256; globalization and, 179, 183; as historical attribute of sovereignty, 34–36; influence vs., 90, 93; preservation of, 26–27. *See also* Sovereignty bargains

Avena case (2005), 139

Bank for International Settlements (BIS), 236

Ban Ki Moon, 243

Bannon, Stephen K., 10, 175–76, 192, 199, 211

Basel Convention on Hazardous Wastes, 124

Basel III capital account requirements, 91

Bellinger, John, 118

Biden, Joseph, 244

Bill of Rights (England), 44

Bill of Rights (U.S.), 126, 127

bin Laden, Osama, 151

Biological Weapons Convention, 85

Biosphere Reserve, 222

Biotechnology, 170

Bipartisan leadership, 57–58, 67–68, 75–76

BIS (Bank for International Settlements), 236

Black Hawk Down episode, Somalia (1993), 154

Blackstone, William, 44

Bloomberg, Michael, 260

Blum, Gabriella, 169

Bodin, Jean, 43

Boehner, John A., 173

Bohlen, Charles, 80

Bolton, John: American exceptionalism and, 49; on arms control, 160; coalition approach to international cooperation, 88; as defender of sovereignty, 29, 46, 148; on funding for international organizations, 245; International Criminal Court, Rome Statute, 112; on outer space code of conduct, 165–66; on Trump's objections to WTO, 193; on war on sovereignty, 8–9

Bond, Carol Ann, 139–40

Bond v. United States (2014), 139–40

Booth, Ken, 29

Borah, William, 67–69, 71

Border Patrol (U.S.), 204–05

Border security, 205–07. *See also* International borders

Bosnian war (1995), 84, 151

Boutros-Ghali, Boutros, 234

Bowers v. Hardwick (1986), 135

Bracero guest worker program, 205

Bradley, Curtis A., 116

Bradley Foundation, 211

Brahimi, Lakhdar, 242

Brandeis, Louis, 260

Brazil: global output of, 92; outer space, competition for, 165

Breitbart News, 10

Brennan, William, 135

Bretton Woods system, 179, 182–87

Brexit, 39, 111, 212, 217–21, 246

Breyer, Stephen, 132–33, 135, 137

Bricker, John, 104–05, 127

Bricker Amendment, 104–05

BRICS Bank, 262

BRICS Contingency Fund, 262

BRICS countries, 92

Bromund, Theodore, 124, 161

Broun, Paul, 225

Bryan, William Jennings, 66, 144

Buchanan, Patrick J., 184, 190–92, 197

Burden sharing: in collective security, 85, 150; within NATO, 81, 145; new members of international organizations and, 92

Burke-White, William W., 110–11

Bush, George H. W.: Americans with Disabilities Act, 98; Gulf War, UNSC authorization for, 147, 153; immigration policy of, 205; internationalism of, 85; Kosovo intervention, 148–49; post–Cold War leadership of, 49, 84; trade agreements, 188–89

Bush, George W.: American exceptionalism and, 49; child support treaty, 138; Container Security Initiative, 157, 159; global interdependence and, 20; immigration policy of, 206–07; international obligations, 138–39; Iraq invasion, UNSC lack of authorization for, 147, 149; Obama on Bush's foreign policy, 89–90; presidential debate (2004), 142–43; Rome Statute of ICC, 111–13; trade policy, 192; UN Convention on the Rights of Persons with Disabilities, 98; unilateral foreign policy of, 85–89; war on terrorism, 87–89, 142–43, 151–52

Calhoun, John C., 55

California: climate change actions of, 260; immigration policy in, 197, 208; terrorist actions in (2015), 198

Camarena, Enrique "Kiki," 214

Cameron, David, 217

Canada, trade agreements of, 187–88. *See also* North American Free Trade Agreement (NAFTA)

Canada-U.S. Free Trade Agreement (CUSFTA), 187–88

Capitalism, 182, 184, 187

Carafano, James Jay, 214

Caribbean region, Monroe Doctrine directed toward, 63–64

Carswell, Douglas, 219

Casey, Lee, 107

Catholic Church, 32–33, 37–38, 114

Cato Institute, 173, 198

CBP (Customs and Border Protection), 157, 159

CEDAW (Convention on the Elimination of Discrimination against Women), 125

Center for Immigration Studies (CIS), 205

Central America: migration to Mexico, 212; migration to United States, 208–09, 211–12, 215

CESCR (Covenant on Economic, Social and Cultural Rights), 126

CFE (Conventional Forces in Europe Treaty), 124

Chamber of Commerce (U.S.), 180

Chan, Margaret, 239

Charles I (king of England), 43

Charming Betsy Doctrine (1804), 101

Chayes, Abram, 141

Chayes, Antonia, 141

Chemical Weapons Act (CWA), 139–40

Chemical Weapons Convention (CWC), 16, 119, 124, 159–60

Chemical weapons, use of, 148, 160

Chertoff, Michael, 162

Chesterton, G. K., 48

China: economic partnership, U.S. exclusion from, 262; global output of, 92; human rights issues of, 246; Libya conflict, criticism of, 152; maritime law, challenges to, 93, 163; Open Door Notes on, 64; opposition to adding members to UN Security Council, 91; outer space, competition for, 165; SARS outbreak in, 239; sovereignty of, 40; Syria conflict, blocking UNSC actions in, 93, 152; trade with, 64, 175, 192–93; UN missions, contributions to, 155

Chinese Exclusion Act (1882), 197, 203

Chisholm v. Georgia (1793), 43

CIS (Center for Immigration Studies), 205

Cities, global activism of, 259–60

Citizenship, 48, 135

Civil Rights Movement, 104

Civil War (U.S.), 56

Clay, Henry, 56

Climate change: C40 coalition for, 259–60; international commitments on, 29; Paris Accord on Climate Change, 9, 252–53, 258, 260–61; sovereign state system vs. world state, 249; UN Framework Convention on Climate Change, 258. *See also* Transnational challenges

Clinton, Bill: American exceptionalism and, 49; foreign policy of, 86; Gulf War, 154; immigration policy of, 205; on international conservation agreements, 222; Kosovo intervention, UNSC lack of authorization for, 147; post–Cold War leadership of, 84; Rome Statute of ICC, 111; trade agreements, 189–90

Clinton, Hillary, 50, 116, 175

Club for Growth, 173

Cluster Munitions Convention, 114

Coalitions: concerns with, 261–63; international organizations, preference over, 86, 88–89, 237, 260; for medicine regulation, 259; minilateral, 149–50, 157, 258, 261–62; as solution to sovereignty issue, 257–60, 263; for war on terrorism, 87–89

Codes of conduct, voluntary, 258

Cohens v. Virginia (1821), 55

Cold War: distribution of power during, 92; effect on military force of UN, 153; end of, 83; India and, 40–41; NATO creation for, 81–82; new world order following, 49, 84; post–World War II peace structure and, 79–80

Collective action. *See* Coalitions

Collective security: burden sharing for, 150; coalitions for, 87–89, 149–50; unilateralism jump-starting, 86; U.S.

participation in, 65. *See also specific organizations for*

Commentaries on the Laws of England (Blackstone), 44

Commerce Department (U.S.), 188

Commission to Study the Bases of a Just and Durable Peace, 248

Common Sense (Paine), 50

Communication: cyberspace security, 167; Internet, 166–69; satellites for, 164–65

Comprehensive Test Ban Treaty (CTBT): opposition to, 161; senate rejection of, 84, 85, 104, 120, 124; U.S. lack of participation in, 14

Compromise of 1850, 56

Confederate States of America, 56

Congo, peacekeeping mission in, 238

Congress: arms control, opposition to, 161, 165; bipartisan leadership in, 57–58, 67–68, 75–76; Bretton Woods Agreements, 182; Chemical Weapons Convention, approval of, 160; Comprehensive Test Ban Treaty, rejection of, 84, 85, 104, 120, 124; Convention on the Rights of Persons with Disabilities, rejection of, 98–99, 104; on foreign command of military, 154; historical powers of, 54; human rights treaty ratification of, 127; on ICC membership, 112; international law and, 98–99, 102–05, 116; international treaties and finances, oversight of, 19, 100, 120, 124, 127, 161; non-self-execution of treaties and, 103, 105, 125, 131; powers of, 57; right to advise and consent during treaty negotiations, 6, 68; "Sense of the House" resolution, 29, 136; Sovereignty Caucus, 9, 52, 225; tariffs, control over, 180; on Trans-Pacific Partnership, 172–75; United Nations, bill to withdraw United States from, 29–30, 155; United Nations relations, 79, 223, 243–44, 248; UN Security Council relations, 77, 143; on world

government, 248; World Trade Organization, opposition to, 190–91

Congressional Research Service, 153

Connally, Tom, 75, 79, 82

Consent of governed. *See* Popular sovereignty

Conservative Political Acton Conference (CPAC, 2017), 30

Constitution, U.S.: arms control treaties, 161; Bricker Amendment to, 104–05; free speech, Internet control and, 168; history of sovereignty and, 53–58; human rights issues, 126; ideals in, 48; as institutional factor of sovereignty, 30–31; international law, 19, 21–22, 62, 86, 98–102, 107, 132–34; international obligations, 13–14, 19, 42; international organizations, 222; League of Nations membership, 2, 4–5; national security concerns leading to, 60–61; separation of powers in, 42, 53–54, 57, 82; structure of, 18–19; Supremacy Clause of, 131; trade agreements as threat to, 173–74, 187. *See also specific amendments*

Constitutional Convention (1787), 53, 54, 61

Container Security Initiative (CSI), 157

Contingent sovereignty, 22, 150–52, 250

Conventional Forces in Europe Treaty (CFE), 124

Convention on Biological Diversity, 120, 124

Coolidge, Calvin, 7, 70–71

Costa v. ENEL (1964), 220

Council for America, 10

Council on Foreign Relations (1931), 71

Counter-Reformation, 32

Counterterrorism. *See* Terrorism and counterterrorism

The Court and the World (Breyer), 137

Covenant of the League of Nations. *See* League of Nations

Covenant on Economic, Social and Cultural Rights (CESCR), 126

CRC (Convention on the Rights of the
    Child), 14, 125, 127–28
Crimea conflict, 92–93, 258
CRPD (Convention on the Rights of Persons
    with Disabilities), 21, 98–99, 104, 126
Cruz, Ted, 140, 167
CSI (Container Security Initiative), 157
CTBT. *See* Comprehensive Test Ban
    Treaty
CTC (Counterterrorism Committee of
    UN), 87
Cultural factor of sovereignty, 30
Currency, 181–83, 192
CUSFTA (Canada-U.S. Free Trade
    Agreement), 187–88
Customary international law, 115–17
Customs and Border Protection (CBP),
    157, 159
CWA (Chemical Weapons Act), 139–40
Cyberspace, 166–69, 259
Cyberwarfare, 168, 259

Daalder, Ivo, 85
A Dangerous Place (Moynihan), 231
Dark web, 167
DEA (Drug Enforcement Agency), 200
Death penalty, 97, 135–36
Declaration of Independence, 43, 50–51,
    53, 62, 222
Decolonization, 33, 226
Dejammet, Alain, 224
DeLauro, Rosa, 172
Delay, Tom, 155
Delegation of authority to international
    organizations, 26, 232–40
DeMint, Jim, 120
Democracy in America (Tocqueville),
    45–46
Democratic Republic of Congo,
    peacekeeping mission in, 238
Democrats: American exceptionalism and,
    50; bipartisan leadership and, 57–58,
    67–68, 75–76; human rights treaty
    ratification of, 127; on League of

Nations, 65–66, 70; on national
    security, 142–43; on Trans-Pacific
    Partnership, 173–75
DePorte, Anton, 51
Deudney, Daniel, 55, 251
Developing countries: globalization and,
    183–84; Internet, lack of control over,
    167
Dewey, Thomas E., 76, 78
Diplomacy: dispute resolution vs., 187–89;
    exceptionalism vs., 126; for immigration
    issues, 215; legal recognition of
    sovereignty and, 33–34; in Middle Ages,
    33; NATO undermining, 83; trade deals,
    alternative to, 185; UN support for,
    148–50; U.S. influence in UN, 245–46
Disarmament. *See* Arms control
Dispute settlement mechanisms: Canada-
    U.S. Free Trade Agreement, 187–88;
    GATT, 24, 188–90; Investor-State
    Dispute Settlement of TTP, 172;
    League of Nations, 4; NAFTA, 188;
    United Nations Convention on the Law
    of the Sea, 164; WTO, 24, 188–89,
    191–92, 194
Dispute settlement understanding (DSU)
    of WTO, 188–89, 191–92, 194
Doha Development Round of WTO, 192,
    259
Dole, Robert, 98–99, 190–91, 234
Doty, Roxanne, 210
Douglas, Stephen A., 46
Drone technology, 151–52, 169–70
Drug Enforcement Agency (DEA), 200
Drug trade, 200, 214
Dublin Regulations, 212
Due process, 111
Duffy, Sean, 167–68
Dulles, John Foster, 76, 248
Dumbarton Oaks negotiations (1944), 76–77

Eagle Forum, 173
East India Company, 37–38
East Timor, conflict in, 151

Ebola outbreak in West Africa (2014–15), 239

Economic and Social Council (ECOSOC), 226–27, 231, 241

Economics: incentives to migrate, 199; inequality in, 201, 214; interdependence in, 72, 187; international cooperation in, 12, 14; nationalism and, 70, 179; political trilemma of world economy, 185–86; pre–World War II, 74. *See also* Globalization; Trade

EEZs (exclusive economic zones), 164

Eighteenth Amendment, 205

Eighth Amendment, 131, 136

Einstein, Albert, 248

Eisenhower, Dwight D., 105

EITI (Extractive Industries Transparency Initiative), 260

Embedded liberalism, 179, 183, 186

Employment: competition from undocumented immigrants, 212; globalization's effect on, 24, 178; migrant labor for, 24, 199, 201, 203–05, 214; trade agreements as threat to, 174

England. *See* United Kingdom

Environmental treaties, 124

Eritrea, refugees from, 212

Ethics: of drone technology, 152; mass atrocity crimes, 151. *See also* Human rights

Ethnic chauvinism, 48

Ethnic identity, 208

Ethnic stereotypes, 202

Eugenics, 204

European Commission (EC), 219

European Court of Justice, 220

Europe and European Union (EU): anti-immigrant sentiments in, 210–11; Brexit, 39, 111, 212, 217–21, 246; history of sovereignty in, 31–33, 39–40; Monroe Doctrine directed toward, 63; pooling authority in, 35, 37, 220; refugee crisis in, 201, 212; as supranationalism, 25, 109–11. *See also* North Atlantic Treaty Organization (NATO); *specific countries*

Exceptionalism: cultural factor of sovereignty as, 30, 253–54; explanation of, 19; history of U.S. sovereignty, 47–52; international law and, 21, 102–03, 107; multilateral obligations and, 13, 41–42; as national identity, 49, 107; NATO membership and, 82; treaty creation and ratification, 125–26

Exchange rates, 181–83

Exclusive economic zones (EEZs), 164

Executive branch of government: arms control treaties, 161; bipartisan leadership and, 57–58, 67–68, 75–76; Bricker Amendment and, 104–05; international law and, 103–04; support for joining United Nations, 78; trade liberalization, 180; UN Security Council relations, 143. *See also specific presidents*

Exemptionalism: expressions of, 125; harm caused by, 128, 262; hypocrisy of, 141; popular sovereignty leading to, 103; U.S. exceptionalism as, 52, 102–03

Exit, Voice, and Loyalty (Hirschman), 245

Extended exclusive economic zones (EEEZs), 129

Extractive Industries Transparency Initiative (EITI), 260

FAIR (Federation for American Immigration Reform), 205

Fair trade, 192–93

Family Research Council, 127

Farewell Address (Washington, 1796), 5, 61, 67, 179

Federalism: Constitution and, 53–54, 60; dangers of, 54; government expansion and, 62; international law vs., 21, 137–40; international obligations vs., 42; post–World War II, 248

The Federalist Papers, 45, 54–55, 61–62, 137

Federalists, 53–54, 60, 62

Federalist Society, 29

Federation for American Immigration
    Reform (FAIR), 205

Feeney, Tom, 136

Fei-Ling Wang, 40

Feldman, Noah, 139

Fidler, David, 239

Fifth Amendment, 131

Financial Action Task Force, 169

Financial Stability Board, 91, 262

Fleischer, Ari, 149

Fonte, John, 9, 113–14

Food and Drug Administration, 259

Foreign exchange transactions, 234–35

Foreign relations law, 101. *See also*
    International law

Foster, Howard, 209

Founders / founding fathers: human rights
    issues in Constitution, 126; on
    international commitments, 1, 3, 17, 50,
    61–62, 67, 180; on international
    cooperation, 50–51; on international
    law, 101; on migrants to United States,
    202; on popular sovereignty, 42–43,
    45–46, 53. *See also* American Revolution

"Four Freedoms" speech (Roosevelt, 1940),
    124

Fourteenth Amendment, 131, 135

France: American Revolution and, 153;
    French Revolution, 45; Treaty of Amity
    and Commerce (1778), 179; UN
    Security Council veto, 88

Franklin, Benjamin, 42–43

Freedom of speech, 127

Free Trade Commission, 188

French Revolution, 45

Froman, Michael, 174

Fulbright Resolution, 75

G-7 (Group of 7), 258

G-8 (Group of 8), 93, 258

G-20 (Group of 20), 91, 258, 262

G-77 (Group of 77), 236

Gaddafi, Moammar, 93

Gandhi, Mahatma, 40–41

Garcia, Denise, 170

Gaulle, Charles de, 111

General Accounting Office (GAO), 191

General Agreement on Tariffs and Trade
    (GATT): benefits of, 181; creation of,
    23–24, 180; dispute settlement
    mechanisms of, 188–90; intrusiveness
    of, 91; Western alliance and, 80

Genetic modifications, 170

Geneva Conventions (1949), 116

Genocide Convention (1948), 104, 105, 124

Geographic isolation of United States, 71–72

Geopolitical position of United States:
    China and, 92–93; as factor in
    sovereignty, 31, 42, 59–60; history of,
    19–20; maritime access, 163–64; national
    security concerns leading to, 60–61;
    Russia and, 92–93; Syrian conflict and, 93

Germany: sovereignty of, 39; UN Security
    Council veto, 88; World War I
    reparations, 236

Gillette, Guy, 76

Gingrich, Newt, 154

Ginsburg, Ruth Bader, 134–35

Global capitalism, 184

Global commons: outer space, 164–66; sea,
    163–64; security of, 23, 145, 162–66

"Global Governance Watch" (AEI and
    Federalist Society), 29

Global government. *See* World government

Globalism, 9, 14, 20, 95, 252

Globalization, 19–20, 172–95; adjusting
    to, 184–87; Bretton Woods system,
    182–87; co-evolution with sovereignty,
    38–39; democratizing, 185–86; as
    factor of sovereignty, 31, 59–60; global
    commons, security of, 163; global
    pandemics, 238–39; hyperglobalization,
    178, 185–86; international borders and,
    206–07; international law and, 21–22;
    maritime access facilitating, 163;
    monetary policy, 181–82; neoliberalism,

183; pace of, 179; post–World War II trade liberalization, 179–81; preparation for, 177–78; public opinion on, 175–76, 184; sovereignty, challenge to, 14–15, 17–18, 95, 107–08, 180, 183; sovereignty bargains and, 23–24, 31, 39, 42, 60, 95, 177, 186; states' rights, influence on, 138; trade, increase in, 176–77; Trans-Pacific Partnership, 172–76; U.S. management of, 11; WTO and, 187–95

Global pandemics, 238–40

Global Parliament of Mayors, 260

Global Recession (2007–08), 24, 91, 184

Global Trends report, 187

Glorious Revolution (England, 1660), 44

Goldsmith, Jack L., 116

Gold standard, 182–83

Gostin, Lawrence, 239

Graham v. Sullivan (2010), 136–37

The Great Betrayal (Buchanan), 191–92

Great Britain. *See* United Kingdom

Great Depression, 72, 74, 181

Greece, refugee crisis in, 201

Greenpeace, 114

Greenstock, Jeremy, 224

Gregory VII (pope), 32

Grew, Joseph, 78

Gross domestic product (GDP), 92

Guatemala, migration to Mexico, 212

Gulf War (1991), 83–84, 147, 153, 154

Gutteres, António, 226, 242

Haass, Richard N., 160, 258

Hamilton, Alexander, 45, 53, 60, 62, 131

Harding, Warren G., 70

Hartz, Louis, 47

Hatch, Orrin, 99, 173

Hay, John, 64

Helms, Jesse, 8, 84–85, 190, 222–25, 244

Henkin, Louis, 105–06

Henry IV (Holy Roman Emperor), 32

Here Come the Black Helicopters! (Morris and McGann), 234–35

Heritage Foundation, 173

Hirschman, Albert, 245

History of sovereignty, 31–58; components of sovereignty, 33–36; European Union and, 39–40; globalization and, 38–39; Middle Ages, 31–33; private corporations and transnational movements, 37–38; in Russia, China, and India, 40–41; U.S. Constitution and, 53–58; U.S. exceptionalism and, 47–52; U.S. popular sovereignty and, 42–47

Hobbes, Thomas, 33, 43–44

Hofstadter, Richard, 10

Holbrooke, Richard, 84, 223

Holland precedent, 140

Holy Roman Empire, 32–33

Home School Legal Defense Association, 98

Hudson Institute, 211

Hull, Cordell, 52, 76, 176

Humanitarian law, 170

Human rights: in Constitution, 126; crimes of, 151; sovereignty and, 126; treaties on, 104–05, 124–28

Human Rights Council of UN, 226–27, 230, 241, 246

Human Rights Watch, 114

Hussein, Saddam, 88, 142, 160

Hyperglobalization, 178, 185–86

IAEA (International Atomic Energy Agency), 16, 89, 226

ICC. *See* International Criminal Court

ICCPR (International Convention on Civil and Political Rights), 105

ICJ (International Court of Justice), 139

Idaho, international law and, 138

Identity. *See* National identity

Ideological factor of sovereignty, 30–31

IEA (International Energy Agency), 91, 236

IMF (International Monetary Fund), 23, 80, 131, 182–83, 262

Immigration Act (1924), 197, 203, 204

Immigration Act (1965), 205

Immigration policy: Bannon on, 10; border security, spending on, 207, 211, 213; of G. H. W. Bush, 205; of G. W. Bush, 206–07; in California, 197, 208; for counterterrorism, 198–99, 205–07; deportations (2009–2015), 211–12; historical, 197, 201–05; League of Nations and, 4; Muslims, travel ban to United States, 10, 24, 198–99; of Obama, 206–07, 209, 211, 213; of Trump, 10, 196–99, 211–14. *See also* International borders

Immigration Reform and Control Act (IRCA, 1986), 205

Import duties, 4–5, 34, 73–74

India: global output of, 92; outer space, competition for, 165; sovereignty of, 40–41

Indian Ocean, pirates in, 258

INF (Intermediate-Range Nuclear Forces Treaty), 124

Infectious diseases, 238–40

Influence: authority vs., 134–35; autonomy vs., 90, 93; as dimension of sovereignty, 8, 12–14, 256; as historical attribute of sovereignty, 35–36; in international organizations, 246; preservation of, 26–27. *See also* Sovereignty bargains

InfoWars, 10

Inhofe, James, 98, 120

Innocent X (pope), 33

Institutional factor of sovereignty, 30–31

Interdependence: alarmism over, 37; economic, 72, 187; exemptionism vs., 52; for global health, 238; impact on sovereignty, 31, 42; international law and, 22; international organizations, need for, 95; League of Nations debate, 69–70; lessons from, 72–74; managing challenges of, 42, 114–15, 179, 215–16; for security, 22, 72, 144, 146; sovereignty's influence over terms of, 34; technological change requiring, 166. *See also* Globalization; Transnational challenges

Intergovernmental Panel on Climate Change (IPCC), 226, 261

Intermediate-Range Nuclear Forces Treaty (INF), 124

International activism, 51–52, 114

International Atomic Energy Agency (IAEA), 16, 89, 226

International Bank of Reconstruction and Development. *See* World Bank

International borders, 24–25, 196–216; border control, 199–201; economic incentives to cross, 199; EU migrant and refugee crisis, 111, 201, 212; Muslim immigrants, U.S. ban on, 10, 24, 198–99; permeability of, 200, 213; risk management for, 214–15; security, spending on, 207, 211; sovereignty, maintaining through, 209–10; sovereignty bargains for, 199, 213, 215–16; terrorism and, 205–07; trade, increase in, 176–77; Trump policy on U.S.-Mexico border, 196–99, 211–14; undocumented immigration across, 208–13; U.S. history of migration, 197, 201–05

International Center for Settlement of Investment Disputers, 173

International Commission on Intervention and State Sovereignty, 151

International commitments: American exceptionalism and, 51–53; benefits of, 14–17; constitutionality of, 13–14, 19, 57; exiting, 16–17, 195, 246, 253; founding fathers on, 1, 3, 17, 50, 61–62, 180; sovereignty and, 2, 7–9, 13, 29; sovereignty bargains and, 15–16; U.S. historical aversion to, 1–2, 13–14, 20; U.S. moratorium on, 10. *See also specific treaties and organizations*

International Convention on Civil and Political Rights (ICCPR), 105

International cooperation: for arms control, 22–23, 162; autonomy and independence vs., 14; in cyberspace,

166–67; Declaration of Independence and, 50; in economics, 12, 14; international law and, 22; as necessity for sovereignty, 250–51; Obama foreign policy and, 89–90; pooling for, 235; sovereignty bargains for, 257, 260–61; U.S. Constitution and, 30–31. *See also* International security; Transnational challenges

International Court of Justice (ICJ), 139

International Criminal Court (ICC): Article 98 agreements with United States, 112; as challenge to U.S. Constitution, 86; India, lack of participation in, 41; Rome Statute, 14, 85, 103, 111–12, 114, 120; as supranationalism, 111–13; U.S. lack of participation in, 14, 29, 85, 122

International Energy Agency (IEA), 91, 236

International Health Regulations (IHR), 238–40

Internationalism: of American public, 254–55; of G. H. W. Bush, 85; disagreement within, 6, 95; League of Nations membership as, 6, 65–66, 70; post–World War II sovereignty and, 72–73; UN membership and, 75, 79

International law, 21–22, 97–141; activism through, 21, 29, 106, 116; Bricker Amendment and, 104–05; challenge to U.S. Constitution, 19, 62, 86, 98–102, 132–33; citing in U.S. court cases, 21–22, 97–98, 107, 109, 132–37, 139; criticisms of, 105–06; in Declaration of Independence, 62; defenses of, 105–06; defined, 100; European Union, supranationalism of, 109–11; federalism vs., 21, 137–40; freedom, infringement upon, 14, 16; general principles of, 191; globalization and, 21–22; gridlock over treaties and conventions, 128–29; human rights treaties, 124–28; International Criminal Court,

supranationalism of, 111–13; international diversity, reconciling, 51–52; Investor-State Dispute Settlement of TTP, 172–74; legal recognition of sovereignty and, 33–34; limits on treaties and conventions, 131; in Middle Ages, 33; multilateral treaties, sovereignty and, 117–24; sovereignty, threat to, 98–101, 106–07, 172; sovereignty bargains for, 21, 99, 102, 106, 134–35, 256–57; state's rights and, 56, 98, 137–40; treaty ratification, 102–04; workarounds for treaties and conventions, 130; WTO and, 187–95

International Monetary Fund (IMF), 23, 80, 131, 182–83, 262

International organizations, 24–25, 217–51; accountability of, 47, 242; alternatives to, 94; Brexit and, 217–21; checks and balances for, 243; coalitions, preference for, 86, 88–89, 237, 260; coalitions undermining, 261; delegation of authority to, 26, 232–40; exiting, 245–47; financial leverage in, 223, 243–45; joining, benefits of, 237–38; limits of, 257; national security, benefits to, 72, 78; persistent objections to actions of, 245; pooling in, 235–36; post–World War II cooperative action and, 74; public opinion on, 218–19, 254–56; reform of, 90–91; remedies for pathologies of, 240–47; sovereignty, threat to, 25–26, 221–22, 225, 246; staff of, 242; sunset provisions for, 241–42; transnational challenges, response to, 93–94, 238–40; United Nations, U.S. experience with, 221–32; U.S. building of, 20, 51, 74, 102, 178, 189; U.S. Constitution and, 222; value conflicts among new members to, 92; world government through, 247–51; World Health Organization as case study, 238–40. *See also specific organizations*

International Seabed Authority, 164

International security, 22–23, 142–71;
arms control and sovereignty, 155–60;
contingent sovereignty of nations,
150–52; of cyberspace, 166–69; drone
use and, 151–52, 169–70; of global
commons, 162–66; international
agreements for, 14; multilateral peace
operations and sovereignty, 153–55;
opposition to arms control, 160–62;
technological changes in, 166–70; UN
Charter for, 147–52
International Security Assistance Force
(ISAF), 88
International Trade Organization (ITO),
180–81
Internet, 166–69
Internet Assigned Numbers Authority
(IANA), 167–68
Internet Corporation for Assigned Names
and Numbers (ICANN), 167, 260
Investor-State Dispute Settlement (ISDS),
172–74
Iran, nuclear weapons of, 89, 143
Iraq: Kuwait, invasion of, 88; U.S. invasion
of (2003), 88, 105, 142–43, 147, 149
Iraqi Governing Council, 89
IRCA (Immigration Reform and Control
Act, 1986), 205
ISAF (International Security Assistance
Force), 88
Islamic people, travel ban to United States,
10, 24, 198–99
Islamic State, 168, 198
Isolationism: in early 20th century, 71;
globalization vs., 186; impracticality of,
78; of India, 41; internationalism vs.,
72–73; League of Nations debate and,
5–7, 65, 69–70; legal, 100; post–World
War II security and, 75–76; pre–World
War II and Pearl Harbor attack, 71–72;
public opinion and, 255; Trump foreign
policy and, 9, 51
ITO (International Trade Organization),
180–81

Jackson, Robert, 32–33
James I (king of England), 43
Japan: attack on Pearl Harbor (1941),
71–72; migration to United States,
204
Jay, John, 43, 45, 101
Jefferson, Thomas: on international
commitments, 3, 17, 50, 62, 101; on
popular sovereignty, 53
Jentleson, Bruce, 146
Johnson, Andrew, 63
Johnson, Boris, 217–19
Johnson, Lyndon B., 205
Johnson, Samuel, 8
Joint Comprehensive Plan of Action
(JCPOA), 143
Jones, Bruce, 162
Judicial branch of government: activism of,
98, 132, 191, 192; citing international
law in decisions, 21–22, 97–98, 107, 109,
132–37, 139–40; on death penalty, 97,
135–36; international law vs., 188;
treaty interpretation by, 101

Kansas-Nebraska Act (1854), 46
Kant, Immanuel, 249
Kellogg-Briand Pact (1928), 71
Kennan, George, 80–81
Kennedy, Anthony, 97, 136
Kennedy, John F., 49, 155–56
Keohane, Robert, 240
Kerry, John, 142–43
Keynes, John Maynard, 57
Kim, Jim Young, 242
King, Larry, 87
Kirkpatrick, Jeanne, 222
Knight v. Florida (1999), 135
Knox, Philander, 68–69
Koh, Harold Hongju, 113
Korean War, 153
Kosovo conflict (1999), 84, 105, 147, 151
Kreps, Sarah, 150
Krishna, Gopal, 41
Ku, Julian, 111, 140

Kuwait, Iraqi invasion of, 148–49
Kyl, John, 29, 107, 110, 126
Kyoto Protocol, 85, 120, 124, 258

Lafayette, Marquis de, 153
Lamborn, Doug, 9, 52
Lankford, James, 167
LaPierre, Wayne, 161
Lawrence, Robert Z., 194
Lawrence v. Texas (2003), 135–36
League of Nations: collective security
    benefits, 69; constraints on sovereignty,
    65–69, 144; reasons for failure of, 3,
    75; rejection of, 7, 69–71, 102; U.S.
    debate over joining, 1–7, 64–71
League to Enforce Peace (LEP), 66
Lee, Mike, 98, 167
Legal recognition of sovereignty, 33–35
Legislative branch of government. *See*
    Congress
Legro, Jeffrey, 74
Lehrer, Jim, 142
Les Six Livres de la République (Bodin), 43
Leviathan (Hobbes), 43–44
Levin, Sander, 194
Lewis, Jeffrey, 155
Liberal internationalists, 8, 13, 65, 73, 126,
    222
Libya conflict (2011), 93, 152
Limited Test Ban Treaty (1963), 124
Lincoln, Abraham, 56
Lindbergh, Charles, 9, 71
Lindsay, James, 85
Lisbon Treaty (2009), 218, 220–21
Locke, John, 43–45, 47
Lodge, Henry Cabot, 1–7, 65–67, 69–70,
    204
London Economic Conference, 74
Lowell, A. Lawrence, 1–7, 204
Lynn, William, 165

Macedo, Stephen, 240
Macedonia, UNPREDEP mission in,
    154–55

Mackinac Declaration (1943), 75
Madison, James, 45, 53–55
Manifest destiny, 48
Mao Tse-Tung, 40
Maritime law, 93, 163. *See also* United
    Nations Convention on the Law of the
    Sea (UNCLOS)
Maritime shipping, 157, 159, 163–64
Marrakesh Treaty (1994), 187, 192
Marshall, John, 46, 55, 56, 101
Marshall Plan, 220, 236
Martin, Trayvon, 126
Mary (queen of England), 44
May, Theresa, 221
McCaul, Michael, 198
McConnell, Mitch, 173
McGann, Eileen, 235
Mead, Walter Russell, 110
Medellin, José, 139
Medellin v. Texas (2008), 139–40
Melville, Herman, 48–49
Merry, Robert, 209
Metcalfe, Daryl, 209
Mexican-American War, 63
Mexico: Bracero guest worker program,
    205; economic improvements in,
    211–12; immigrants from Guatemala,
    212; immigrants to United States, 196,
    207–08, 213; Trump-proposed border
    wall, 196–99, 211, 214; U.S. relations,
    9, 25, 197, 199, 214–15. *See also* North
    American Free Trade Agreement
Middle Ages, 31–33
Middle East, refugees from, 198–99
Migration: anti-immigrant sentiments in
    Europe, 210–11; asylum seekers, 201,
    208–09; international cooperation for,
    215–16; national identity, threat to,
    201–02, 208, 210–11, 216; nationalism,
    effect on, 201–03; undocumented,
    208–13; U.S. history of, 197, 201–05.
    See also Immigration policy;
    International borders; Refugees
Migratory Bird Treaty (1918), 138

Military (U.S.): drone use, 151–52, 169–70; foreign command of, 153–55; globally deployed, vulnerability of, 86; international commitments of, 101–02; NATO obligations, 82–83; protection of soldiers abroad, 112; spending on, 84; UN Charter on use of force, 147–48; UN Security Council, provision of troops to, 77, 145, 153, 155, 237–38. *See also specific wars and conflicts*

Miller v. Alabama (2012), 136

Mine Ban Treaty (1997), 14, 103, 114, 124

Minilateral coalitions, 149–50, 157, 258, 261–62

Minilateral institutions, 15, 27, 94

Missouri v. Holland (1920), 138

Monarchies, 43–44

Monetary policy, 179–82

Monnet, Jean, 111

Monroe, James, 63

Monroe Doctrine: expansion of United States, 63–64; League of Nations extension of, 4–5, 67–70; NATO as alternative to, 81; philosophy of United States, 82; United Nations and, 79

Montreal Protocol on Ozone-Depleting Substances, 124

Moravcsik, Andrew, 125–26, 240

More, Thomas, 249

Morgenthau, Hans, 100, 248

Morris, Dick, 235

Moynihan, Daniel Patrick, 231

Multinational corporations, 38, 172, 174, 178

Mundt, Karl, 75

Muslims, travel ban to United States, 10, 24, 198–99

Nader, Ralph, 190

NAFTA (North American Free Trade Agreement), 9–10, 24, 173, 187–88

NAM (Non-Aligned Movement), 39–41, 236

NAT (North Atlantic Treaty), 82

National Center for Home Education, 127

National Foreign Trade Council, 180

National identity: exceptionalism as, 49, 107; internationalism vs., 6; migrants as threat to, 201–02, 208, 210–11, 216; sovereignty debates and, 8, 18

National Intelligence Council, 187

Nationalism: economic, 70, 179; effect on sovereignty, 33; ethnic and racial stereotypes in, 202; foreign command of military, 154; globalism vs., 95, 252; internationalism vs., 6; migration, effect on, 201–03; political rhetoric on, 10; racism in, 48; terrorism, response to, 87; white nationalist movement, 10, 48; world government vs., 247, 250

National Origins Act (1924), 204–05

National Quota Act (1921), 204

National Rifle Association, 114

National security: border security and, 205–07; international organizations determining, 144; opposition to arms control, 160–61; outer space code of conduct, 165; sovereignty bargains for, 144–46, 150, 153, 155–57

National Security Entry-Exit Registration System (NSEERS), 206

National Security Strategy (2002), 87–88

National Security Strategy (2008), 90

Native Americans, sovereign rights of, 56–57

NATO. *See* North Atlantic Treaty Organization

Nehru, Jawaharlal, 41

Neoliberalism, 183

Neutrality, 41, 61–62

Neutrality Acts (1930s), 71

New, Michael G., 154–55

New sovereigntists, 29–30, 225

New York: climate change actions of, 260; September 11 terrorist attacks (2001), 87–88, 206

New York v. United States (1992), 137

Niblett, Robin, 219

Nishimura, Mika, 156

Nixon, Richard, 183, 200

Non-Aligned Movement (NAM), 39–41, 236

Nongovernmental organizations (NGOs): competition with states, 37–38; increase in, 38; Russian objections to, 40; as threat to sovereignty, 106, 113–14, 116, 141; UN treaty negotiations, influence in, 113

Nonintervention policies of UN Charter, 151

Non-self-execution of treaties and conventions, 103, 105, 125, 131

North American Free Trade Agreement (NAFTA), 9–10, 24, 173, 187–88

North Atlantic Treaty (NAT), 82

North Atlantic Treaty Organization (NATO): alternatives to, 80–81; Article V of, 83, 87; benefits to United States, 81; burden sharing within, 81, 145; creation of, 20, 80–81; Kosovo conflict (1999), 105; Libya intervention (2011), 152; 9/11 terrorist attacks response of, 87; Trump's view of, 145; U.S. role in, 82–83; war on terrorism, role in, 88

North Korea: cyberattacks of, 168; nuclear weapons of, 89, 157, 161

Northwest Ordinance (1787), 63

Notter, Harley, 74

Nowrasteh, Alex, 198

NSEERS (National Security Entry-Exit Registration System), 206

Nuclear energy, 157

Nuclear Non-Proliferation Treaty (NPT), 41, 131, 156–57

Nuclear Security Summit, 258–59

Nuclear weapons: arms control and disarmament agreements, 155–56; of Iran, 89, 143; monitoring, 89; of North Korea, 89, 157, 161; testing, CTBT against, 161; of United States, 83, 157

Nuclear weapons states (NWS), 157

Nullification Crisis (1832–33), 55–56

Nye Committee hearings, 71

Obama, Barack: on American exceptionalism, 49; arms control treaties, 161; Asian Infrastructure Investment Bank, opposition to, 262; on Brexit, 217, 219; Convention on the Rights of Persons with Disabilities, 99; global interdependence and, 20; immigration policy of, 206–07, 209, 211, 213; international organization reform of, 90–91; Iraq, dismantling nuclear weapons of, 143; Libya intervention, UNSC authorization for, 147; medicine regulations and, 259; multilateral foreign policy of, 89–90; Nuclear Security Summit, 258–59; outer space code of conduct, 165; Paris Accord on Climate Change, 253; Rome Statute of ICC, 111, 113; Syrian refugees, acceptance of, 198; Trans-Pacific Partnership, 172, 174; UN funding issues and, 244; on U.S. stewardship of Internet, 167–68; war on terrorism and, 151–52

O'Connor, Sandra Day, 135–36, 137

OECD (Organization for Economic Cooperation and Development), 91, 92, 234, 236

Office of the United States Trade Representative (USTR), 185

OIOS (Office of Internal Oversight Services of UN), 243

Olney, Richard, 64

Open Door Notes (Hay), 64

Operation Camarena, 214

Optional Protocol to the Vienna Convention on Consular Relations (VCCR), 139

Organization for Economic Cooperation and Development (OECD), 91, 92, 234, 236

Organization for the Prohibition of Chemical Weapons (OPCW), 159–60

Otter, Butch, 138

Outer space, 164–66

Outer Space Treaty (1967), 165

Paine, Thomas, 48, 50

Pakistan: human rights issues in, 246; war on terrorism and, 151, 231

Palestine, UNESCO membership and, 244

Palestinian Authority (PA), 244

Paquet Habana case (1900), 116

Paris Accord on Climate Change, 9, 252–53, 258, 260–61

Paris Peace Conference (1919), 1–2, 6–7, 68

Partial Test Ban Treaty (PTBT), 156

Pascual, Carlos, 162

Patriotism, 211

Patten, Christopher, 87

Paul, Ron, 155, 210

Peace of Augsburg (1555), 32

Peace of Westphalia (1648), 32–34, 40, 250

Peace operations: of United Nations, 84, 237–38, 244; of UN Security Council, 231; U.S. sovereignty and, 153–55, 171

Pearl Harbor, attack on (1941), 71–72

Peña Nieto, Enrique, 197

Penn, William, 247

People with disabilities, 21, 98–99, 104, 126

Perot, H. Ross, 190

Pew Research Center, 255

PHEICs (public health emergencies of international concern), 238–40

Philpott, A. J., 1

Pillay, Navi, 126

Pinckney, Charles, 54

Pirates in Indian Ocean, 258

Pletka, Danielle, 225

Political ideology, 18

Political trilemma of world economy, 185–86

Polk, James K., 63

Pooling in international organizations, 26, 35, 37, 220, 235–36

Popular sovereignty: American exceptionalism, expression of, 30; in Constitution, 26, 53, 55, 222;

explanation of, 18, 41; immigrants as threat to, 213; international law vs., 21, 103, 112, 120–21, 131; national identity and, 201–02; NATO membership and, 82; public opinion on, 254–55; source of, 42–47; spread of, 34

Populist nationalism, 10

Portugal, criticism of U.S. policy on treaties, 131

Preemptive strike, 142–43, 171

Presidential campaign (1920), 70

Presidential campaign (1944), 76–78

Presidential campaign (2004), 142–43

Presidential campaign (2008), 90

Presidential campaign (2016): America First rhetoric of, 9, 23, 95, 127, 254; American exceptionalism and, 49–50, 52; immigration policy promises, 196–97; NATO support, debate over, 145; Russian involvement in, 167; trade politics, 175, 177

Principles for Responsible Investment, 242

Program for Public Consultation, 254–55

Proliferation Security Initiative (PSI), 88–89

Protectionist policies, 73, 175–76, 194

Protestantism, 32, 49

PTBT (Partial Test Ban Treaty), 156

Public Citizen, 174–75

Public health emergencies of international concern (PHEICs), 238–40

Public opinion: on immigration, 196, 201, 206, 210; on international organizations, 218–19, 254–56; on trade and globalization, 17, 175–76, 184

Putin, Vladimir, 40, 92–93

Quinlan, Andrew, 234

Rabkin, Jeremy, 50–51, 110, 191–92, 194–95

Racism: Bricker Amendment and, 104–05; migration and, 202; in white nationalism, 10, 48

Rarick, John R., 221

Reagan, Ronald, 49–50, 178, 205, 208

Reciprocal Trade Agreements Act (RTAA, 1934), 180

"Re-Declaration of Independence: Petition to protect U.S. Sovereignty," 10

Reformation, 32

Refugees: admissions process for, 198; from Central America, 211–12; EU crisis and, 111, 201, 212; suspension of U.S. admission, 10, 24, 198–99; total world-wide, 201

Rehnquist, William, 97

Religious influence in United States, 49

Remittances, 201

Report of the Ebola Interim Assessment Panel, 239–40

Republicans: American exceptionalism and, 49; bipartisan leadership and, 57–58, 67–68, 75–76; on foreign command of military, 154; on human rights treaties, 127; international commitments, aversion to, 29–30; on international law, 132; on League of Nations, 65–69; on multilateral treaties, 117; national security and, 142–43; on outer space code of conduct, 165; on trade, 175; on Trans-Pacific Partnership, 172–75; UN peace operations, restrictions on, 84; WTO creation, support for, 187

Reservations, understandings, and declarations (RUDs) in treaties, 125, 127, 131

Responsibility to Protect (R2P), 151–52

Revolutionary War (U.S.). *See* American Revolution

Reynolds, Robert, 75–76

Rice, Condoleezza, 86

Risch, James E., 126

Rivkin, David, 107

Rodrik, Dani, 185–86

Rogers, Mike, 29–30, 155

Rohrabacher, Dana, 172

Rome Statute of International Criminal Court (ICC): role of, 114; unsigning of, 85, 112; U.S. rejection of, 14, 103, 111–12, 120

Roosevelt, Franklin D.: bipartisan leadership and, 58; "Four Freedoms" speech, 124; international institution building, 20, 51, 74, 102, 254; on isolationism, 71, 72; post–World War II cooperative action of, 73–74; reelection of, 78; trade policy of, 180; UN creation and, 74–77

Roosevelt, Theodore, 49, 65–66, 68

Root, Elihu, 68

Roper v. Simmons (2005), 97, 136–37

Ros-Lehtinen, Ileana, 225, 244–45

Rousseau, Jean-Jacques, 45

Rudolph, Christopher, 216

Ruggie, John, 116, 179

Rumsfeld, Donald, 87

Rusk, Dean, 8, 118, 156, 240

Russia: 2016 U.S. presidential election, influence in, 167; Arctic Ocean, claim on, 163–64; arms control treaty violations of, 161; Crimea, invasion of, 92–93, 258; cyberattacks of, 168; G-8, suspension from, 258; global output of, 92; Libya conflict, criticism of, 152; outer space, competition for, 165; sanctions on, 93; sovereignty of, 40; Syria conflict, blocking UNSC actions in, 93, 152; Ukraine conflict and, 92–93; UN Security Council, opposition to adding members, 91; U.S. relations, 92–93. *See also* Soviet Union

Rwanda, conflict in, 151

Ryan, Paul, 173

San Bernardino, California, massacre (2015), 198

Sanders, Bernie, 173, 175, 177

Santorum, Rick, 98

SARS (severe acute respiratory syndrome), 89, 239

Satellites, 164–65

Scalia, Antonin, 97–98, 132, 135–36

Schengen Agreement, 212

Schooner Exchange v. *McFaddon* (1812), 46

Scowcroft, Brent, 148–49, 153

Second Amendment, 161

Second Treatise on Government (Locke), 44

Security. *See* International security; National security

Security Assistance Force (SAF), 87–88

Security Council (UN): adding members, opposition to, 91; creation of, 226; ICC, referrals to, 113; negotiations over power of, 76–77; nuclear weapons of Iraq, dismantling, 143; peace operations of, 231; reform of, 92; Resolution 1540, 89; secretary general, selection of, 242; Syrian conflict, response to, 93, 152; terrorism, combating, 87; troops, provision of, 77, 145, 153; U.S. national security conflict with, 146–47; U.S. position in, 131, 241; use of force, authorizing, 145, 147, 148–52, 171; veto provision of, 76, 80; war on terrorism, 88–89, 146

Self-determination: Brexit, causes of, 219; in India, 40; popular sovereignty and, 202; sovereignty and, 33, 37; UN Charter principle of, 148

Self-reliance, 144, 146, 257

Self-rule. *See* Popular sovereignty

Senate Foreign Relations Committee, 8, 103

"Sense of the House" resolution, 29, 136

September 11, 2001, terrorist attacks, 87–88, 206

Sessions, Jeff, 175, 192, 209

Seventeenth Amendment, 55

Severe acute respiratory syndrome (SARS), 89, 239

Shakespeare, William, 43

Shanghai Cooperation Organization, 262

Shipping containers, 157, 159, 215

Shipping lanes, 163–64

Sims, Kathleen, 138

Slaughter, Anne-Marie, 110–11, 115

Slaves and slavery, 46, 56, 116

Smith, Bob, 222

Smoot-Hawley tariff, 73–74

The Social Contract (Rousseau), 45

Socialism, 127

Somalia: conflict in, 84; Convention on the Rights of the Child, 125; pirates in, 258; refugees from, 212; sovereignty in, 34; UN peace operation in (1993), 154; war on terrorism and, 151

Sources of sovereignty, 41–58; exceptionalism, 47–52; popular sovereignty, 42–47; U.S. Constitution, 53–58

South Africa, global output of, 92

South Carolina, secession from Union, 56

South China Sea, 163

South Korea, U.S. defense commitment to, 103

Sovereignty, 18, 28–58; arms control as threat to, 160–62; Brexit, causes of, 218–21; coalitions to preserve, 257–60, 263; contingent, 22, 150–52, 250; dimensions of, 12–13; in European Union, 31–33, 39–40, 109–11; explanation of, 31–32; in French Constitution, 45; globalization as challenge to, 14–15, 17–18, 95, 107–08, 180, 183; human rights issues and, 126; ideological factors of, 30–31; immigration and, 209–10; infectious disease reporting vs., 238–40; institutional factors of, 30–31; international commitments and, 2, 7–10, 13, 29; international law as threat to, 98–101, 106–07, 172; international organizations as threat to, 25–26, 221–22, 225, 246; international security, 150–52; as multi-dimensional concept, 11–13, 256; of nations threatening United States, 150–52; Republicans and, 29–30; self-reliance to preserve, 61;

transnational challenges and, 17–18, 36, 93; Trump policy and, 9–10, 117, 175–76; world government vs., 249–50; World Trade Organization as threat to, 189–95. *See also* History of sovereignty; Popular sovereignty; Sources of sovereignty

Sovereignty bargains: for arms control, 22–23, 81, 155–56, 159–60, 162; in coalitions, 86, 88–89; for collective security, 85, 170; for cyberspace control, 168; dimensions in, 12–13; explanation of, 15–18; global interdependence and, 20; globalization and, 23–24, 31, 39, 42, 60, 95, 177, 186; for international border security, 199, 213, 215–16; for international cooperation, 15–16, 257, 260–61; international law and, 21, 99, 102, 106, 134–35, 256–57; international organizations and, 26, 238, 246; League of Nations participation, 64–66, 68; maritime law and, 164; minilateral institutions easing, 94; for national security, 144–46, 150, 153, 155–57; NATO participation, 81; necessity of, 263; for outer space access, 164, 166; post–World War II cooperative action as, 74; technological innovation, threat of, 166; trade law, 193–94; transnational challenges and, 93; for treaty participation, 117–18, 120, 155; for UN participation, 77, 84–85; for WTO participation, 189

Sovereignty Caucus, 9, 52, 225

Sovereignty or Submission (Fonte), 9, 114

Sovereignty triangle, 12–13. *See also* Sovereignty bargains

Soviet Union: UN creation and, 76–77; UN Security Council veto of, 80. *See also* Cold War

Space-based systems, 164–65

Spain: revolutions in colonies of, 62; war with United States, 64

Spiro, Peter, 29

Stalin, Joseph, 80

Stamp Act (England, 1765), 44

Stanford v. Kentucky (1989), 135

States' rights: in Articles of Confederation, 54; Civil War resulting from, 56; in Declaration of Independence, 53; globalization, influence of, 138; international law and, 98, 137–40; in U.S. Constitution, 19, 42, 55

Stedman, Stephen, 162

Steel imports to United States, 192

Steel Safeguards case (2003), 192

Steinberg, James B., 149

Stereotypes, racial and ethnic, 202

Stettinius, Edward, 78

Stiglitz, Joseph, 183

Stockholm Convention on Persistent Organic Pollutants, 124

Straddling Fish Stocks Convention, 124

Strategic Arms Reduction Treaties (START I and II), 124

Sudan, peacekeeping mission in, 238

Sugar Act (England, 1764), 44

Summers, Lawrence, 183

Sunset provisions for international organizations, 241–42

Supranationalism, international law as: European Union, 109–11; International Criminal Court, 111–13. *See also* World government

Supreme Court (U.S.): on death penalty, 97, 135–36; international law in decision making of, 97, 107, 132–37, 139–40. *See also specific cases*

Sweden, criticism of U.S. policy on treaties, 131

Syrian conflict: chemical weapons used in, 148, 160; refugees resulting from, 198, 212; UN Security Council actions, 93, 152; U.S. involvement in, 147–48

Taft, Robert, 75, 82, 182

Taft, William Howard, 66, 69

Taliban, 87–88

Taming Globalization (Ku and Yoo), 140

Tariffs, 73–74, 91, 175, 180, 192–93

TheTeaParty.net, 173

Technological innovation: biotechnology, 170; border security spending, 207; cyberspace security, 166–69; cyberwarfare, 168, 259; drones, 151–52, 169–70; migration, facilitating, 201; outer space, 165

Tenth Amendment, 137–39. *See also* States' rights

Territorial seas, 164

Terrorism and counterterrorism: border control and, 25, 197–99, 207, 214; California massacre (2015), 198; collective security organizations' response to, 87, 151; Container Security Initiative for, 157, 159; cyberattacks, 169; immigration policy, 198–99; prisoners-of-war privileges and, 116; September 11, 2001 terrorist attacks, 87–88, 206; as transnational threat, 144–45; Trump executive order on immigration and, 10, 198–99; U.S. unilateral response to, 87–89; war on terrorism, 87–89, 142–43, 146, 151–52, 231. *See also* International security; Transnational challenges

Texas: annexation of, 63; international obligations, 139

Thatcher, Margaret, 178

Thomas, Clarence, 97, 135, 140

Thornburgh, Richard, 99

Thurmond, Strom, 190

Tianxia, 40

Tichenor, Daniel J., 204

Tocqueville, Alexis de, 45–46, 48, 137, 253

Totalitarianism, 45

TPP. *See* Trans-Pacific Partnership

Trade: with China, 64, 175, 192–93, 262; constitutionality of agreements, 173–74; dispute settlement mechanisms for, 172, 187–88; illegal drugs, 200, 214; increase in, globalization and, 176–77;

international commitments, 61–62; international organizations for, reform of, 91; under League of Nations, 4–5; liberalization of, 172–76, 178, 182; origins of, 179–82, 261; postwar internationalism, 73–74; public opinion on, 175–76; terms of interdependence and, 34; Trump foreign policy and, 9–10; welfare state and safety nets resulting from, 38. *See also* Globalization; *specific trade agreements and organizations*

Trade Policy Agenda, of Trump administration, 176

Transatlantic Trade and Investment Partnership (TTIP), 217

Transgovernmental networks, 114–15

Transnational challenges: city coalitions for, 259–60; coalition vs. international organization use in, 88–89; infectious diseases, 238–40; international cooperation for, 2, 11, 29; international law for, 108; international organizations for, 237; national security and, 144–45; Obama foreign policy for, 90; piecemeal vs. comprehensive approaches to, 259; public opinion on, 255; sovereignty and, 17–18, 36, 93. *See also* Arms control; Terrorism and counterterrorism

Transnational organizations: customary international law, 115–17; nongovernmental organizations, 113–14; unaccountable transgovernmental networks, 114–15. *See also specific organizations*

Trans-Pacific Partnership (TPP): debate over membership, 172–75; U.S. withdrawal from, 9–10, 175–76, 262

Transparency International, 242

Treaties and conventions: for arms control and disarmament, 41, 120, 124, 131, 155–59; benefits to Americans, 118–19; Congressional oversight of, 19, 100, 120, 124, 127, 161; democracy, expression of, 108–09, 117–18; exceptionalism and, 125–26; federal responsibility for, 101, 103–04; gridlock over, 128–29; on human rights, 124–28; increase in ratification of, 118; limits on, strategies for, 131; non-self-execution of, 103, 105, 125, 131; ratifying, 21; reservations, understandings, and declarations (RUDs), 125, 127, 131; sovereignty bargains for, 117–18; U.S. rejection of, 119–20; workarounds for, 130. *See also* International law; *specific treaties*

Treaty of Amity and Commerce (1778), 179

Treaty of Lisbon (2009), 110

Treaty of Versailles (1919), 236

Tribal rights, 56–57

Trop v. Dulles (1958), 97, 135

Truman, Harry S.: bipartisan leadership and, 58; Bricker Amendment and, 104–05; international institution building, 20, 51, 102, 254; on isolationism, 72; NATO and, 82; trade liberalization and, 180; UN approval by, 78–79

Trump, Donald J.: American exceptionalism and, 51; antiglobalization rhetoric, 175, 184–85; on border security, 24; on Brexit, 218; burden sharing within NATO, 81; election of, 9, 95; executive orders of, 9–10, 117, 198–99, 245; on international commitments, 9, 30, 244–47; national security vision of, 145; new sovereigntists and, 30; Paris Accord on Climate Change, withdrawal from, 252–53, 260; Syria intervention, UNSC lack of authorization for, 147–48; Trans-Pacific Partnership, withdrawal from, 176, 262; treaties, moratorium on, 117; on undocumented immigration, 196–99, 211–14; WTO,

objections to, 192–95. *See also* Presidential campaign (2016)

TTIP (Transatlantic Trade and Investment Partnership), 217

Ukraine conflict, 92–93

UN Charter: approval of, 78; on armed forces, 84, 147–48; creation of, 102, 124; on domestic jurisdiction, 34, 76; financial and legal obligations of member states, 245; human rights crimes, nonintervention vs., 151; public opinion on, 255; UN central organs created by, 226; U.S. position in, 131, 241; on world government, 251

UN Committee on Disarmament, 236

UN Convention against Torture, 131

UN Convention on the Elimination of All Forms of Racial Discrimination, 105

UN Convention on the Elimination of Discrimination against Women (CEDAW), 125

UN Convention on the Rights of Persons with Disabilities (CRPD), 21, 98–99, 104, 126

UN Convention on the Rights of the Child (CRC), 14, 125, 127–28

UN Counterterrorism Committee (CTC), 87

UN Economic and Social Council (ECOSOC), 226–27, 231, 241

UN Framework Convention on Climate Change (UNFCCC), 258

Unilateralism: G. W. Bush foreign policy as, 85–86, 89–90; impracticality of, 78; international law vs., 103; as isolationism, 50, 65; political and military self-reliance as, 61–62; post–Cold War, 83–84; in war on terrorism, 87–88

UN International Covenant on Human Rights, 127

United Kingdom (U.K.): exit from EU, 39, 111, 212, 217–21, 246; history of government in, 43–45; United Nations creation and, 76–77; War of 1812, 62

United Nations (UN): arms control treaties, 160–62; arms trafficking reduction, 85; Assistance Mission in Afghanistan, 89; autonomy of United States, 84–85; budget of, 226, 231, 243–44; Cold War, effect of, 79–80; collective security and, 22; creation of, 20, 74–79, 102; expansion of, 226–27, 255; Gulf War (1991), 83–84; human rights treaties, 104–05, 124–28; Macedonia, Preventive Deployment mission in, 154–55; member state self-interest, 227, 230–31; new members of, 91–92; nongovernmental organizations' influence in, 113–14; peace operations of, 84, 237–38, 244; Responsibility to Protect (R2P) citizens of, 151–52; revenue sources of, 234–35; shared authority within, 35; skepticism of, 86; veto provision of, 76, 79, 80. *See also* United States–United Nations relations; *specific bodies and conventions*

United Nations Commission on International Trade Law, 173

United Nations Convention on the Law of the Sea (UNCLOS), 14, 21, 119–20, 164

United Nations Educational, Scientific and Cultural Organization (UNESCO), 221–22, 244

United Nations General Assembly (UNGA): conflict among members, 231, 236; creation of, 226; expansion of UN through, 226–27; U.S. relations with, 241

United Nations Industrial Development Organization (UNIDO), 241

United Nations Organization (UNO), 102

United Nations Relief and Rehabilitation Agency (UNRRA), 241

United Nations Security Council (UNSC), 143, 147–48, 149–50, 152, 153, 171

United States: citizenship in, 48; collective security leadership by, 65, 84; Constitutional conflicts with global leadership, 30–31; expansion of, 63; globalization and, 11, 20, 177–78; history of sovereignty in, 39–41, 60–61; human rights treaties, 124–28; immigration history in, 197, 201–05; international institution building by, 20, 51, 74, 102, 178, 189, 254; lack of participation in treaties, 13–14; Mexican relations, 9, 25, 197, 199, 214–15; military spending, 84; NATO, role in, 82–83; neutrality of, 61–62; public opinion on, 255; Russia, "reset" policy, 92–93; Spain, war with, 64; terrorist attacks in, 87–88, 198; trade policy in, 192; war on terrorism, 87–89, 142–43, 146, 151–52, 231. *See also* American Revolution; Exceptionalism; Military; National security; Popular sovereignty; *specific wars and conflicts*

United States–United Nations relations: human rights issues, 126; multilateral peace operations and U.S. sovereignty, 153–55; national security conflict with UNSC, 146–47; remedies for, 240–41; as threat to U.S. sovereignty, 25–26, 221–22, 225; Trump on, 10; U.S. bill to withdraw from, 29–30, 221; U.S. contributions, 10, 226, 243–45; U.S. position in UNSC, 131, 241

United World Federalists, 248

Universal Declaration of Human Rights (1948), 124, 126

UN Office of Internal Oversight Services (OIOS), 243

UN Trusteeship Council, 226

U.S. Agency for International Development (USAID), 232

U.S. Term Limits, Inc. v. Thornton (1995), 55
USTR (Office of the United States Trade Representative), 185
Utopia (More), 249

Vandenberg, Arthur, 58, 71, 75–76, 79, 82
Vaubel, Roland, 236
Versailles Peace Treaty (1920), 7, 70, 104
Vienna Convention on Consular Relations (VCCR), 139
Vietnam War, 147
Virginia Plan, 61
Voeten, Eric, 148
Voluntary commitments, 27, 103, 253, 258–59, 261
von Raab, William, 214

War: cyberwarfare, 168, 259; democracy, effect of, 50; preventive, 88; public opinion on, 255. *See also specific wars*
War of 1812, 62
War on drugs, 200
War on terrorism, 87–89, 142–43, 146, 151–52, 231
Warren, Earl, 135
Warren, Elizabeth, 172
Washington, George: Farwell Address (1796), 5, 61, 67, 179; on international commitments, 3, 17, 50, 61–62, 101, 180; on migrants to United States, 202; Revolutionary War, 153
Washington Naval Conference (1921–22), 71
Washington Treaty to establish NATO, 83
The Watchtower over Tomorrow (documentary), 78
Weaponization of outer space, 165
Weapons of mass destruction (WMD), 14, 16, 22–23, 89, 142–43, 162
Webster, Daniel, 55
Wedgwood, Ruth, 261
Weiss, Thomas G., 248
Welles, Sumner, 75

West Africa, Ebola outbreak in (2014–15), 239
White Jacket (Melville), 48–49
White nationalism, 10, 48
WHO (World Health Organization), 89, 119, 231, 238–40
William of Orange (king of England), 44
Willkie, Wendell, 75, 77
Wilson, Pete, 197, 208
Wilson, Woodrow: American exceptionalism and, 49; League of Nations and, 1–4, 6–7, 65–67, 69–70; post–World War I international organization, 51
Winthrop, John, 42
Wittes, Benjamin, 169
Wood, Gordon, 45, 48
Wood, John Travers, 221
World Bank: bias of, 230–31; creation of, 23; G-20, effect of, 262; role of, 182; U.S. relations, 243; voting system of, 131; Western alliance and, 80
World government: consideration of, 247–51; European Union as, 109–11; fear of, 210, 221, 225, 247; International Criminal Court as, 111–13; international organizations vs., 26; League of Nations as, 68; nongovernmental organizations as, 113–14; post–World War II environment for, 75, 248; sovereignty as obstacle to, 37, 39, 46; United Nations as, 75–76, 104, 223
World Health Organization (WHO), 89, 119, 231, 238–40
World Heritage Sites, 222
WorldNetDaily, 10
World Summit (2005), 151
World Trade Organization (WTO), 187–95; Appellate Body (AB) of, 189–95; creation of, 24, 187; dispute settlement understanding (DSU) of, 188–89, 191–92, 194; Doha Development Round of, 192, 259;

World Trade Organization (WTO) (*cont.*)
House resolution to withdraw from, 191;
sovereignty, infringement on, 189–95;
sovereignty bargains for, 118–19; tariffs,
invalidation of, 192; as threat to
constitution, 187; Trump's objections to,
176, 192–95

World War I, 1, 71, 236

World War II: Bracero guest worker
program during, 205; credibility of U.S.
diplomacy during, 57; economic climate
preceding, 74; Pearl Harbor, Japanese
attack on, 71–72; postwar
internationalism, 72–73, 75–76;
postwar trade, 179–82; United Nations
creation after, 74–79; world government
advocacy, 248

WTO. *See* World Trade Organization

Xi Jinping, 92–93

Yemen, war on terrorism and, 151–52

Yoo, John, 111, 140, 160, 165–66

Young, Don, 222

Zimmerman, George, 126